THE BIBLE
in Art

THE NEW TESTAMENT

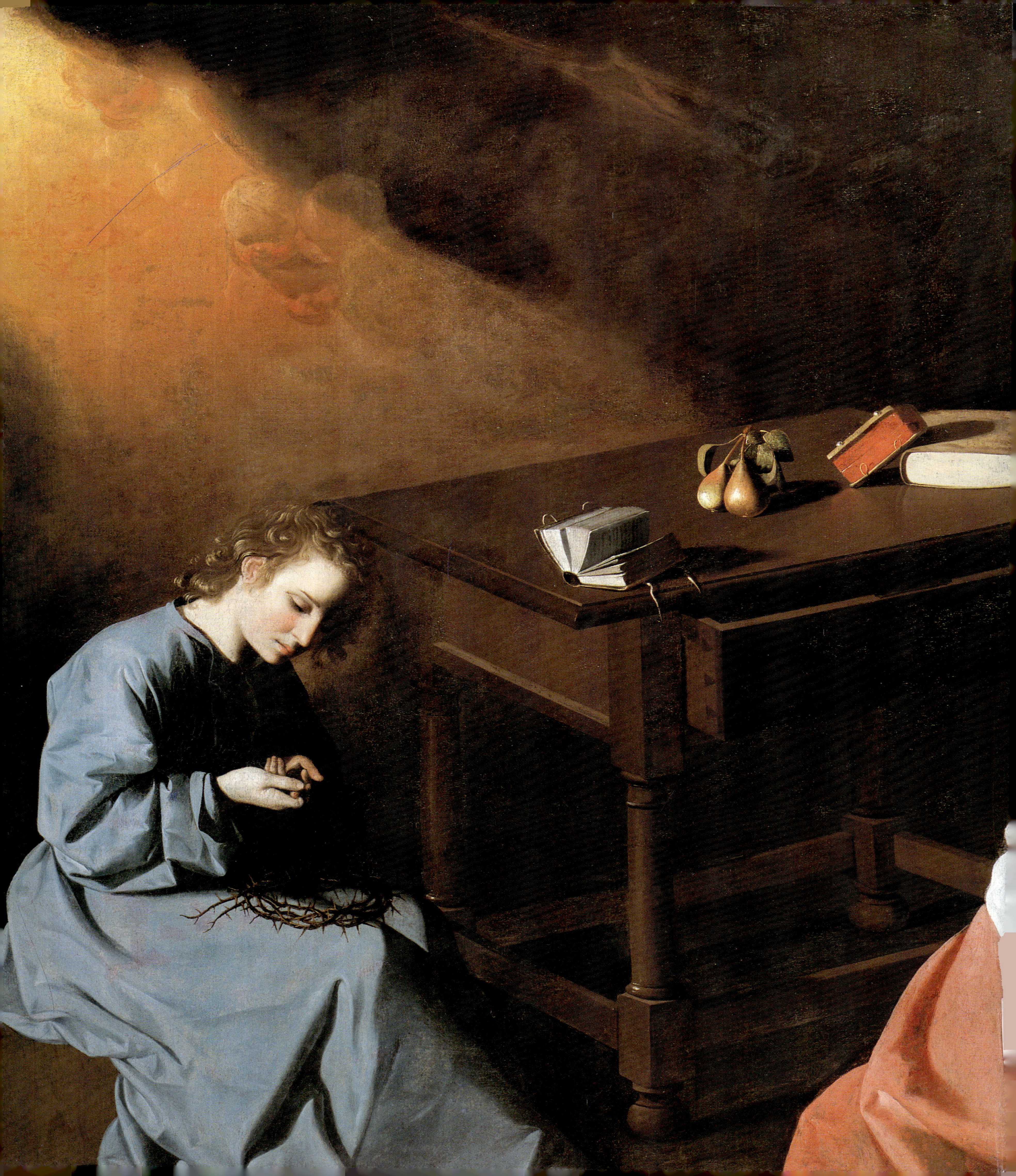

THE BIBLE
in Art

THE NEW TESTAMENT

RICHARD MÜHLBERGER

PORTLAND HOUSE
New York

This 1990 edition was published by Portland House, a division of Dilithium Press, Ltd., distributed by Outlet Book Company, Inc., a Random House Company, 225 Park Avenue South, New York, New York 10003

8 7 6 5 4 3 2 1

ISBN 0-517-03364-X

Printed and bound in Hong Kong

The Bible in Art: The New Testament was prepared and produced by Moore & Moore Publishing, 11 W 19th Street, New York, New York 10011

Photo Credits

Artothek, Munich: 47, 91, 146, 160-161; The Art Institute of Chicago: 119, 125, 126, 136; The Cleveland Museum of Art: 48; The Detroit Institute of Arts: 28-29, 40, 134-135, 164-165; The Frick Collection: 119, 129; Indianapolis Museum of Art: 14-15; The Isabella Stewart Gardner Museum: 69; The Metropolitan Museum of Art: 18, 32, 84, 97, 121, 148, 154-155; Museo de Arte de Ponce, Puerto Rico: 140; The Museum of Fine Arts, Boston: 118, 130, 157; The Museum of Fine Arts, Springfield: 24, 152-153; National Gallery of Art, Washington DC: 33, 54-55, 56, 68, 70-71, 82-83, 88, 92-93, 94-95; The Saint Louis Art Museum: 85, 98-99; Sarah Campbell Blaffer Collection: 162; Superstock International, Inc.: 10-11, 16, 20-21, 22, 25, 26-27, 30-31, 38, 39, 41, 44-45, 49, 62, 63, 65, 74-75, 78, 79, 86, 87, 89, 100-101, 102-103, 106, 109, 112-113, 116-117, 122, 127, 132-133, 136, 139, 141, 142, 150-151, 159, 163, 167, 168-169; Superstock/Bridgeman 36-37, 52-53, 81, 114, 110-111, 149, 166; The Toledo Museum of Art: 66-67, 72-73, 124; Worcester Art Museum: 34, 42, 60-61

PAGE 2 ZURBARAN: *The Holy House of Nazareth* (detail)

AN M&M BOOK

Project Director & Editor: Gary Fishgall
Senior Editorial Assistant: Shirley Vierheller;
Editorial Assistants: Maxine Dormer, Ben D'Amprisi, Jr.;
Copyediting: Bert N. Zelman, Joan Agranoff of Publishers Workshop Inc.
Photo Research: Maxine Dormer, Jana Marcus
Designer: Binns & Lubin
Separations and Printing: Regent Publishing Services Ltd.
Typesetting: Dynographics, Inc.

Measurements of the paintings when known, are in inches, height before width.

Contents

Introduction

There was a time, and it was not so many years ago, when a painting inspired a lively interaction between an artist and the beholder of his work. It was a unique form of communication often cutting across time and space, even centuries and continents, but it was as intimate as a whispered exchange between two chums.

To foster this dialogue, the artist invested his time in the act of creation. He may have taken less than a day, as Vincent van Gogh did with *The Good Samaritan* (see p. 89) or two full years as did Albrecht Dürer with *Four Apostles* (see pp. 160–161). But the *amount* of time was less important than the talent, imagination, and passion reflected in the result.

For his part, the viewer also invested time. He sat in front of a work of art and studied it. He discussed it with his family and friends. He considered it in relation to other interpretations of the same subject—how it differed, what it drew from. And he remembered it so that he could subsequently compare it with other works from the same artist.

Art became an exciting part of human affairs by this reciprocal give and take. It enriched the lives of art lovers—people of every station and stratum of society—and it enabled an artist's vision to survive long after the artist himself had ceased to exist. *Ars longa, vita brevis.* It is the hope of the author that this book will rekindle the delicious, provocative, and challenging exchange between painter and public.

This volume was conceived as a way of bringing together one of mankind's most profound books, the New Testament, with some of Western civilization's greatest paintings. It shows how visual interpretations of the Bible have varied throughout the ages and how, at the same time, the appeal of these sacred stories has remained constant.

Demonstrating the ageless appeal of the scriptures is not without obstacles, however. Some subjects have had greater appeal for artists and their patrons than others. There are, for example, literally thousands upon thousands of paintings relating to the conception and birth of Jesus, and equal numbers that depict his last days. There are far fewer works devoted to the interval between these two momentous chapters. A number of the miracles have inspired paintings, but the parables, and certain high points in the ministry of Jesus, such as the Sermon on the Mount and the Transfiguration, have been treated infrequently. The abundance of some subjects and the dearth of others has to do with the great liturgical cycles of prayer, praise, and instruction that have prepared worshippers for Christmas, Epiphany, Holy Week, and Easter since Christianity's early days; all of the episodes that do not directly impact upon these major events—at least when it comes to art—are fill-ins. Nevertheless, the objective of this writer was to cover as much of the New Testament as possible. While the choices for some stories were fewer than for others, ample paintings with which to meet this goal were there for the finding.

We have sought to explore works from a wide range of epochs and to include paintings from at least a few relatively unknown artists. A number of the greatest religious painters, such as Giotto and Zurbarán, are represented by several examples. So too are Rubens and Poussin, whose reputations are not so much based on their religious subjects as on their secular ones, but who managed to depict Gospel stories that others eschewed. There are five paintings by Rembrandt, clearly showing this writer's prejudice for the great 17th-century master, but also testifying to the extraordinary range of biblical subject matter that he explored. The 17th century is the era best represented (37 paintings), with the 16th and 15th centuries also well covered (22 and 15, respectively). Six paintings are from earlier periods, four from the 18th century, ten from the 19th, and three from the 20th. Because illuminated manuscripts, as well as stained glass windows, mosaics, cloisonné, and other decorative arts are not within the purview of this book (one exception is made), it is easy to understand why there are not more examples from the great age of faith, the medieval period.

If the contents of this book were an index to the spirituality of various periods of history, the predominance of works from certain centuries would offer an intersting, and perhaps surprising, commentary. But there is no correlation between the art represented on these pages and the state of religious conviction during the periods they cover. Rather, the contents reflect issues having to do with art history and aesthetic merit. Seventeenth-century art is simply more plentiful than, say, 14th century art so we have included more examples of the former than the latter. And while there is ample religious art from the 18th century, so much of it is dry, repetitious, and dull that it begs to be passed over. The same can be said of 19th-century religious art. But the latter was also a period of new ideas, borne by the likes of Delacroix, Manet, van Gogh, and Gauguin, so an aggressive effort to find and include works by these artists was made, even though they are not primarily known as painters of Bible subjects.

The selections for this book were also controlled to a degree by the ready availability of imagery. Hence paintings were drawn primarily from museum collections. This practical consideration further explains the book's preponderance of 17th-century art, for many of the royal collections that eventually became Europe's public museums began to be assembled in that century with works of then-contemporary masters. When American museums were founded some 200 years later, they modeled themselves after their European antecedents.

Many Bible stories are not to be found herein because exciting paintings devoted to them were not available. Some stories are represented by two or more paintings, enabling us to compare and contrast different interpretations from the same source material. While such an approach has been adopted as the primary means of teaching art history, every effort has been made to avoid academic pretensions. You will find information drawn from the history of art in nearly every entry in this book, but more attention is paid to the images themselves. The aim is not so much to "explain" art as it is to help the reader *experience* art. For those who are seriously interested in this pursuit, this book can be a start. The next step is to imitate the viewer described at the opening of this *Introduction.* Go to a museum and connect with a painting, perhaps with one discussed on the following pages. It may be that this book will also inspire readers to reexamine the Scriptures. And that is fine too. Certainly, the summaries contained herein should not substitute for a reading of the originals. While full appreciation of the paintings demands knowledge of the Scriptures, the latter do not require illustrations to enrich their power and beauty. Incidentally, all quotations from the Bible cited in this volume are from the Revised Standard Version.

The author is grateful to Gary Fishgall for his guidance in formulating the discussions of the paintings and for his help in editing the text. Thanks are also extended to Jana Marcus for her assistance in finding illustrations, and to Maxine Dormer for her work in the production of this volume.

This book is dedicated to the artist's mother, who got him interested in these stories in the first place.

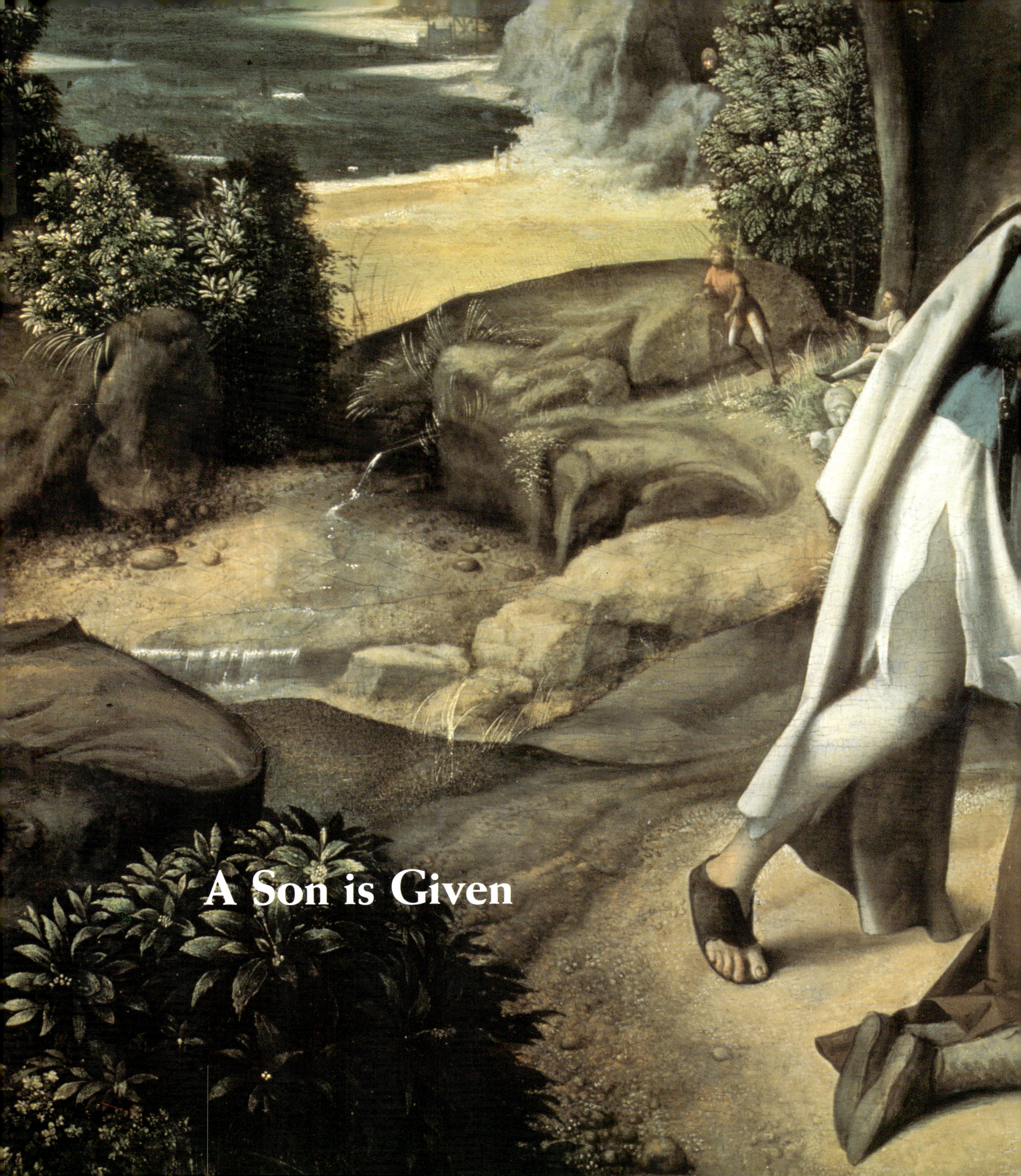
A Son is Given

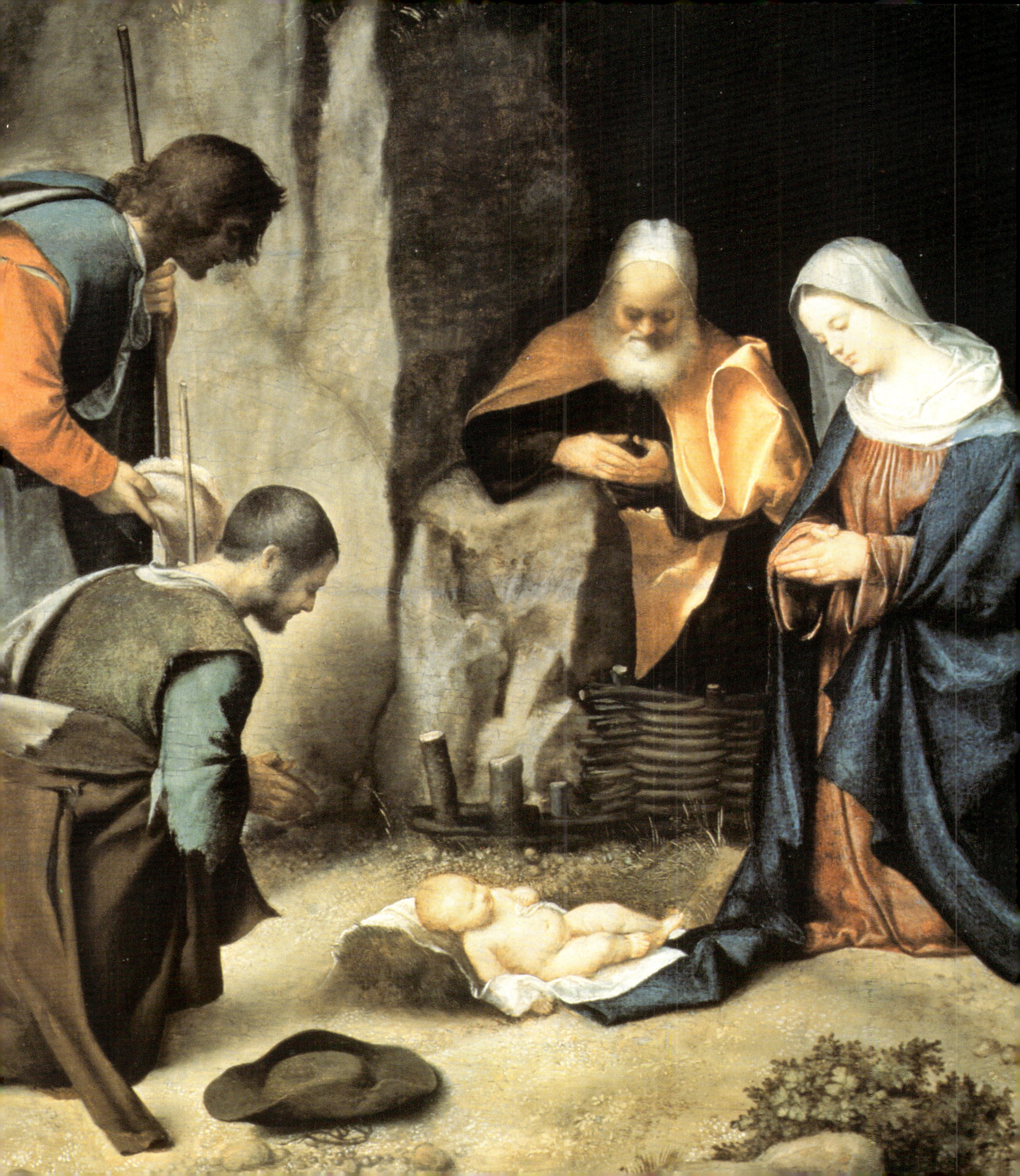

PRECEDING PAGES
GIORGIONE: *The Adoration of the Shepherds* (detail)

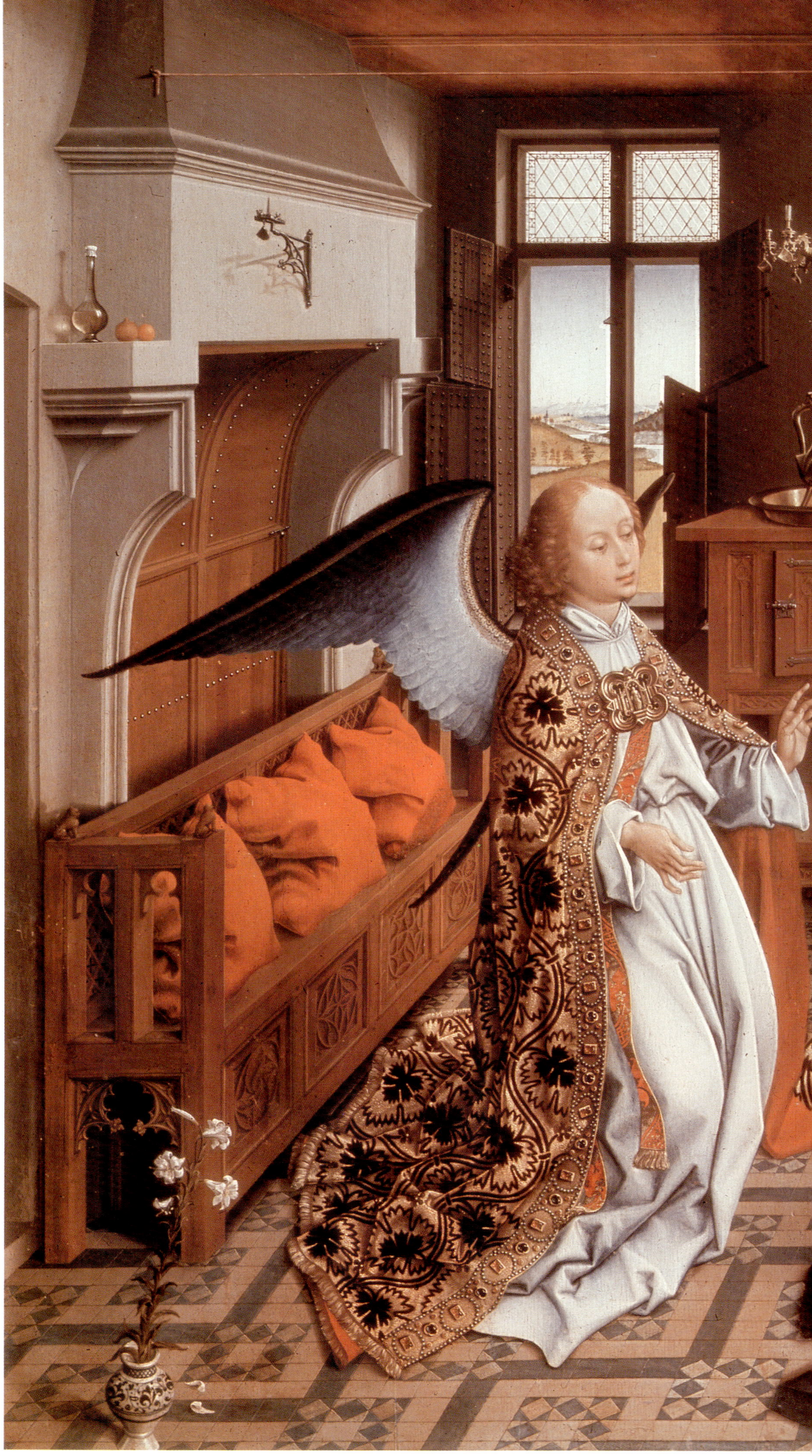

The Annunciation
ROGER VAN DER WEYDEN, Flemish,
1399/1400–1464
Musée du Louvre, Paris. Wood panel. 34 × 36½ in.

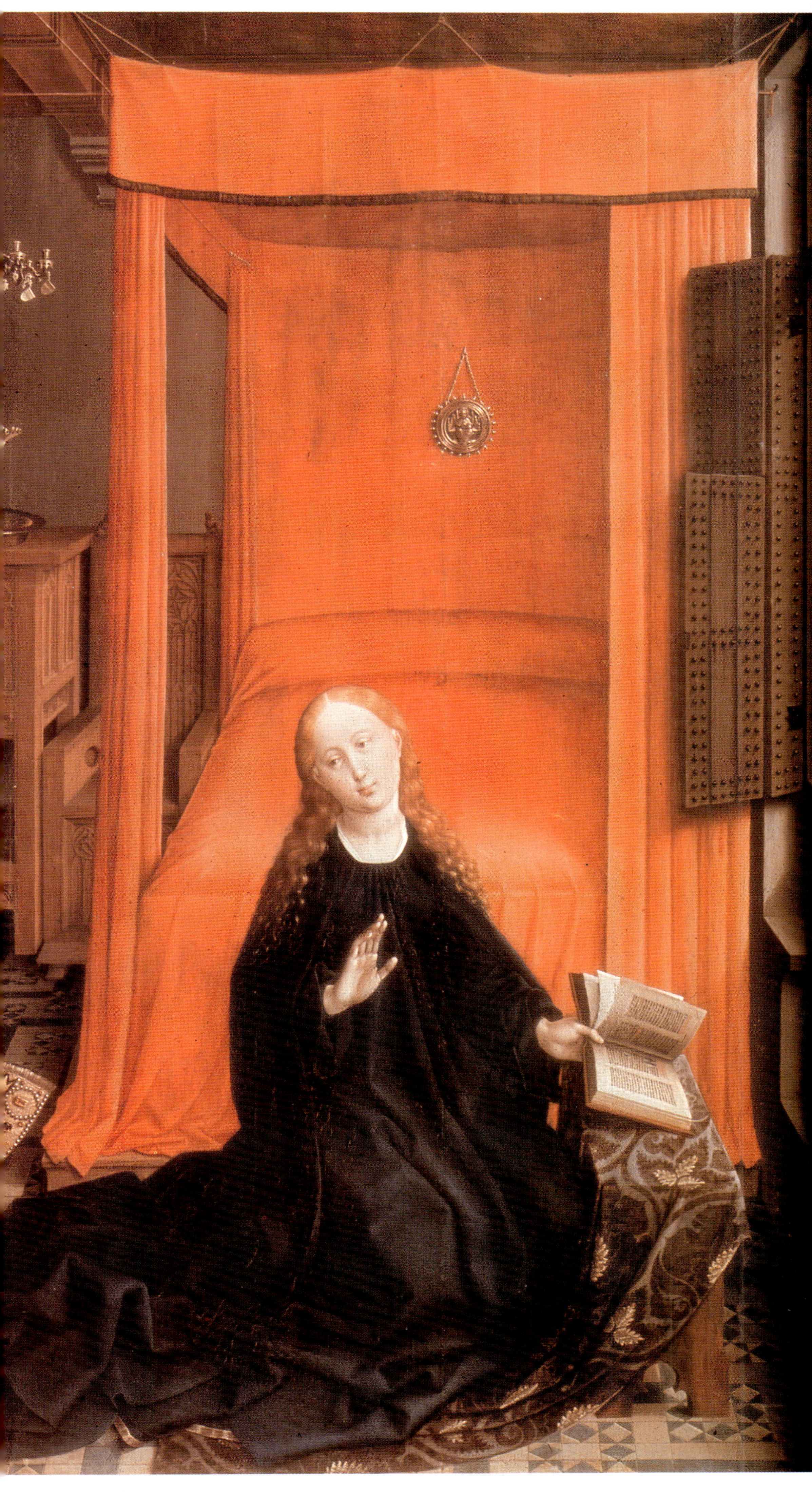

The Annunciation

The miraculous conception and birth of Jesus are not the first stories of the New Testament Gospels. Two of the writers, Mark and John, ignored these events entirely, and Matthew started off with the genealogy of Joseph. But to the pious throughout the centuries the image of the angel Gabriel appearing to the Virgin Mary and saying, "Hail, O favored one, the Lord is with you!" marks the start of the story of Christian redemption. It was one of the most frequently painted of all New Testament subjects.

In his *Annunciation*, Roger van der Weyden, among the most influential artists of his day, depicts the holy pair Mary and Gabriel, not at the moment when the birth of the "Son of the Most High" is foretold, but at the moment of her response: "How can this be, since I have no husband?" (Luke 1:34). The question is like that of a schoolgirl to her teacher. Indeed, in Roger's interpretation, she has been studying; her thumb holds her place as she puts down her Bible to converse with Gabriel. He, dressed like a priest at High Mass, answers, "The Holy Spirit will come upon you, and the power of the Most High will overshadow you; therefore the child to be born will be called holy, the Son of God" (Luke 1:35).

Roger makes this story totally believable. Even though the two figures seem to almost float on the volumes of fabric that make up their robes (the one aspect of the painting that suggests an otherworldly presence), they are in a very real setting.

The bedroom of an upper-class family of 15th-century Brussels is shown in exacting detail. Painted for a society that employed many hands in the manufacture of textiles, the rich fabrics in Gabriel's finely appointed garments and on Mary's prie-dieu would have been greatly appreciated as much for their quality of design and depth of color as for their worth per yard. The room is filled with enchanting still-life passages, like the delicate glass vase on the mantel that catches light in its liquid contents and reflects it against the wall. White lilies, always associated with the Virgin in art, stand in another vase on the floor. But the great bed—the type reserved for the master and mistress of a household—is the central element in the room. With hangings and coverings of red, a color symbolic of earthly love, it is empty. This is a reminder that the conception will be chaste and miraculous.

As much as Roger emphasizes corporeal substance in his setting, his Italian contemporary Giovanni di Paolo in his *Annunciation* lays stress on the theological significance of the event. The mansion that he has contrived as a setting for his telling of the story seems almost too insubstantial to contain a miracle, yet at the same time it suggests a tabernacle for the keeping of something sacred. It probably was inspired by the scenery for one of the "miracle plays" that were sweeping Italy with great popularity at the time Giovanni painted this picture. Performed in churches, these entertainments featured portable and rather flimsy tableaux to serve as backdrops for the popular stories of the life of the Virgin Mary, Jesus, and the saints that were acted out in broad, stylized form. Here, on center stage, we see Gabriel and the Virgin seemingly in confrontation over the announcement of her pregnancy. As though impatient with her unwillingness to believe that she is the chosen of God, the angel crosses his arms and explains, "with God, nothing will be impossible" (Luke 1:37).

The setting opens to the outdoors where rabbits, an age-old symbol of fecundity, romp among flowers and grass. And there, in quite surprising nakedness, are also Adam and Eve. They are being ushered from the east gate of Eden. God the Father hovers above them in circles of light that might have found their inspiration in Dante's cosmology. Like Gabriel, he seems perturbed. But *his* news is not salutary. "You are dust, and to dust you shall return" (Genesis 3:19) were his last words to Adam. The presence of this disturbing scene connects the story of Jesus to the events and prophesies of the Old Testament. The New Testament itself is full of this kind of allusion, such as St. Paul's words, "as in Adam all die, so also in Christ shall all be made alive" (I Corinthians 15:22). In early Christian theological writings, Mary was sometimes called "the second Eve."

In this symbolic, theologically discursive, and emotionally brittle painting, there is one very down-to-earth passage that is almost Flemish in its simplicity, and one wonders why Giovanni instead of Roger thought of it. Joseph sits in a room to the left of center. Bald, cold, and seated on a simple three-legged stool, he reminds the viewer that the miracle of the conception is set within a real, not an ethereal, context. He and his betrothed were poor, and no one would have described them as the perfectly matched couple. The Feast of the Annunciation, which celebrates the event shown in the center room, is celebrated on March 25. The Italian viewers of this painting would have expected a fire to be raging and sending smoke into the morning air at that time of the year, so Giovanni does not disappoint them. His fire also allows Joseph to warm his hands.

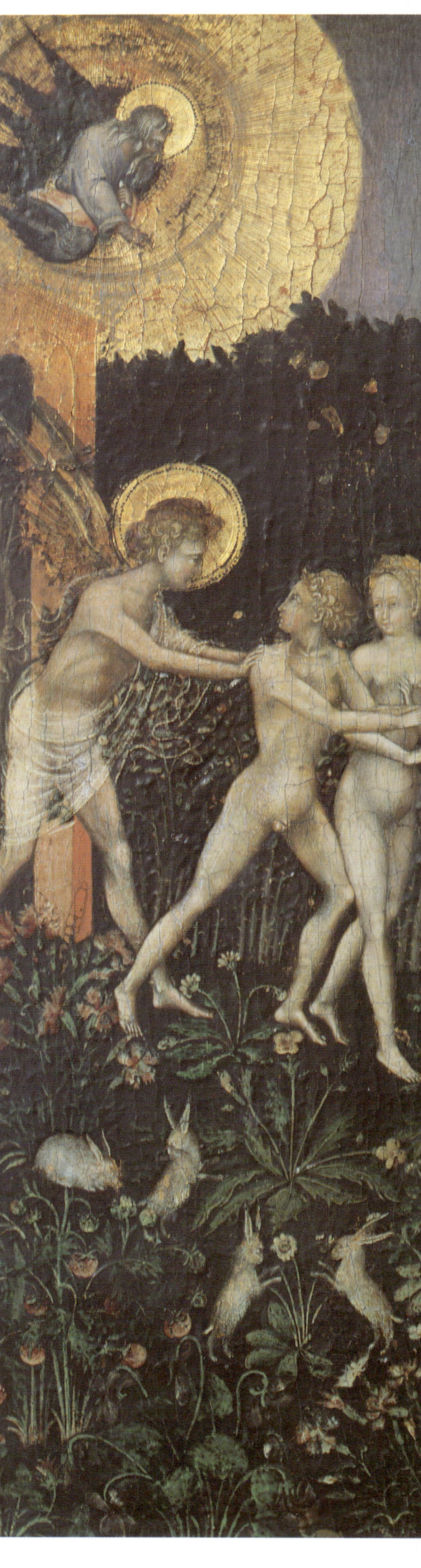

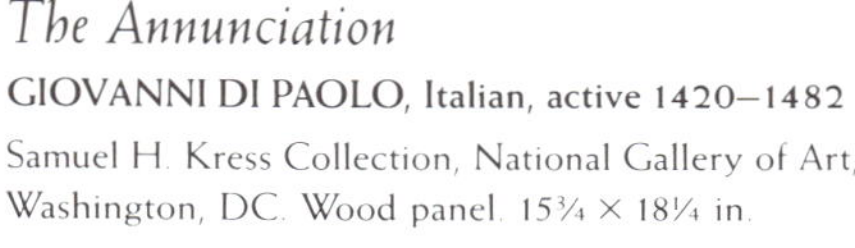

The Annunciation
GIOVANNI DI PAOLO, Italian, active 1420–1482
Samuel H. Kress Collection, National Gallery of Art, Washington, DC. Wood panel. 15¾ × 18¼ in.

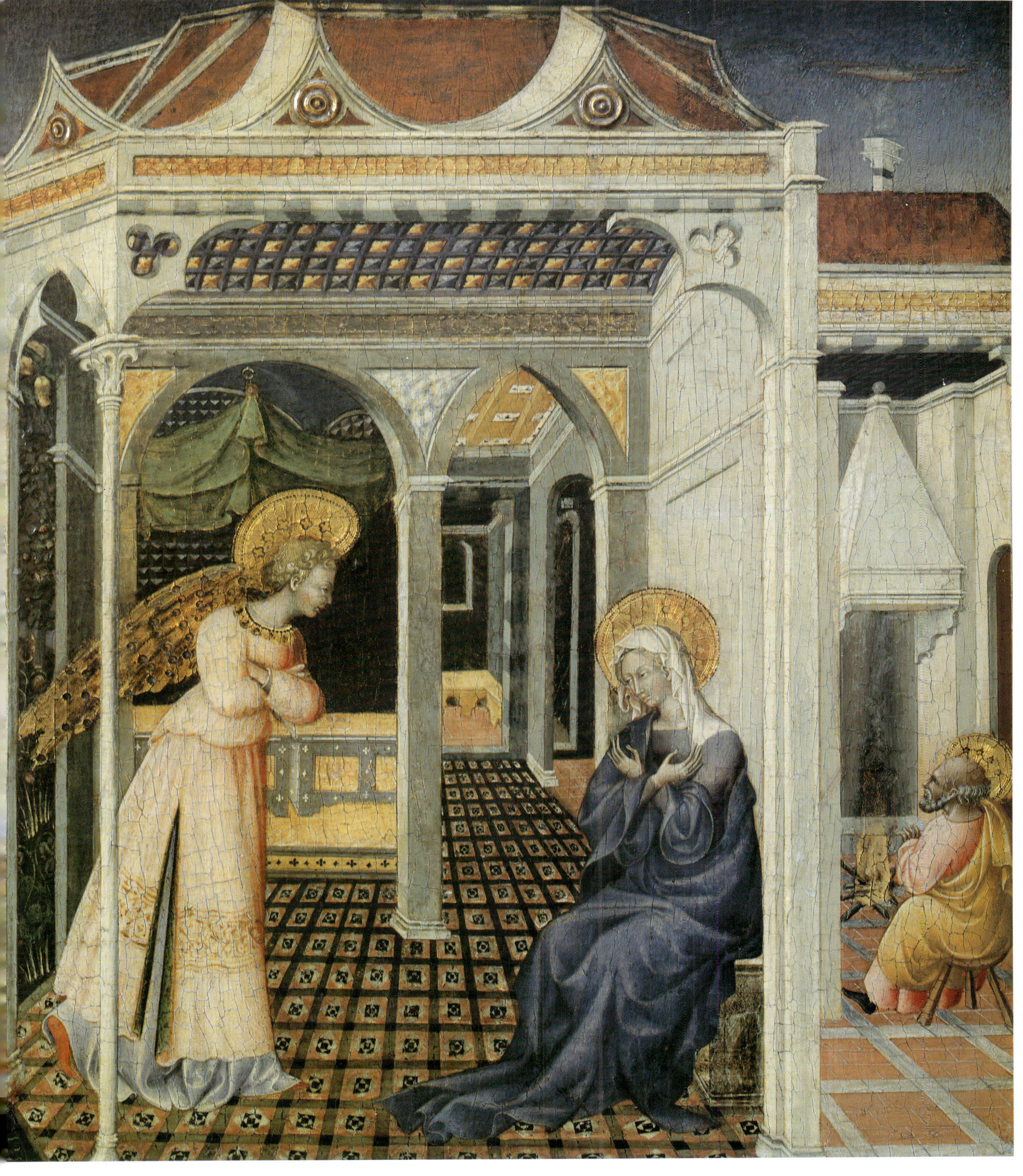

The Dream of St. Joseph

In art, Joseph usually stands aside. He frequently takes on the role of butler when the three kings visit his wife and her child Jesus, and he seems content to worship the child with the shepherds in paintings that depict their adoration. But the first chapter of The Gospel According to St. Matthew is devoted to this placid, yet solid citizen and, in the rare paintings that illustrate these verses, he enjoys the same attention regularly lavished on Mary. Here he receives his heavenly reward: clouds, angels, and God the Father himself!

Joseph was a carpenter from Bethlehem who settled in Nazareth, where this workshop scene is set. His tool shelf separates the room into halves of equal visual importance. The clouds, spilling with angels from the Father on high, unite the scene and seem to make Mary more a part of Joseph's dream than a real presence.

Matthew began his history of the life and works of Jesus with a lengthy geneology, tracing Christ's descent from Abraham and David. Then he proceeded to relate one of the most human episodes in the Bible—the impact of the immaculate conception on Mary's fiancé. Mary and Joseph were betrothed. In those days, an engagement of marriage usually required a public announcement and a marriage contract. So when Joseph realized Mary was pregnant, he sought to break the agreement as was allowed by Jewish law in cases of alleged adultery. Matthew wrote, "being a just man and unwilling to put her to shame," he planned to do this quietly. But before he had time to act, "an angel of the Lord appeared to him in a dream, saying, 'Joseph, son of David, do not fear to take Mary your wife, for that which is conceived in her is of the Holy Spirit; she will bear a son, and you shall call his name Jesus, for he will save his people from their sins'" (Matthew 1:19–21).

Luca Giordano, who depicts Joseph's dream here, was a celebrity in his day because of the speed with which he could paint. His nickname, Fa Presto, means, "do it quickly." It was said that he could decorate the entire ceiling of a palace dining room in one day; audiences would gather to watch him do so. He probably painted this work at the end of a decade-long stint in Spain, where he decorated numerous palaces. The diagonal of brilliant light-filled clouds with angels tumbling from them, as seen here illuminating the entire scene, is typical of his ceiling decorations. Although the Bible states that only one angel visited Joseph in his dream, Fa Presto has found it difficult to resist the temptation to multiply them and to add the figure of God the Father as well. This gives even more importance to Joseph than Matthew accorded him. Perhaps this version of the story comes from one of the many apochryphal books that were written to enlarge the biblical narratives. They date as early as the beginning of the fifth century. The *History of Joseph the Carpenter* was one of these and became the basis for a cult of Joseph, making his feast day on March 19 one of great celebration.

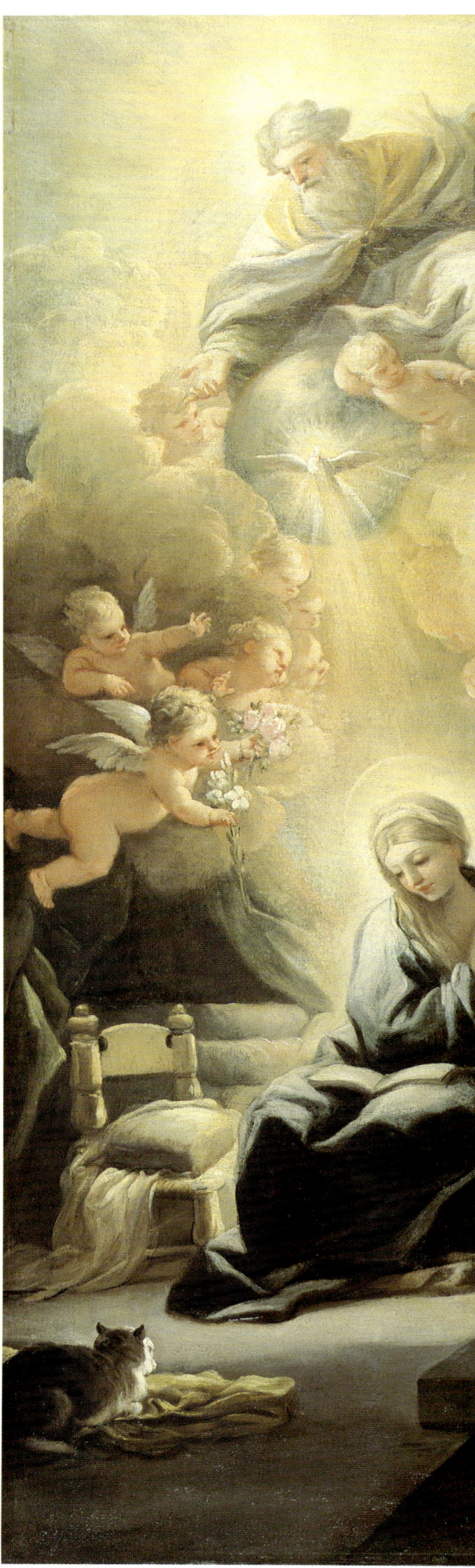

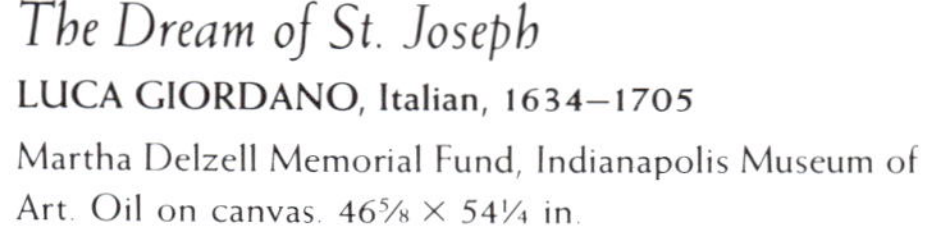

The Dream of St. Joseph
LUCA GIORDANO, Italian, 1634–1705
Martha Delzell Memorial Fund, Indianapolis Museum of Art. Oil on canvas. 46⅝ × 54¼ in.

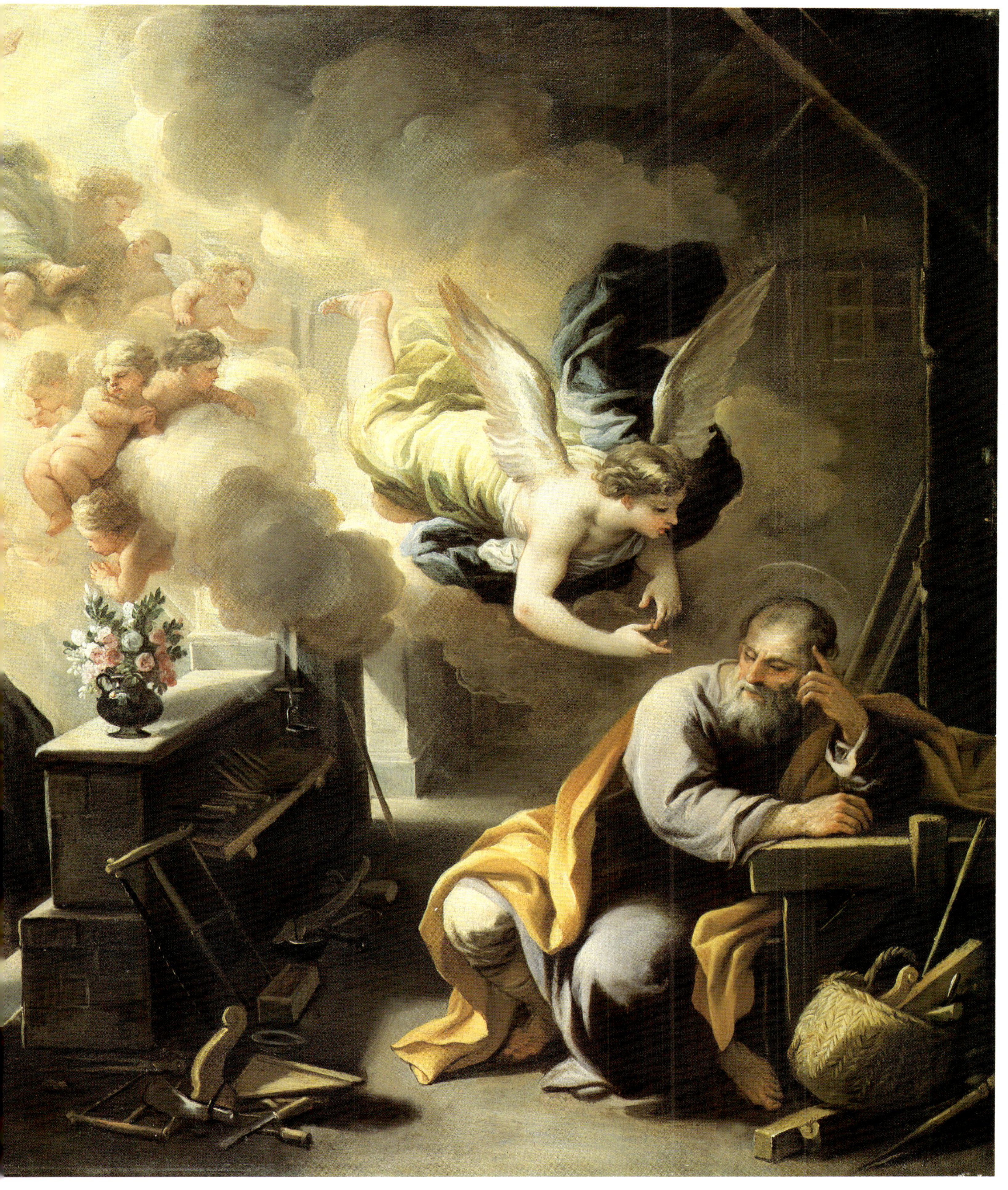

The Marriage of the Virgin

Painted when he was only 19 years of age, *The Marriage of the Virgin* is Raphael's first great masterpiece. He proudly put his name and the year in Roman letters and numerals over the central door of the great temple in the background: RAPHAEL VRBINAS MDIIII, Raphael of Urbino 1504. At the time, he was considered a prodigy, with only a local reputation in Tuscany and Umbria. The lucid organization of this painting, based on a flawless interpretation of linear perspective, and the reserved nobility of its figures, summarizes every artistic ideal of the 15th century while also presaging Raphael's later fame as architect to the Vatican and the leading artist of the High Renaissance.

The marriage of the Virgin was only implied in the Bible, but the second-century Protevangelium of James ignored what little the Gospels did report (see *The Dream of St. Joseph*, pp. 16–17) and told how Mary's suitors lined up in the temple and drew rods for her, and how the rod of Joseph blossomed. He carries it here, while another, once-ardent suitor breaks his unneeded limb across his knee. Posed elegantly, like a ballet dancer, Joseph is barefooted, a sign of his humility as he takes on the awesome responsibility of raising the holy child of his virgin wife. The marriage has a magnificent setting in an idealized Renaissance piazza before a perfectly proportioned temple. This is not because Raphael was ignorant of the humble state of Joseph and Mary and the poor environment in which they no doubt were forced to live, but because he wished to glorify the lives of these two humble people who cooperated so unselfishly in God's grand design for the salvation of the world.

The Protevangelium of James was not used by artists until the 16th century, when it was believed that it was an earlier work than the four Gospels, but the fanciful account of Mary's engagement and marriage had already been collected in Jacobus de Voragine's *Legenda Aurea*, which had been available to the literate since the end of the 13th century. This particular story was so widely accepted by Raphael's time that it was considered "Gospel truth" by most people. Not until the Reformation was there much critical evaluation of early apocryphal literature, and even Luther and Calvin were in disagreement over the value and legitimacy of some of the texts. Nonetheless, these imaginative apocryphal writings provided the stories for numerous artistic masterpieces.

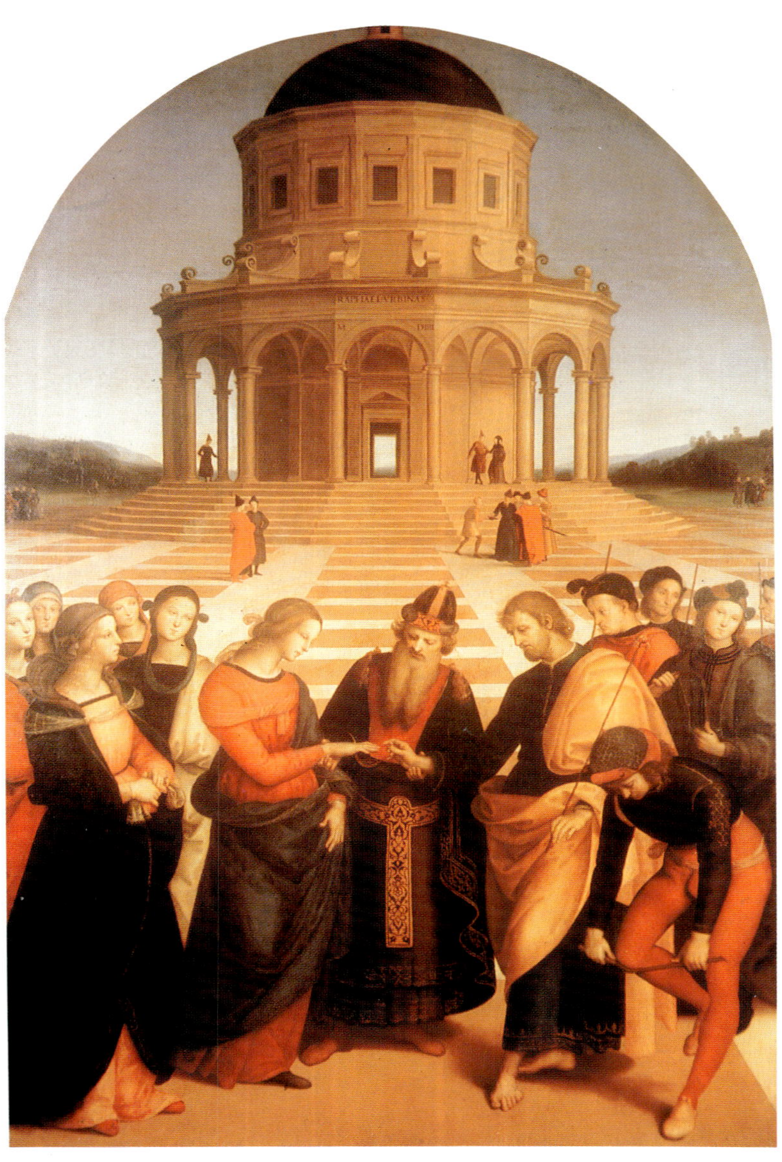

The Marriage of the Virgin
RAPHAEL, Italian, 1483–1520
Pinacoteca di Brera, Milan. Oil on wood panel.
67 × 46½ in.

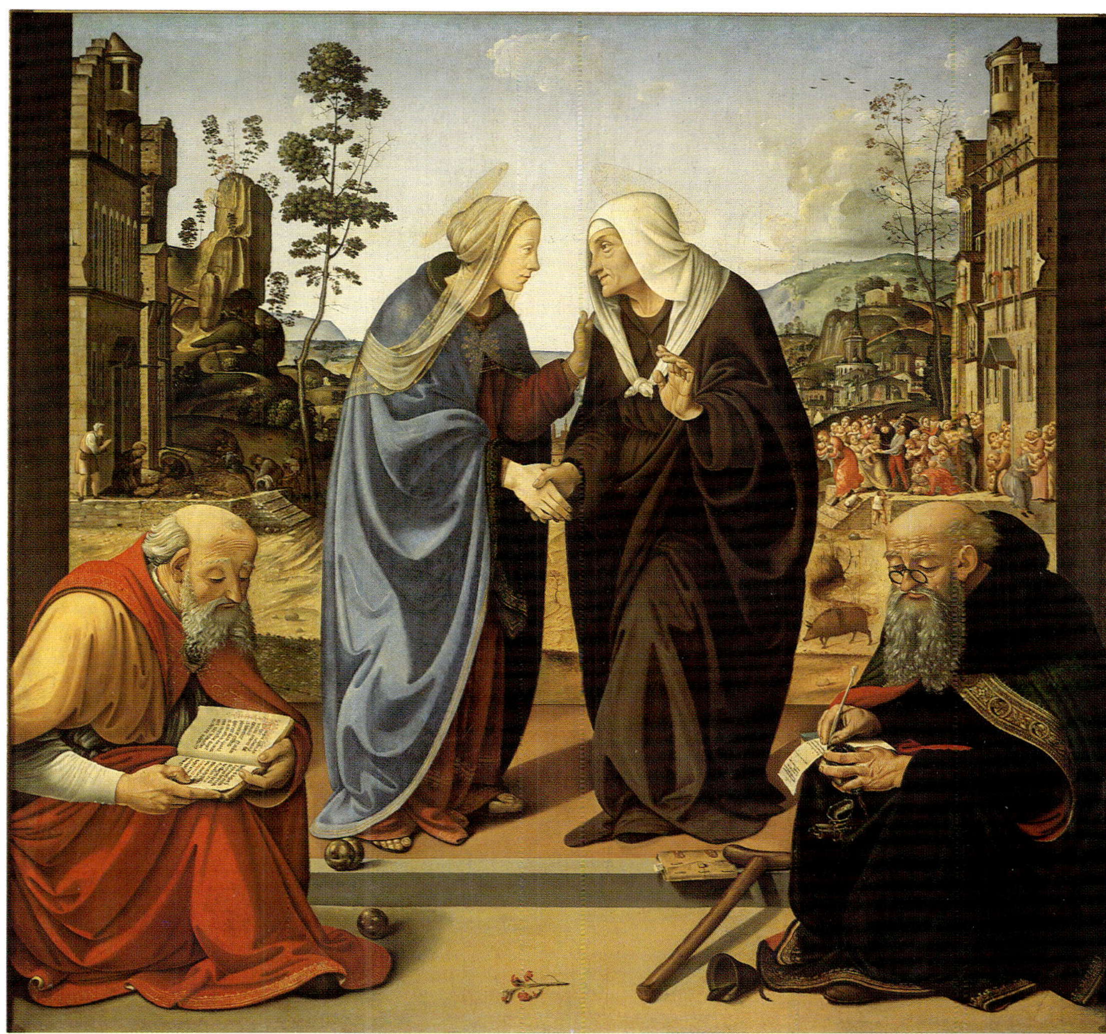

The Visitation with St. Nicolas and St. Anthony Abbot
PIERO DI COSIMO, Italian, 1462–ca. 1521
Samuel H. Kress Collection, National Gallery of Art, Washington, DC. Wood panel. 72½ × 74¼ in.

The Visitation of Mary and Elizabeth

This tender meeting was the inspiration for the Ave Maria and the Magnificat, two of the most enduring prayers of Christendom, after the Lord's Prayer itself.

At the same time he announced the conception of Jesus, the angel Gabriel told Mary that her cousin Elizabeth, the elderly wife of Zechariah, had become pregnant. Mary immediately rushed to Elizabeth's house and called out a greeting. At the sound of Mary's voice, Elizabeth's baby "leaped in her womb"; Elizabeth, filled with the Holy Spirit, exclaimed with a loud cry, "Blessed are you among women, and blessed is the fruit of your womb" (Luke 1:41–42). These words, coupled with the greeting of the angel Gabriel at the Annunciation, "Hail, O favored one, the Lord is with you!" (Luke 1:28) form the basis for the Ave Maria.

Mary's answer to her kinswoman has come down to us as the Magnificat. The measured cadence of its psalm-like poetry is repeated daily at Vespers, or Evening Prayer, by millions of Christians who follow the liturgical ritual of the early church. "My soul magnifies the Lord, and my spirit rejoices in God my Savior," she said, "for he has regarded the low estate of his handmaiden" (Luke 1:46–48). It is this spirit of humble submission to God that Piero di Cosimo captures in his painting.

Mary and Elizabeth shake hands, rather formally. But Elizabeth's left hand, held up in greeting, will soon be around Mary's shoulder in a warm embrace. Mary has already lifted her free hand to hold her older cousin. Beneath them lies a sprig of red carnations, a flower with double symbolism for this scene. On the one hand, the red prefigures the blood that will accompany the executions of both of these women's sons; on the other, the carnation—the flower of betrothal—signifies that the marriages of these women are coming to fruition with their pregnancies.

The two male saints are probably in this painting because it was commissioned for a church or an altar dedicated to them; they actually have nothing to do with the narrative. Engaged in literary pursuits, their presence here seems to resonate of the great prayers that will emerge from Mary and Elizabeth's words.

Above Saint Nicholas in the distance is the Nativity of Jesus with shepherds adoring the newborn child. To the right is the "Massacre of the Innocents," the slaughter of all the male children of Bethlehem that was ordered by Herod as a way of preventing a newborn king from rising up who might challenge his rule (see pp. 46–47). The architecture of both background scenes is based on the fortress-like palaces of Florence, where the artist lived.

Piero heightens the quiet formality of this scene through the use of perfect symmetry. The Renaissance espoused balance in all things, including the composition of music and painting. The intellectuals of Florence, seeing this image hanging above an altar in a church or chapel, would have expected the same kind of formality in its composition as they would have mandated in the arrangement of candlesticks and other accoutrements on the altar. While Piero was a favorite of the intellectuals, his *Visitation* also served the needs of the masses. They too would have appreciated—and been inspired by—this joyous reunion, although the philosophical ideas behind its composition would have been lost on them.

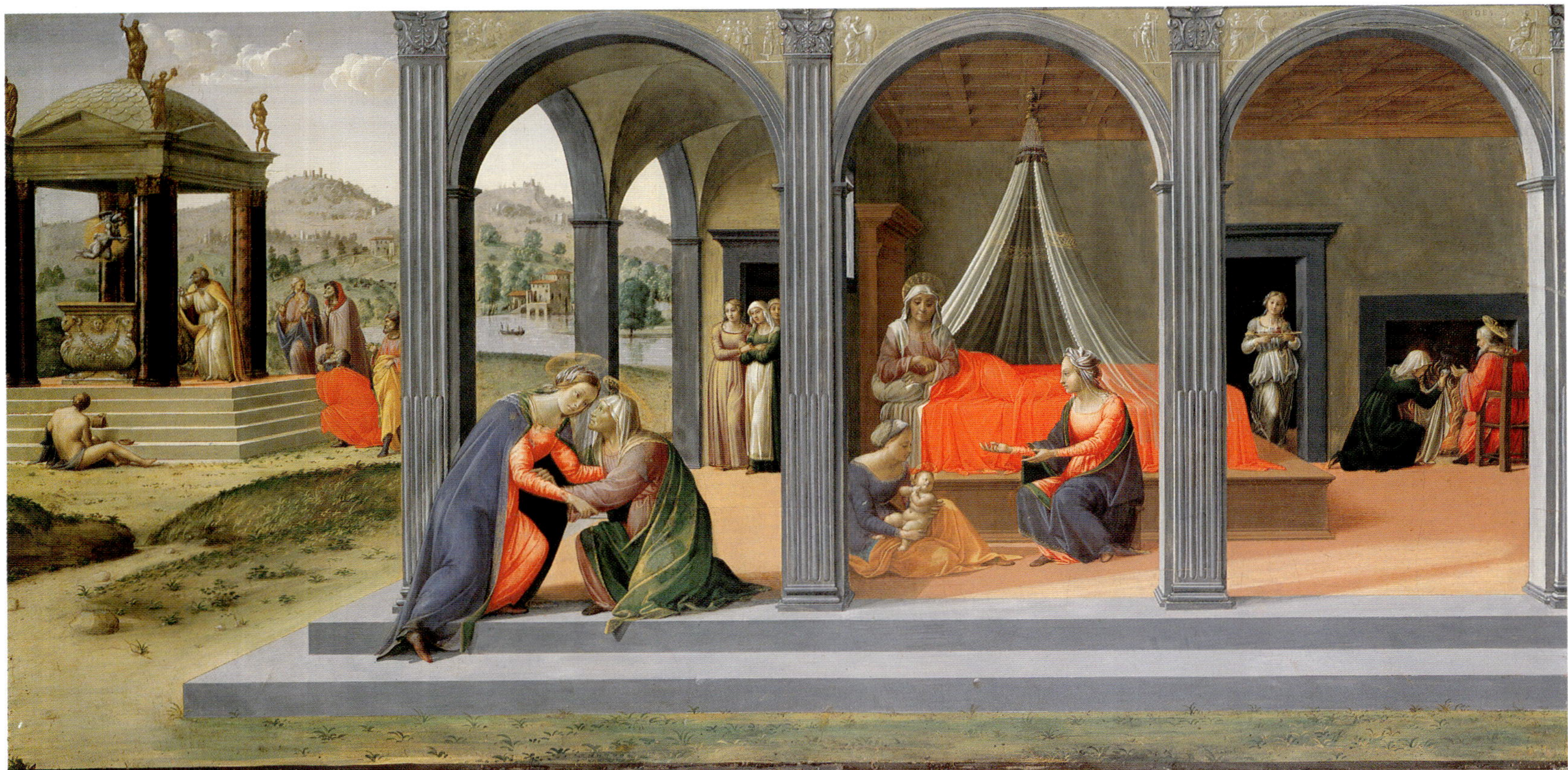

The Birth of St. John the Baptist from *Scenes from the Life of St. John the Baptist*
FRANCESCO GRANACCI, Italian, 1469–1543
Metropolitan Museum of Art, New York, Gwynne Andrews, Harris Brisbane Dick, Dodge, Fletcher, and Rogers Funds, funds from various donors, Ella Morris Depeyster Gift, Mrs. Donald Oenslager Gift, and gifts in memory of Robert Lehman, 1970. (1970.134.1). Oil on wood panel. 31½ × 60 in.

The Birth of St. John the Baptist

Elizabeth, the wife of Zechariah the priest and a kinswoman of Mary the Mother of Jesus, was advanced in years. She must have been the subject of much derision during her lifetime, for she was barren. To be childless was considered a curse by a society that placed great importance on the bearing of heirs. So when she finally brought forth a son "Kinsfolk heard that the Lord had shown great mercy to her, and they rejoiced with her" (Luke 1:58). This moment of shared happiness is shown by Francesco Granacci as quiet and dignified, befitting Elizabeth's station and age. The artist has captured the most beautiful expression of pride on Elizabeth's face, as she begins to free her hands from their resting place, tucked into her sleeves.

Light enters the simple but rich room from a window above the bed. It illuminates Elizabeth's head, the baby, and the face and breast of the visitor. This guest is also linked to Elizabeth by the triangular drape of the elegant white and gold bed hanging. Filigreed halos of gold hover over the heads of the mother and child, symbols of sainthood, but the visitor is not so marked. Nonetheless, she is dressed in the traditional red and blue garb of the Virgin Mary, and the account of St. Luke has her visiting Elizabeth during the last three months of the old woman's pregnancy. She was very likely present in Zechariah's house at the time of the birth. Perhaps the artist decided not to bestow sainthood on her until she had given birth to Jesus.

The baby here is St. John, whose birth was foretold by the angel Gabriel to Zechariah, John's elderly father. Zechariah didn't believe the heavenly message and, for his lack of faith, God made him speechless for nine months. At the time of the announcement, the name of the boy was ordained, as was his role in life: "He will turn many of the sons of Israel to the Lord their God, and he will go before him in the spirit and power of Elijah . . . to make ready for the Lord a people prepared" (Luke 1:16–17). Possibly still stunned by this news, the old man was not present at his son's birth.

The Census in Bethlehem

"In those days a decree went out from Caesar Augustus that all the world should be enrolled. . . . And all went to be enrolled, each to his own city" (Luke 2:1–5). Joseph complied with the rest of his countrymen and went from the small village of Nazareth to Bethlehem, the city where King David had been born, because Joseph was of the house and lineage of David. His journey was only 7 miles but it was a difficult one, for Mary was nine months pregnant.

The Caesar Augustus of Pieter Bruegel's era was King Philip II of Spain, and from time to time he too ordered the census in his provinces, including Bruegel's Flanders. Census and taxation were then almost synonymous, and war taxes were regularly exacted. Bruegel had to pay them like everyone else, and resented them like everyone else. His disenchanted bitterness at such repression emerges in a number of his paintings. In *The Census in Bethlehem*, he seems to be in perfect sympathy with the vassals who must trudge through the cold to give homage in taxes to a foreign master.

In this masterful work, Bethlehem becomes a Flemish town of 1566. Mobs of people gather at the local inn that has been commandeered by the tax officials. A mother and her child in bright red have just left the registration window, and now a man lays down his levy to be collected by the official in a fur-trimmed coat. A second official checks the ledgers to be sure the right payment has been made. In front of the inn, pigs are being slaughtered to feed the large crowds expected in the course of the day. While this will make a delicious meal for the weary travelers of 16th-century Flanders, it would have been repugnant in Bethlehem where Jewish dietary laws would have forbidden such a repast. But this may be the only false note in an otherwise convincing picture.

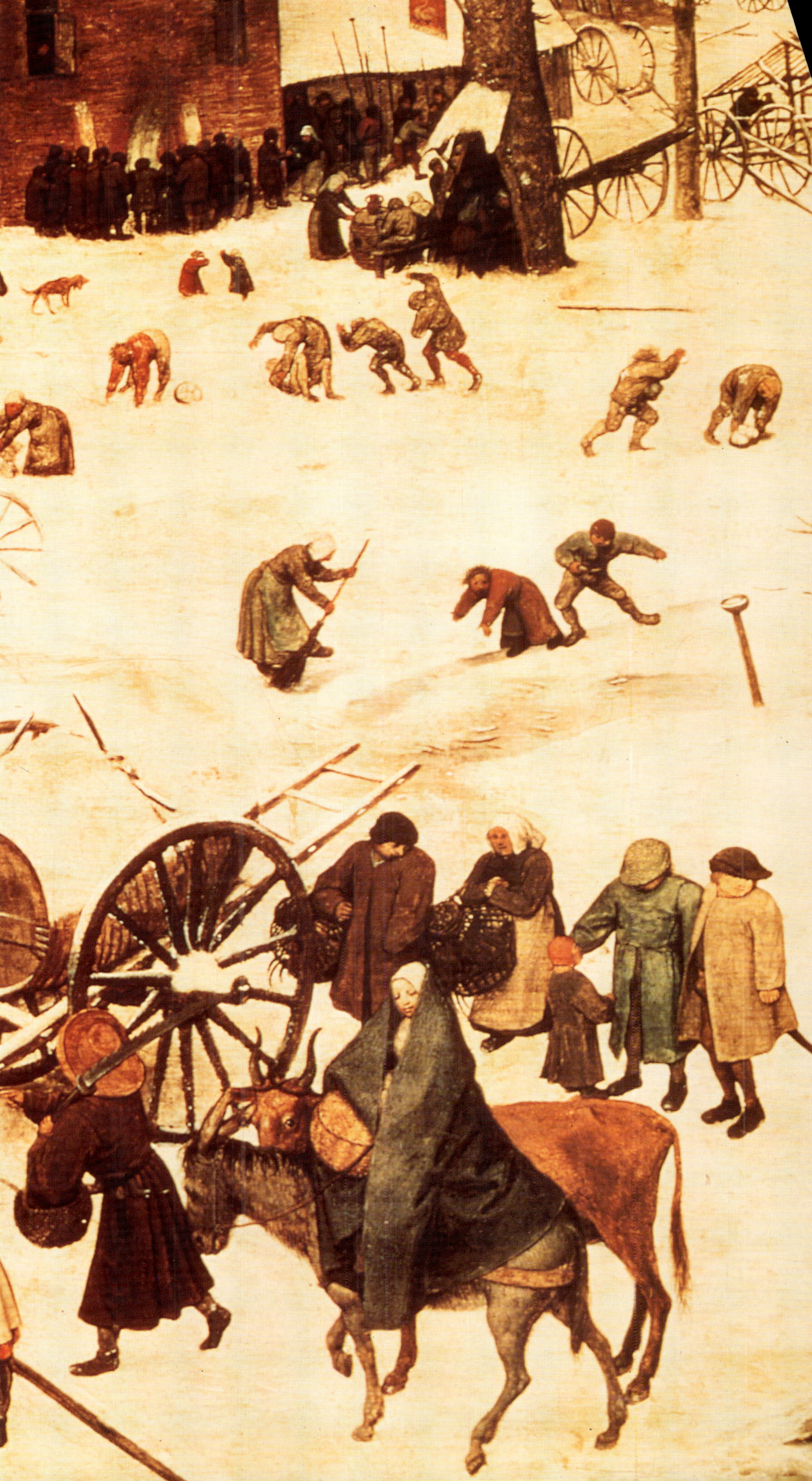

DETAIL
The Census in Bethlehem

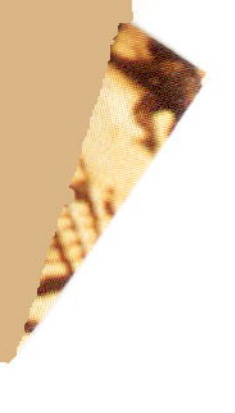

Although the inn promises warmth and food, the rest of the scene is cold and gloomy. Travelers, laden with baggage on their backs, make their way across a frozen river above the inn. Some stop to warm their limbs in front of bonfires that have been lighted at the side of a great step-gabled brick house near the center of the painting. More come from other parts of the compass, across the snow-packed earth. Among them is the Virgin Mary, atop a donkey pulled by Joseph. An ox walks alongside. This is the last leg of their slow journey from Nazareth, and they are picking up their pace as the inviting sounds and smells from the inn beckon them. This sacred party is almost lost in the elaboration of detail that Bruegel presents. In the world of Caesar Augustus they were anonymous among the masses. And so they appear here.

A hovel stands to the right of the center of the painting; a small cross leans precariously from the peak of its roof. This is no doubt meant to be the place where Mary will give birth to her holy son. According to Luke, while they were in Bethlehem, "the time came for her to be delivered. And she gave birth to her first-born son and wrapped him in swaddling cloths, and laid him in a manger, because there was no place for them in the inn" (Luke 2:6–7).

The Census in Bethlehem
PIETER BRUEGEL THE ELDER, Flemish, ca. 1525–1569
Koninklijke Musea voor Schone Kunsten van Belgie, Brussels. Oil on wood panel. 46 × 65¼ in.

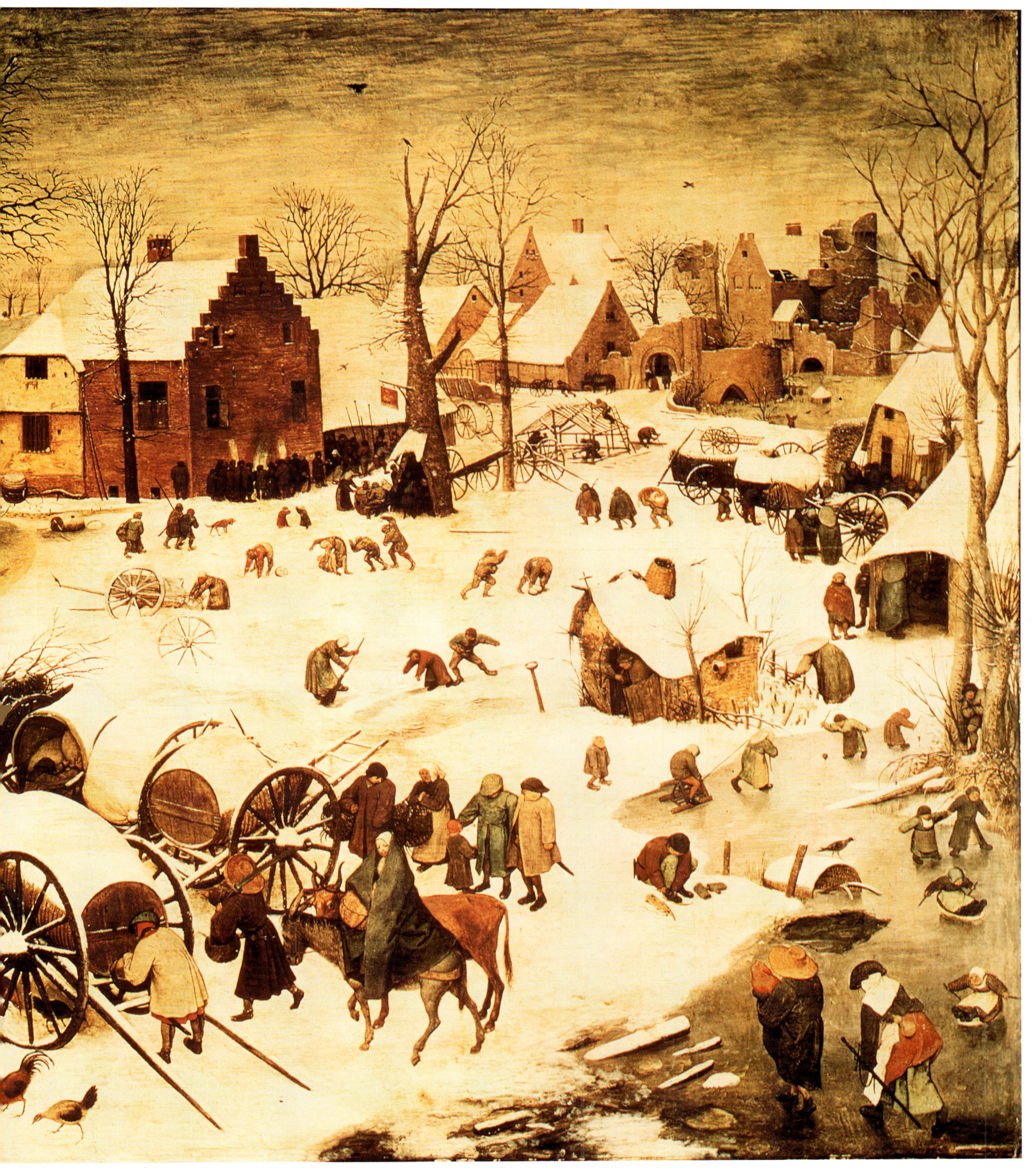

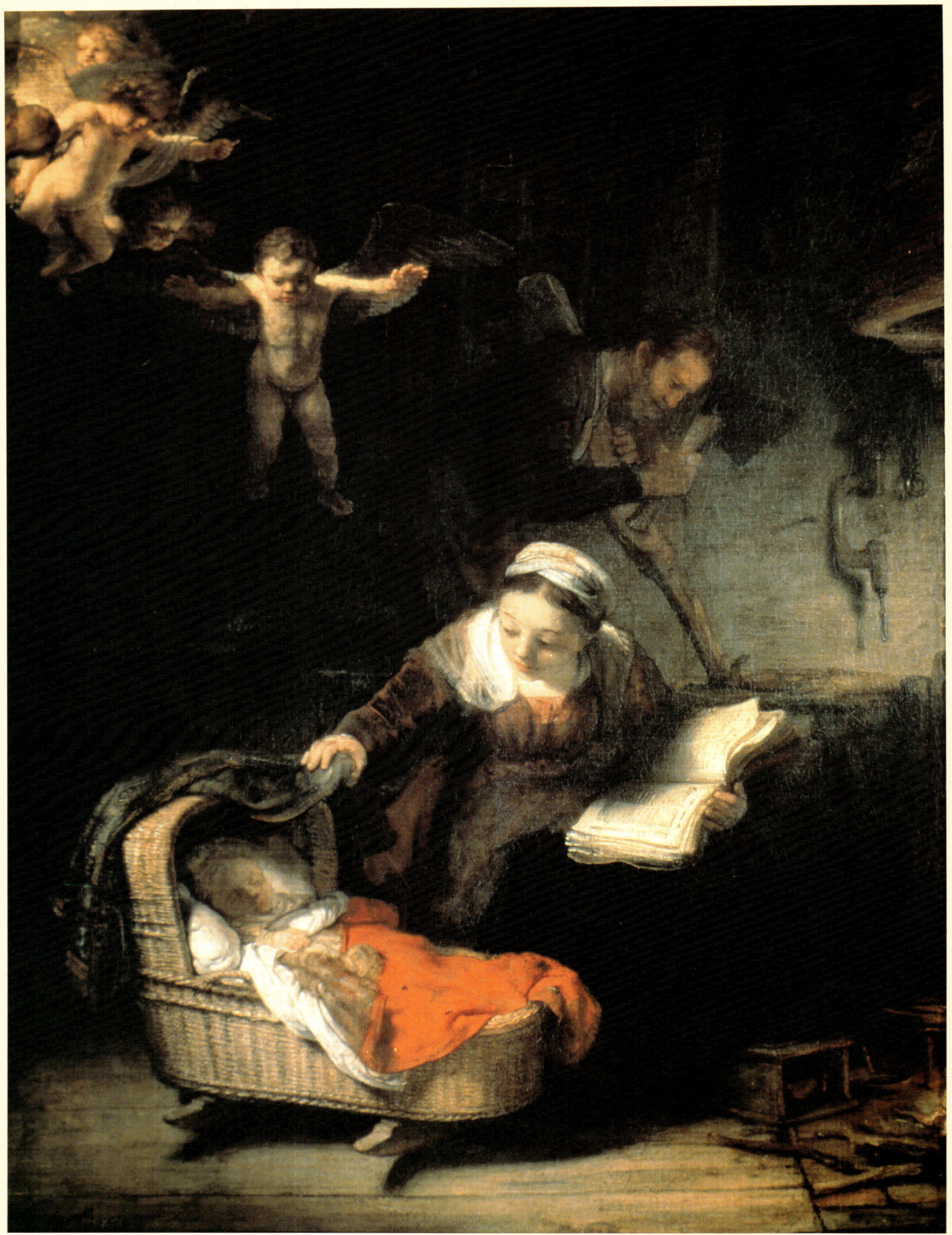

The Holy Family with Angels

Religious scenes imbued with grandeur and idealized figures did not appeal to most 17th-century Dutchmen. They were practical people, with their feet solidly on the ground, and they liked paintings that were about everyday life. Familiar things, things within their own grasp, appealed to them especially. Rembrandt's baby angels in this otherwise realistic domestic scene may have stretched the limits of his countrymen's acceptance, but the artist tempers his vision by having the cherubs jump into the house of Mary and Joseph like children leaping into a pool of cool water, rather than having them descend from heaven on clouds, as in the manner of an Italian or French artist of the day.

From the great number of extant Rembrandt drawings, it seems that the artist spent a good deal of his time studying human expressions and postures by sketching what he saw. Strangely, though, not many of his drawings are directly related to his paintings. This is not the case, however, with *The Holy Family with Angels*. At least three drawings are known in which the artist worked out the relative locations of the figures in relationship to the cradle, so this painting has been considered one of the most carefully planned in the great master's output.

Rembrandt had profound feeling for family life. The eighth of nine children in the poor family of a miller and a baker's daughter, he himself fathered five children, three of whom died in infancy. At about the time he painted this tender picture, he was deeply in love with Hendrickje Stoffels, a simple country girl who had come into his life as a maid. Eventually, she became his model, his common-law wife, and the mother of his daughter, whose birth was probably the inspiration for this work. Hendrickje was most likely the model for the Virgin Mary.

The scene is Joseph's workshop. He can be dimly seen in the background behind Mary, hacking away at wood, as he plies his trade. A drill, which Rembrandt paints with great detail, casts a shadow on the wall from which it hangs. Light comes from a fire in the lower corner of the painting. It is a cold day, and Jesus is covered with a red blanket lined with rabbit fur. His mother adjusts another blanket to keep out drafts that might come through the back of the wicker cradle. Mary has been reading the Bible, an occupation for a young woman that would have been highly respected and applauded by Rembrandt's contemporaries. The great tenderness and maternal concern with which she attends to her child would also have been seen as a model for others.

The Holy Family with Angels
REMBRANDT VAN RIJN, Dutch, 1606–1669
Hermitage, Leningrad. Oil on canvas. 46 × 35¾ in.

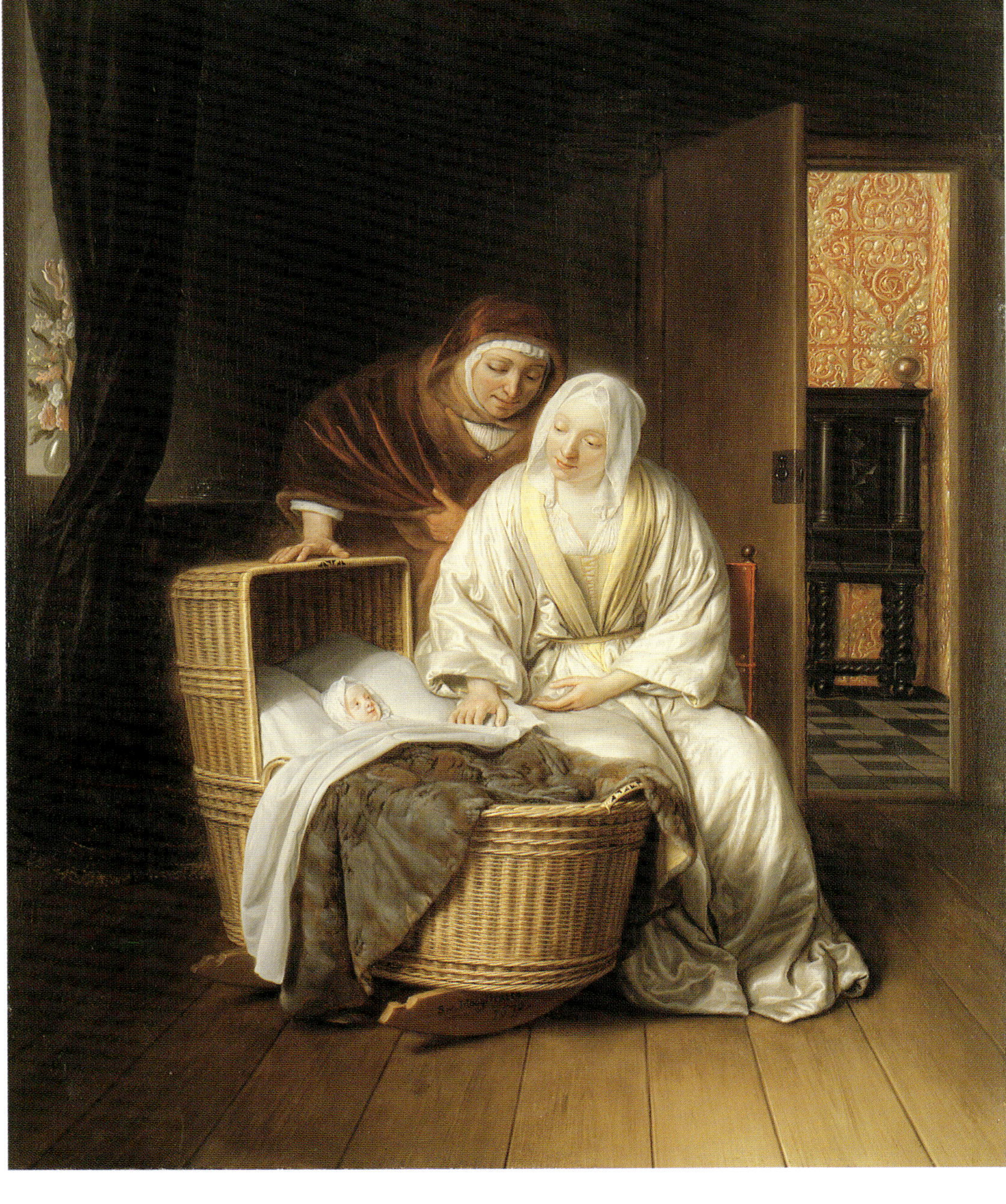

The First Born
SAMUEL VAN HOOGSTRATEN, Dutch, 1627–1678
James Philip Gray Collection, Museum of Fine Arts, Springfield, Massachusetts. Oil on canvas. 27½ × 22¼ in.

The First Born

Most Calvinist Dutchmen of the 17th century would not have felt comfortable with an overtly religious painting, even one as simply stated as Rembrandt's *The Holy Family with Angels* (see pp. 24–25). Religious art reminded them of Catholicism and of the Spanish king whose yoke they had only recently cast off. The Bible stories were familiar and dear to them, however, so veiled references to its stories and lessons are found throughout Dutch art.

In *The First Born*, Rembrandt's student Samuel van Hoogstraten reveals a typical upper-class Dutch interior of the mid-17th century. The partially opened door lets the viewer examine the light-filled entrance hall with its tooled-leather wall coverings enriched with gold, and massive ebony sideboard. In the main room of the house, a mother sits next to the cradle where her first-born lies sleeping. An older woman bends over to look more closely at the infant. The fur coverlet over the baby, the rich silk fabric of the mother's gown, and the woven willow of the cradle are all meticulously rendered. The artist has signed his name and the date 1670 on the rocker of the cradle, which tells art historians that the painting was completed the year after his famous teacher's death.

While this scene ostensibly is a calm and tender slice of Dutch domestic life, it can be interpreted as a picture of the Virgin Mary, her mother Anne, and the infant Jesus in a contemporary setting. The vase on the window sill at the far left contains white lilies that symbolize Mary's virginity, and it would have been entirely consistent with artistic practice in 17th-century Holland to invest a painting with two levels of meaning and significance. This picture is clearly about maternal love and pride, but it is also a reminder of the greatest biblical exemplar of that love.

Samuel van Hoogstraten was an art theorist. His treatise on perspective was widely read and was utilized in the training of young artists. The receding parallel lines of the floorboards are a lesson from that book. Based on strict one-point linear perspective, they allow the viewer to gauge the depth of the room and they also lead the eye to the cradle. The viewer, therefore, becomes a participant in the scene, walking across the hardwood planks of the floor to approach the women and the child.

Christmas Night

Paul Gauguin, one of the most radical painters of his day, gives a personal view of the night of Christ's birth. It is not a historical re-creation, nor the famous story retold. It is a night he knew while he lived among the pious Breton peasants early in his career. Or, at least, it is his sentimental memory of what a Christmas night would have been like for them, for he painted it upon his return to Paris soon after his first disastrous attempt to find paradise in Tahiti.

The primitive and elemental in art had taken on a special appeal for Gauguin as he searched for a style of his own. He particularly liked the carved stone "calvaries" of Brittany in the northwest of France. These were crucifixion scenes beside the roads, created to inspire the peasants. And, indeed, it was common to see countryfolk stop at them to pray. Carved by masons unschooled in art, they were notable for their simplicity and directness. Part of one can be seen in Gauguin's *Christmas Night*, picturing perhaps not the crucifixion but a nativity scene.

Two farm girls pass the shrine, eager to get home for the celebrations of Christmas eve. The cattle they herd brings to mind the animals at the manger whose breath warmed the holy family the first Christmas night. The soft pink glow of the setting sun, reflected off the snow and coloring the path at the bottom of the picture, continues a mood of warmth and comfort. Gauguin colors his scene without the use of shadows, giving an unearthly feeling to this rural reverie.

Christmas Night
PAUL GAUGUIN, French, 1848–1903
Collection Josefowitz, Lausanne, Switzerland. Oil on canvas. 28½ × 33 in.

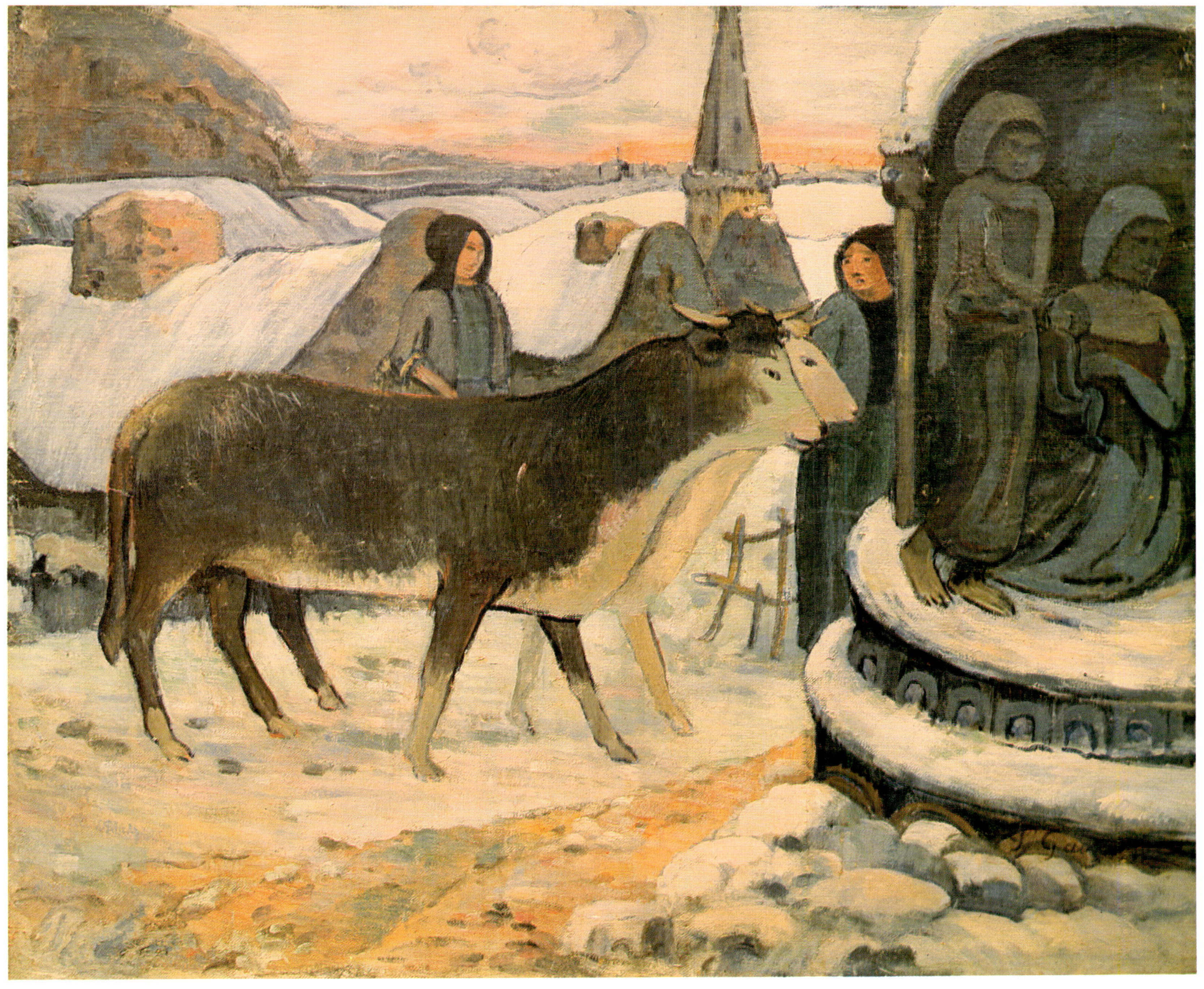

Angels Appearing to Shepherds

Bethlehem was a small town surrounded by fertile fields where animal husbandry and agriculture were the bases of existence. Its citizens lived modestly and knew one another's business. So word must have spread quickly when angels appeared to a group of shepherds to announce that "to you is born this day in the city of David a Savior, who is Christ the Lord. And this will be a sign for you: you will find a babe wrapped in swaddling cloths and lying in a manger" (Luke 2:11–12).

It is this magical moment that Nicolas Berchem depicts in *Angels Appearing to Shepherds*. The shepherds respond with wonder and adoration as they behold the beautiful messengers of God and hear their happy tidings. All except one shepherdess who sleeps, a reminder perhaps that the word of the Gospel was not accepted by all.

This heavenly vision is in startling contrast to the dead trunks of a tree, and the light from above is far more brilliant than the small fire burning inside the improvised tent. Berchem was known for the exacting detail of his animals and peasant figures—which is certainly evident in this painting—and he was also highly regarded as a hardworking artist, responsible for executing about 800 paintings during his very successful career.

As discussed in Rembrandt's *The Holy Family with Angels* (see pp. 24–25). 17th-century Holland was a newly Protestant country which boasted no glorious altarpieces, ceiling decorations, or wall murals extolling the church and telling the story of the Redemption like those Berchem had seen during sojourns in Rome. He was somewhat daring, therefore, in transferring the spirit of the latest, most exuberant Roman Catholic church decoration to this enchanting and inspiring scene.

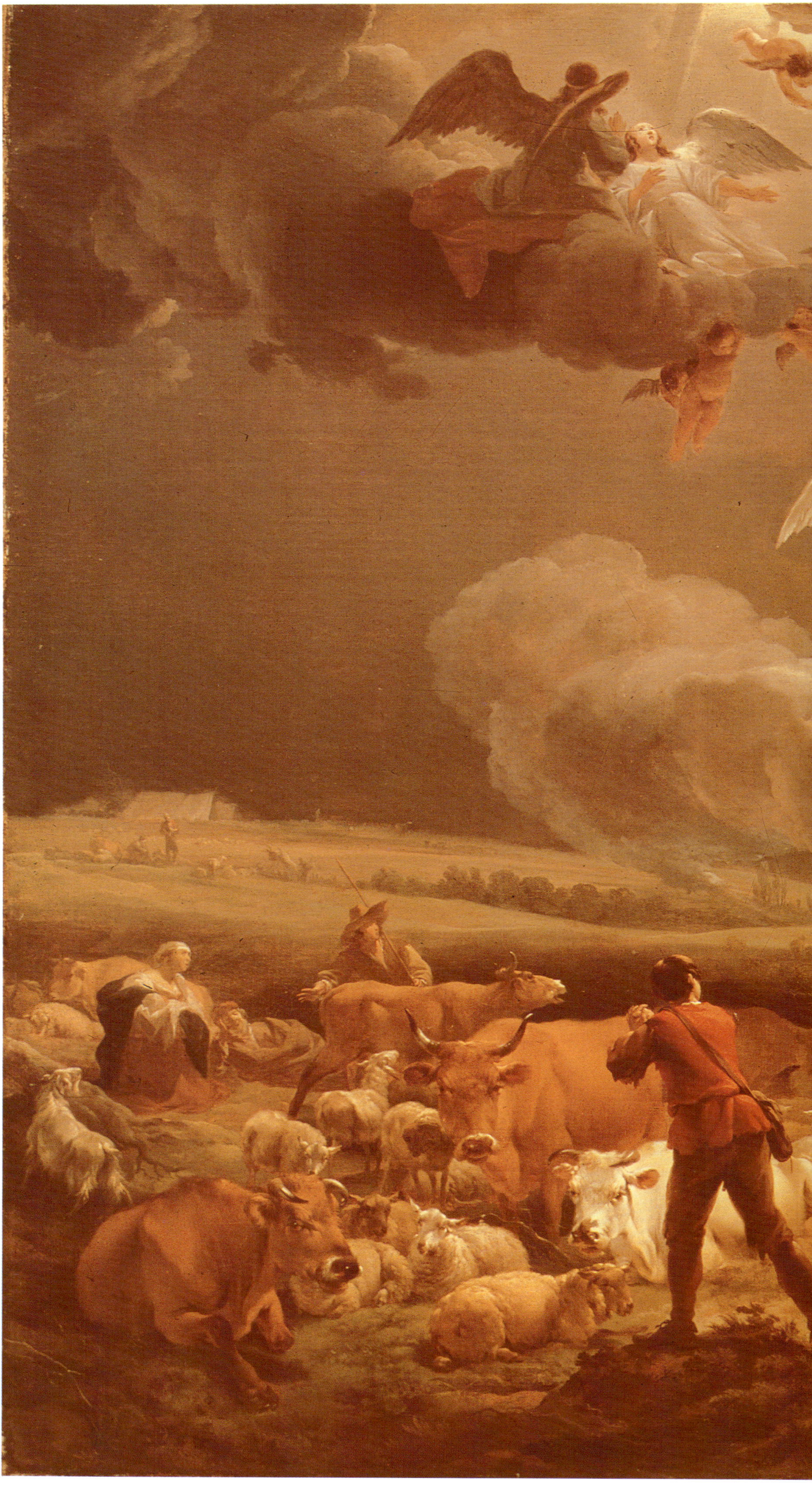

Angels Appearing to Shepherds
NICOLAS BERCHEM, Dutch, 1620–1685
City of Bristol Museum and Art Gallery, England. Oil on canvas. 43½ × 58 in.

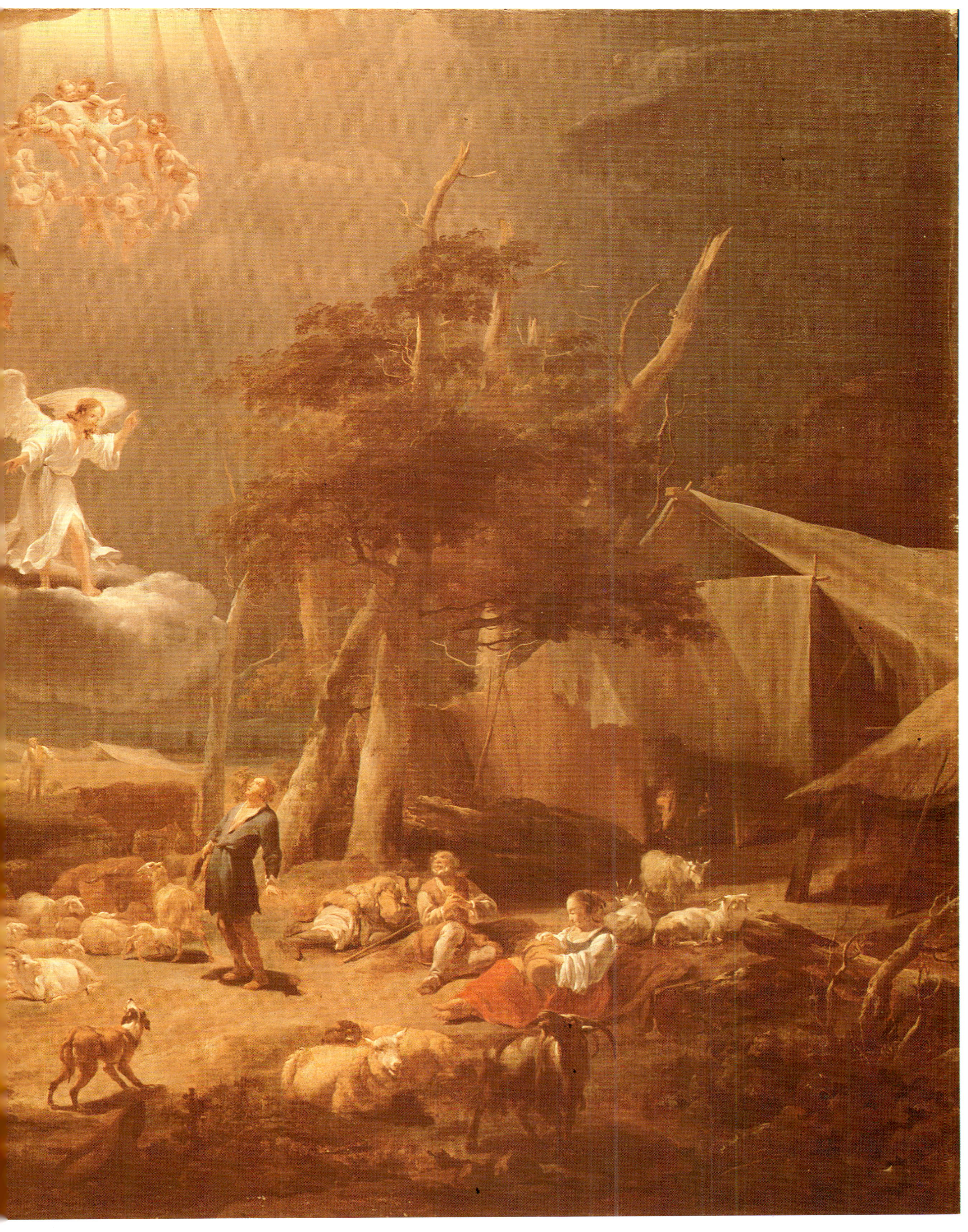

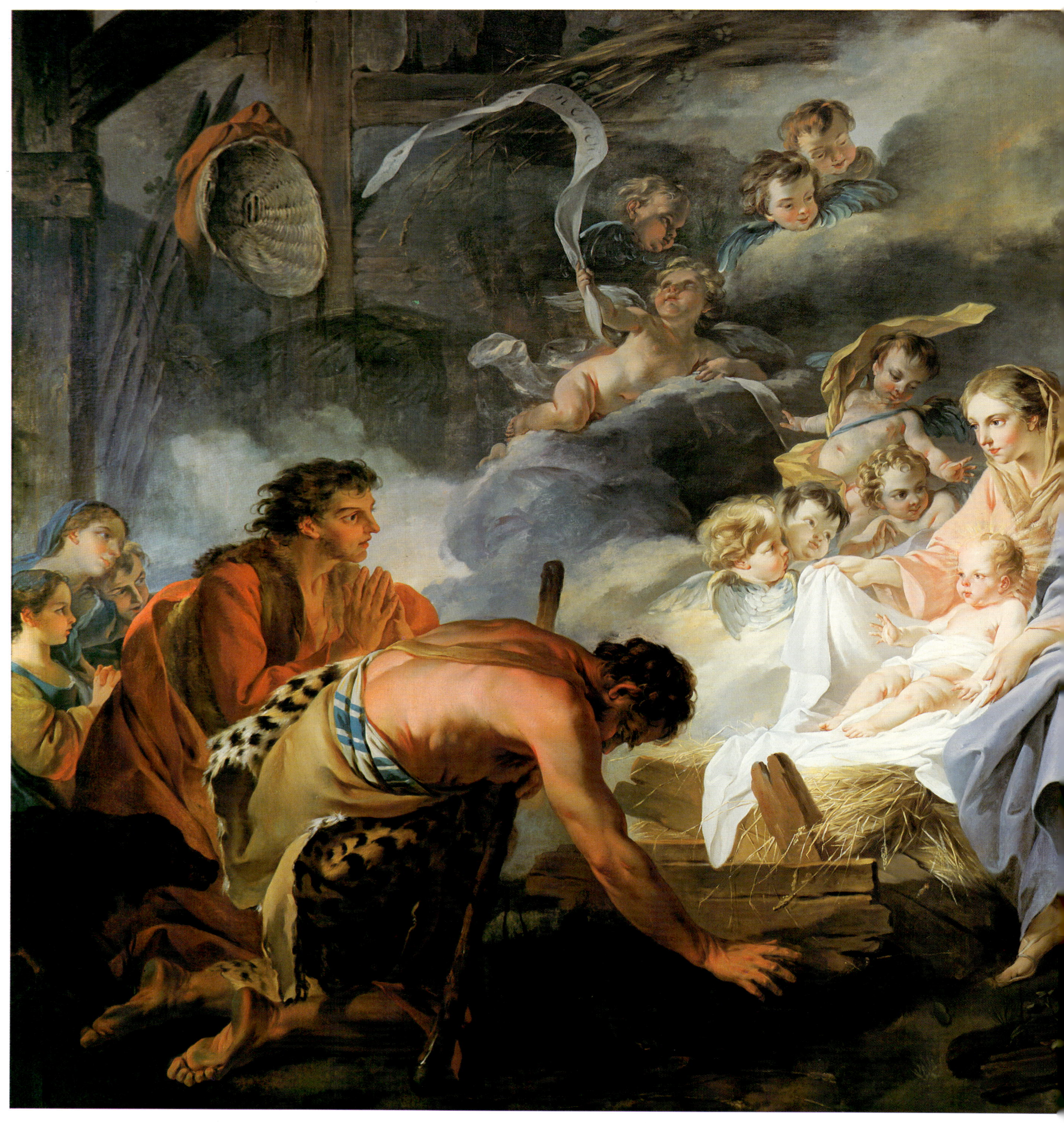

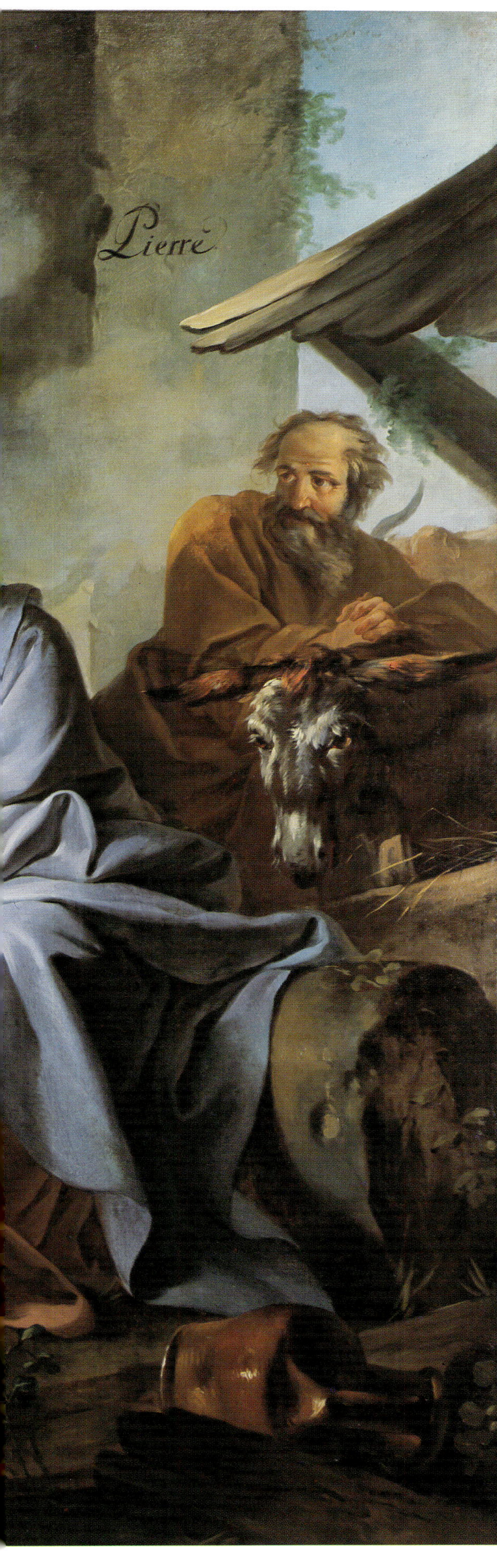

The Adoration of the Shepherds

In *The Adoration of the Shepherds*, the holiness, the magic, and the profound religious significance of the Nativity are captured by Jean-Baptiste Marie Pierre, who served the court of King Louis XV of France. Although Luke said that the angels returned to heaven after announcing the birth of Christ to the shepherds, Pierre has them accompany the humble men in their adoration. Actually, this is probably the shepherds' second visit to the nativity scene. Luke said they came, saw, went to tell others, and then returned, "glorifying and praising God for all they had heard and seen . . ." (Luke 2:20).

To present him better to the adoring shepherds, Mary has uncovered the child. He is the source of the wonderful light that illuminates the heads of the angels playfully spiraling up from the manger and their banner on which is written "Hosannah." The cool blues and yellows of the Virgin's robe, the clouds, and the straw are surrounded by the hot and earthy tones of the witnesses, strongly contrasting the divine aspects of the event with the earthly. As she looks toward the worshipful shepherds, Mary's face is filled with wonder and acceptance, but Joseph seems less sanguine as he cringes from all the attention that has come into his simple life, leaning his weight against a donkey.

Jean-Baptiste Marie Pierre has invented a barn-like setting for his *Adoration of the Shepherds*, but there is an old tradition that the birthplace of Jesus was a cave in Bethlehem. This notion stems from the fact that caves were used in biblical times to house cattle at night. Indeed, church writers as early as Justin Martyr in the second century and Origen in the third categorically stated that the birth took place in a cave. Thus, a cave under the great Basilica of the Holy Nativity is shown today to pilgrims who want to see this potentially famous spot. Apparently this theory of Jesus' birthplace is one to which the Venetian artist Giorgione subscribed as one can see in his version of the same story on the following pages.

Not only does he set his scene in a cave, he also depicts a warmer climate than do most artists who have pictured this scene; it is December, but the holy family is outdoors. The visit of the shepherds is also unusual for they seem reverential but not awestruck, as the French artists customarily depicted them. Rather, in Giorgione's work they appear to be doing something customary. Perhaps these simple men returned day after day to see how the baby was doing.

The self-assured quiet of this painting allows the viewer's eye to wander, taking in every detail without ever completely abandoning the central event which is pushed far off the center of the canvas. Verdant bushes and trees, fresh running water, and the towers and villas dotting the countryside to the left of the shepherds are all imbued with the same dignity that characterizes the figures at the mouth of the cave. Above them are little angels of the day—heads of children with golden wings—that were a convention in religious art by the time Giorgione lifted his brush to this canvas.

Jean-Baptiste Marie Pierre also uses cherubic angels—about 250 years later than Giorgione—but more to the effect of a cho-

The Adoration of the Shepherds
JEAN-BAPTISTE MARIE PIERRE, French, 1713–1789
Gift of Elizabeth Shelden in memory of her son Allan Shelden III, The Detroit Institute of Arts, Founders Society Purchase, Elizabeth, Allan and Warren Shelden Fund in memory of Allan Shelden III. Oil on canvas. 110 × 129¾ in.

rus in a grand opera. Moreover, he chooses to view his scene from below, as though he were front-row-center in an orchestra seat of a theater, while Giorgione views his *Adoration* from above, as though hovering like the heavenly creatures around the cavern. Both of these vantage points somewhat separate the viewer from the moment—one would have to be on the ground to share in it directly—but they allow one the most privileged views possible. Despite the fullness of his composition, Giorgione keeps the focus on the object of veneration by framing it with the only bright colors in the painting, the tattered red sleeve of the standing shepherd, the red and blue of the Virgin's garb, and the rich golden yellow of Joseph's cape. Jean-Baptiste uses brilliant light to the same end in his *Adoration*.

Dead by his 32nd year, Giorgione left no more than 20 works for future generations to enjoy. This one is cardinal to his oeuvre for its mature vision, its utter sincerity, and its ability to convince the viewer of the veracity of the event depicted. It is hard to believe that he painted directly with pigment on canvas, without preparatory drawings to guide him. He most assuredly had the scene etched in his mind's eye before he began.

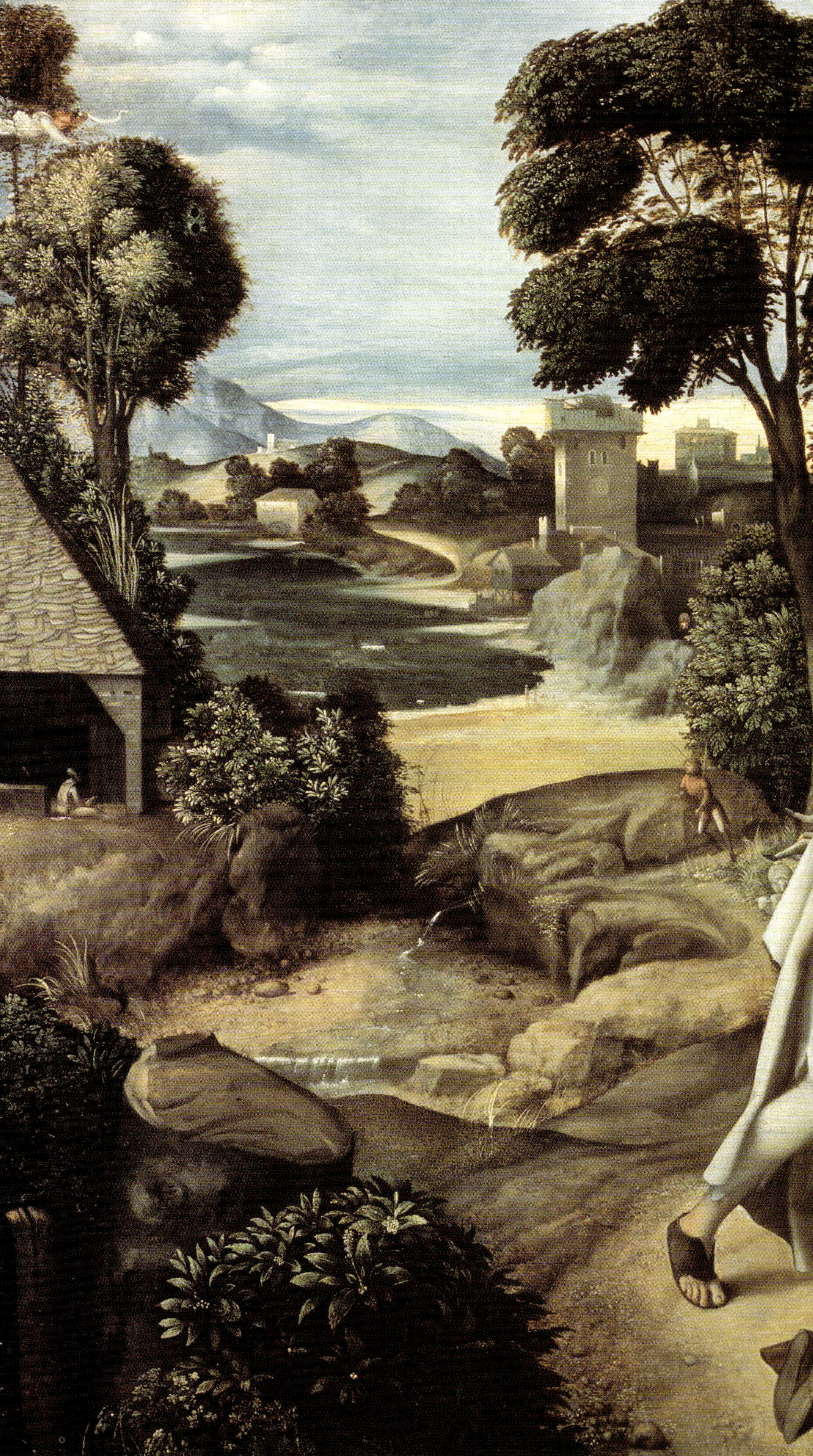

The Adoration of the Shepherds
GIORGIONE, Italian, ca. 1478–1510
Samuel H. Kress Collection, National Gallery of Art, Washington, DC. Wood panel. 35¾ × 43½ in.

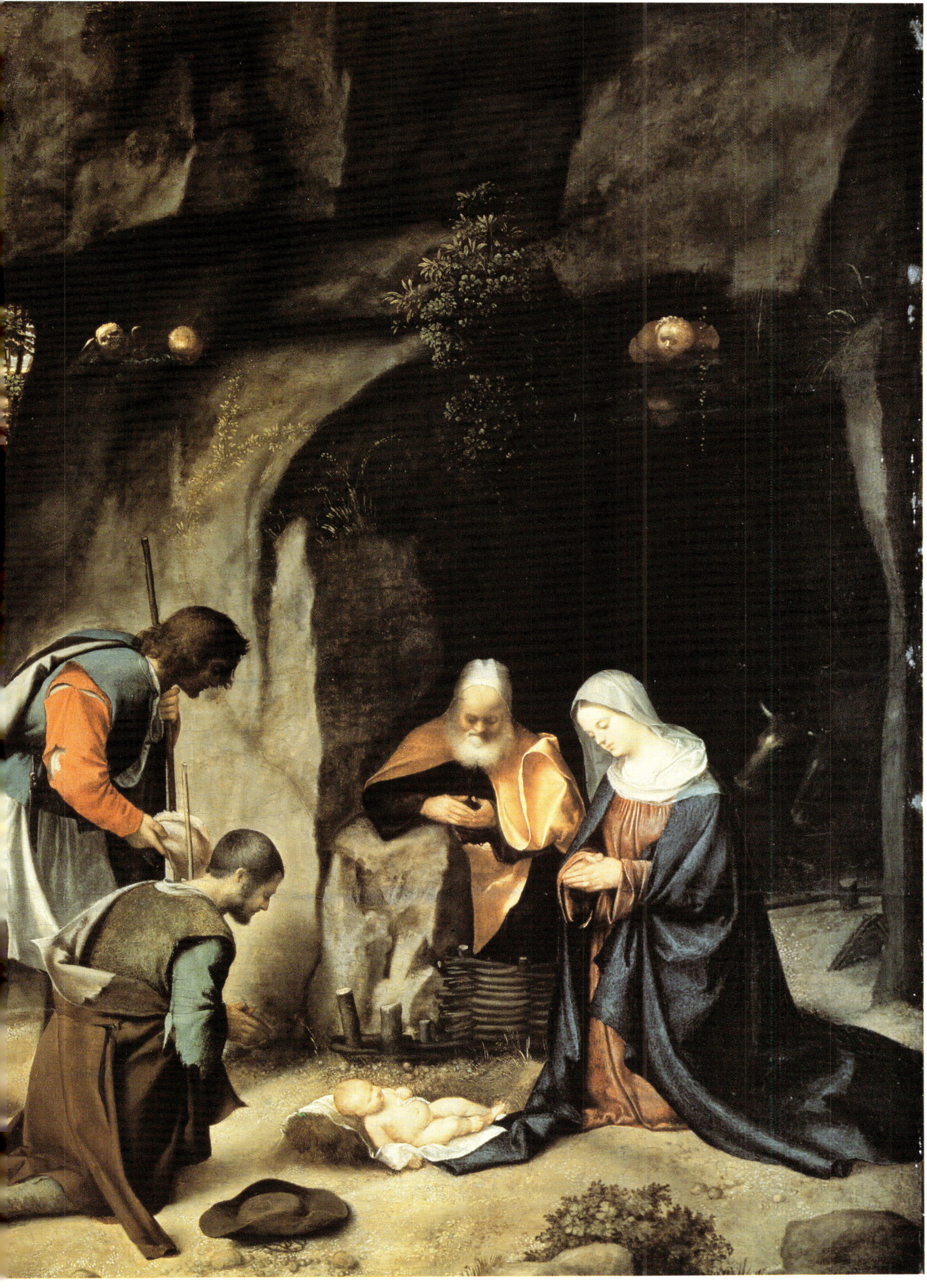

The Madonna and Child

Probably the majority of images in Christian art are portraits which find their earliest inspiration in the art of ancient Rome. But the Romans were interested in lifelike portraiture. Christianity developed a transcendental art that held sway for over a thousand years. Ugolino da Siena's *Madonna and Child* typifies this style at its sweetest.

This sacred picture and the thousands that came before it, known as icons, were considered a window to God, not a likeness. Indeed, because Jesus was not a man but God-made man, no artist dared picture him as a real, earthly human. The same apprehension applied to depictions of saints, since their lives were changed by God.

The stylistic convention that grew out of Christian theology retained the aspects of the human—eyes, ears, nose, hair, etc.—but it also changed them. The head and limbs were elongated well beyond normal human proportions. The eyes were almond-shaped and disproportionately large relative to the width of the face, for ancient religions believed that the eyes were the seat of divinity. Fingers were elegantly stretched, and other parts of the body highly stylized.

While these formulas were de rigueur throughout the orthodox Christian world, degrees of individuality crept into the images. The artists of Siena were among the most important innovators, softening the usual depiction with visual ideas that represented one of the last stages of this art in Italy. A more human concept of the Christian martyrs began with the teachings of St. Francis of Assisi, who died about 100 years before this image was painted. As his followers understood more of Jesus' human dimensions—and those of the saints of the New Testament—worshippers wanted portraits rather than symbols.

The famous painting by Raphael reproduced on p. 33 retains the spirit of imperial Rome, but is softer, more alluring, and more approachable than any official portrait ever dared to be. Known as *The Alba Madonna* because it was once owned by the powerful Alba family of Spain, it pairs John the Baptist, the son of Mary's cousin Elizabeth and her husband Zechariah, with Jesus, linking them through the tall, thin cross that both of them hold, and by the embrace of the virgin mother. John wears the robe of camel's hair that the Bible describes in Mark 1:6, as very like the garment Elijah wore in the Old Testament, and Jesus, his cousin, is naked.

Raphael was 27 years of age when he painted this memorable icon. He had just become chief painter to Pope Julius II in Rome. Only four years later, he was to be placed in charge of all artistic projects for the Pope, including the supervision of architectural work, the decoration of vast spaces, and the execution of numerous large paintings. He was also in charge, at his own request, of overseeing historic Rome. In this capacity, he saved many important ancient buildings from destruction; when he died unexpectedly at the age of only 37, he was buried in one of them, the Pantheon. His knowledge of antiquity is evident in *The Alba Madonna*; the sandals of the Virgin are exactly the kind worn in the first century of the Christian era.

Raphael was no slave to antiquity, however. He admired it as one glorious moment in the history of humanism, the philosophy that places man at the center of the universe as God's agent, responsible for God's creation. Using all he knew of ancient art, as well as the lessons he learned from his older contemporaries Michelangelo and Leonardo da Vinci, he created a bold but soft new style. It became the model for generations of artists, just as the Byzantine icon had been the paradigm for centuries before the Renaissance.

Raphael also turned to antiquity for the format of his painting. Coins and medals bearing imperial images were round, and so this work suggests an official portrait. By positioning the holy family in a vast and empty field, he infuses the painting with an aura of spaciousness and timelessness, as though these handsome creatures will be preserved, as he has depicted them, for an eternity.

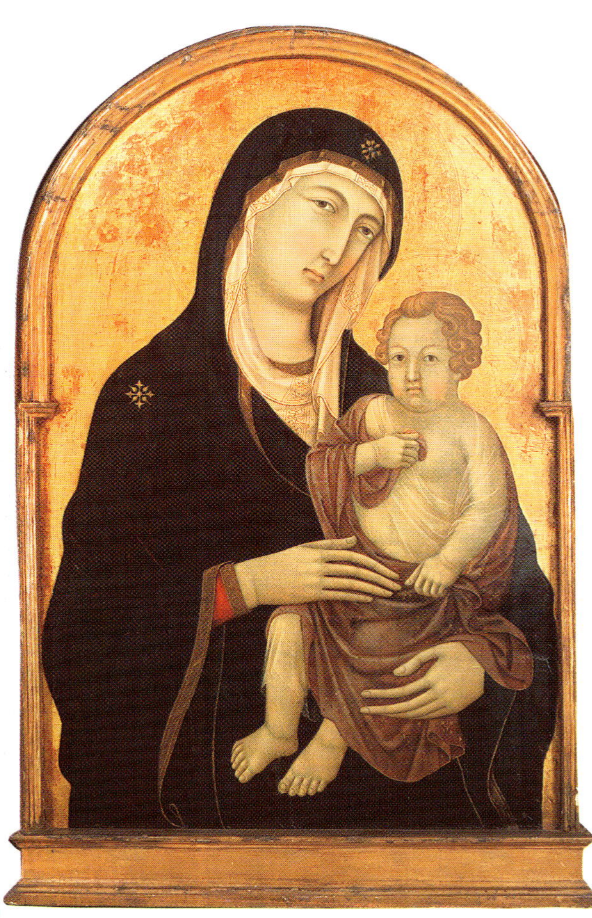

Madonna and Child
UGOLINO DA SIENA, Italian, active 1317–1327
The Robert Lehman Collection, Metropolitan Museum of Art, New York. Tempera on wood panel. 35⅛ × 23 in.

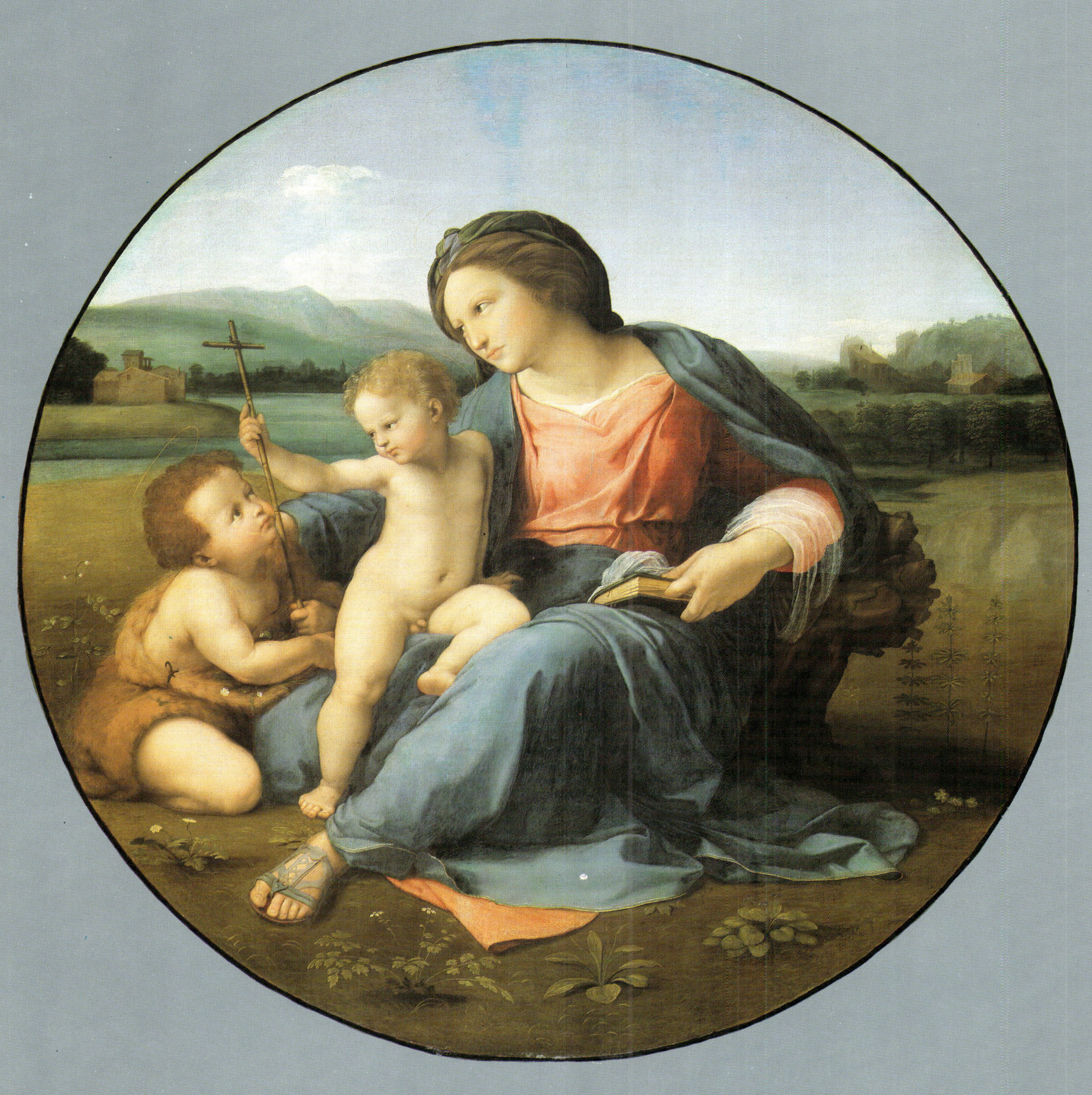

The Alba Madonna
RAPHAEL, Italian, 1483–1520
Andrew W. Mellon Collection, National Gallery of Art, Washington, DC. Oil on canvas. Diameter, 37¼ in.

The Virgin and Child with Angels in a Garden

Because Christ is more approachable when he is remembered as a baby in his mother's arms, artists of every generation and every Christian country adopted the Madonna and Child as their own. The tenderness of such images had a great deal to do with the success of Christian proselytizing of the nomadic and warring tribes of Europe during the first millennium of the Christian era.

But by the late Middle Ages, the direct and straightforward presentation of the holy mother and her child had become overlaid with a courtly and symbolic philosophy of love. The 13th century idealized maidenhood. Woman was heroine, goddess, and mascot at the same time. Jousts were dedicated to her. Knights carried her handkerchief or a lock of her hair with them to the Crusades, and the man who adored her and did not touch her received spiritual elevation for his dedication and restraint.

It was for a court society with such platonic ideals that Stefano da Verona painted this charming and fetching picture, in which the worship of Woman becomes fused with the cult of Mary. Although clearly of elevated status in a voluminous gown of white silk, the Virgin is a paradigm for all young women. She is not enthroned. Rather, she sits on a cushion on the ground, an indication of her humility. The deepness of her meditation with her son has brought angels to their presence, filling her garden with joyful music. God the Father, high above in a mandorla of gold, completes the family portrait.

The garden too takes on mythic proportions. Both the enclosure itself and the flowers are symbols of virginity. Indeed, cloistered gardens were part of every monastery and convent where the living models of virginity said their prayers, meditated, and found recreation. Moreover, women of the courts of Europe were frequently pictured reading, talking quietly, or listening to music in enclosed gardens. The protected garden also recalls the Garden of Eden, and the prophet Jeremiah's comparison of the redeemed soul with a watered garden (Jeremiah 31:12). Given these myriad layers of meaning, every Christian is exhorted by this painting to create a holy garden in his or her heart where Jesus and his mother can live in praise and jubilation.

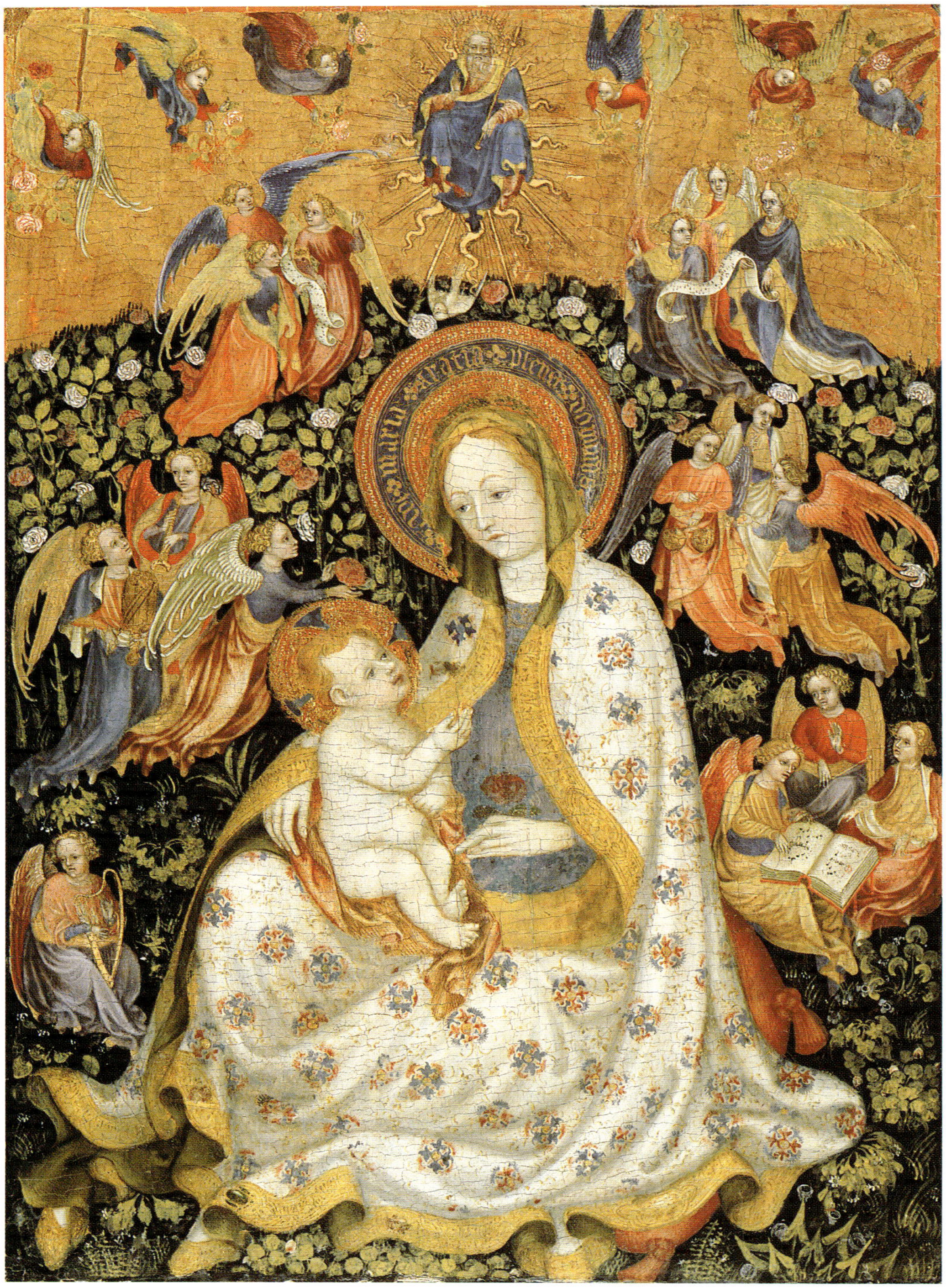

The Virgin and Child with Angels in a Garden with a Rose Hedge

STEFANO DA VERONA, Italian, ca. 1374–1438 or later

Worcester Art Museum, Massachusetts. Tempera on wood panel. 24 × 17 in.

The Journey of the Magi to Bethlehem

Because Benozzo Gozzoli focuses sharply on every single detail of this picture, the scene is overwhelmingly ornate. Its appeal is in the lavishness of the trappings and costumes, and these compete with one another in dizzying spectacle. No pretense is made to symbolize the sacred context of the story being told. With enormous assuredness that to be very rich and handsome is to be nearer to God, the artist plays out the pageant in the conventions of his, not the Magi's, day. This is a banker's painting, commissioned for a banker's private chapel at the start of the Renaissance in the city where that intellectual rebirth began. The banker was Cosimo de' Medici and the city was Florence.

The Medici, when this picture was painted, were fast becoming the most important family in all of Italy, the first time since ancient days that private wealth exceeded princely wealth. The Medici were cunning politicans, so in public they were less conspicuous in their show of riches than the subjects in this painting. Their palace, a silent and imposing fortress, presented a public facade of dark gray, rusticated stones, but in its interior, reserved for the inner circle of the Medici, the family could show off. Still, any guest who was awed by the gold and splendor of this work, or of the others that the Medici had commissioned for their personal pleasure, also knew that his hosts regularly exceeded all others in Europe in philanthropy.

Florence was accustomed to public spectacles, and many of its important feast-day celebrations were funded through Medici largess. Benozzo Gozzoli got his ideas for this painting from participating in those great pageants. He was asked by Cosimo to decorate the entire second-floor chapel of his new palace. Originally, tapestries had been planned, and that idea might have inspired Gozzoli to orchestrate such a highly patterned work in which the procession marches down one side of the chapel and ends up at the altar where a painting of the

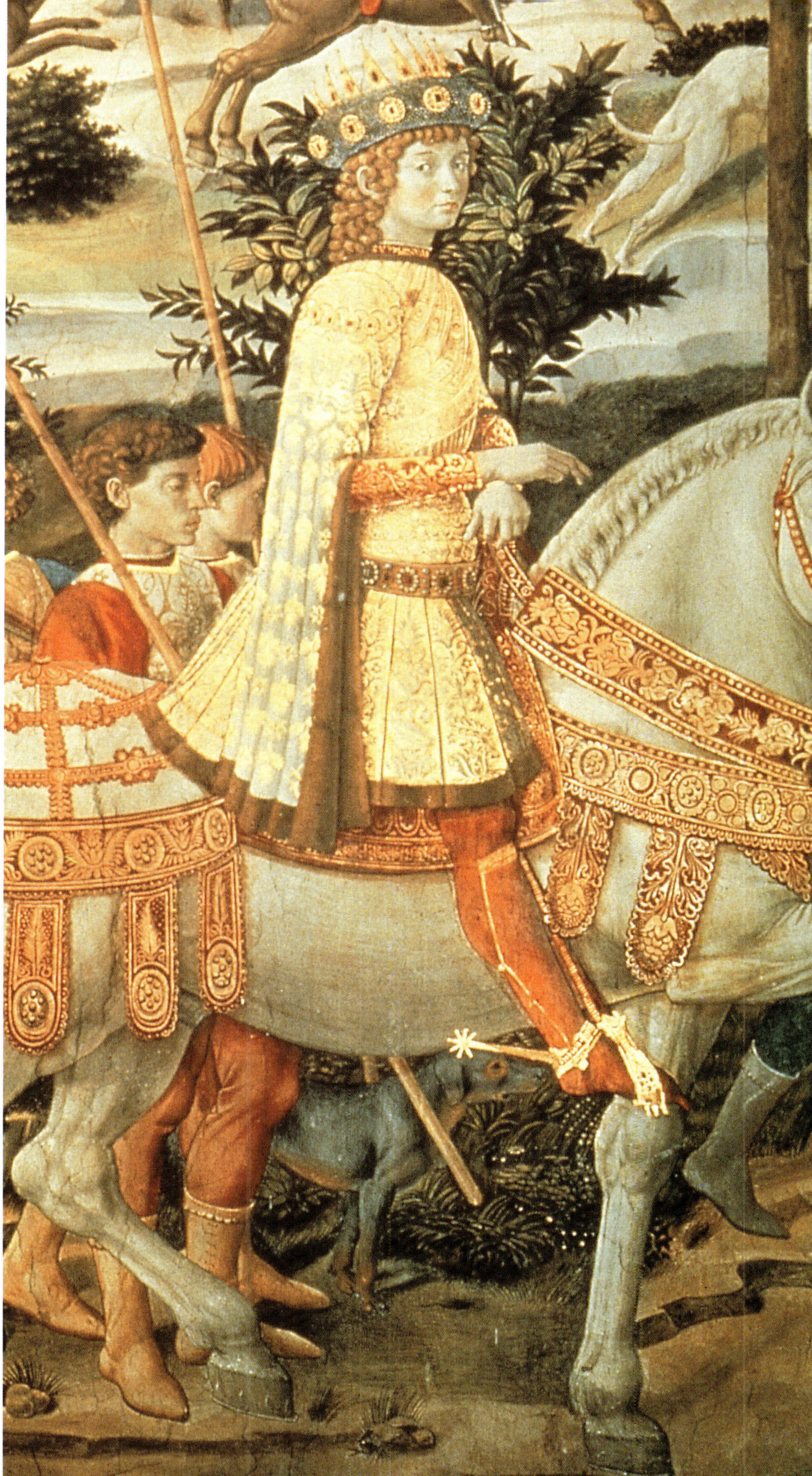

DETAIL
Journey of the Magi

Madonna and Child brings them to a halt. He finished the painting just in time for Cosimo and his family to enjoy it when they moved into the palace in 1459.

Turning from the setting in which the painting hung to the setting of the painting itself, a medieval walled city rises high on a hill in the distance. Perhaps it represents Jerusalem, and the procession from it is the last stage in the Magi's long trip. The rich multitude that attends them snakes its way across a wilderness of barren, gray rocks where palm and orange trees flourish and hunters pursue deer. Many of the richly clad riders wear red caps.

It is difficult to figure out exactly who are the Magi and who are not. Two equestrians at the left, seen from the front, wait for the others to catch up. Their horses stir nervously and do not want to pause. One of these men holds high a covered vessel of gold, and the other guards this treasure with a drawn sword. A young nobleman, wearing a crown and fur-trimmed cloth of gold, rides on a prancing gray steed. He and his mount are seen in profile, with six young pages striding along in attendance. "Ah, yes," the guest in the Medici palace would have realized, "that is the face of Cosimo himself." Indeed, the entire work is filled with portraits of family and household members.

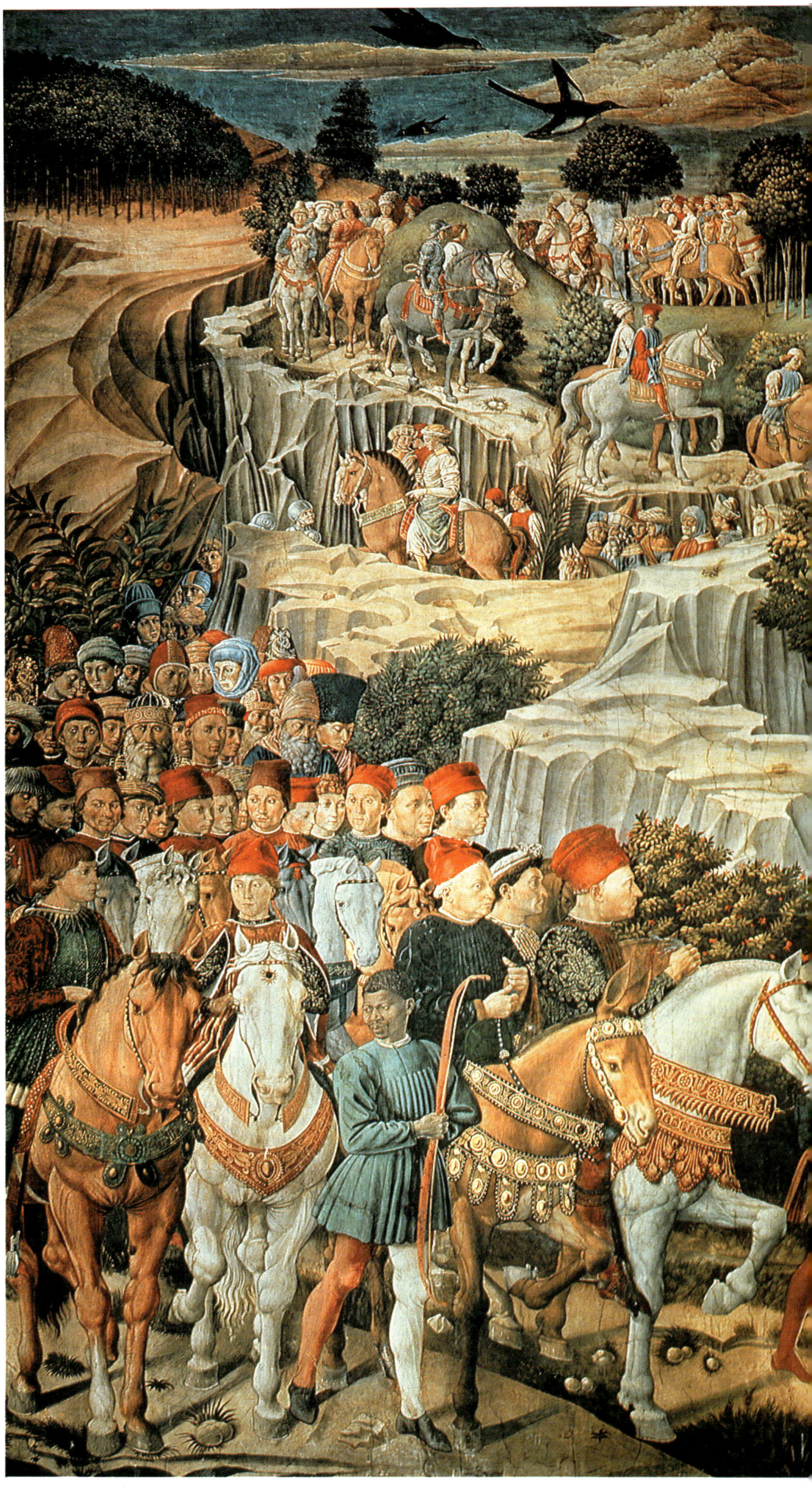

Journey of the Magi
BENOZZO GOZZOLI, Italian, 1420–1497
Palazzo Medici-Riccardi, Florence. Fresco.

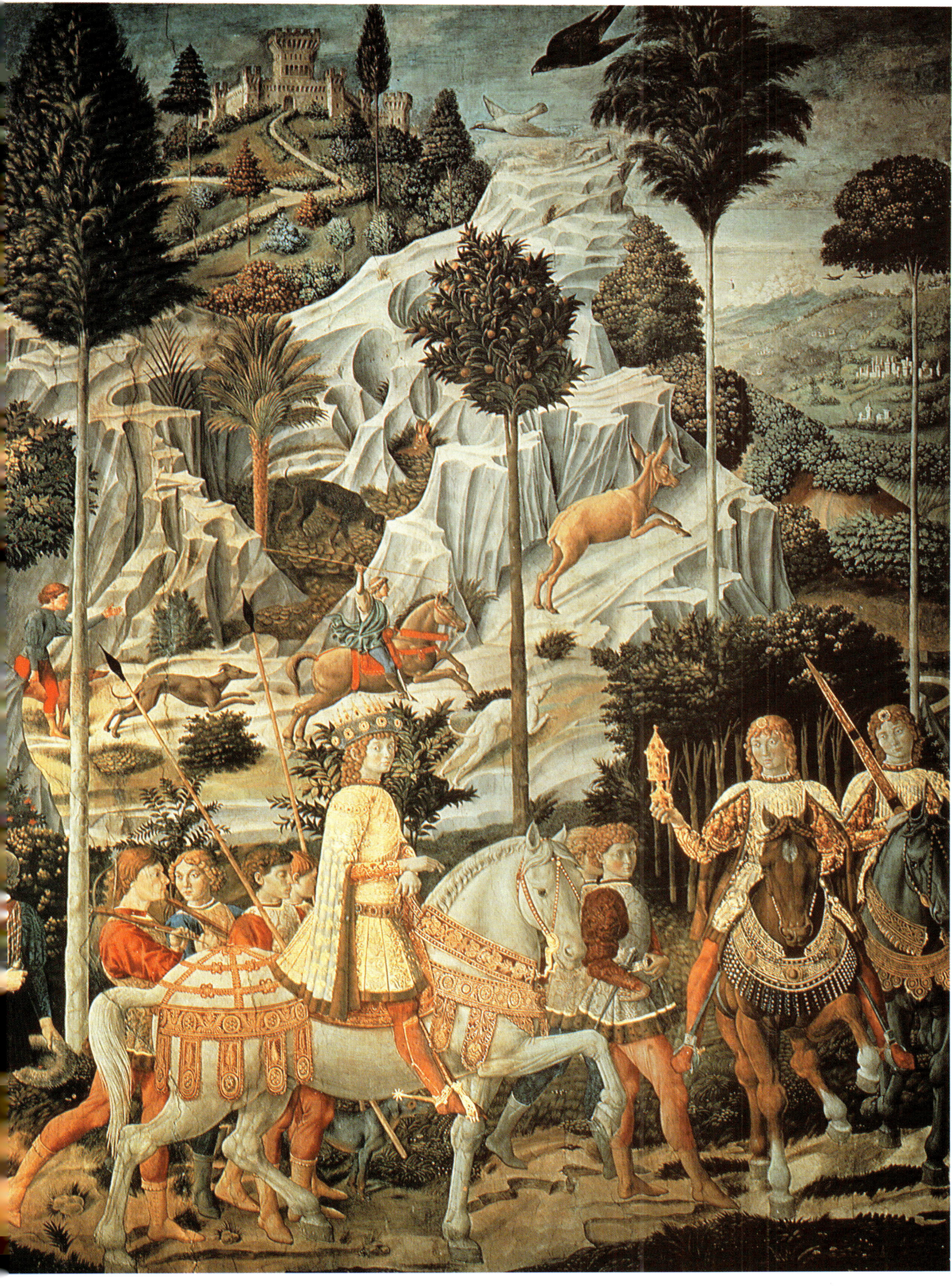

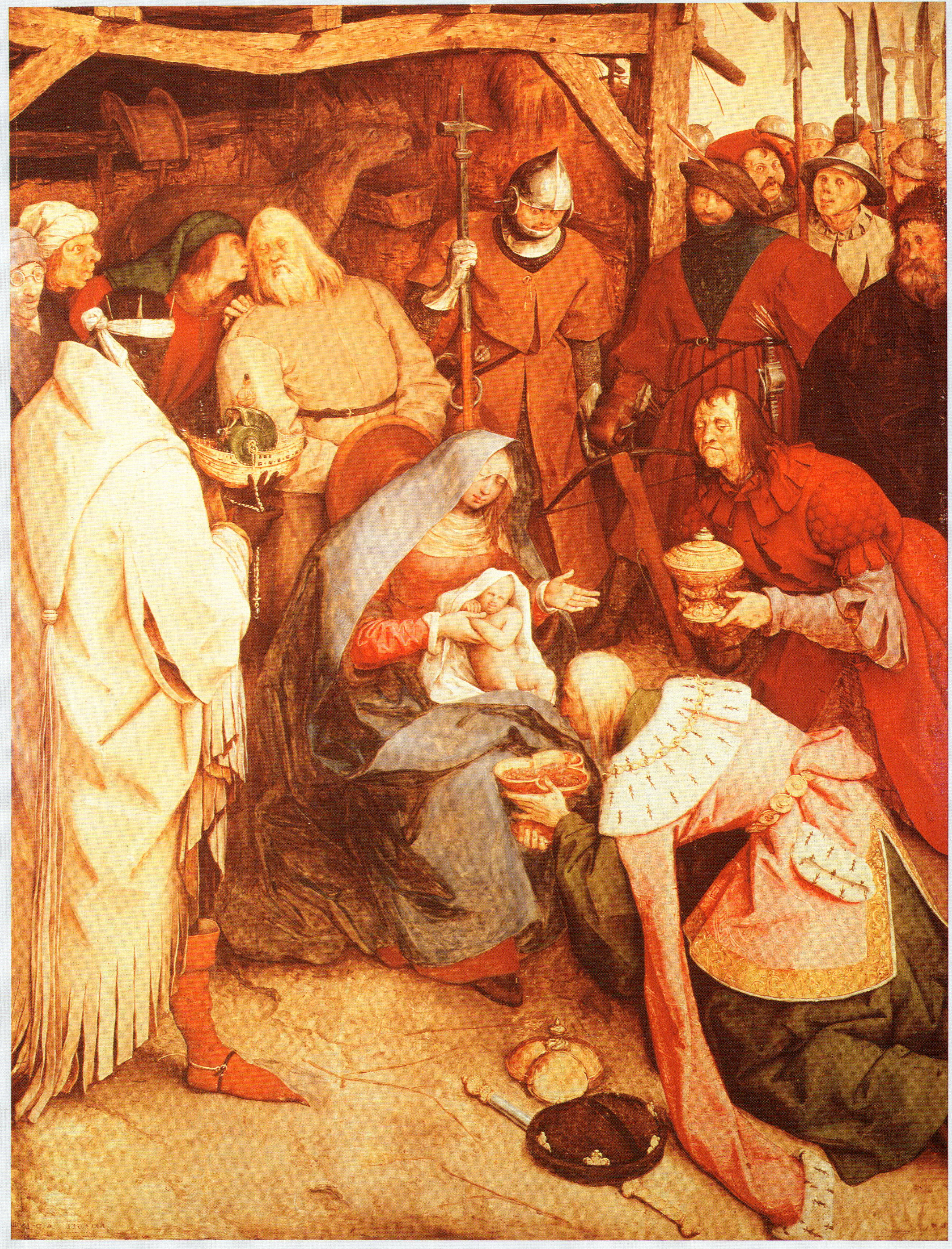

Adoration of the Magi

Only Matthew reported that wise men paid a visit to the baby Jesus. He did not say they were kings; that tradition stemmed from Isaiah, who prophesied that "nations shall come to your light, and kings to the brightness of your rising" (Isaiah 60:3). Nor did Matthew number them; that bit of mathematics was based on their gifts of gold, frankincense, and myrrh. The episode was expanded in devotional literature during the Middle Ages, as so many Bible stories were. Names, and even ages, were given to the sages—Melchior (60), Balthasar (40), and Caspar of Sheba, a black (20)—and the story of their journey was extravagantly embroidered.

The visit of the Magi was significant for it marked Jesus' first appearance, or epiphany, to the Gentiles, in contrast to the earlier visitation to the shepherds, which was Jesus' manifestation to his own people. Because they were unfamiliar with the prophecy of Jesus' birth in Bethlehem, it was assumed that the Magi were not Jews. They had to ask in Jerusalem where Jesus could be found. For centuries the celebration of their visit on January 6 was a far greater holiday than Christmas. To this day in many Latin countries, Epiphany, or Three Kings Day, remains the more festive of the celebrations and is the time for the exchange of gifts.

In *The Adoration of the Kings*, Pieter Bruegel, like most artists, concentrates on the richness of the attire of these exotics, but he ignores the star that amazed them and eventually led them to Jesus. Diego Velázquez, on the other hand, is much too sober an artist to care about finery, and his star is veiled by trees and clouds in the far distance. His concern is the response of the wise men to the boy king, in contrast to Bruegel's lively interest in the anonymous man who stands behind the Madonna and Child gossiping with old Joseph about Caspar's extraordinary gift. (Velázquez is kinder to Joseph than Bruegel, showing him as a handsome young man, which contradicts every tradition about him.) The lighting of the subjects in these works strongly supports the intent of each painting. The Flemish work is anecdotal and, since it elaborates considerably on both the Bible and tradition, Bruegel casts it in an overall, generalized light, so that nothing can be missed. The Spanish painting, by contrast, is designed to inspire worship by making an example of the kings for the pious. Velázquez, therefore, endows his realistically observed light with spiritual overtones, reflecting it off of Jesus and Mary.

Three decades separate the lives of Bruegel and Velázquez, and their art has little in common but deep human sympathy and understanding. Both men are ranked as the very greatest creative spirits of their respective ages. Bruegel's appellation as the rube "Peasant Bruegel" came soon after his death, diminishing the strong reputation he had in life. But historians today recognize him as more than a comic painter. His novel treatments of proverbs and the 12 months, which he made into genre subjects, are among the most profound works of the 16th century. Velázquez became the chief painter to the young king Philip IV of Spain just four years after completing this *Adoration of the Magi*. With his young wife, who likely posed for the Virgin Mary in this work, he moved from Seville to Madrid where he was granted more privileges than any artist of the age. Both men personally knew the greatest intellectuals and most powerful rulers of their times, so they must have felt comfortable in depicting the Magi as either sages or kings.

Adoration of the Kings
PIETER BRUEGEL THE ELDER, Flemish, ca. 1525–1569
National Gallery, London. Oil on panel. 42¾ × 33 in.

Adoration of the Magi
DIEGO VELÁZQUEZ, Spanish, 1599–1660
Museo del Prado, Madrid. Oil on canvas. 81 × 49½ in.

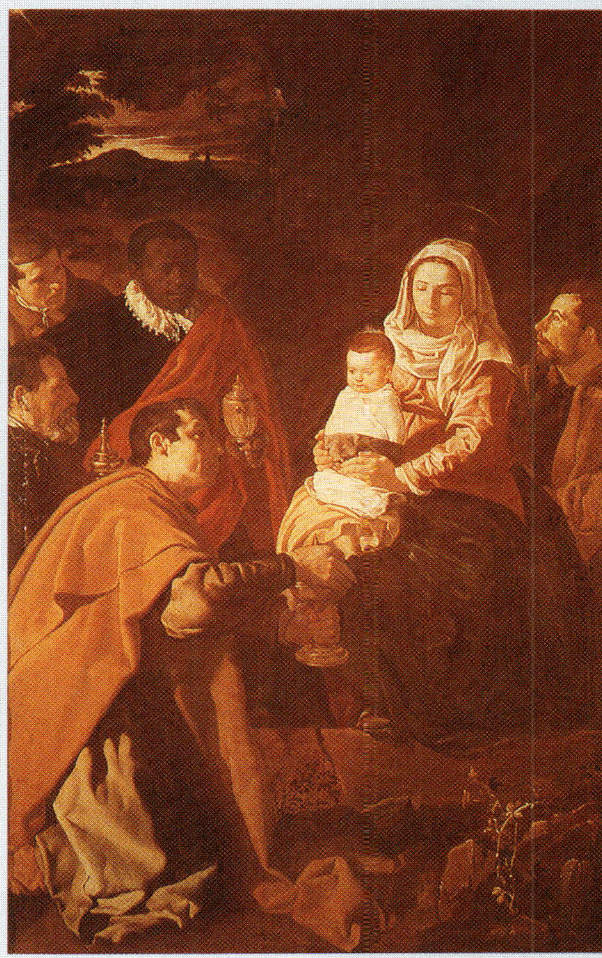

The Circumcision

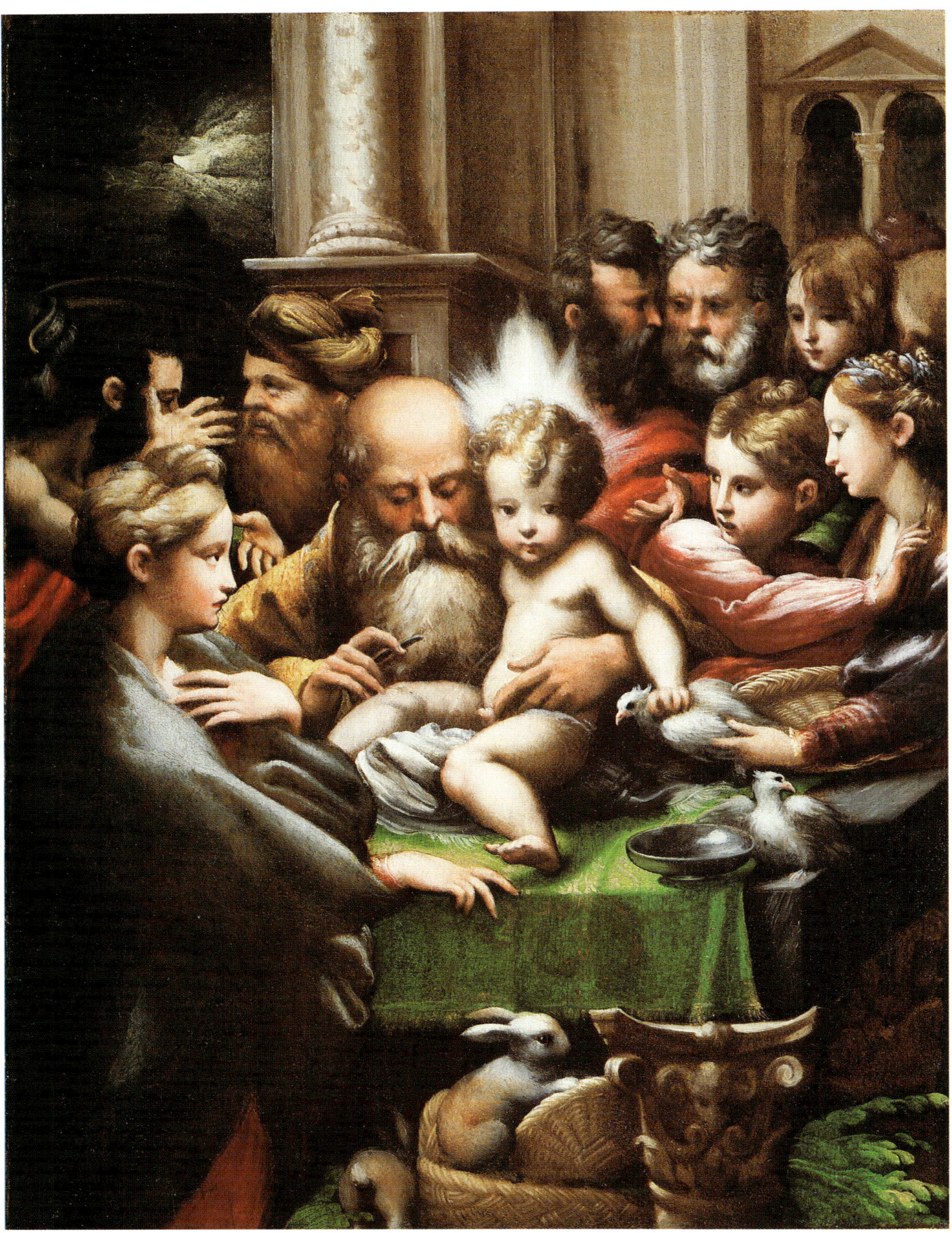

The Circumcision
PARMIGIANINO, Italian, 1503–1540
Gift of Axel Beskow, The Detroit Institute of Arts. Oil on wood panel. 16½ × 12⅜ in.

Jesus was circumcised and given his name when he was eight days old. Parmigianino assumed that this initiation rite, to which every Jewish male since Abraham had been submitted, occurred in the Temple, but the New Testament did not give particulars in its one-sentence account (Luke 2:21). In fact, Joseph or Mary could have performed the operation at home, but Parmigianino shows it being administered by the *mohel* in a public setting, with Mary making offerings of twin doves and rabbits.

There are only two sources of light in the scene, from the full moon outside with scudding clouds veiling it (Parmigianino took the liberty of making this a night scene to make use of this effect), and from the head of the Christ Child. His heavenly aura is noticed by some of the company around him and they are amazed. The old functionary holds his scalpel and concentrates on planning his cut, unaware of the radiance of the child in his arms.

Although one would imagine that the sanctuary is immense, the artist fills the picture so that there is barely breathing room between his participants, and the distance from Jesus to the back wall cannot be measured in terms of real space. The figures in the back row, consisting of family friends and neighbors, appear to be right up against the distant temple portico. Logically, the back wall would be much farther away, given its size relative to the figures and to the great column that rises above the bald head of the *mohel*. This compressed space intensifies the animation of the crowd, heightening the atmosphere of religious wonder. The painting was one of the first to be executed in this taut restless style, which eventually dominated mid-16th-century Italian art, spread to other countries, and became known as Mannerism.

The Presentation in the Temple

Soon after the circumcision, the holy family traveled to Jerusalem for the rite of purification. As the priest blessed the baby as "holy to the Lord" (Luke 2:23), a sacrifice of two turtledoves was made to symbolize the dedication of the child. In Philippe de Champaigne's *The Presentation in the Temple*, Joseph, who stands at the far left, only partially in the picture, has tucked these birds away in his robe as he and Mary encounter the old man Simeon.

According to Luke, God had revealed to Simeon that he would not die until he had seen the Messiah, and on this day he was inspired to go to the Temple. Taking Jesus up into his arms, he uttered a psalm of praise that is one of the most moving in Christian literature: "Lord, now lettest thou thy servant depart in peace, according to thy word; for mine eyes have seen thy salvation which thou hast prepared in the presence of all people, a light for revelation to the Gentiles, and for glory to thy people Israel" (Luke 2:29–32). Later he told Mary that Jesus was "set for the fall and rising of many in Israel." He added that a sword would pierce through her own soul also (Luke 2:34).

Simeon's song is known as the Nunc Dimitis after the first two words of its text in the Latin Vulgate, and it has been part of weekly Christian worship since the fourth century. Philippe de Champaigne places the viewer at the foot of the steps, where he or she can participate in the moment when these words were first spoken. Indeed, from this vantage point, one can see how deeply impressed the strangers around Simeon are by the conviction of his message. Through his depiction of Mary and Joseph, one sees that they truly did marvel at what was said about Jesus, as Luke reported (Luke 2:33).

A Flemish-born Frenchman, the artist was as much regarded during his lifetime for his piety as for his talent. Official court portraitist to King Louis XIII, he may well have modeled the faces of Simeon, Mary, Joseph, and the observers on real people. Certainly, the realism of the figures in this majestic work support that assumption.

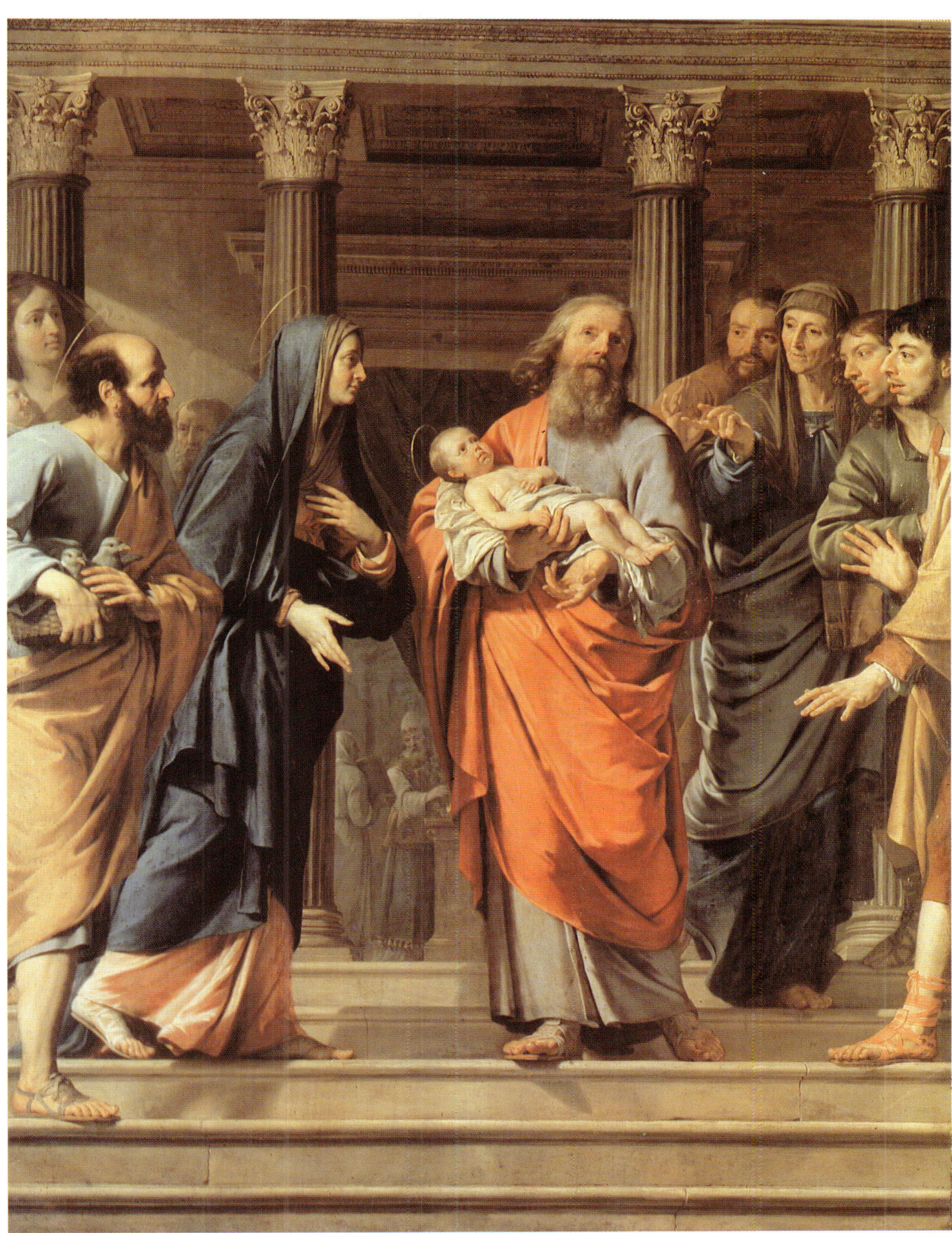

The Presentation in the Temple
PHILIPPE DE CHAMPAIGNE, French, 1602–1674
Koninklijke Musea voor Schone Kunsten van Belgie, Brussels. Oil on canvas. 102 × 78 in.

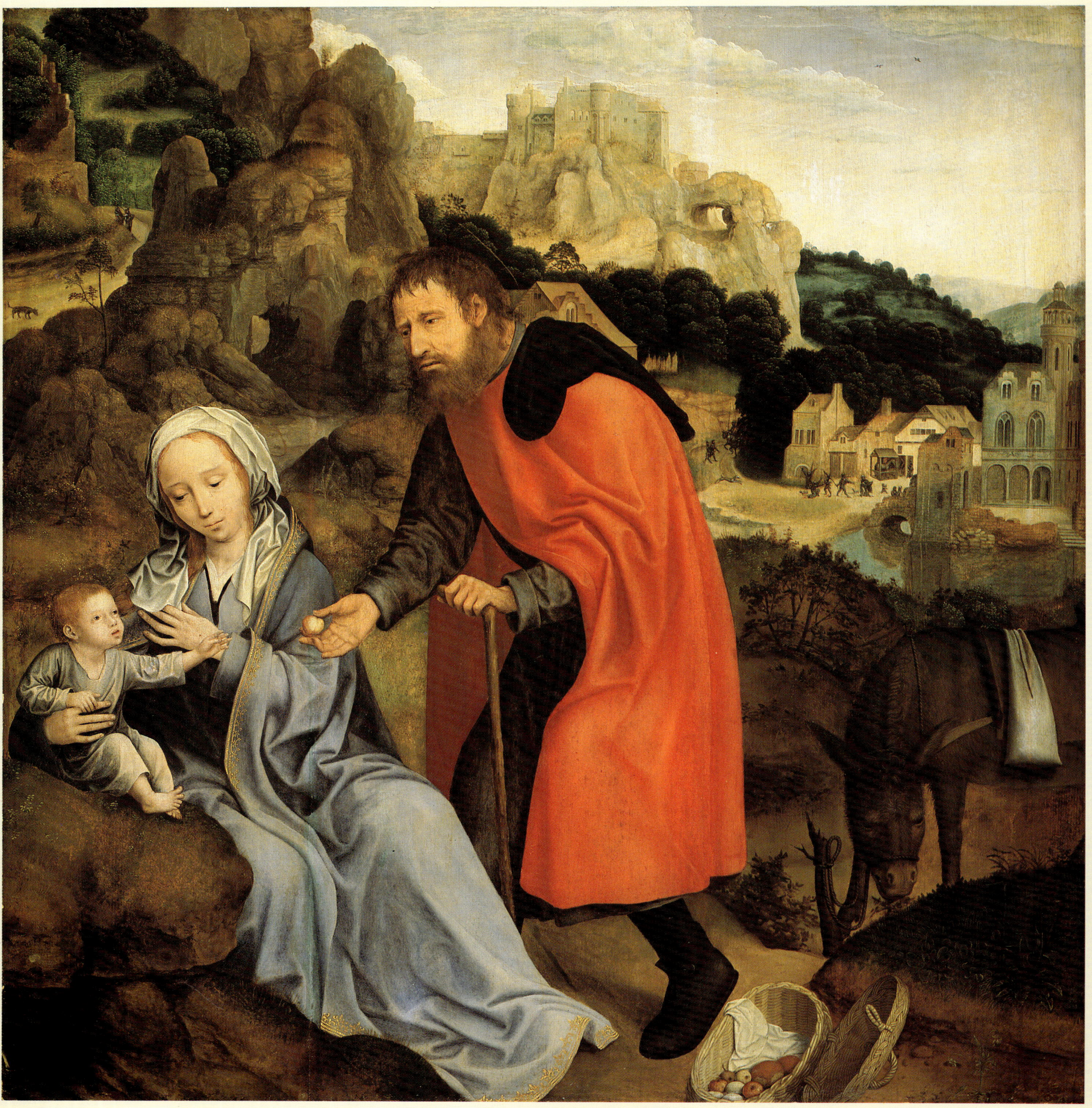

The Flight to Egypt

No sooner had the wise men left the holy family than an angel came to Joseph in a dream and commanded him to flee, for Herod, king of Judea, believed the newborn "king of the Jews" would usurp his throne. Obediently, Joseph "rose and took the child and his mother by night, and departed to Egypt, and remained there until the death of Herod" (Matthew 2:14–15).

Although this is a story about Joseph fulfilling his paternal obligations, and thus the will of God, the apochryphal literature that popularized it by the early 16th century stressed the sacrifices made by Mary during the trip and the miracles that happened to answer every dilemma she encountered. Artists, too, usually focused on the Virgin. In his *Flight to Egypt*, however, Quentin Massys places Joseph at the center of the story, handing fruit to the baby.

Joseph is dressed as a pilgrim, and any 16th-century viewer of this scene would have quickly contrasted the lowlands of his country with the high craggy landscape in the picture and assumed it to be a foreign place. But the painting was actually not done for a Flemish patron. It was part of an altarpiece commissioned of the artist for a monastery in Portugal dedicated to the so-called Seven Sorrows of Mary. Appropriately, in this picture, she is crying. So is Joseph, which is exceedingly unusual. Their sadness comes from the fruit, a reminder of the fruit of Eden and a symbol of Jesus' passion and suffering on the cross.

A careful examination of the activity taking place in front of the village pictured in the middle distance reveals the slaughter of children commanded by Herod (see pp. 46–47). The holy family escaped this fate by only a few days.

Claude Lorrain has also depicted *The Flight to Egypt*, but at first glance it is not a religious picture at all. Once the little figures of Joseph, his wife, and child are found in the vast and sublime beauty of this landscape, however, one could easily expect an angel to attend to the needs of those who were fortunate enough to traverse it.

The landscapes of Claude Lorrain influenced painting as well as garden design for hundreds of years. Fragments of ancient ruins, great vistas across water, and especially atmospheric lighting were his contribution to these fields. But landscape painting, to the Italian and French academics, was not a very high form of art. It was merely an imitation of nature. History painting was ranked as more important, for it had moral value for the beholder and it took imagination to make the stories of the past come to life. Therefore, Claude Lorrain has made his landscape into a history painting by placing the cluster of sacred personages on its right edge. It is safe to assume that he would have been content to be a pure landscape painter, but he added historical or biblical figures as a concession to the art criticism of his day. His source for this little respite during the flight to Egypt was one of the many apocryphal accounts of this journey, such as the lengthy one in the Gospel of Pseudo-Matthew, which dates from the eighth or ninth century.

The Rest on the Flight to Egypt
QUENTIN MASSYS, Flemish, 1465/66–1530
Worcester Art Museum, Massachusetts. Oil on wood panel. 32⁷⁄₁₆ × 31⅛ in.

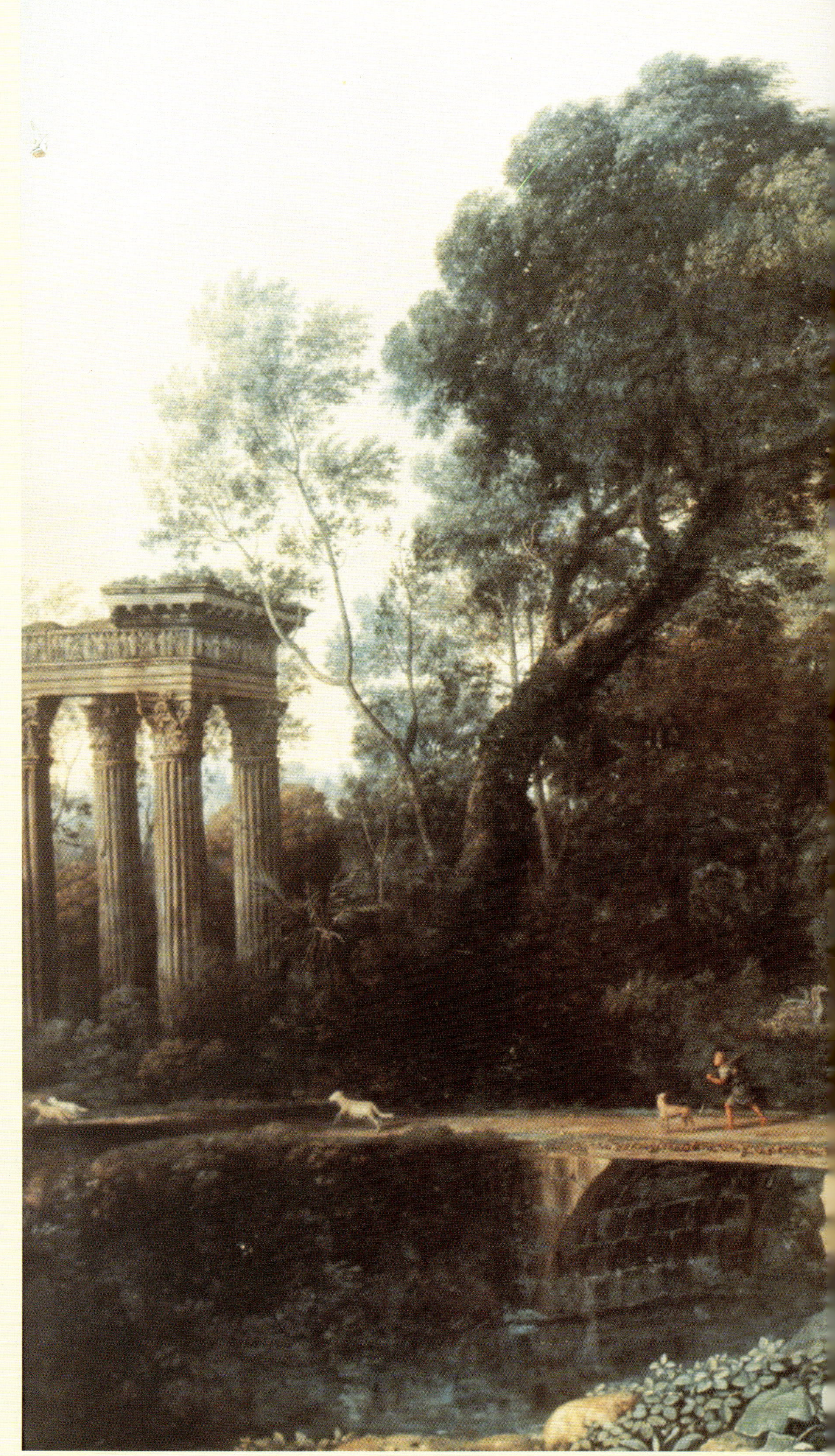

Landscape with Rest on the Flight to Egypt
CLAUDE LORRAIN, French, 1600–1682
Hermitage, Leningrad. Oil on canvas. 44¾ × 62 in.

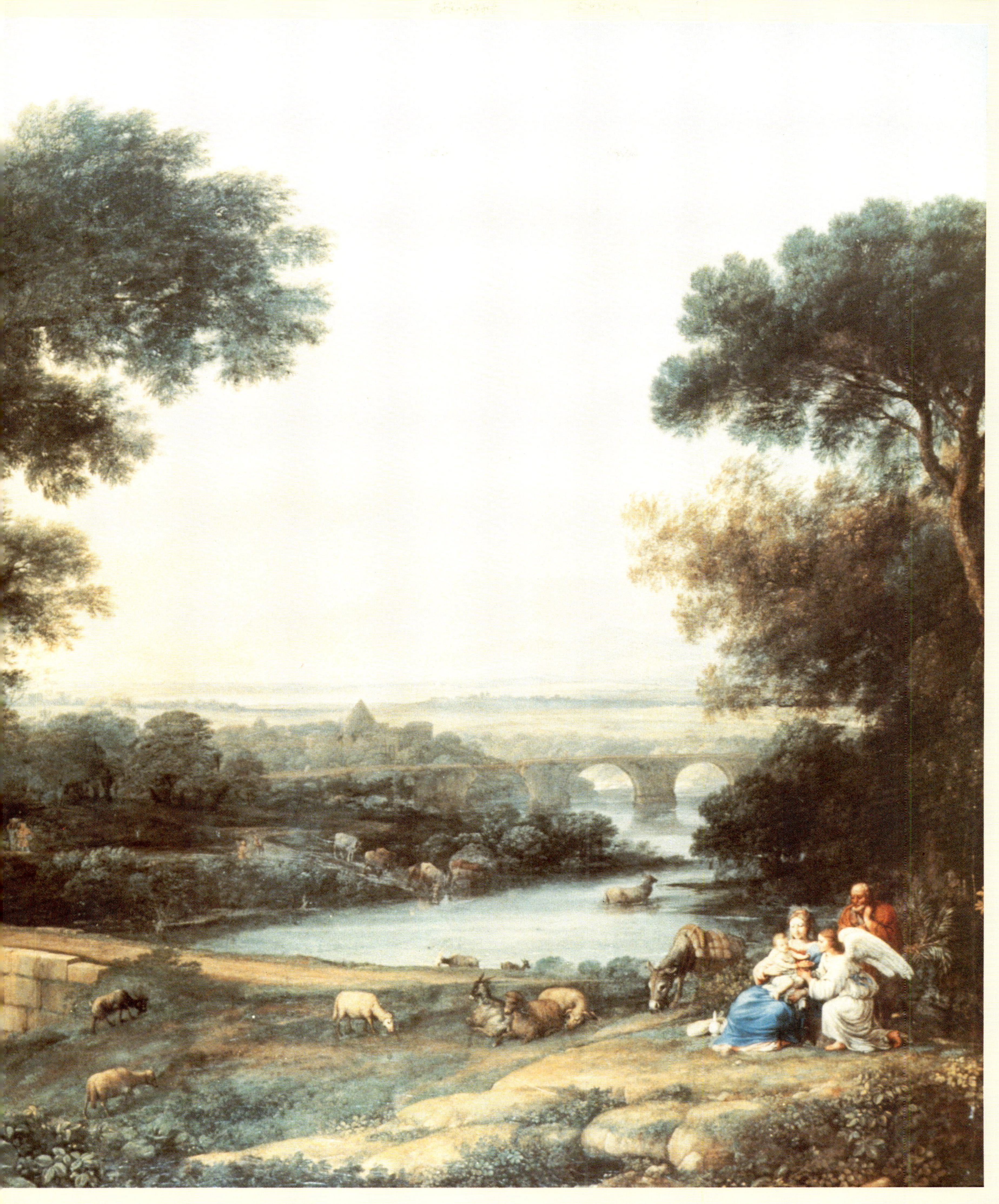

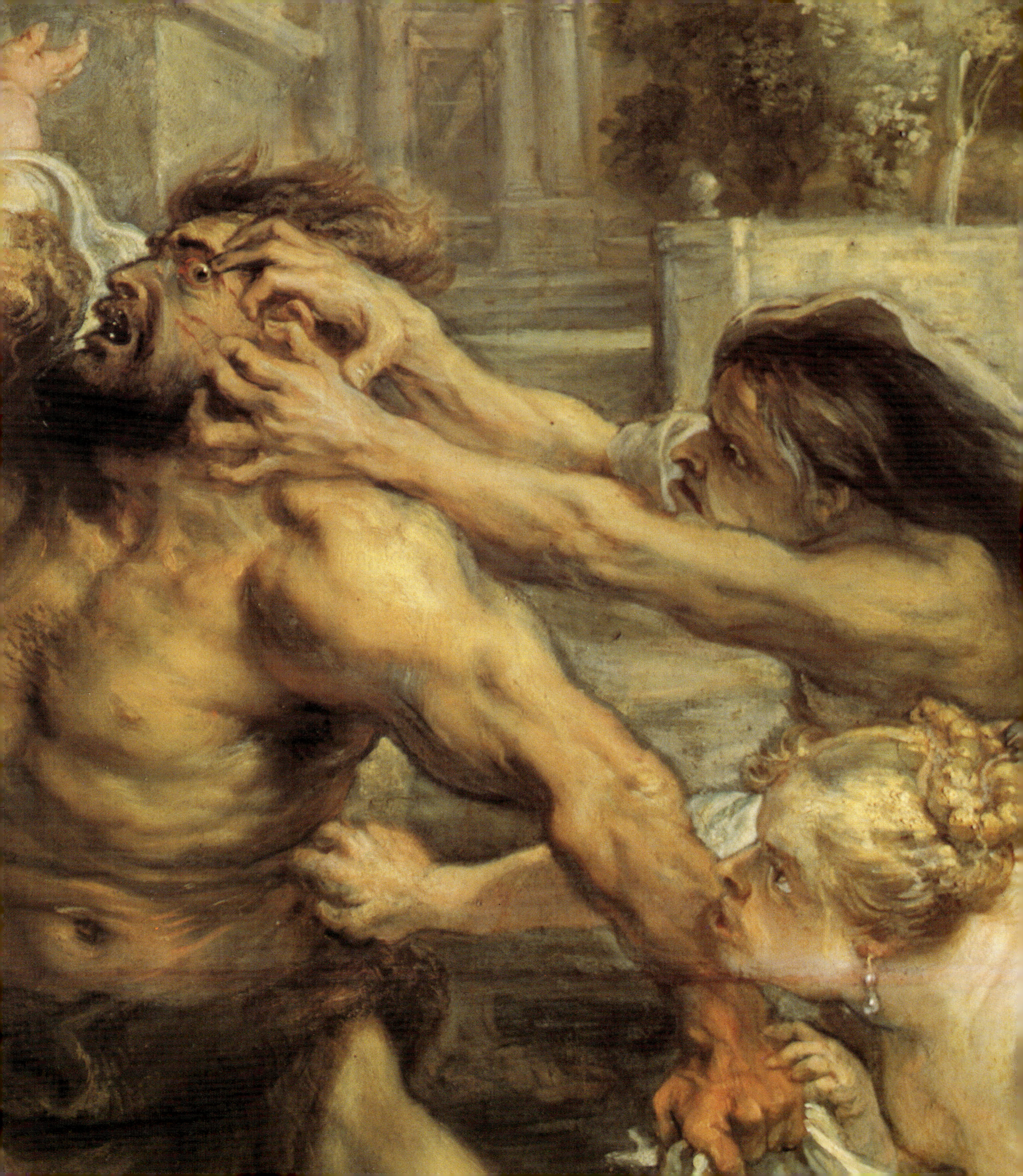

The Slaughter of the Innocents

Because Herod, the king of Judea, was nominally a Jew, he would not have built a Roman temple with a great porch like the one Peter Paul Rubens pictures in *The Slaughter of the Innocents*, but he was responsible for the magnificent reconstruction of the Temple in Jerusalem and many public buildings throughout his realm. The round, domed building in the left background is probably meant to be the synagogue of Bethlehem. Near the temple porch, a notice in Hebrew is posted, ordering the execution of all male children two years old and under. It is for this wanton act that Herod is remembered, while his building programs are virtually forgotten.

The intrigues in Herod's court were unending. He progressed through marriages with ten women, had at least one of them murdered, ordered three of his own sons killed, and changed his will six times. The New Testament understated his reaction when the Magi came to Jerusalem and asked for the birthplace of "the king of the Jews" by saying, "he was troubled" (Matthew 2:3). In fact, he panicked. He tried to trick the wise men into leading him to the child, but they were warned of his plan in a dream and did not cooperate with him. Then Joseph, the stepfather of Jesus, heard from an angel in another dream that Herod was trying to find the child in order to destroy him and he took Jesus and Mary to safety in Egypt (see pp. 42–45). In the meantime, Herod, convinced his throne would be stolen by the new king, flew into a furious rage. To make sure that he destroyed the usurper, he commanded the slaughter of all of Bethlehem's sons.

Few subjects held more appeal for artists wishing to display their mastery of contrasting heightened emotions and thrilling action, and Rubens was equal to the challenge. He has organized his depiction of this rampage in a great spiral of overlapping activity, with a regally dressed woman in the center, her outstretched arms leading the viewer to the angels who are waiting ready to receive the children into heaven. Fathers behind the women keep their distance, but threaten with stones as mothers wail and plead. One of the latter tries to scratch out the eyes of a soldier; another grabs an attacker's hair; a third bites a murderer's arm. Children scream, thrash out, and are piled up like carcasses from the hunt, while soldiers bare their ugliest faces and flex muscular arms and legs against the unexpected strength of the women. Their lances rise above the holocaust; though instruments of death, they repeat the angles formed by the matrons' pleading arms.

Rubens excelled at this kind of lavishly conceived, highly dramatic extravaganza. He knew opulence firsthand, for not only was he the most successful artist of his day but he was also a leading diplomat, welcome in every court of Europe. The age of the Baroque loved his operatic excesses, but at the same time embraced the more realistic art of Caravaggio and meditated before the stark paintings of Zurbarán. It was an era when splendid court spectacles were a chief symbol of power and when the word *quietude* entered the language as the only way to express the feelings evoked by a typical Dutch landscape. What all of this contrasting art has in common is a love of physicality and a faith in the wonders of God.

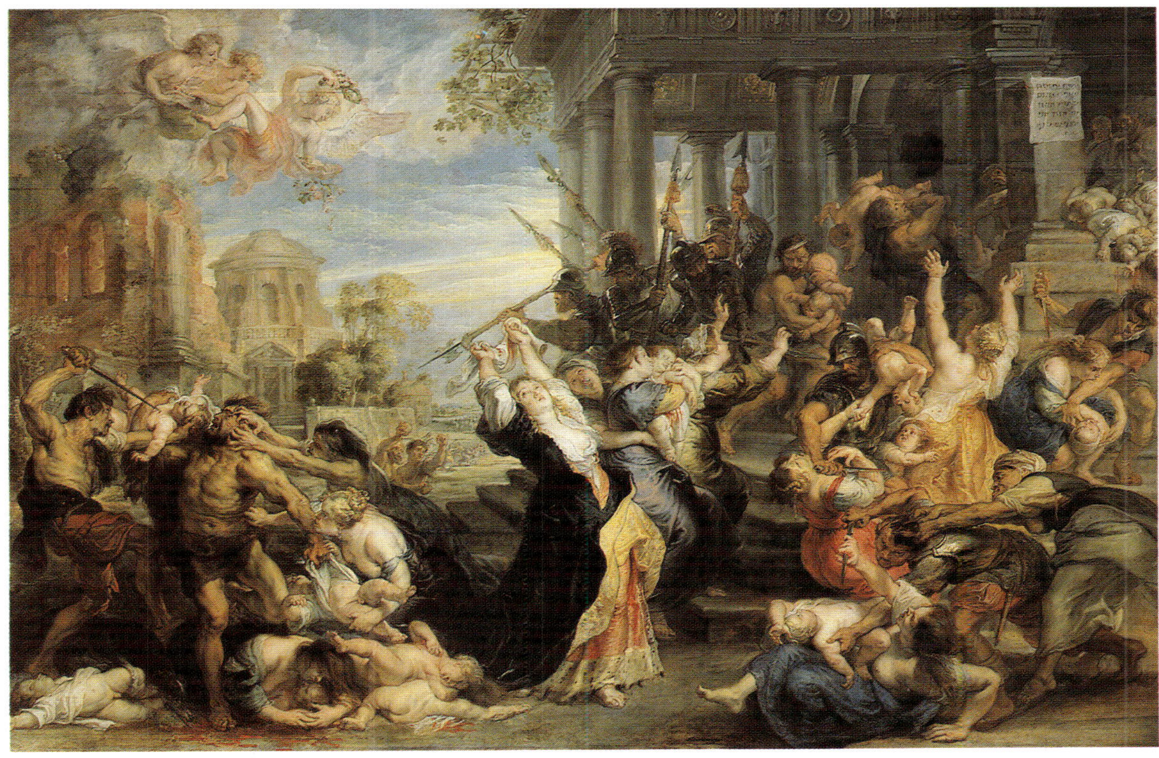

The Slaughter of the Innocents
PETER PAUL RUBENS, Flemish, 1577–1640
Alte Pinakothek, Munich. Oil on wood panel. 78 × 119 in.

◁
DETAIL

Christ Among the Doctors

Jesus' family was steadfast in making its annual pilgrimage to Jerusalem to celebrate the Passover, and when the boy was 12 years old he and Mary and Joseph trekked to the capital again. This time they were part of a large caravan of relatives and acquaintances. After the holiday observances, the travelers had jo neyed an entire day back toward Nazareth before they discovered that Jesus was missing. It took three days of frantic searching before his parents found him in the temple "sitting among the teachers, listening to them and asking them questions" (Luke 2:46).

In *Christ Among the Doctors*, Matthias Stomer shows Jesus with the elders, three of whom argue heatedly with the boy, while the fourth listens with respect. Jesus points upward with his right hand in a posture that was reserved in ancient art for the emperor making proclamations. His body is as erect as his gesture. The Gospel writer stated that "all who heard him were amazed at his understanding and his answers." An ancient tradition held that Jesus was omniscient from birth, so artists often portrayed him with the face of an old man. Matthias Stomer, instead, shows him as though filled with such wisdom that he himself cannot comprehend it all.

By pointing to heaven, Jesus is referring to the authority of his father, just as he did in answer to his mother when she found him and complained about his unexcused absence: "How is it that you sought me out? Did you not know that I must be in my Father's house" (Luke 2:49). From this moment forward in the story of his life, there is never again a mention of his earthly father Joseph. It is assumed that he died during Jesus' teen years.

Matthias Stomer, a Dutchman, lived in southern Italy most of his adult life. His work combined a Dutch feeling for personality and realism with the latest Italian manner of simplifying a story by focusing only on its most salient moment. In this, as in his other mature works, Stomer concentrates all of his talent on making the figures believable. His painting of the costume of the elder with the open book on his lap makes the textures of these gorgeous fabrics tangible, while the lively pattern of hands in the center of the painting tells viewers as much about what is happening in this scene as do the intense expressions on the faces.

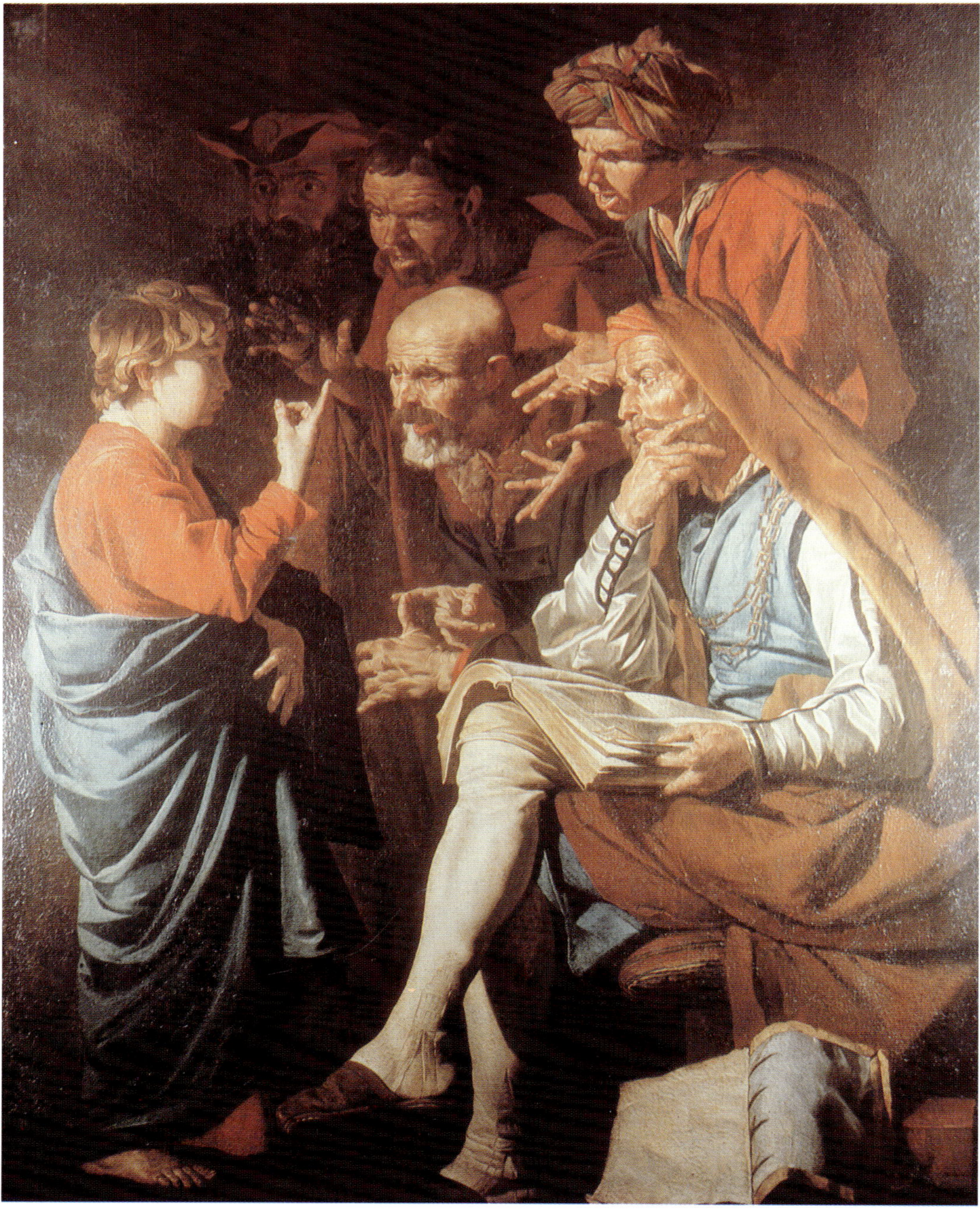

Christ Among the Doctors
MATTHIAS STOMER, Dutch, ca. 1600–after 1650
Alte Pinakothek, Munich. Oil on canvas. 80 × 59 in.

The Virgin and Child in the House of Nazareth

Since the Bible reveals little of Jesus' teenage years, theologians created detailed accounts of his adolescence and these, in turn, inspired meditations that were read to the pious at specified times of the year. Obvious and heavy-handed in their symbolism, they nevertheless became believable when treated by a great artist like Zurbarán. He bases this scene on one of them.

Jesus has made a crown of thorns like the one he will be forced to wear near the end of his life. He pricks his finger on it and examines a drop of blood coming from the wound. Observing this, Mary is filled with sorrow, for she divines the events to come. Furthermore, the needle with which she is sewing evokes the nails that will be used to affix Jesus to the cross. The doves at her feet are a reference to the offering presented in the Temple when Simeon warned her that a sword would also pierce her soul (Luke 2:35).

Zurbarán was one of the greatest still-life painters of all time, and he delights his viewers with several incomparable still-life passages in this haunting work. To be sure that all of them are in view, he has tipped the table off kilter. The symbolism of the pears on the table is an obscure reference to the Passion, and the books derive from the Gospel report that Jesus "increased in wisdom and in stature, and in favor with God and man" (Luke 2:52). Jesus' small workbasket, Mary's large one spilling with linens, and the bouquet of lilies and other flowers complete the accessories which impart so much information about this holy household.

There are two windows. The one above Mary looks out to passing clouds. Another one, out of sight, lets in a golden ray that catches the angelic profile of Jesus and lights the tear running down Mary's cheek. The artist's understanding of the life of the spirit was profound, and the pathos he invests in this particular vignette makes it especially memorable.

The Virgin and Child in the House of Nazareth
FRANCISCO DE ZURBARÁN, Spanish, 1598–1662/64
The Cleveland Museum of Art, Leonard C. Hanna, Jr. Fund. Oil on canvas. 65 × 85⅞ in.

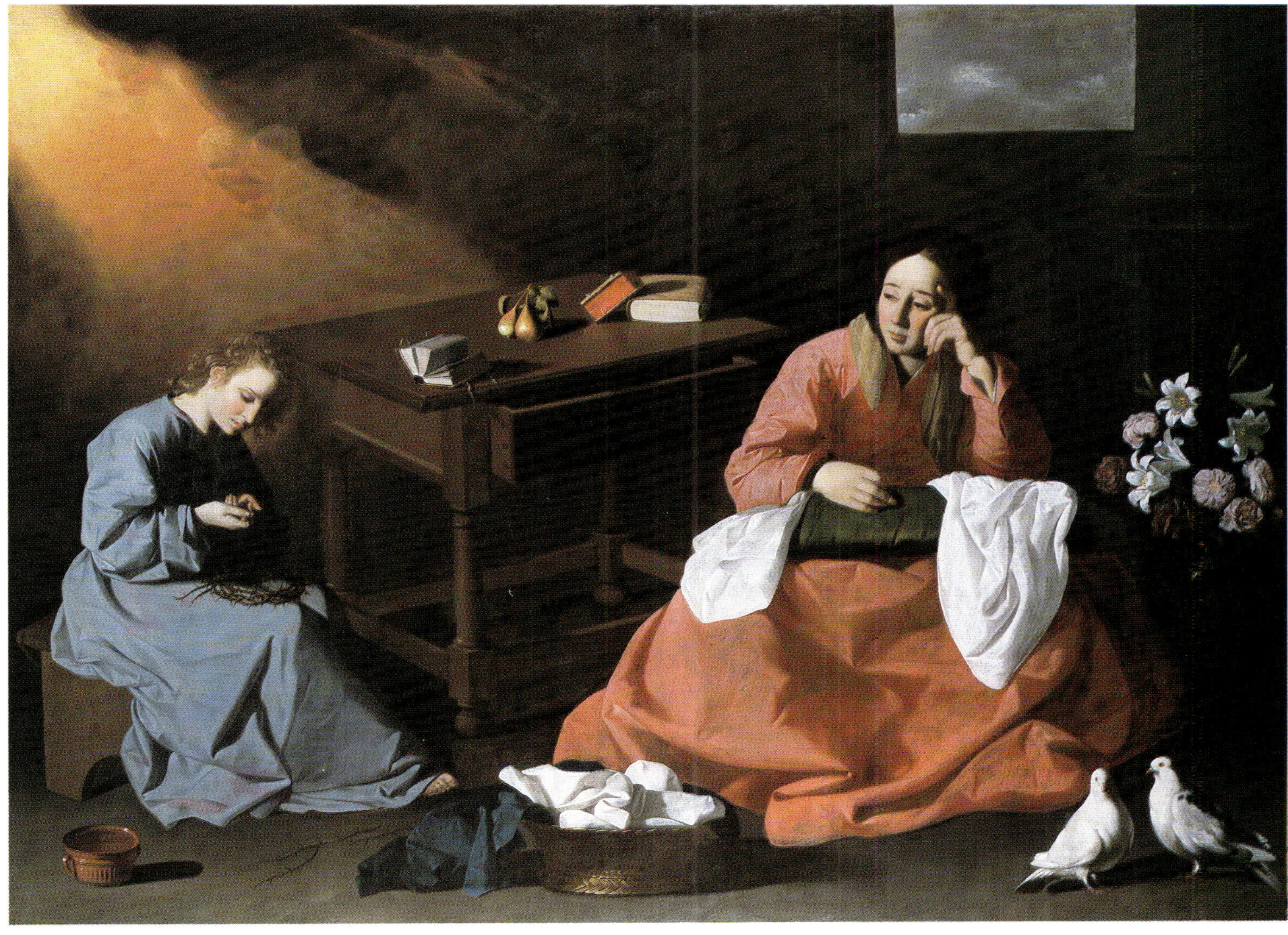

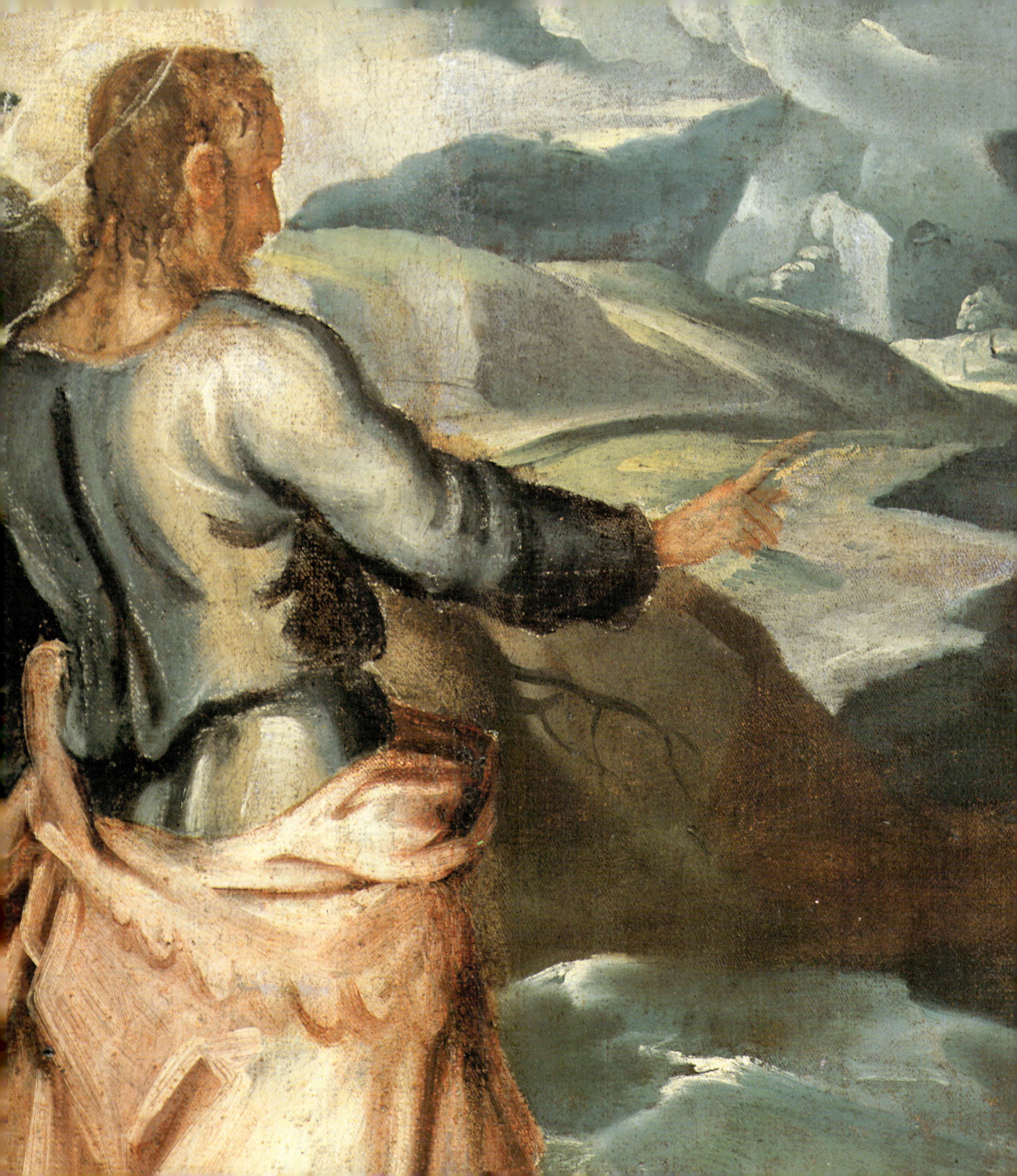

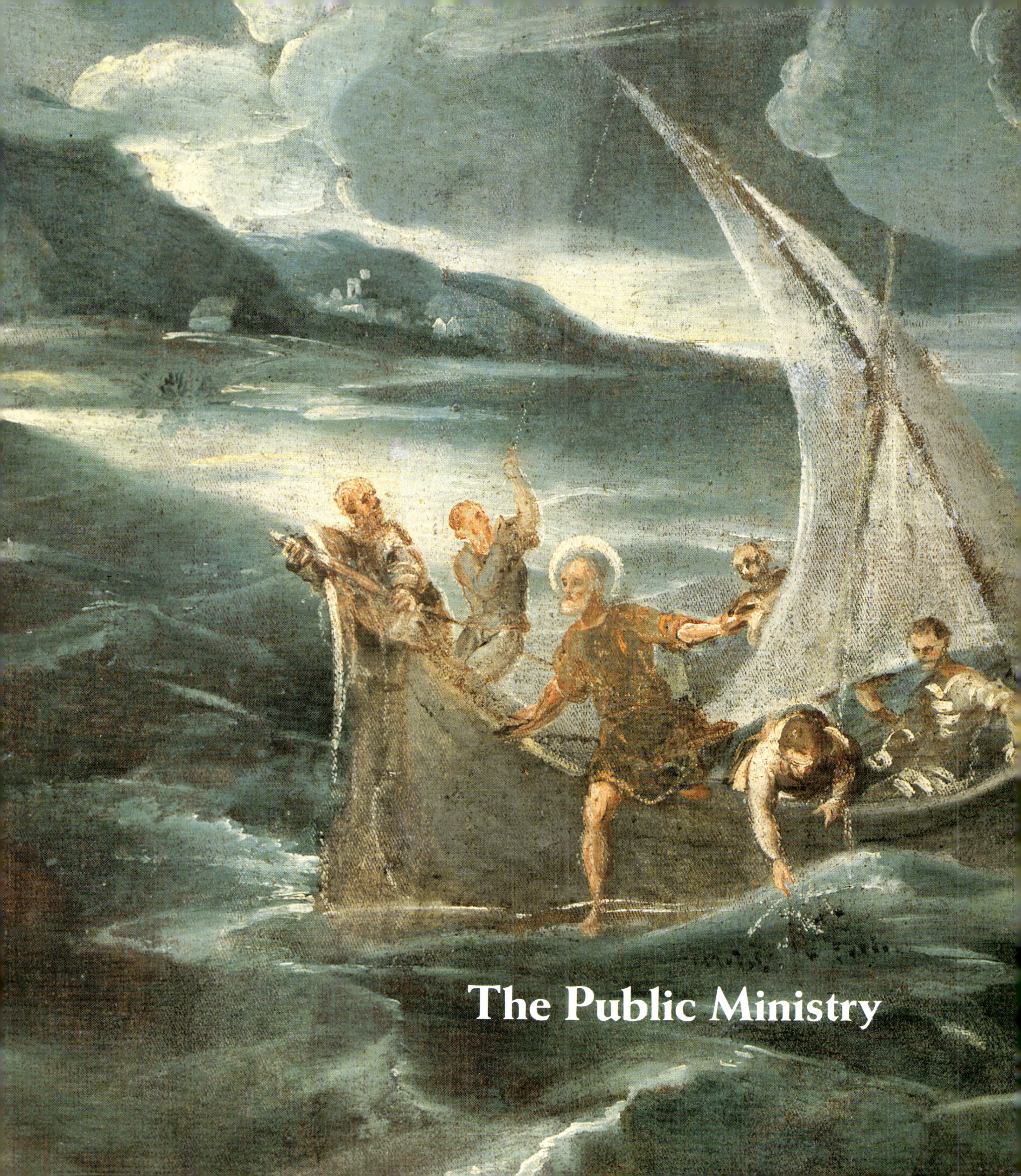

The Public Ministry

PRECEDING PAGES

TINTORETTO: *Christ at the Sea of Galilee* (detail)

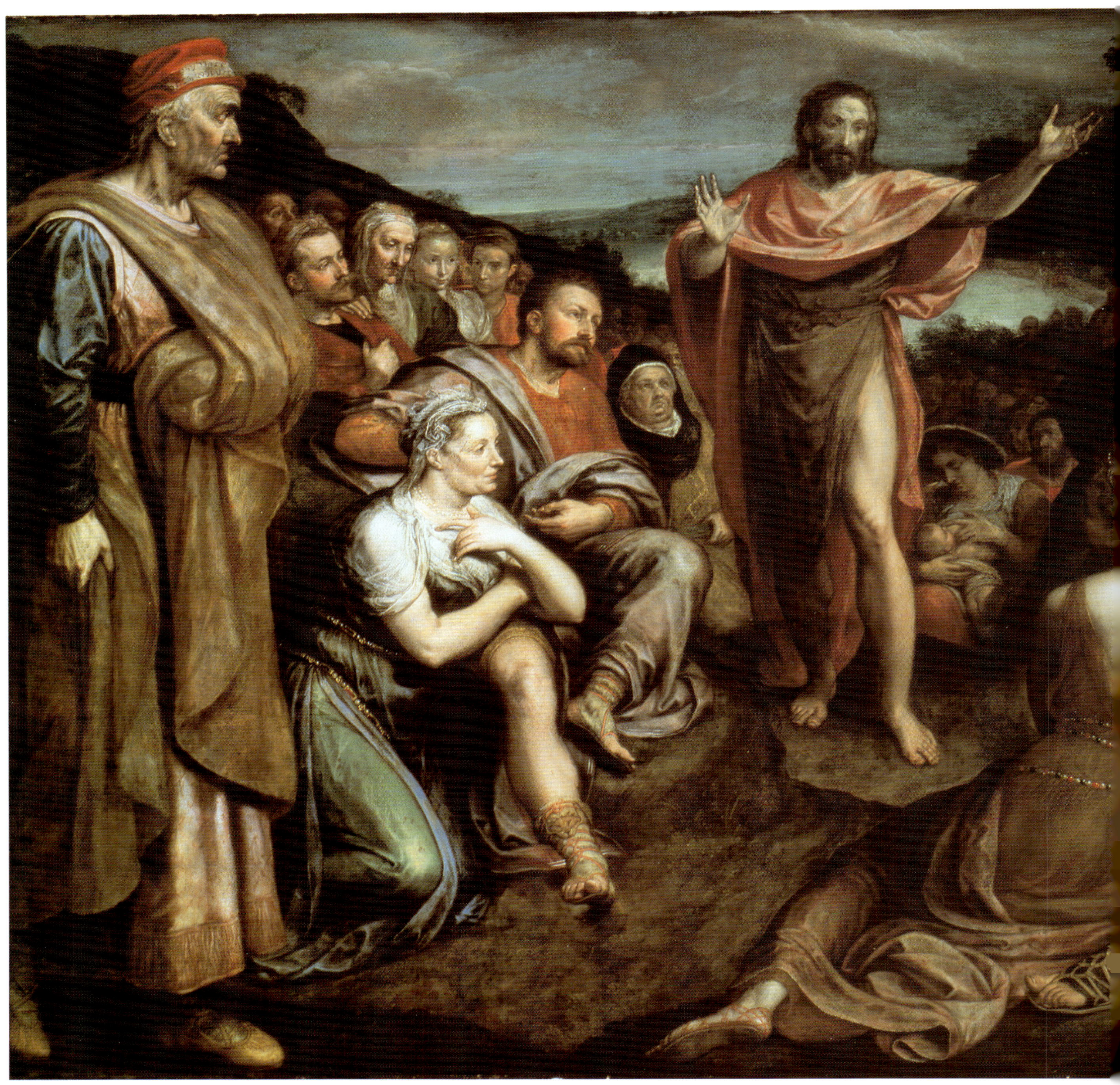

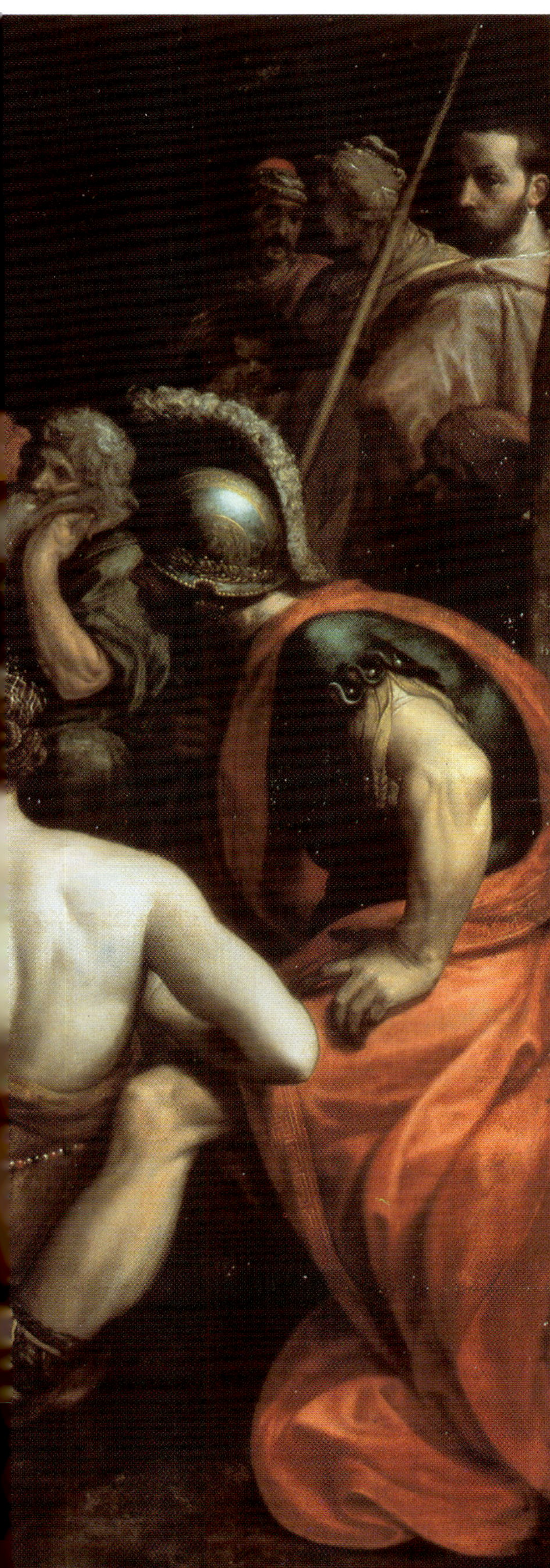

The Sermon of St. John the Baptist

The biblical descriptions of John the Baptist are so graphic and rich that it has always beggared an artist's imagination to bring forth an image that compares to the power of the word. Mistaken for Elijah and described by himself as "the voice of one crying in the wilderness" (Matthew 3:3; Mark 1:3; Luke 3:4; John 1:23), the words and acts of John's brief career are almost as well known as those of Jesus. Hermit, preacher, and cousin to the man whose way he prepared, he was heard by everyone from Herod to the lowliest peasants. Josephus, the Jewish historian who lived soon after John's execution, wrote that "he had great influence over the people, who seemed ready to do anything that he should advise." His advice, however, was hard. He told them to repent, to share their goods, and to be content with their wages, but he also "preached good news to the people" (Luke 3:18).

Frans Pourbus has two specific ideas in mind for his depiction of John preaching. First, he wants to emphasize the variety of people who were drawn to the Baptist. "All the country and all the people of Jerusalem" (Mark 1:5) were too vast an audience to picture, so he settles for a few types—couples, children, the old, and the young. He includes a soldier because soldiers specifically came to John and asked what they should do to gain salvation. (He told them not to rob anyone [Luke 3:14].) This small multitude of serious and reflective people makes a visual frame for the Baptist himself.

The artist's second intention is to illustrate the sermon that John is in the midst of preaching. "After me comes he who is mightier than I," said the Baptist, "the thong of whose sandals I am not worthy to stoop down and untie. I have baptized you with water; but he will baptize you with the Holy Spirit" (Matthew 3:11). Gesturing dramatically with his hands, his brow furrowed, it is probably this moment that is pictured. From his face, it is clear that the Baptist deeply believes his own prophecy.

Pourbus directs John's attention to the tallest man in the painting. Standing aside from the others, his body filling the height of the canvas, he is marked as a Sadducee by the Hebrew text written on the white band of his red hat. John called this man and his conservative and politically powerful party a "brood of vipers" (Matthew 3:7). No wonder the accused appears skeptical of John's new world.

Sermon of St. John the Baptist
FRANS POURBUS THE ELDER, Flemish, 1545–1581
Musée des Beaux-Arts, Valenciennes, France

The Baptism of Christ

As very young children Jesus and John the Baptist may have romped together, but thereafter tradition has it that the cousins went their separate ways. Jesus learned carpentry in Nazareth from his stepfather Joseph, and John lived on locusts and wild honey in the desert as he prepared to herald the coming of the Messiah. When each was 30 years of age, their paths crossed once more, and what happened was recorded by all four Gospel writers. John was preaching and baptizing in the Lower Jordan River, near one of the major crossroads of the country. His sermons demanded that people repent, and the pouring of water over them was symbolic of forgiveness. When Jesus approached him to be baptized, John, realizing the blameless reputation of his cousin, said, "I need to be baptized by you" (Matthew 3:14). Nonetheless, he consented to perform the ritual for Jesus, and it is this moment that Nicolas Poussin captures in *The Baptism of Christ*.

The Bible reported that when John poured water over Jesus the heavens immediately opened, the spirit of God descended like a dove, and a voice from heaven said, "This is my beloved son, with whom I am well pleased" (Matthew 3:17). This austere French artist grants the viewer the dove, which has drawn the attention of a few of the baptism's witnesses, but there is no evidence of a miracle. Instead, Poussin presents a beautiful, controlled, and ever so self-conscious scene. He refers to the biblical story, but he seems primarily interested in creating a figure study. Baptisms provide a better excuse for nudity than the subjects of most sacred tales.

Poussin was the mainspring of the classical tradition in French art. He spent most of his life in Rome, and was probably thinking of the Tiber when he portrayed the river in this painting. Between 1644 and 1648 he was preoccupied with a series of solemn paintings that depicted the seven sacraments of the Roman Catholic church, of which this was the first.

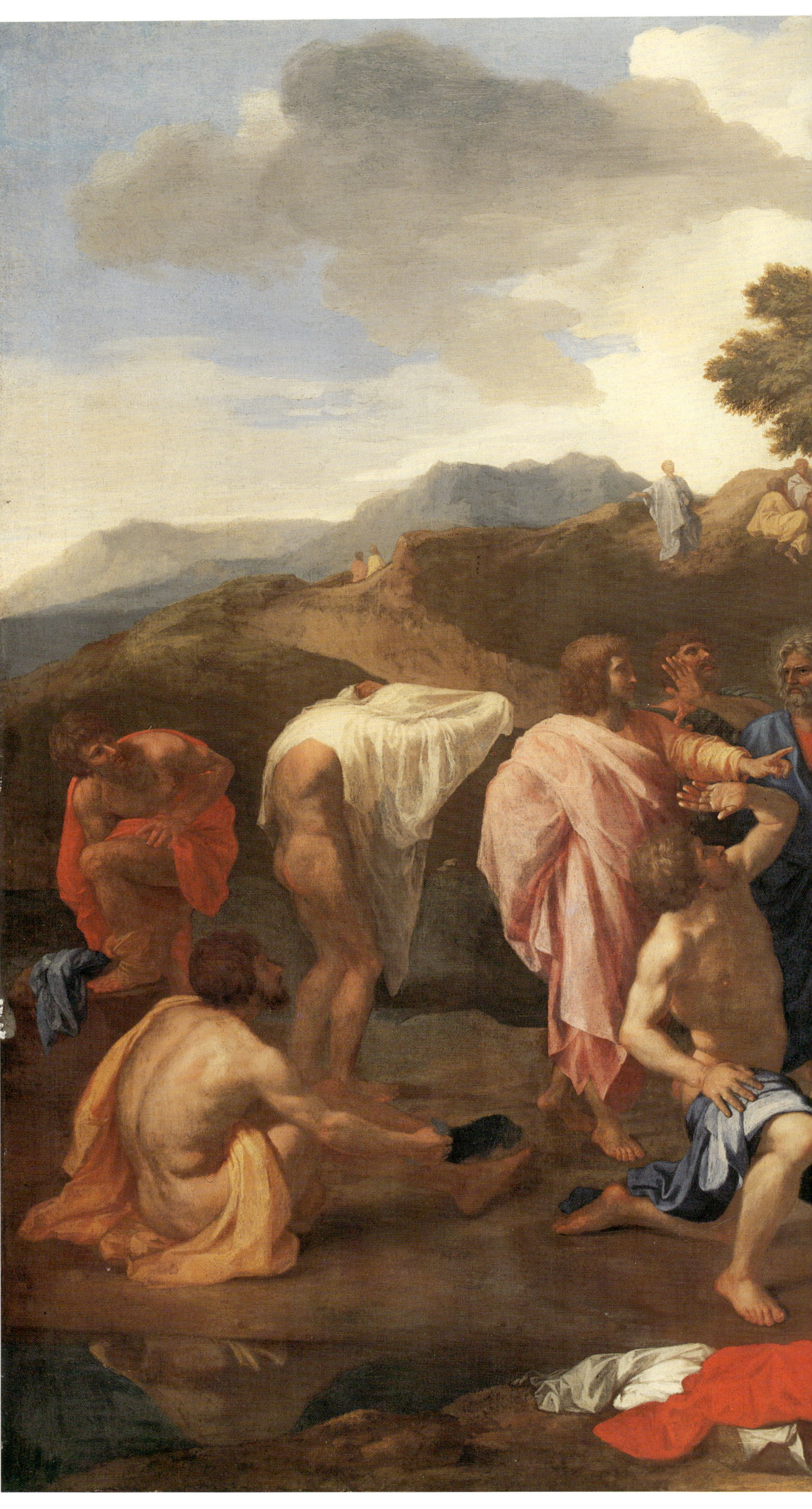

The Baptism of Christ
NICOLAS POUSSIN, French, 1594–1665
Samuel H. Kress Collection, National Gallery of Art, Washington, DC. Oil on canvas. 38 × 48 in.

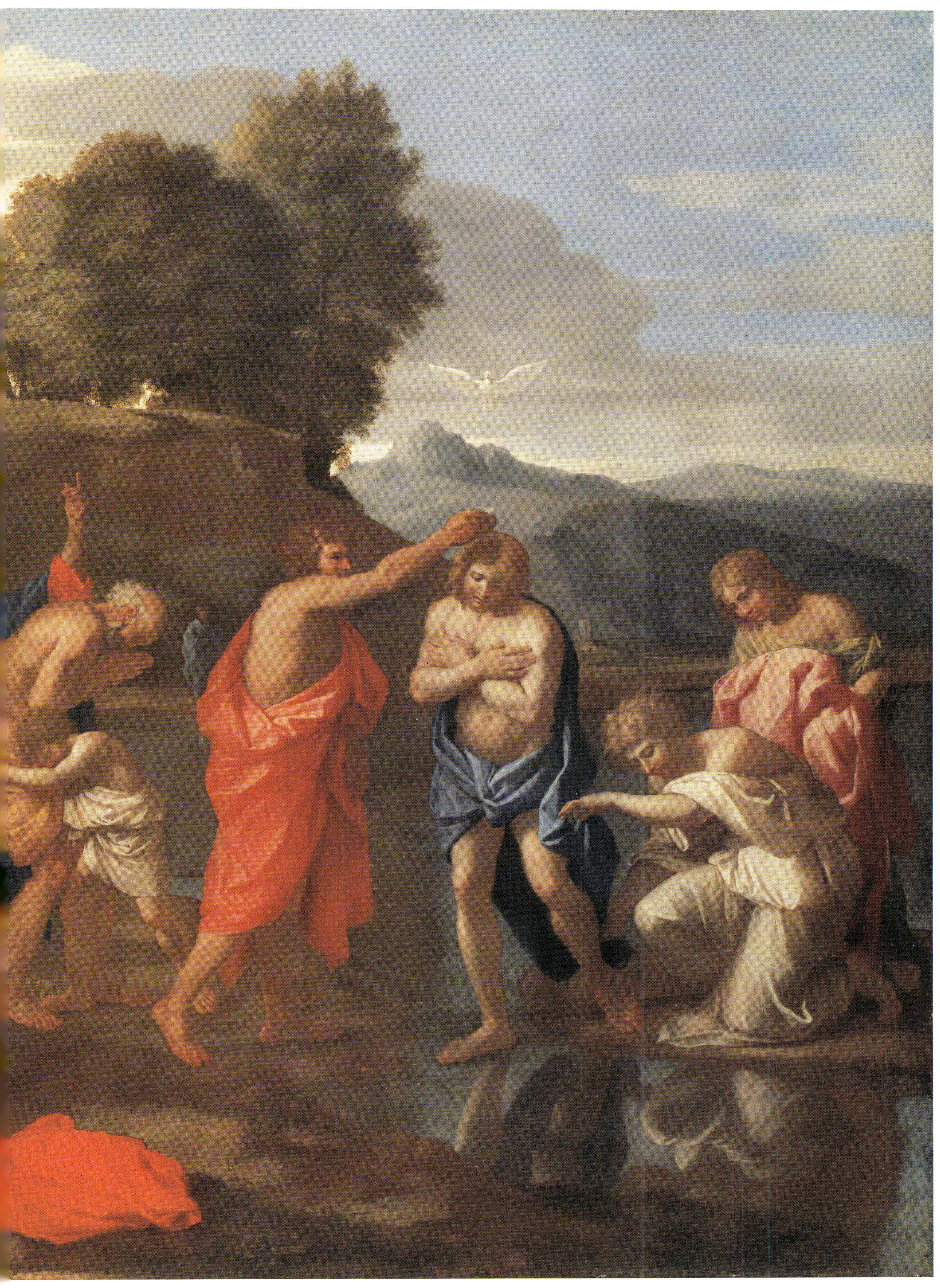

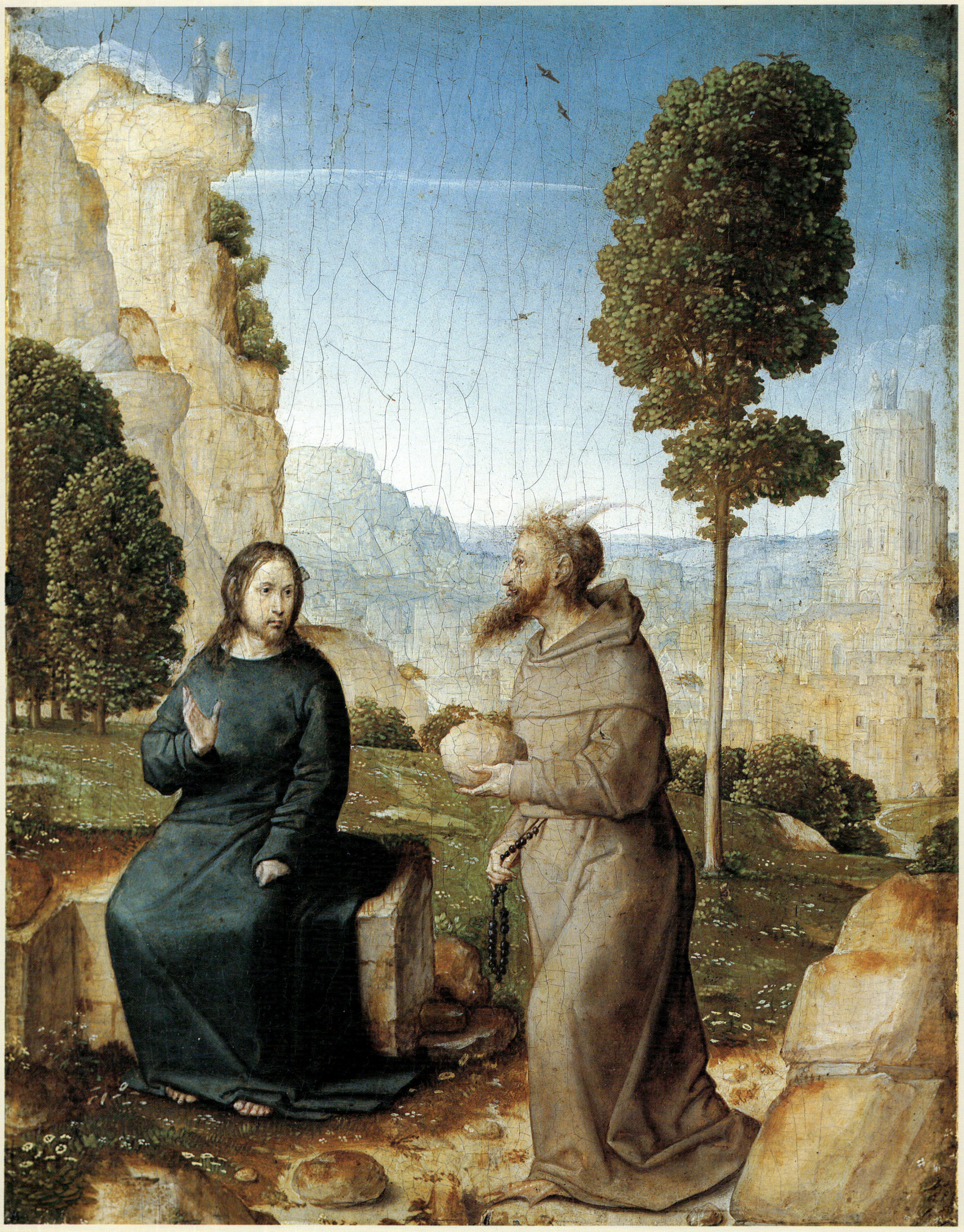

The Temptation of Christ in the Wilderness

Jesus had not eaten for 40 days. He was not strong enough to stand. A man offered a stone to him and said, "If you are the Son of God, command this stone to become bread." Jesus was almost tricked by the man's religious costume and he reached out. But he must have noticed the horns and the webbed feet under the disguise. "Man shall not live by bread alone," he replied. And the devil immediately swept him up to a high place and showed him "all the kingdoms of the world in a moment of time" and offered them to Jesus if he would only worship him. The answer was another quotation: "You shall worship the Lord your God, and him only shall you serve." Finally, from the pinnacle of the Temple in Jerusalem, Jesus was challenged to throw himself down, putting himself in the care of the angels. "You shall not tempt the Lord your God," was his reply. "And when the devil had ended every temptation, he departed from him until an opportune time" (Luke 4:1–13).

Juan des Flandes shows all three temptations, two of them dimly in the background. Although the verses that describe what happened are among the most surreal and perplexing in the entire New Testament, the artist takes them literally. But he finds room for fancy (and perhaps some sarcasm) by dressing the devil as a mendicant monk grasping a rosary. His imagination is able to soar a bit in his treatment of the distant mirages, and in his portrait of Jesus the artist seems to have been fasting himself, so convincing is his depiction.

Temptation of Christ in the Wilderness
JUAN DES FLANDES, Flemish, active by 1496–1519
National Gallery of Art, Washington, DC. Wood panel. 8¼ × 6⅛ in.

The Sermon on the Mount

Claude Lorrain was a French artist who spent most of his life in Rome. He never went to the Holy Land, so the landscape in this painting is imaginary. The mount itself, abruptly rising, its ascent filled with caves, and with expansive vistas on either side, is based on the artist's reading of the Bible. Compressing the actual geography of Israel, he depicts, on the left, the Dead Sea and the winding course of the Jordan River beyond it. On the right, the small villages represent Tiberias and Nazareth on the Sea of Galilee, with Mount Tabor in the distance.

Since his baptism, Jesus' fame had spread and great crowds had begun to follow him as he journeyed through the small villages around the country. One day he climbed to the top of a mountain where he could sit among his disciples and talk to this multitude. It is this scene that Claude Lorrain presents. At 8½ feet wide, he had plenty of room on his canvas to paint both the immense natural space and the many followers of Christ. Those to the left and in the distance are too far away to perceive their reactions in great detail. But the impact of the great healer's words may be found on the faces of the colorful figures to the right as they gaze, point, and quietly comment to one another.

Jesus, atop the mountain, wears blue and spreads out his arms in a traditional gesture of blessing. Perhaps he is enumerating the Beatitudes, with which he began the Sermon on the Mount. "Blessed are the poor in spirit," he said, "for theirs is the kingdom of heaven" (Matthew 5:3). These words were followed by the prayer invoked by Christianity ever since: "Our Father, who art in heaven, hallowed be thy name . . ." (Matthew 6:9). Later in the sermon, Jesus laid down his strict laws of morality, telling the people to love their enemies, to judge not lest they be judged, and to "let the day's own trouble be sufficient for the day" (Matthew 6:34). At the very end of his long and challenging address, the site itself seemed to inspire him. "Every one then who hears these words of mine and does them will be like a wise man who built his house upon a rock; and the rain fell, and the floods came, and the winds blew and beat upon that house, but it did not fall, because it had been founded on the rock" (Matthew 7:24–25).

Claude Lorrain left it to other artists to try to give pictorial palpability to the many lessons contained within the Sermon on the Mount. For him it was enough to suggest the universality of these teachings through the metaphor of this vast and almost endless landscape. It is only the envelopment of the distant hills in light that prevents the viewers' eyes from seeing eternity.

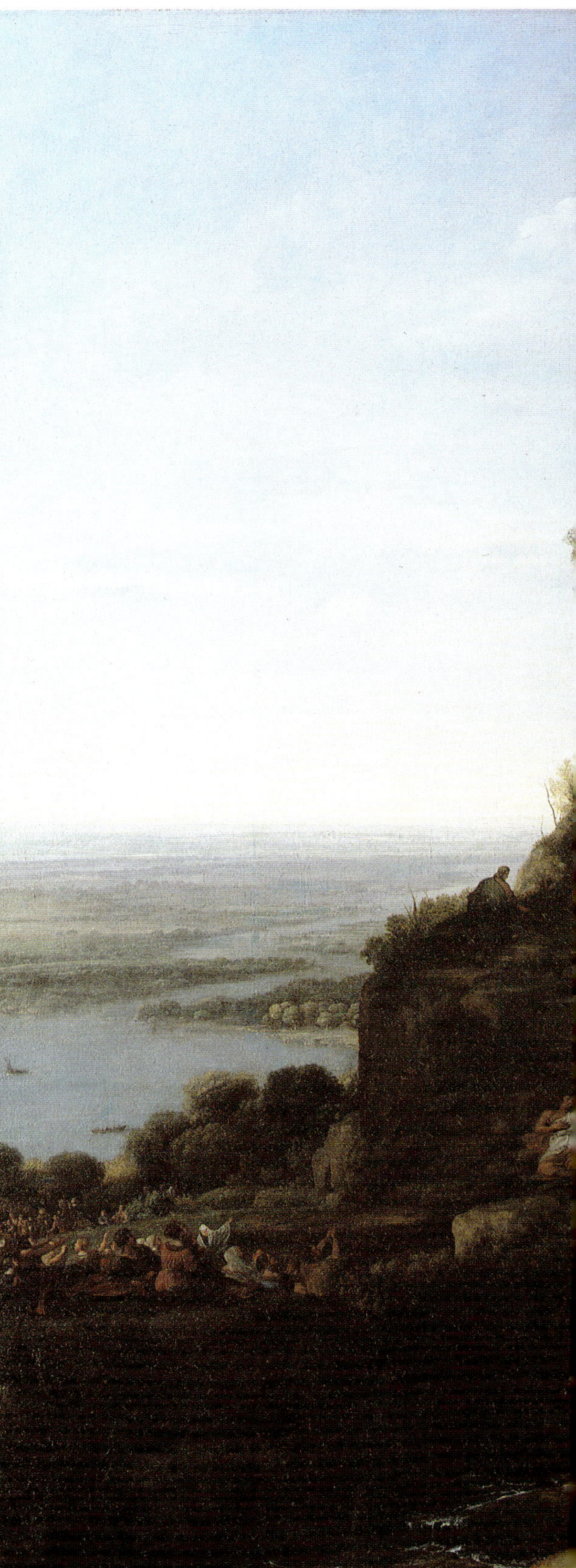

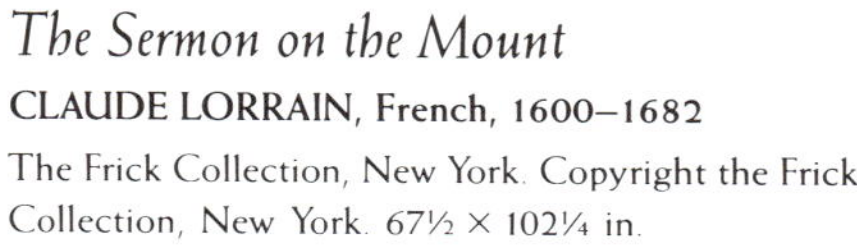

The Sermon on the Mount
CLAUDE LORRAIN, French, 1600–1682
The Frick Collection, New York. Copyright the Frick Collection, New York. 67½ × 102¼ in.

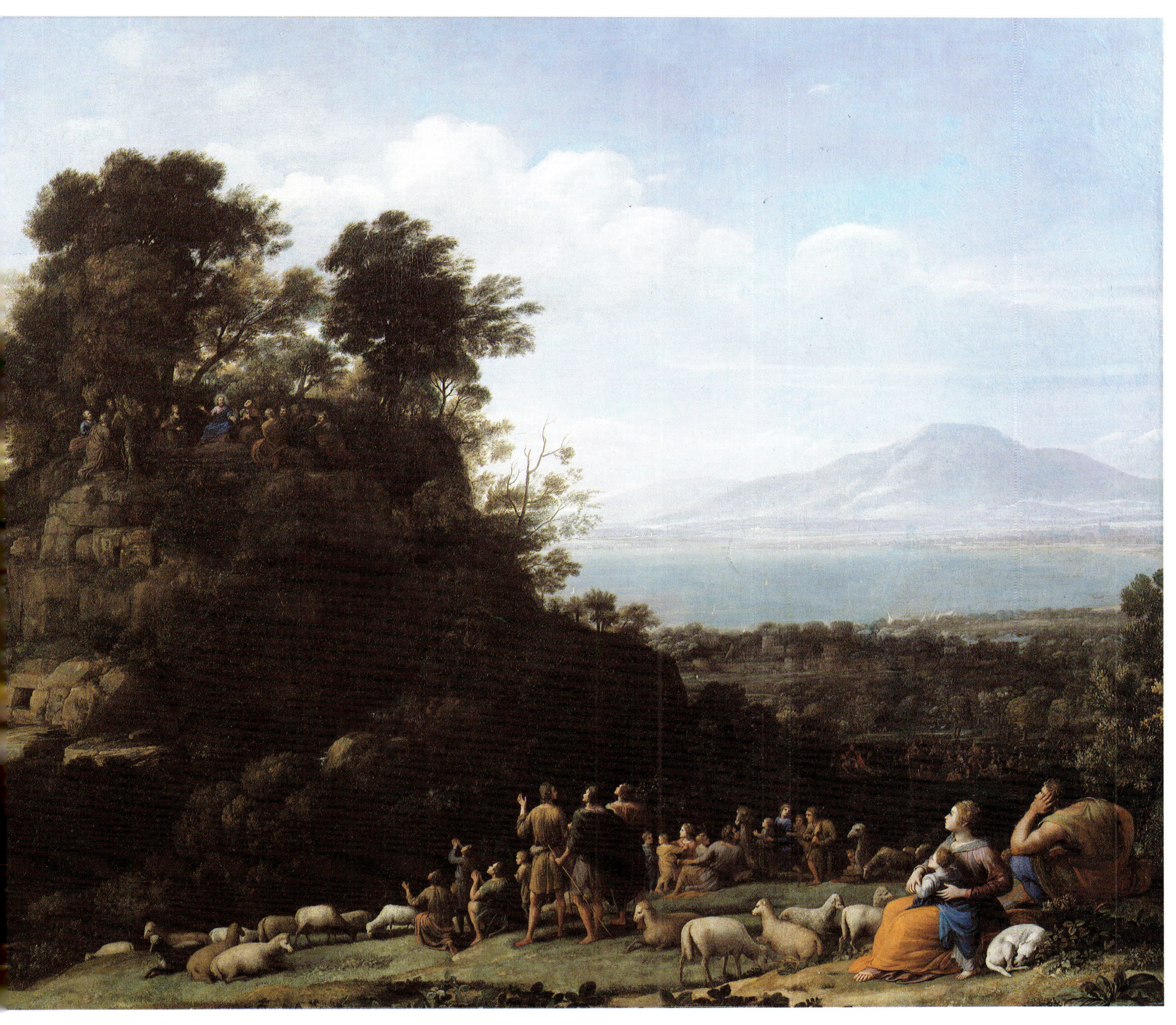

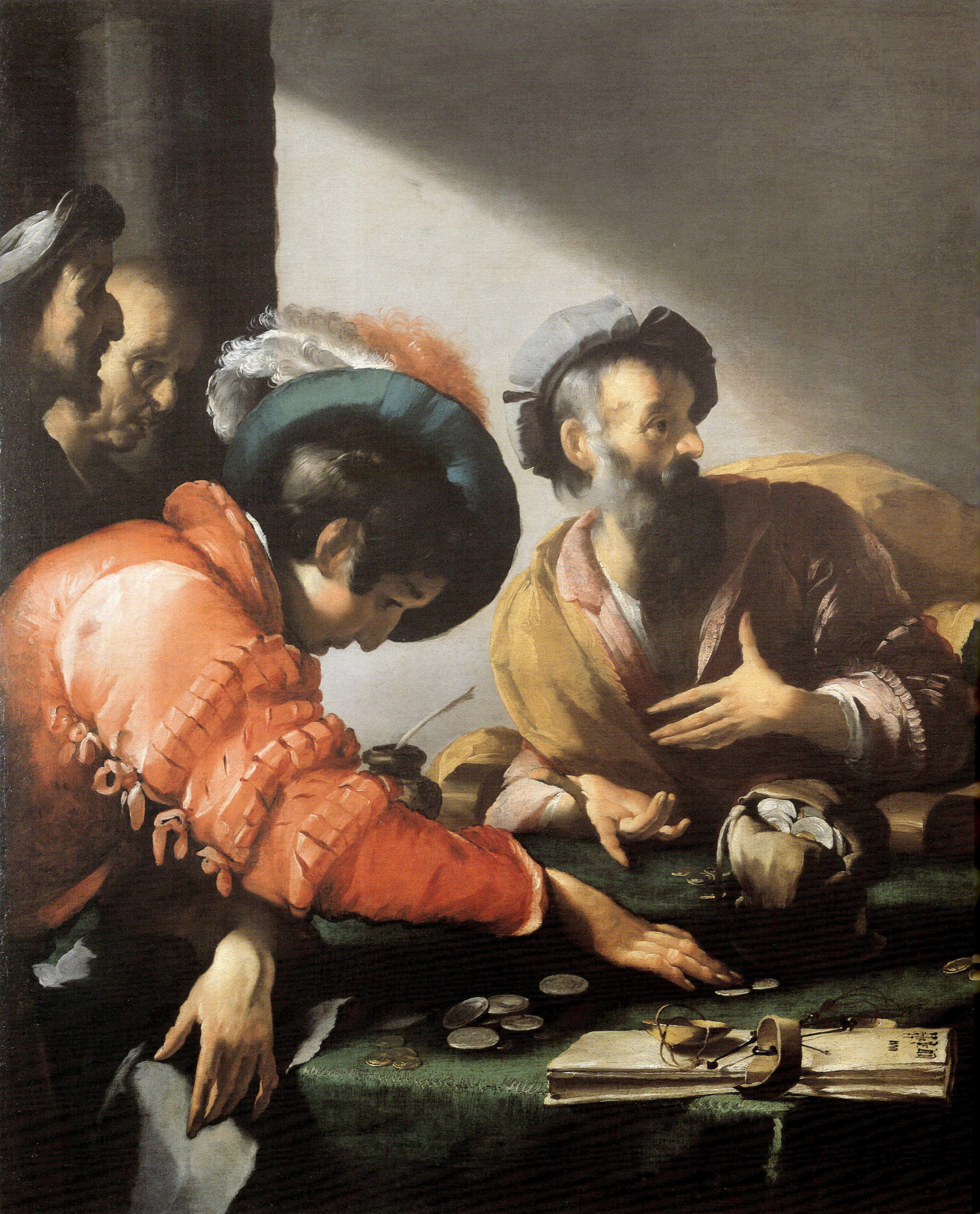

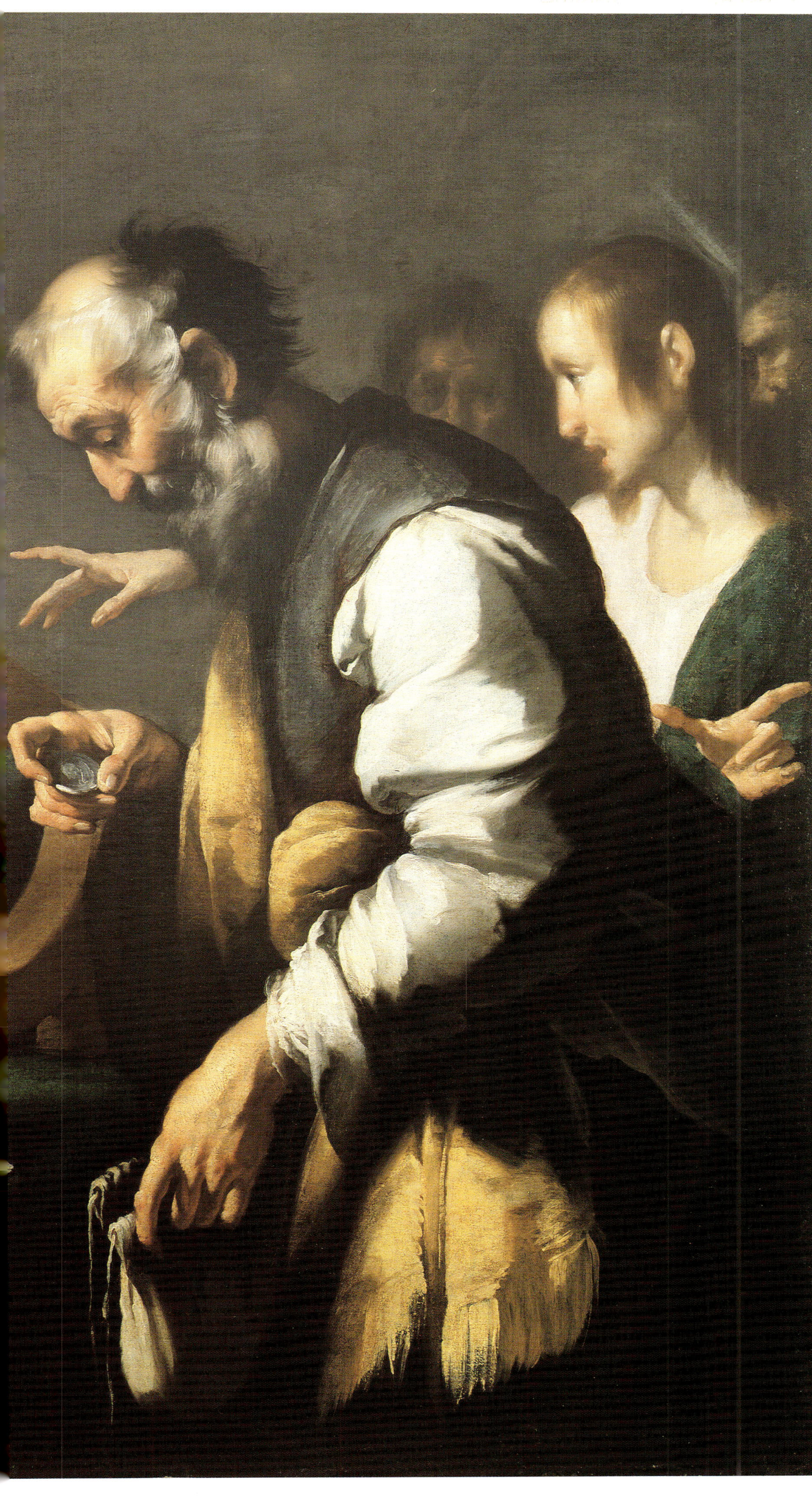

The Calling of St. Matthew

The early 17th century gave rise to a revolutionary style of painting. Taking its cue from the popular opera theaters of the day, this style places the viewer front-row-center. The dramatis personae are close to the edge of the stage, which is not deep. Light hits those who are central to the action, and all that is not essential has been eliminated or cast in deep shadow. The gestures are broad. But unlike opera the characters are from the streets and wear the garb of their daily occupations.

This compelling style emerged at a time when the Roman Catholic church needed to reinvigorate the faithful, for the Protestant Reformation was making thousands of converts to its tenets every month. Bernardo Strozzi, himself a monk earlier in his life, was one of many artists who came to the service of Rome, but setting the way for all of them was Caravaggio, whose *The Calling of Saint Matthew* inspired Strozzi's painting of the same name. While the subject is the same, the exuberant color, bravura brushwork, and startling depiction of Jesus' face are Strozzi's own.

Matthew was a tax collector, one of Jesus' original disciples and purportedly the author of the first book of the New Testament. He told the story of his own "calling" thus: "Jesus . . . saw a man sitting at the tax office, and he said to him, 'Follow me.' And he rose and followed him" (Matthew 9:9). Strozzi turns this dry bureaucratic account into a great duet. Jesus, however, is placed stage left (the viewer's right), where he is upstaged by a member of the "chorus," the man counting the receipts of the day. This figure cuts off the observer's view of Jesus' arm, disembodying the hand that is reminiscent of Michelangelo's hand of God in the Sistine Chapel. Still, Jesus stands out because his face is painted as though slightly out of focus in an otherwise sharply delineated scene. This soft blur, and the halo over his head, clearly mark him as supernatural. Matthew, caught in a bold triangle of light and framed by two figures, is palpably real in contrast.

The Calling of St. Matthew
BERNARDO STROZZI, Italian, 1581–1644
Worcester Art Museum, Massachusetts. Oil on canvas. 56¼ × 73⅞ in.

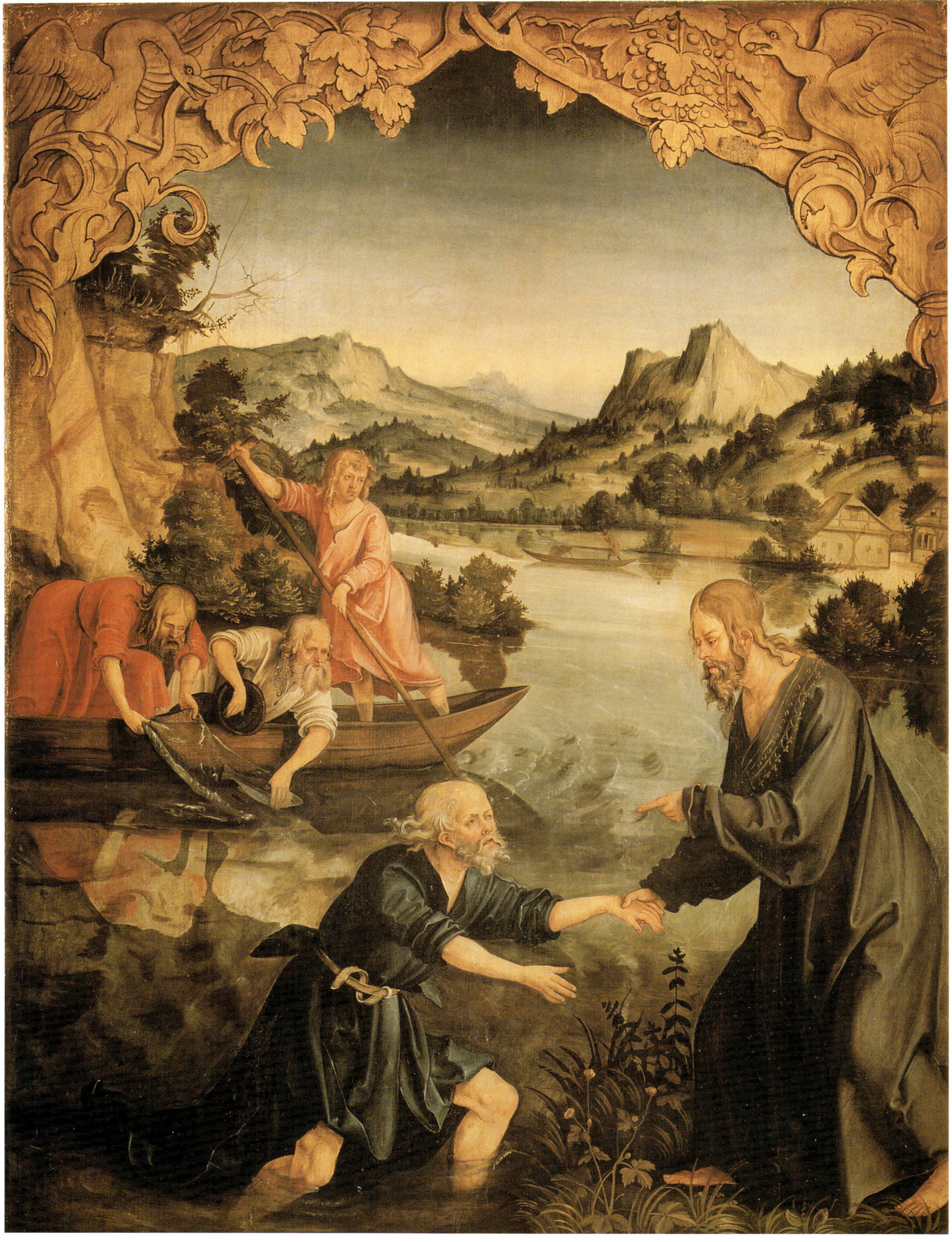

The Miraculous Draught of Fishes

Although he sets his picture on the shoal of an alpine lake, and frames the upper portion with a painted border meant to resemble a popular style of wood carving in 16th-century Germany, the provincial artist Hans Suess von Kulmbach has drawn largely on biblical narrative to create his version of *The Calling of Saint Peter*. The three men in the boat are Simon, later to be renamed Peter, and his partners James and John, the sons of Zebedee.

At the end of a long and fruitless night of fishing, they were washing their nets when Jesus asked if he could sit in their boat to instruct the crowd that was following him. All became silent so they could hear his words, and when he finished preaching he surprised everyone by asking Simon to throw his nets out into the water again. Simon complained that they had been fishing for hours and had taken in nothing, but he knew their visitor, for Jesus had just cured his mother-in-law of a fever the day before. He did as he was instructed. The nets quickly filled to breaking, and the boats began to sink from the weight of the fish.

Simon's reaction was one of utter astonishment and fear. He fell to his knees, begging, "Depart from me, for I am a sinful man, O Lord." Jesus calmly told him not to be afraid for "henceforth, you will be catching men." Kulmbach pictures this very moment. Unusual is his rendition of the advanced age of Simon and the stooped and haggard appearance of Jesus.

Peter Paul Rubens, the great Flemish artist whose career flourished about 100 years after Hans Suess von Kulmbach's, turns to the same subject but treats it more heroically. The figures are brawny and rise out of the sea almost like mythological beings. Like Hans Suess von Kulmbach, Rubens is interested in the relationship between Simon and Jesus, but he also wants to show the magnitude of the miracle. He does this by carefully depicting the net and the fish in it, in contrast to his generalized and sketchy treatment of the water, sky, and costumes of the fishermen.

Rubens did not intend for this painting to stand by itself as a work of art. He meant it to be a disposable working drawing to guide an engraver in reproducing it for wide distribution. Quickly executed in pencil, pen, and oil paint on three enjoined sheets of paper, it survived because the engraving was not made. Later, a collector applied the paper to canvas to preserve it, and today the work demonstrates the spontaneous power of Rubens's genius as a storyteller. The result of the miracle, by the way, was that Simon, James, and John left everything and followed Jesus (Luke 5:1–11). Meanwhile, the crowd that had gathered to hear Jesus preach no doubt had a wonderful fish fry.

The Miraculous Draught of Fishes
PETER PAUL RUBENS, Flemish, 1577–1640.
National Gallery, London. Pencil, pen, and oil on paper, applied to canvas. 21⅝ × 33¼ in.

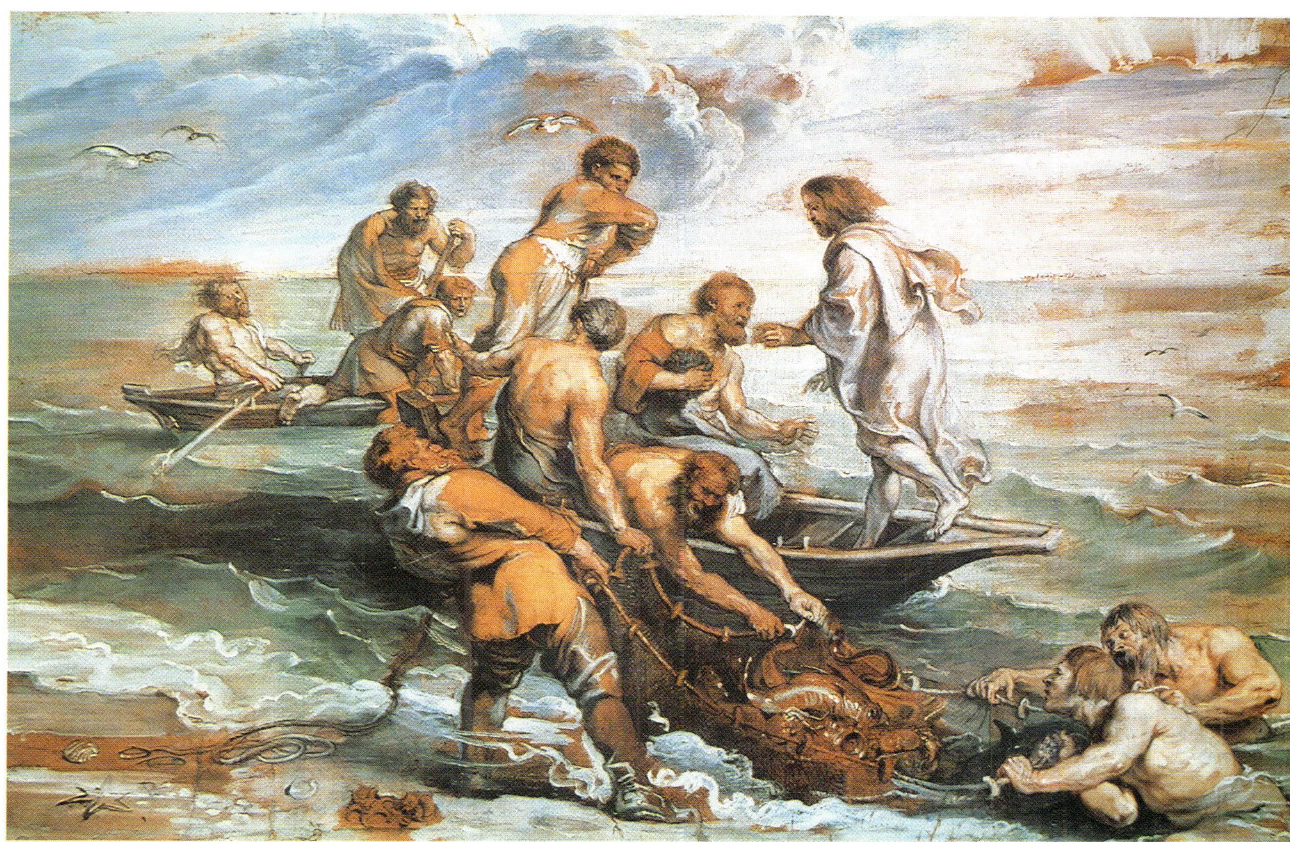

The Calling of St. Peter
HANS SUESS VON KULMBACH, German, ca. 1480–1521/22
Galleria degli Uffizi, Florence. Oil on canvas. 51½ × 39¾ in.

The Marriage Feast at Cana

John, who was the closest to Jesus of the disciples, related the highlights of the first three days of Jesus' public life in his Gospel. On the third day, Jesus, his mother, and the newly chosen disciples were guests at a wedding in the town of Cana in Galilee. The caterers ran out of wine. Mary expected Jesus to do something about this, but he said "My hour has not yet come," as though hesitant to perform his first miracle. Nonetheless, his canny mother instructed the servants to do whatever he told them.

At the moment pictured, Jesus is instructing the servants to fill six great jars to the brim with water. The vessels' contents immediately turned into wine—120 or maybe even 180 gallons of it, according to John's estimation. The conclusion of the story is also shown. As though suddenly aware of his supernatural powers, Jesus commands that a sample of the wine be tasted by the steward of the feast. We see this sommelier in the background, calling to the bridegroom, "Every man serves the good wine first; and when men have drunk freely, then the poor wine; but you have kept the good wine until now" (John 2:10). The bride, like Mary, is aware that it is Jesus who has provided this extraordinary hospitality. With eyes lowered, she silently praises him. Mary looks at him like a proud mother. The groom's reactions are not as clear. Could he be counting on his fingers, trying to remember just how much wine he did order?

Juan des Flandes made this an intimate scene by showing only part of the wedding table, and by keeping the scale of the painting very small (it is not even 12 inches tall). The purity of the table cloth, the careful placement of napkins, bread, and saltcellar, the soft shadows cast by the golden glow of light, and especially the concentration of Jesus, the groom, and the servant on the pouring of the water, all make this an event of more gravity than would be expected at a Jewish wedding. The artist, however, was following the Gospel writer's description of the scene as religious and serious. Indeed, he wrote that the stone jars had once been used in the rite of purification by which a mother was cleansed after childbirth. He further maintained that by manifesting his glory in this miracle, Jesus made his disciples believe in him.

The magical scene is reflected in the convex mirror that hangs behind the bride and groom. Typically, Flemish artists used such locales for self-portraits, suggesting, perhaps somewhat coyly, that they painted the scene from life. Juan des Flandes, instead, places himself outside the loggia—if scholars are correct in believing the man in the yellow cloak is the artist. Having read the biblical text so carefully, perhaps he identified himself with John, the reporter.

The Marriage Feast at Cana

JUAN DES FLANDES, Flemish, active by 1496–1519

The Jack and Belle Linsky Collection, Metropolitan Museum of Art, New York. Oil on wood panel. 8¼ × 6¼ in.

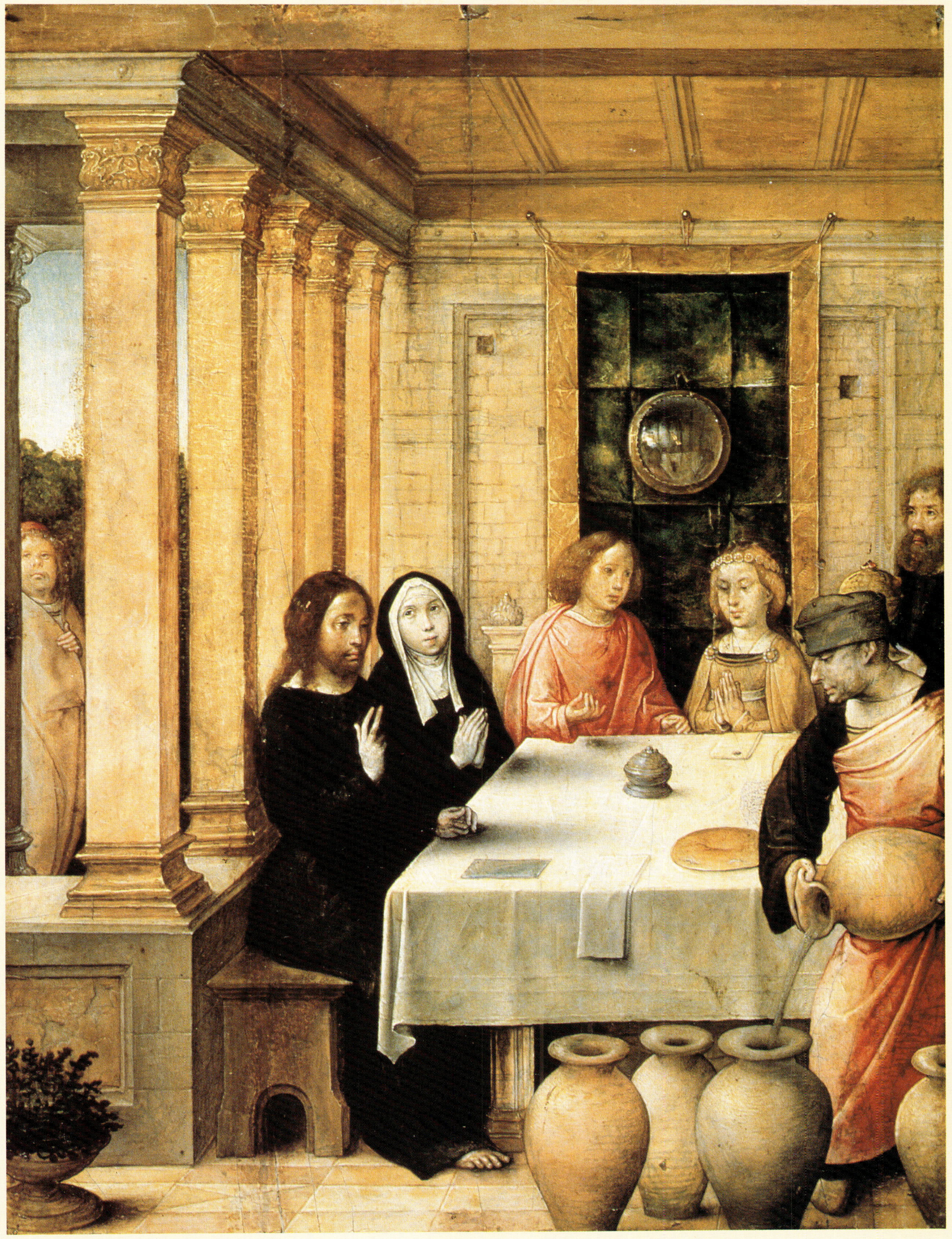

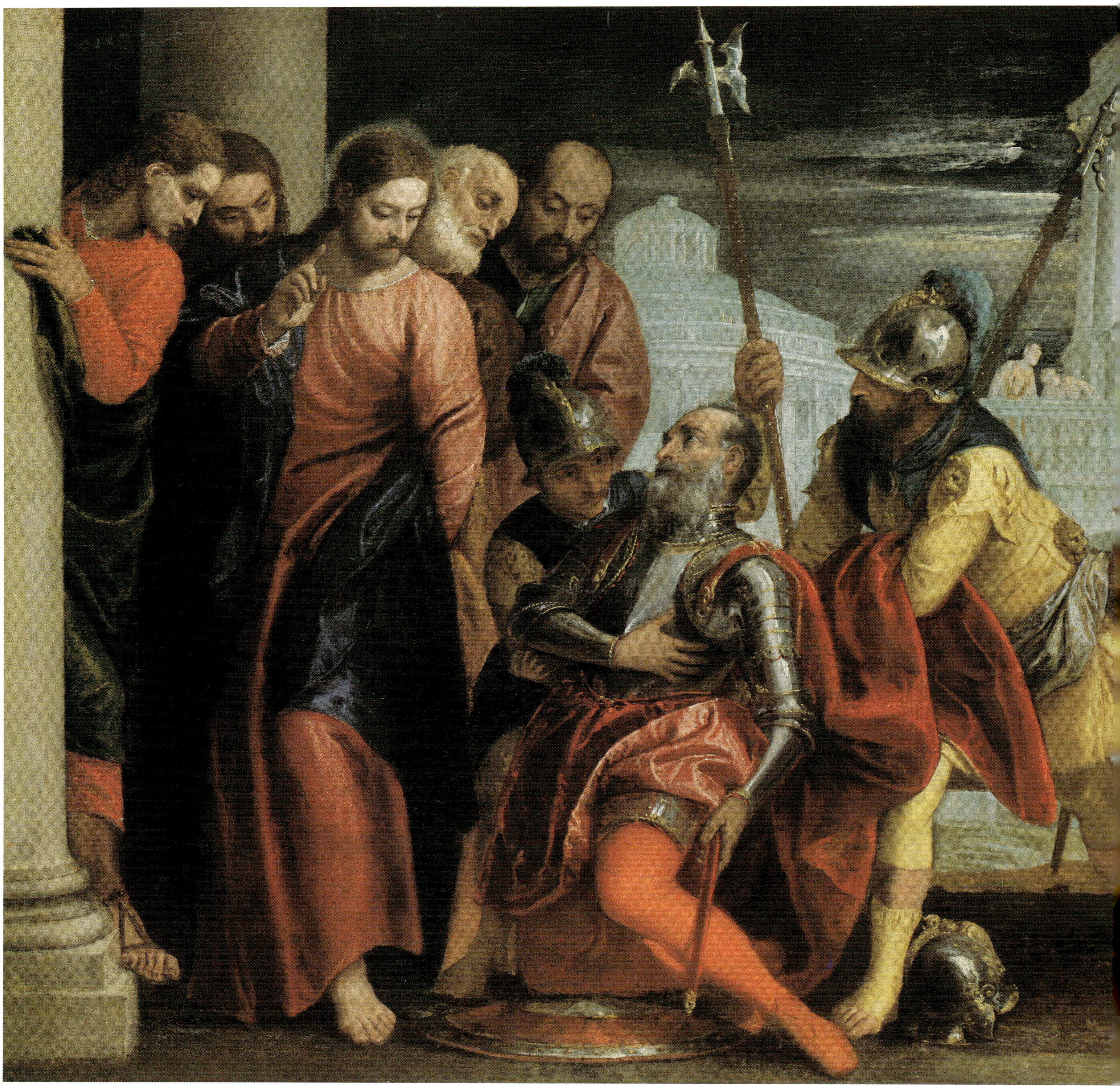

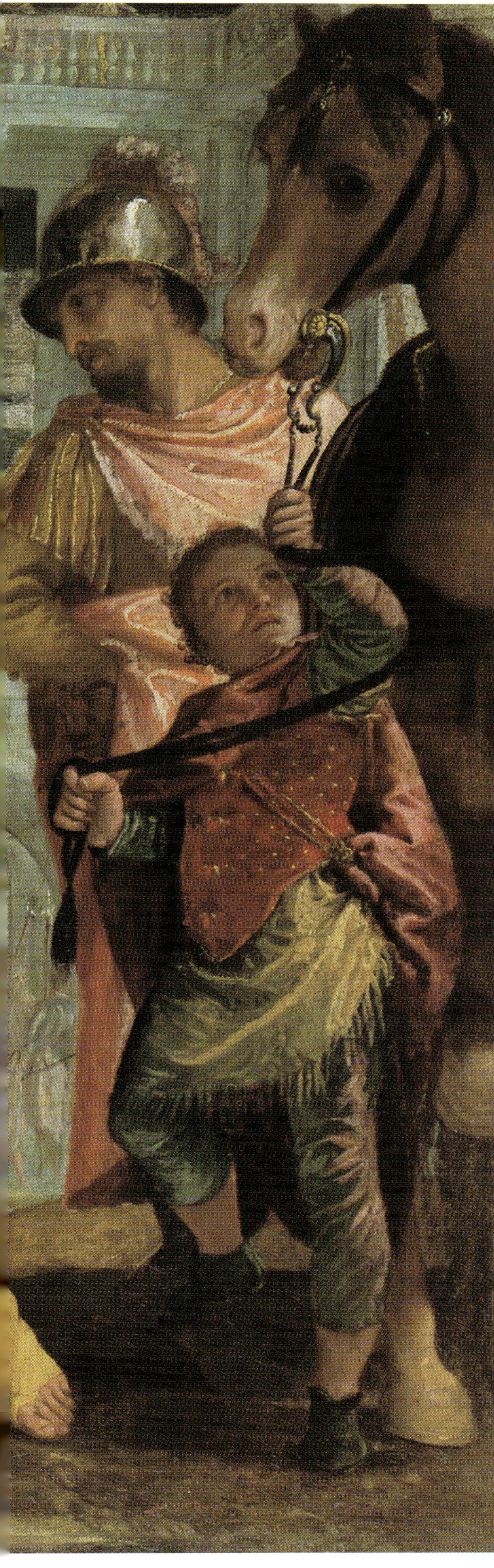

Christ and the Centurion

The Gospel writer called Capernaum Jesus' "own city" (Matthew 9:1), so when the town's Roman military commander came to Jesus for a favor the Savior may have already known that the man loved his adopted country and had indeed built the town's synagogue. He asked Jesus to heal his personal slave who was near death. Jesus gladly offered to go to the centurion's house to do this. "Lord," the soldier responded, "do not trouble yourself, for I am not worthy to have you under my roof . . . but say the word, and let my servant be healed" (Luke 7:6–7). He then assured the centurion that, because of his faith, his servant had already recovered. In the depiction of this scene by Paolo Veronese, Jesus is politely parting from his remarkable supplicant. The commander has thrown his shield to the ground and is being helped to kneel on it by two of his military colleagues, while the disciples look on, decidedly confused over why a Roman would behave like this in front of Jews.

Veronese dresses all the soldiers in the finest armor of his own day. It was exactly the kind of metalware that his viewers would have wanted for themselves or for the men in their families. In an odd but wonderfully natural detail the disciple on the far left, who is too short to see over the others, has propped himself up against the tall column, his sandal barely securing a toehold on the plinth. The centurion's horse, a servant boy, and a military aide stand to the right. The upward movement of their bodies counters the bent postures throughout the rest of the composition. Here Veronese introduces an elegance of pose that ennobles and elevates the narrative.

Capernaum was a modest though regionally important small city. The domed building in the background is probably the town's synagogue. Archaeologists have uncovered the actual structure, and while it still has glorious Corinthian columns, it never had a dome, something Veronese could not have known in the 16th century.

Christ and the Centurion
PAOLO VERONESE, Italian, ca. 1528–1588
The Toledo Museum of Art, Ohio. Gift of Edward Drummond Libbey. Oil on canvas. 39⅛ × 52½ in.

The Healing of the Paralytic

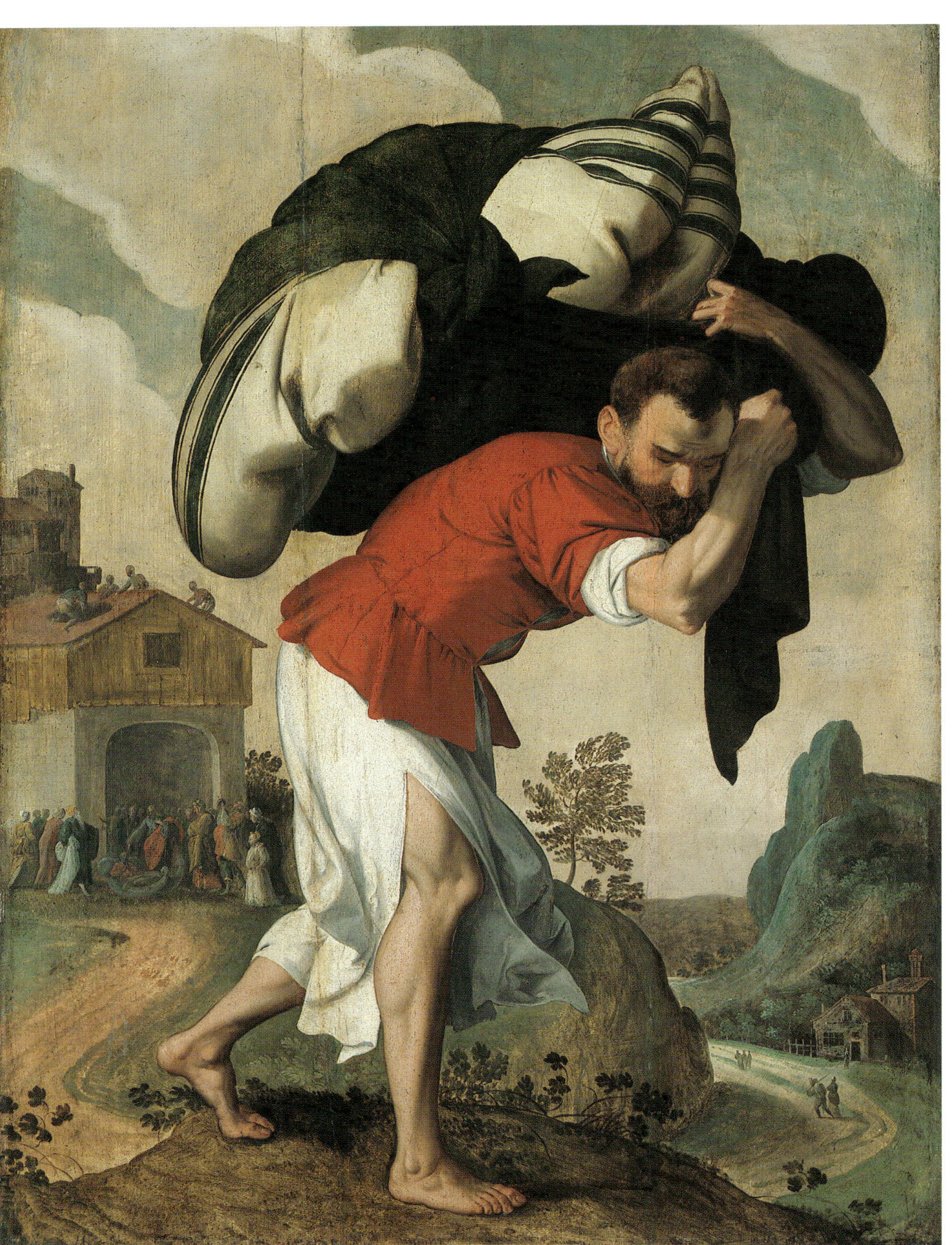

The Healing of the Paralytic
UNKNOWN NETHERLANDISH ARTIST, **16th century**
Chester Dale Collection, National Gallery of Art, Washington, DC. Wood panel. 42½ × 29⅞ in.

The idea of "Jesus at home" is difficult to imagine, for his home was never described in the Bible. But Mark did use the phrase "at home" in his story of the crowd that came to Jesus' residence to hear him and be healed by him. According to his Gospel, there were so many visitors that the house could hold no more, not even outside the door. Four men had brought a paralytic, hoping Jesus would cure him. When they saw the multitude, they climbed to the roof, made an opening in it, and lowered the afflicted man into Jesus' presence. He was moved by the faith of these men and told the paralytic that his sins were forgiven. Some religious teachers who were in the crowd thought Jesus guilty of blasphemy, for only God could forgive sins. Perceiving their thoughts, Jesus asked, "Which is easier, to say to the paralytic 'Your sins are forgiven,' or to say 'Rise, take up your pallet and walk'?" Then, to demonstrate that he indeed had the power both to forgive sins and cure, he said to the paralytic, "Rise, take up your pallet, and go home" (Mark 2:9–12). The man was healed immediately and did as he was told.

The anonymous artist of the 16th-century Netherlands who painted *The Healing of the Paralytic* shows Jesus in front of a barn-like house, having just cured the man whose friends are still on the roof. The newly restored man, deep in meditation over what has happened to him, walks away under the voluminous load of his featherbed. The great shape of this bulging mass, cinched by a dark blanket, appears almost a part of the man's body, as it must have seemed during the many years he had lain on it. It is an ironic commentary. Though he is free of his crippling disability, he is still bound to his most personal possession, which now is clearly a burden. And though he is cured and like other men at last, he hurries from their company. It is as though the artist has made a parable out of this miracle.

Christ in the Storm on the Sea of Galilee

Rembrandt executed only one seascape during his highly productive career, the tempestuous one reproduced here. In it, the artist shows a sea as dark as night. Churning sheets of water break against a broad boat, the spray made brilliantly luminous by daylight off to the left. So powerful is the effect that this might be called a portrait of a storm rather than a seascape.

In showing the upturned boat as it rides the crest of a wave, Rembrandt enables the viewer to see Jesus and the 12 disciples inside. The short trip across the Sea of Galilee was a blessed respite from the surge and demands of the multitudes that had been following Jesus for days. Tired, the great healer slept. A storm arose, and furious waves tossed the boat to and fro, but he did not awaken. Some of the disciples were fishermen, but even the most experienced sailors among them could not control the vessel in such a raging tempest. Many of them cowered, and one became sick over the side of the boat. Finally, they wakened Jesus, and that is the moment Rembrandt has chosen to depict.

"Master, master," they are calling, "we are perishing." According to the Scriptures, "Jesus rebuked the wind and the raging waves; and they ceased, and there was a calm." Having taken care of the dangers of nature, he turned to his disciples and asked, "Where is your faith?" The men were frightened by what had happened, but they were also awed, asking one another, "Who is this, that he commands even wind and water, and they obey him?" (Luke 8:24–25).

In this relatively early work, Rembrandt marked the date 1633 on the ship's rudder and gave his own face to the disciple who clasps his cap to his head. Rembrandt had just moved from his hometown of Leiden to the cosmopolitan center of Amsterdam and was beginning to make a name for himself. During this exhilarating period, he regularly recorded his own image. That he should include a self-portrait in this dramatic scene, however, signifies more than a consistency with his artistic predilections of the moment. Rather, he was presenting a bold and gratuitous lesson in narrative painting to his fellow artists. It was tantamount to saying that an artist had to personalize and internalize events of the past if he wished to bring them to life on canvas. That was a fine idea for an emotional soul like Rembrandt, but most of his compatriots took a more objective approach to art. Still, Rembrandt must have felt confident that he had convinced them with this unforgettable work.

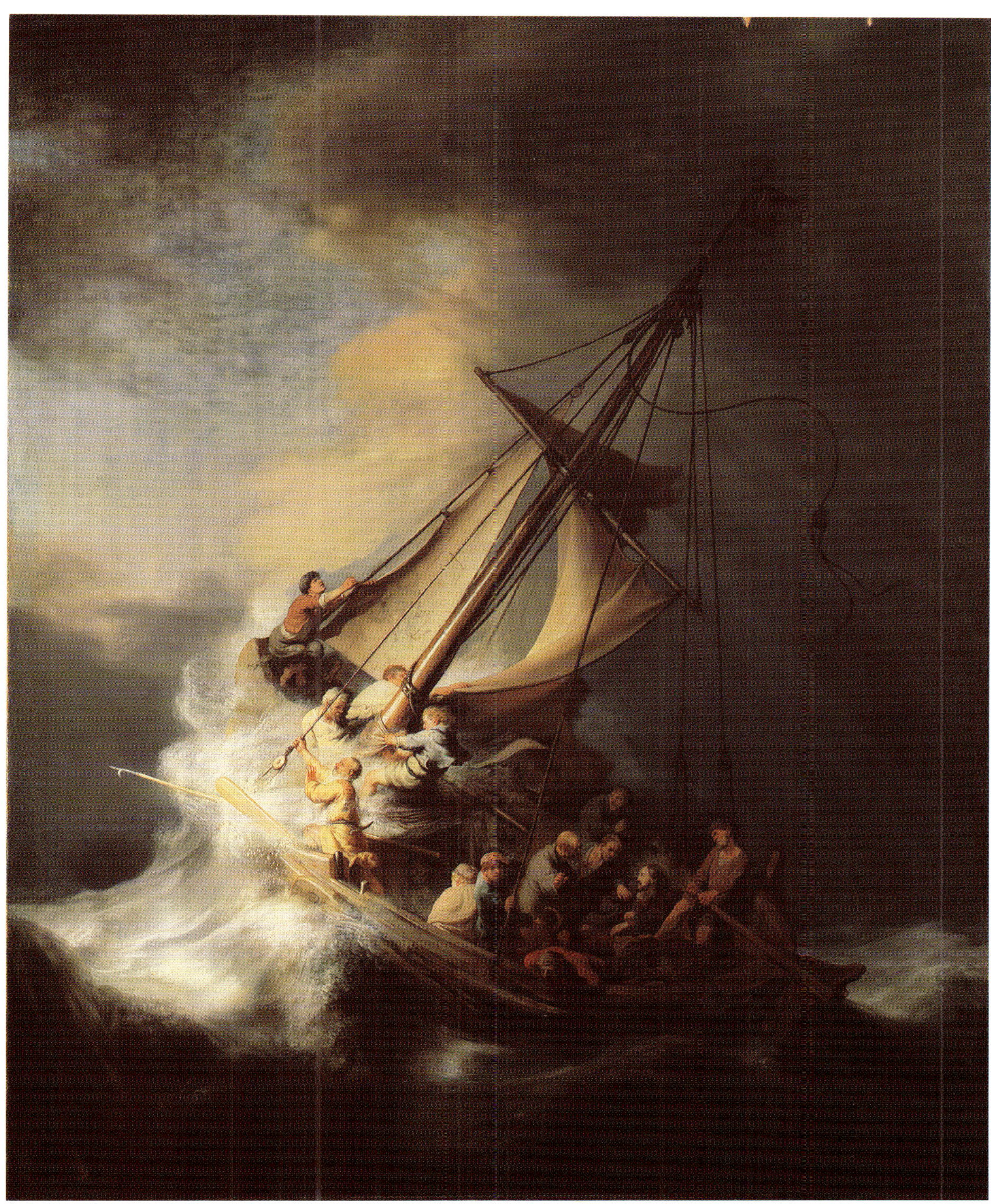

Christ in the Storm on the Sea of Galilee
REMBRANDT VAN RIJN, Dutch, 1606–1669
The Isabella Stewart Gardner Museum, Boston. Oil on canvas. 63½ × 51 in.

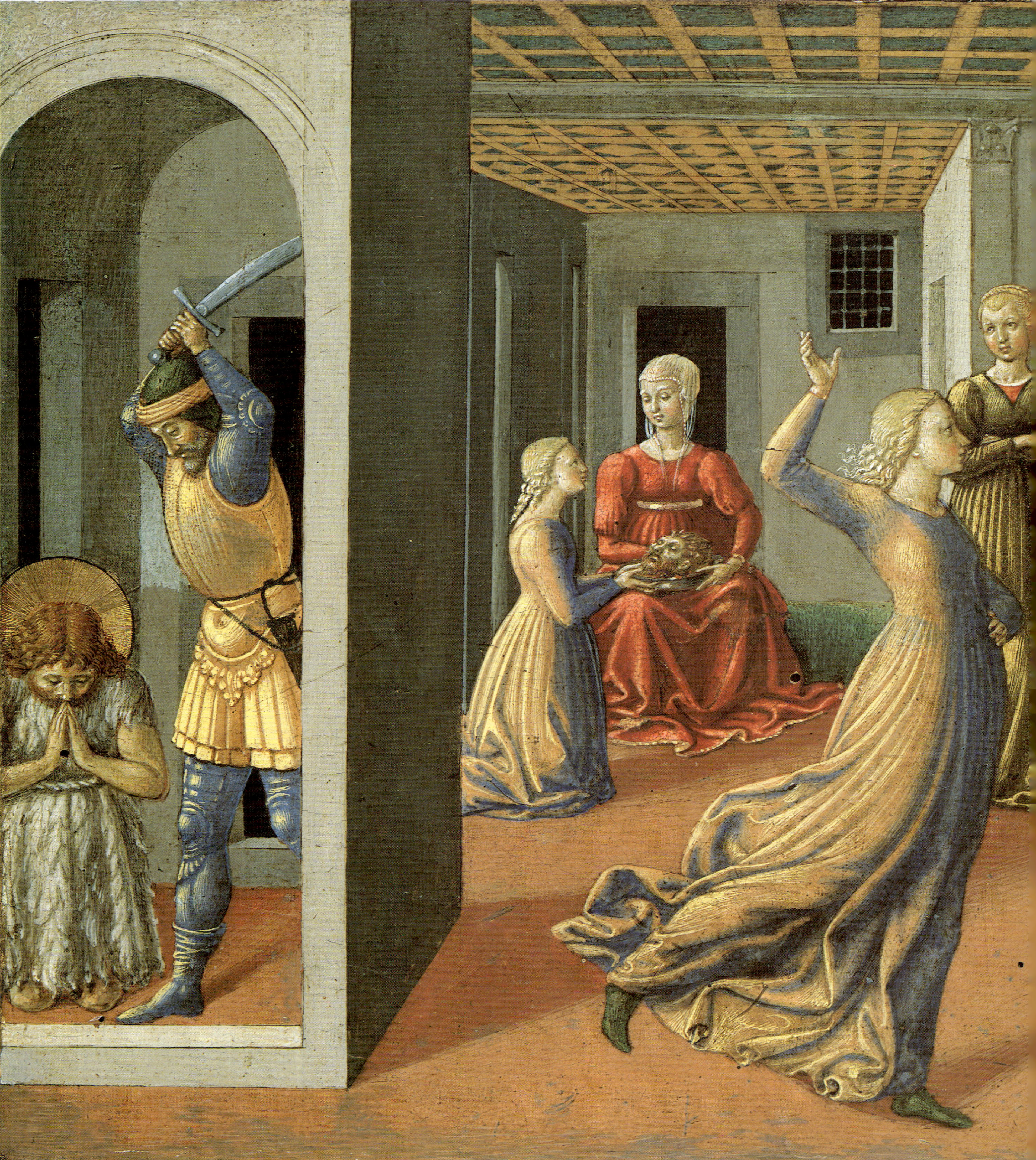

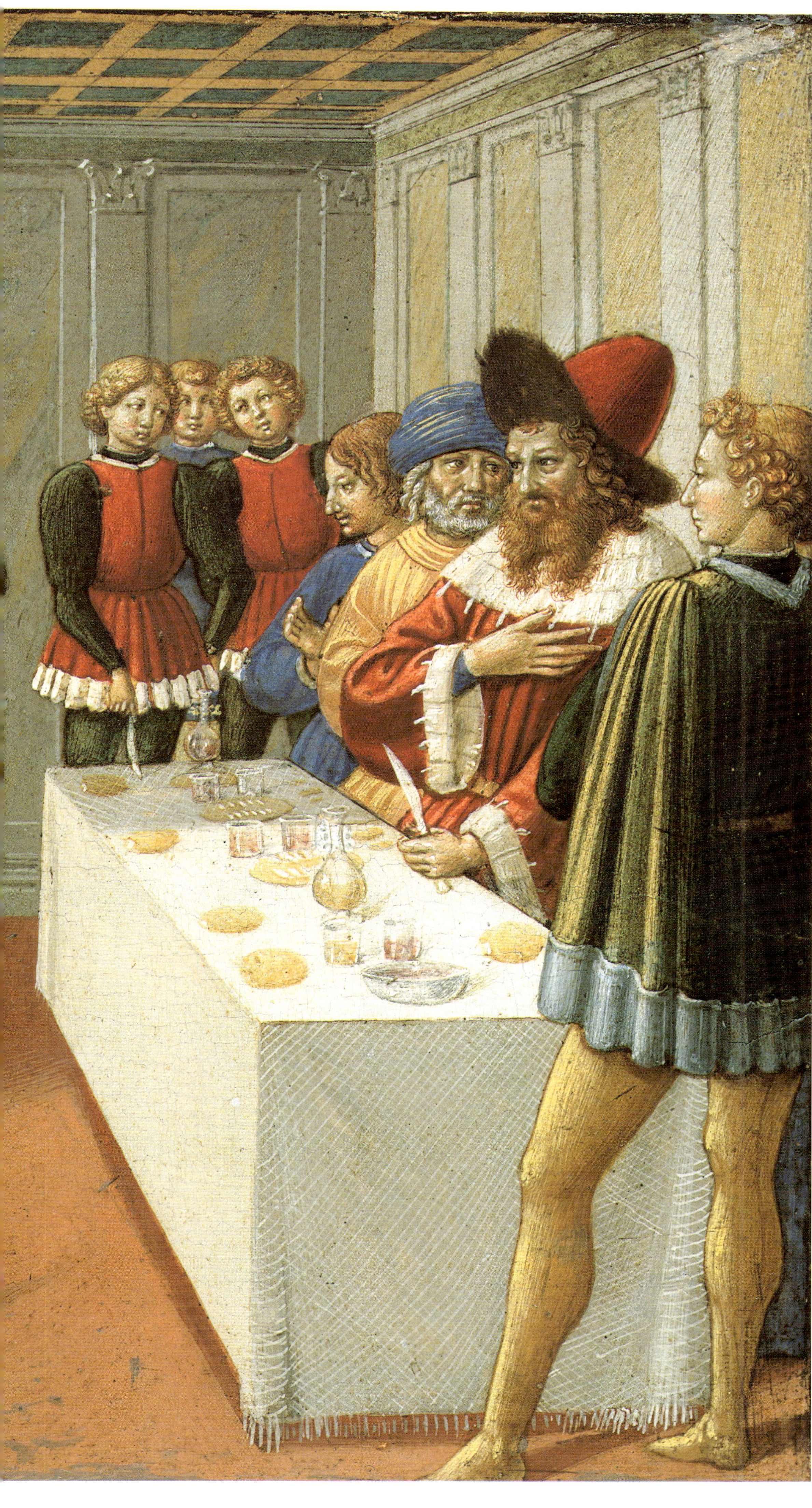

The Dance of Salome

The name of Salome is not mentioned in the New Testament, but her dance is. Because it so pleased her stepfather Herod Antipas and the guests at his birthday party, people throughout the centuries have assumed that it was wickedly sexy, if not also highly artistic. It has been celebrated by many famous artists, writers, and composers as the only truly sensual episode in the New Testament.

What is known from the Gospel writers Matthew, Mark, and Luke, the earliest sources of information on this subject, is chilling. Antipas married Herodias, his cousin and sister-in-law (divorced wife of his half brother). Such an intrafamilial marriage was forbidden by Jewish law, and John the Baptist rebuked him for it, earning Herodias's enmity. She demanded the imprisonment of the itinerant preacher, probably as a troublemaker and subversive. It is here, in *The Dance of Salome*, that artist Benozzo Gozzoli takes up the story. Herodias's daughter Salome is dancing before Antipas to entertain him, his courtiers, officers, and the leading men of Galilee. The young dandy in tights and short green cape openly admires her body, while her uncle takes on a lascivious look and makes a rude gesture with his knife. Painting for a conservative 15th-century religious audience, Gozzoli does not attempt to picture the dancer as anything more than graceful and beautiful. Still, the impact of her performance on the wakening body of the adolescent page boy at the end of the long table is testament to her sensuality.

When the dance was finished, the grateful Antipas asked Salome to request anything, even half of his kingdom, and he would grant

The Dance of Salome
BENOZZO GOZZOLI, Italian, 1420–1497
Samuel H. Kress Collection, National Gallery of Art, Washington, DC. Wood panel. 9⅝ × 13½ in.

it to her. She conferred with her mother and came back demanding the head of John the Baptist on a serving tray. Antipas admired the preacher and was saddened to order his execution, but, as can be seen on the far left of the painting, it was done. Behind her own dancing image, Salome appears a second time, kneeling before her mother and presenting her with the severed head.

Serial narrations, such as in *The Dance of Salome*, were common in late medieval and early Renaissance painting, but the introduction of linear perspective and the use of cast shadows made the task more difficult. Because the room looks real, and the figures in it seem to occupy actual space, it takes a strong imagination to accept this as not one moment in time, but three.

While Gozzoli tells the story of Salome and John the Baptist in a factual way, Mattia Preti reinterprets it. He portrays Salome as a teenager, her innocence slipping away. She holds the gruesome tray but feels nothing. Herodias suddenly has a turning of the stomach as Salome presents the head of the Baptist to her. With a wide gesture of his arm and hand, Antipas seems to say, with disdain, "As you commanded, my dear." Clearly, the party is over.

The disciples fetched the body of John and buried it, then they went to Jesus and told him what had happened. Matthew remembered that after Jesus heard the terrible news he withdrew in a boat "to a lonely place apart" (Matthew 14:13). He was allowed to mourn in private. What he did and how he acted were not reported, nor has his sorrow over the execution of his cousin ever been shown in art.

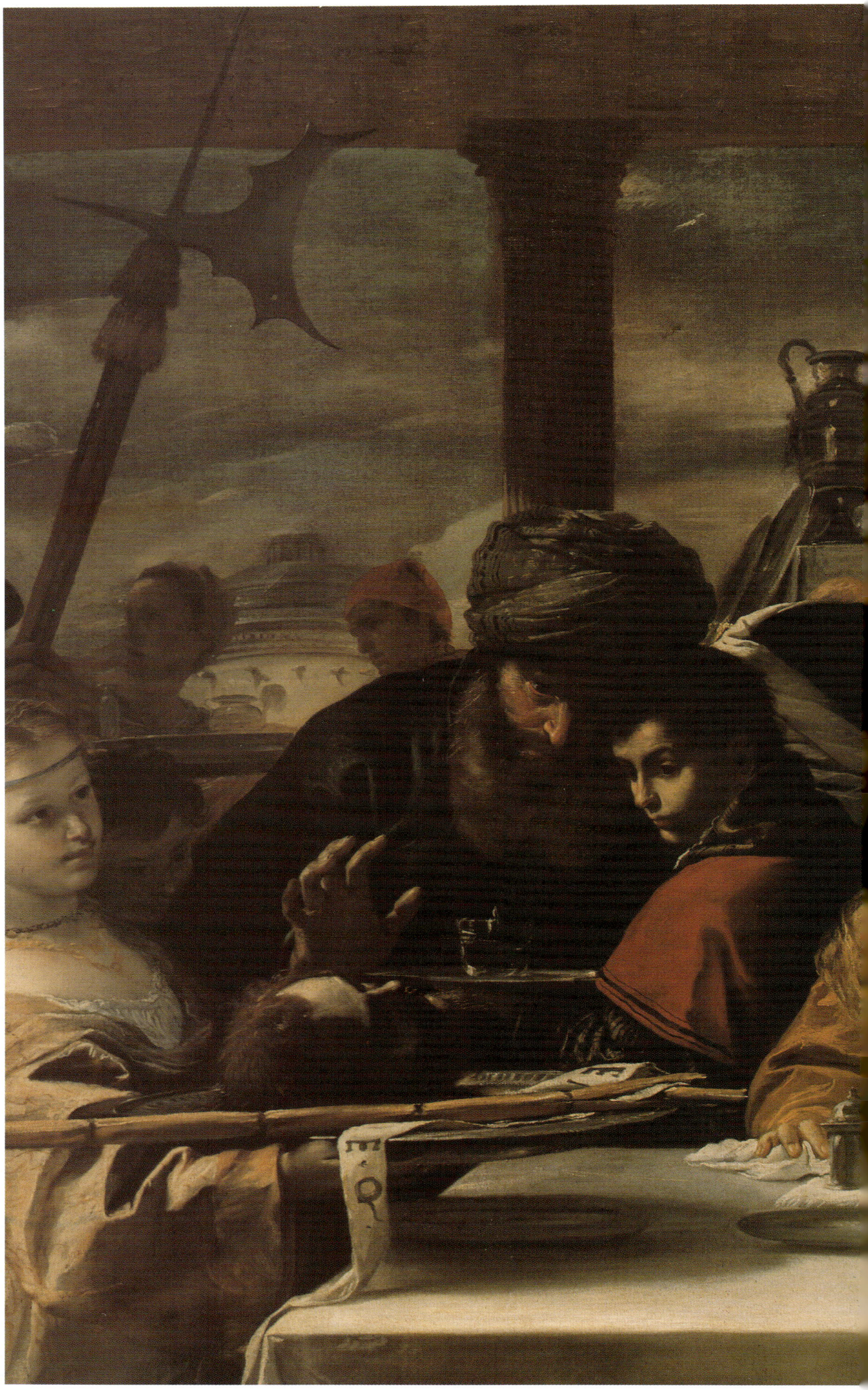

The Feast of Herod

MATTIA PRETI, Italian, 1613–1699

The Toledo Museum of Art, Ohio. Gift of Edward Drummond Libbey. Oil on canvas. 70 × 99¼ in.

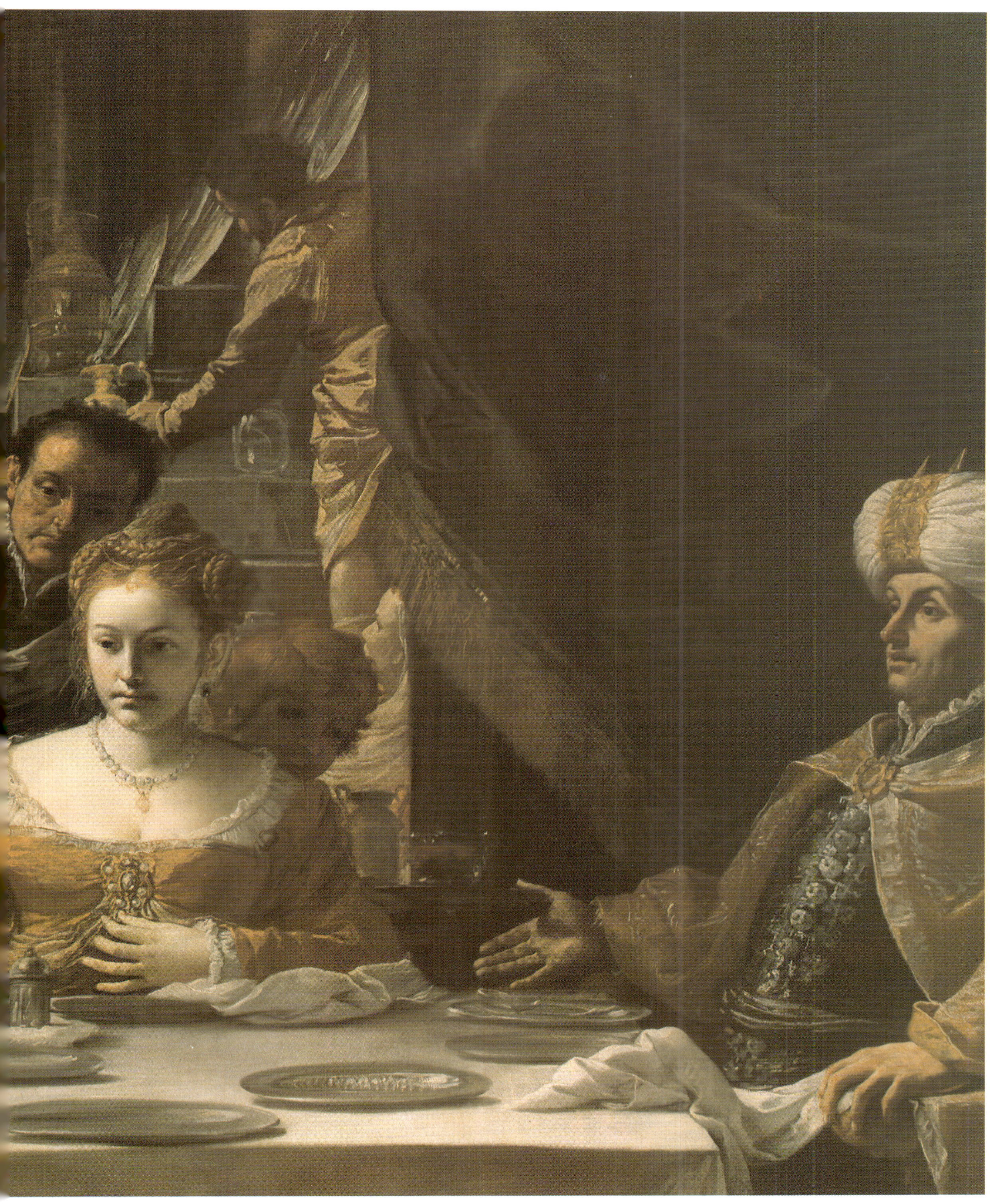

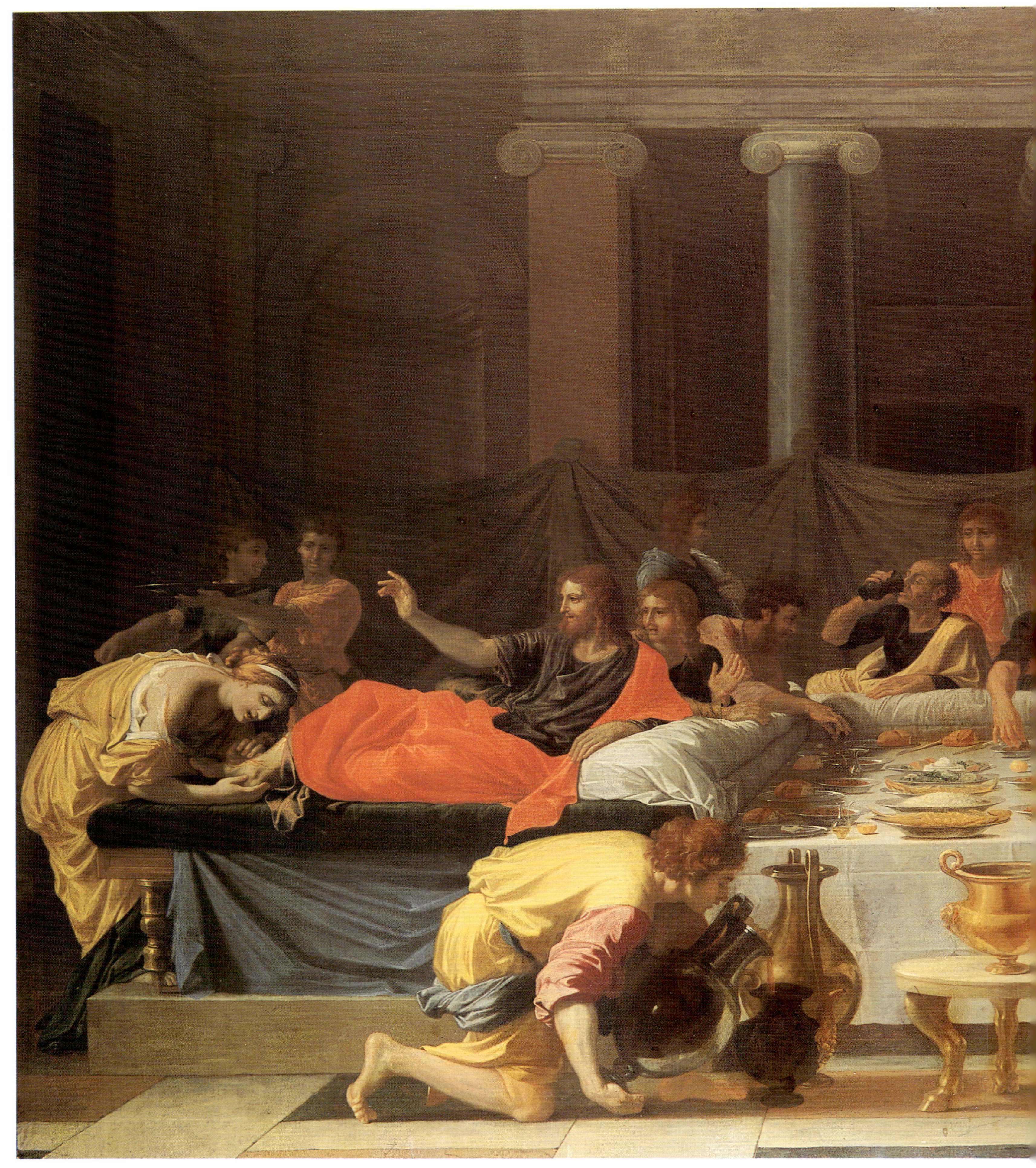

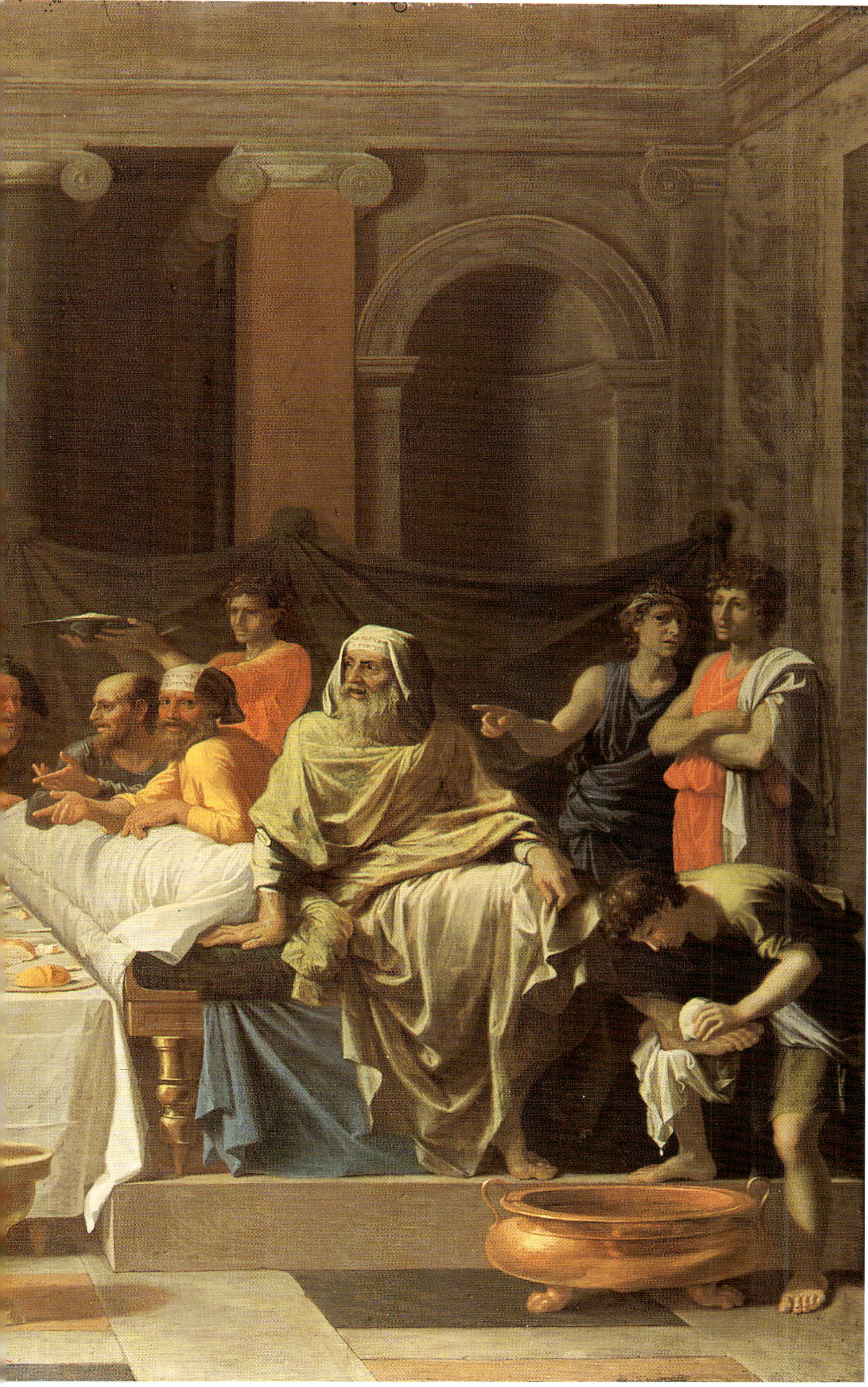

Mary Magdalene Anointing Jesus' Feet

A Pharisee named Simon invited Jesus to his house for dinner. The Bible says Jesus accepted and "sat down with him." A known prostitute of the city found that Jesus was at the Pharisee's home and showed up. Standing behind Jesus, weeping, she washed his feet with her tears, dried them with her hair, and anointed them with ointment she had brought in an alabaster flask. Jesus turned to the woman and said, "Your sins are forgiven. . . . Your faith has saved you; go in peace" (Luke 7:44–50).

In *Mary Magdalene Anointing Jesus' Feet*, Nicolas Poussin translates this event into a Roman banquet, with couches instead of chairs, as was the custom in Rome and in many of its colonies. He shows a servant washing the feet of one of the guests, an older man swathed in tan robes, to underscore the affront of the host's neglect of Jesus. The Pharisees insisted on ritual purity, so it was odd that the host did not extend this simple and common courtesy to Jesus, the man he addressed as Rabbi.

Since at least the sixth century, the woman has been identified as Mary Magdalene, one of the witnesses of the Resurrection of Jesus. There is, however, no evidence save the weight of tradition that the woman *is* the Magdalene, or that she was a prostitute. Whether this romantic conception of her is true or not, it has resulted in many glorious paintings.

In his own lifetime, Poussin was considered the great teller of fables. He carefully researched every detail of every painting. Living in Rome most of his adult life, he found out what the architecture and accessories were like in historic times and slavishly adhered to the models he unearthed. Although these take center stage in his painting of Jesus and the Magdalene, the reactions of the diners bring attention to the figure of Christ, as does the bright red of his robe.

Mary Magdalene Anointing Jesus Feet
NICOLAS POUSSIN, French, 1594–1665
Collection of the Duke of Sutherland, on loan to the National Gallery of Scotland, Edinburgh. Oil on canvas 46½ × 70½ in.

▷
DETAIL
FOLLOWING PAGE

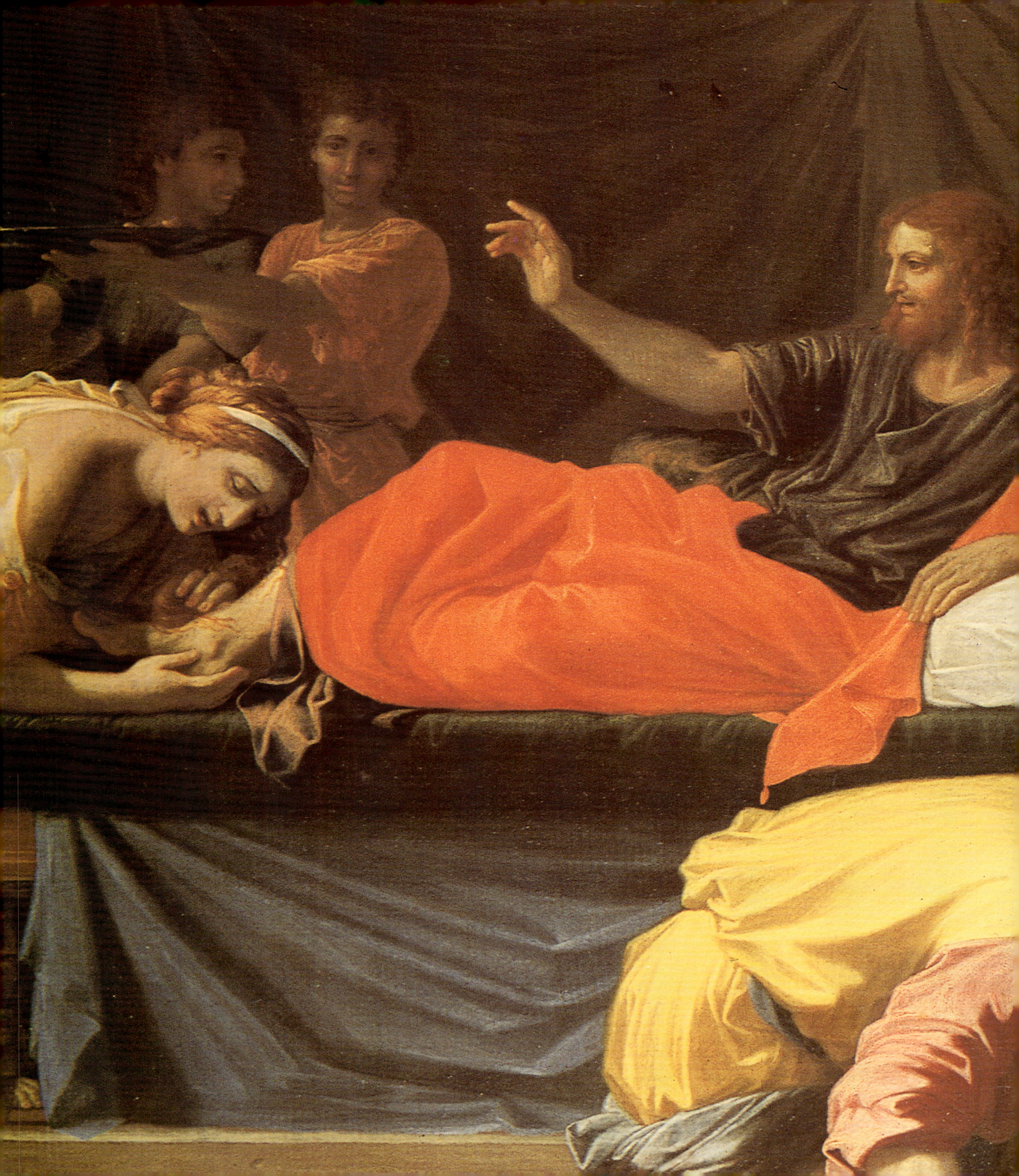

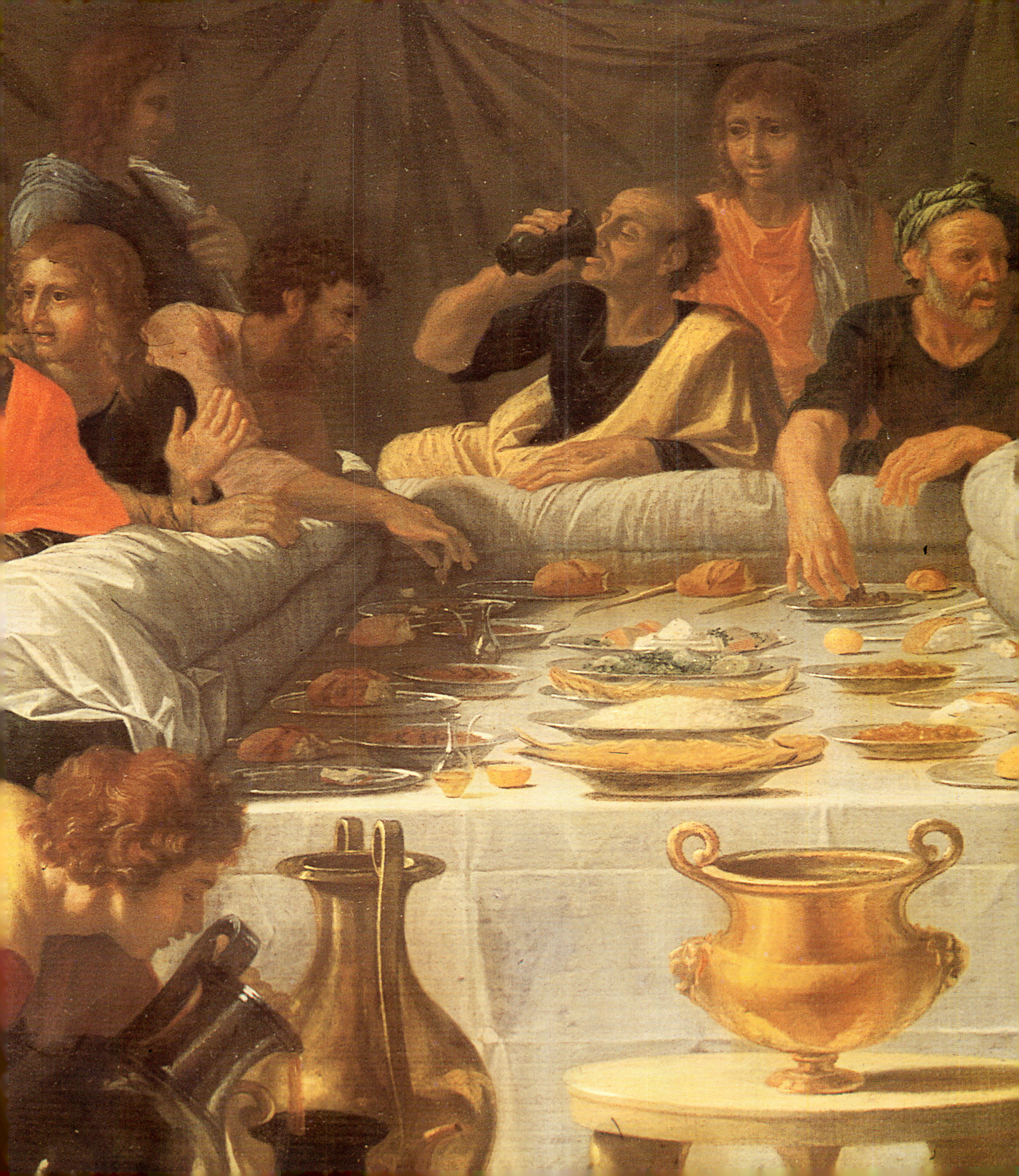

The Repentant Magdalene

The saints, particularly those who knew Christ during his lifetime, played an enormous role in the development of Christian culture. Sinful humans, or those in need, often prayed to patron saints for assistance rather than directly to God. These elevated individuals were thought to particularly favor those who visited places that had been sanctified by their presence or by their burials. Churches were dedicated to them, music was written in their honor, and devotional pieces were produced in their image. Over the centuries, artists have painted a great variety of icons to the saints, but few are as stunningly realistic as this one of the Magdalene by Caravaggio.

Called the Magdalene after the town on the Sea of Galilee where she once lived, she was one of the women who ministered to Jesus and helped him. She was present at the crucifixion and burial of Jesus and was the first to arrive at the tomb on Easter morning, as well as the first to speak with Jesus after his resurrection. Luke identified her as one "from whom seven demons had gone out" (Luke 8:2), probably the reason that over time she came to be associated with the prostitute who anointed Jesus' feet with ointment (see pp. 74–75). That flask of ointment is seen in Caravaggio's depiction of her. Next to it lies her jewelry, including a broken strand of pearls. This magnificent memento mori, probably invented by Caravaggio expressly for her, is an appropriate reminder of life's brevity and eternity's infinite reach.

Caravaggio spent not one moment considering what the garment of a first-century prostitute would be. Instead, he dresses the Magdalene in heavy silk damask of the type that only very rich ecclesiastics, noblewomen, and the most successful courtesans of his day could afford. It is likely, though, from the large size of the pattern, that this particular cloth would have been used for wall and chair covering rather than garments. Her blouse is also very fine, and she has frayed the left sleeve, probably while yanking jewelry from her wrist, neck, and ears. There is a hint of red around the small hole in her ear where a pearl was affixed a moment ago. Her hands are also reddened, and a tear streams down her cheek. Tradition holds that her penitence never ended; after a career as a missionary she retired to a cave near Marseilles in France and died a hermit.

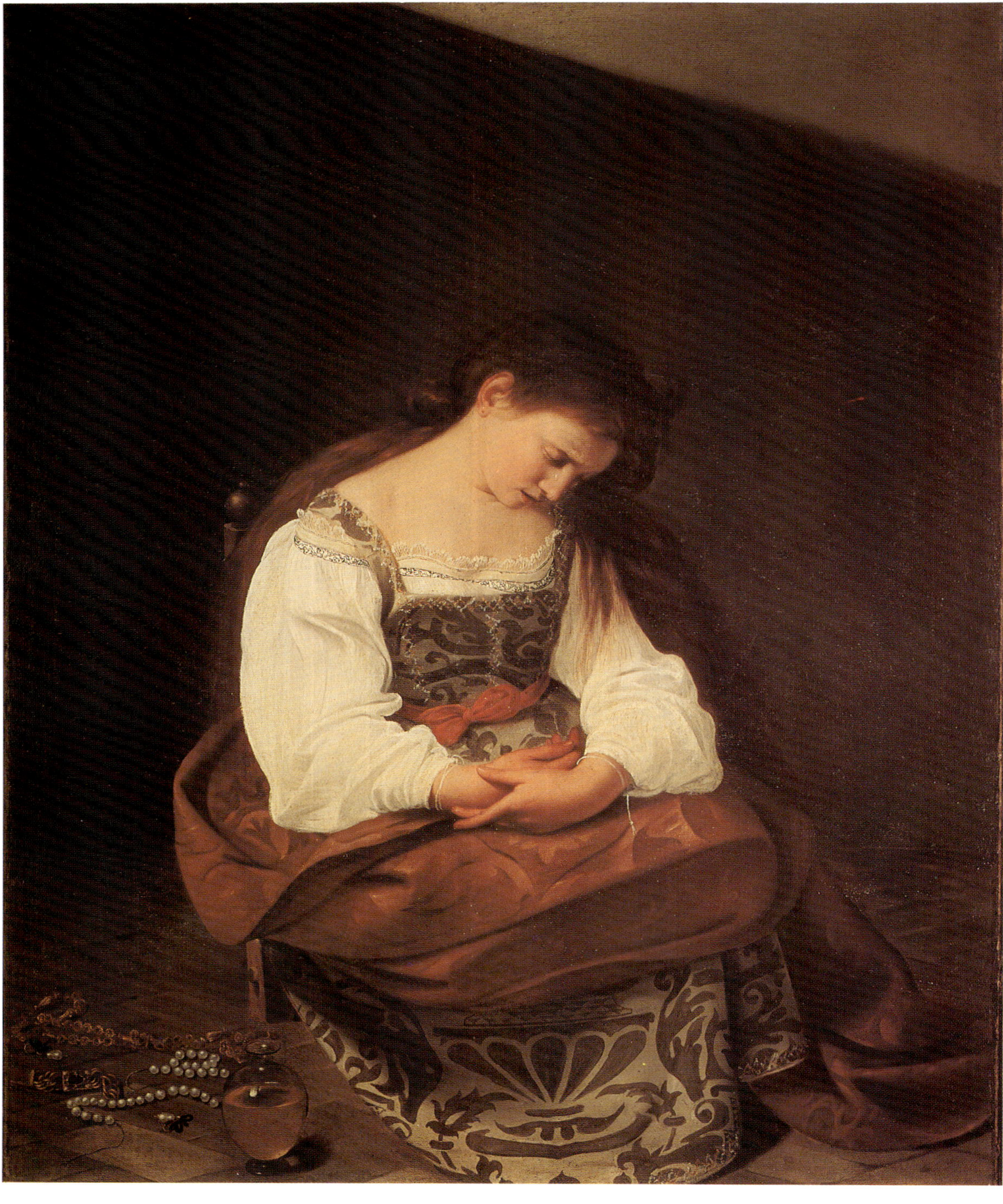

The Repentant Magdalene
CARAVAGGIO, Italian, 1573–1610
Galleria Doria Pamphili, Rome. Oil on canvas. 42 × 38½ in.

Christ and the Samaritan Woman at the Well

Water assumed a symbolic significance in the New Testament. With it, John the Baptist washed away the sins of the penitent, and Jesus said only those "born of water" can enter the kingdom of God (John 3:5). In an encounter at a well that Jacob built, Jesus offered a Samaritan woman "the living water of eternal life" (John 4:10–14). In the hot and arid mountain territory of Samaria where she lived, his promise that those who drank it need never thirst again would have had irresistible appeal. Like all the women of her town, she had to draw water twice daily from the well and trudge with it a quarter of a mile or so back to her home, a burden she would no doubt have been happy to relinquish.

It is not certain why Jesus had to pass through Samaria; it was hostile territory for Jews. But he went there with his disciples and rested at this famous old well. When the Samaritan woman arrived she was surprised that Jesus spoke to her, for Jews and Samaritans were enemies. The conversation they had was remarkable because it marked the first time that Jesus confessed to anyone that he was the Messiah. Because he told the woman many things about her private affairs, she believed him and told many of her neighbors. They asked Jesus to stay, and during the two days that he was in Sychar, many were converted.

A little-known 19th-century Danish portrait painter, Christian Andreas Schleisner, executed this direct and sympathetic telling of the story. It had particular meaning to fundamentalists, for it emphasized the godhead of Jesus and his example as a missionary. In the background is a picture-book version of a biblical city, but Schleisner achieves something out of the ordinary in his evocation of early evening mist. He gives credibility to the conversation that took place between these two strangers by making it seem commonplace, while his setting, with its gorgeous atmospheric effects, is nothing short of otherworldly.

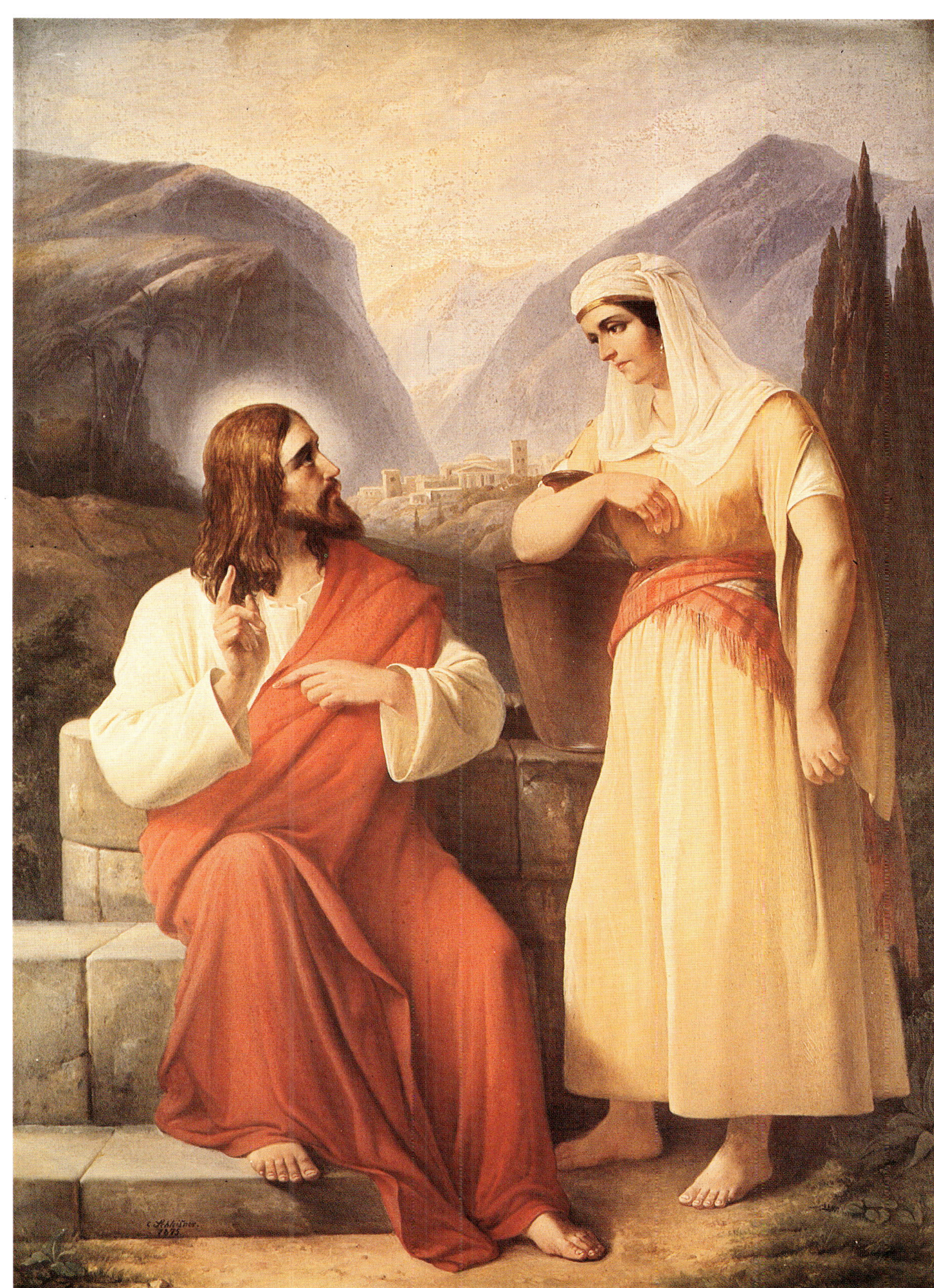

Christ and the Samaritan Woman at the Well
CHRISTIAN ANDREAS SCHLEISNER, Danish, 1810–1882
Valgmenigheds Church, city unknown, Denmark

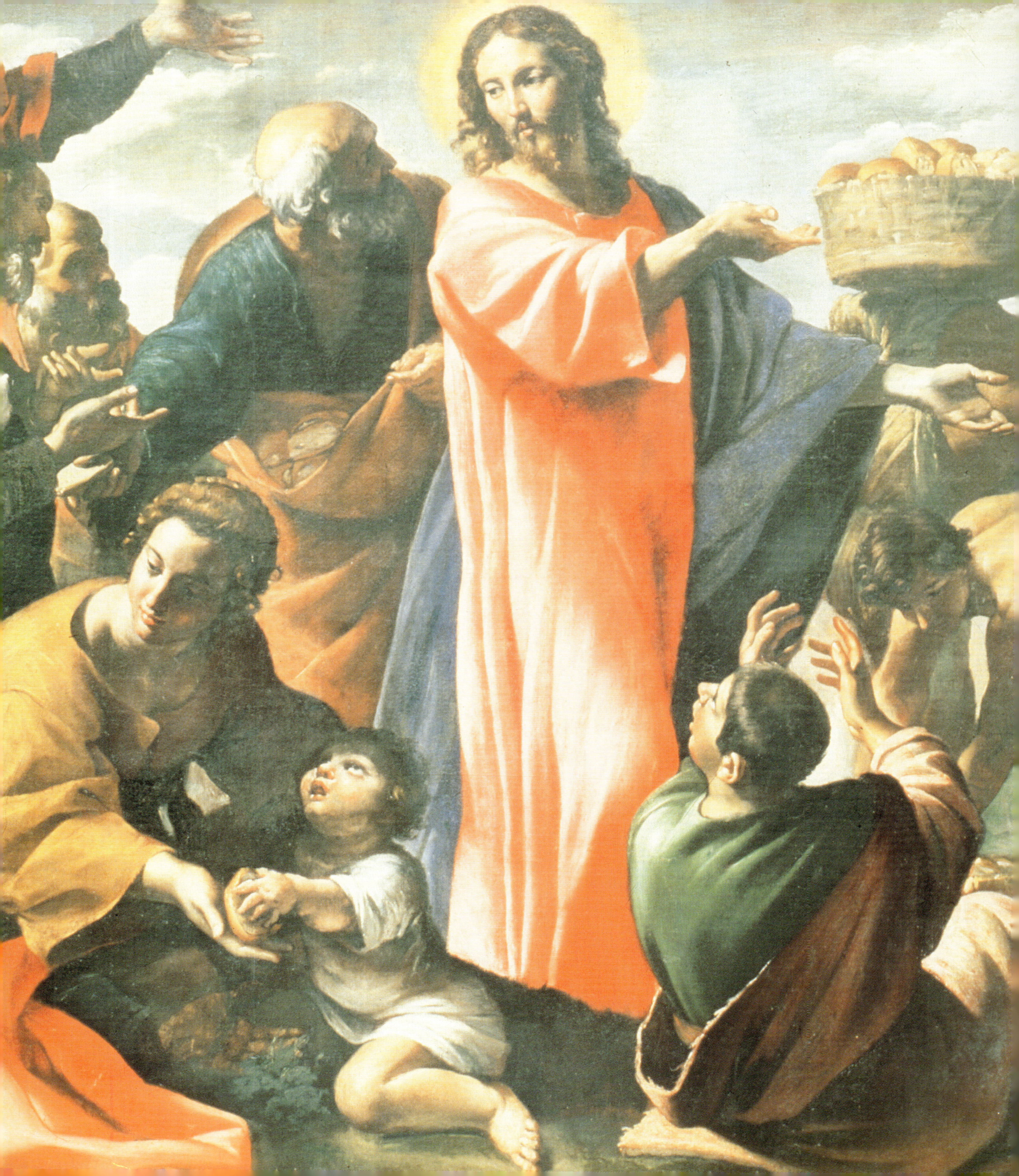

The Miracle of the Loaves and Fishes

The innate hospitality of the people of the Holy Land has not changed since the time of Jesus. The rule then as now was to give your best to your guests. Motivated by a strong desire to make the stranger at home in his household-at-large, Jesus regularly produced refreshment for those around him. His first miracle was one of hospitality—changing water into wine so a young couple could start off its wedding day living up to the high standards of their society (see pp. 64–65). Twice he fed thousands by multiplying the meager rations that were available, and later, at the Last Supper, he asked his followers to repeat for all time the breaking of bread and the sharing of wine (see pp. 112–115).

Five thousand people had followed Jesus to a lonely place (actually the same place where he had just mourned the death of his cousin, John the Baptist). He had been healing the sick all day long, and night fell before anyone expected it. His disciples suggested that he send the crowds into neighboring villages to eat and find lodging. "They need not go away; you give them something to eat," was Jesus' response. They had only five loaves of bread and two fishes. Jesus asked for these, looked up to heaven, blessed the food, and gave it back to his disciples to distribute to the crowd. Jesus organized the distribution of food carefully, dividing the people into groups of 50. Everyone ate and was satisfied, and there were 12 baskets of leftovers (Matthew 14:15–21).

In Giovanni Lanfranco's *The Miracle of the Loaves and Fishes*, Jesus, calm, beautiful, and every inch the host, instructs one of his disciples. The folds of his garments are overflowing with bread, while more is being carried by other disciples in baskets. Lanfranco has captured the wonderful reactions of the people. In the far background they are ecstatic, reaching out their arms in exultant praise. A mother, at the lower left, her child clinging to her, implores Jesus, but we may assume from the expression on her face that her need is not for food alone but for a cure or spiritual help. The man behind her explains to another that heaven is the source of these gifts. Lanfranco gives the occasion a sacramental tone, as though this miracle, near the time of Passover, prefigures the Last Supper, which was in fact a Passover Seder.

The Miracle of the Loaves and Fishes
GIOVANNI LANFRANCO, Italian, 1582–1547
National Gallery of Ireland, Dublin. Oil on canvas.
91 × 169 in.

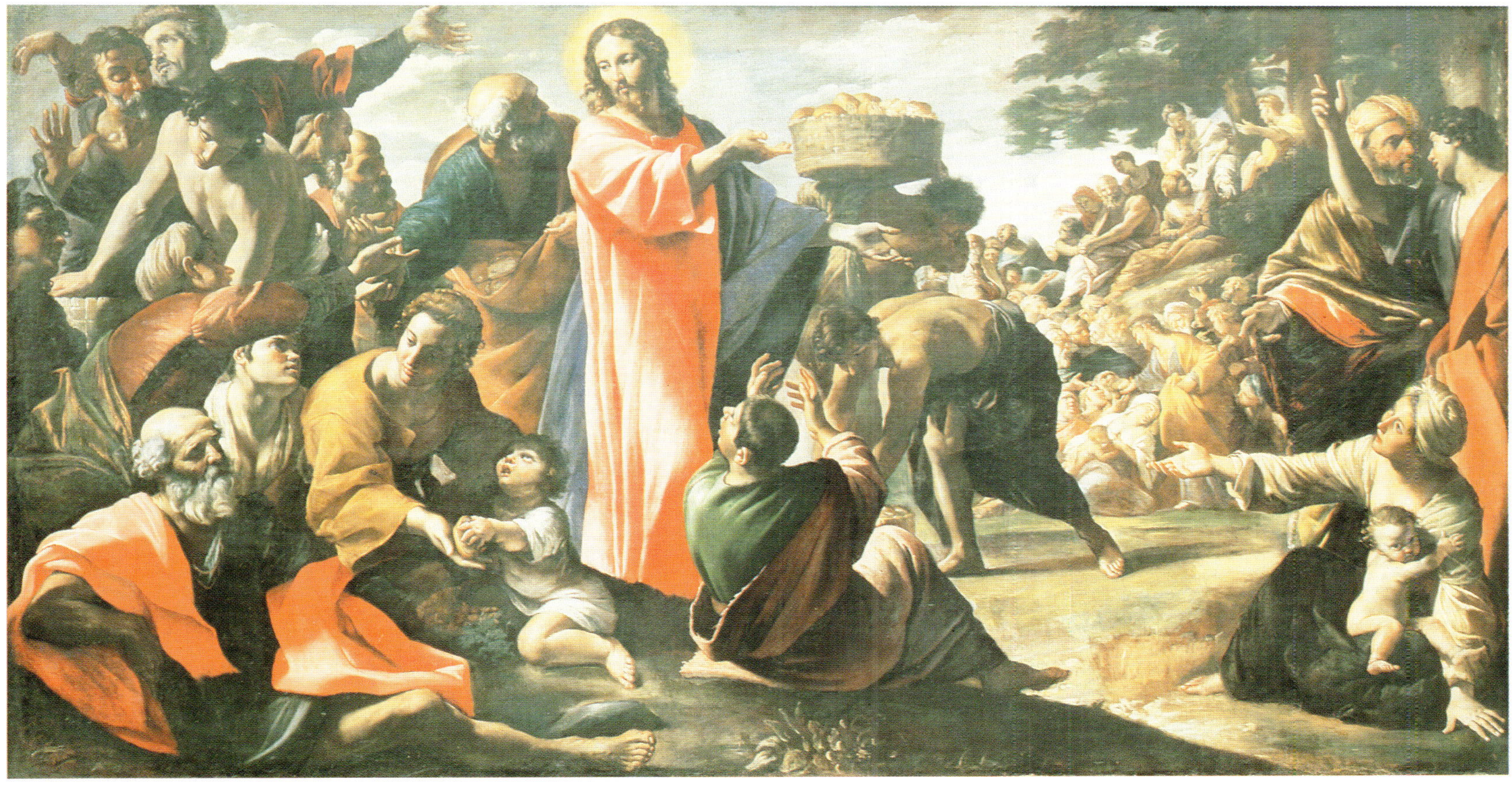

◁
DETAIL

Christ at the Sea of Galilee

A long stormy night had passed, and the disciples were wearily struggling against the gale in their boat when Jesus came toward them, walking on the water. They thought he was a ghost, but he called out, "Take heart, it is I; have no fear." The fisherman Peter expressed both his fear of the apparition and his concern at their desperate straits with the challenge: "Lord, if it is you, bid me come to you on the water." So Jesus called him. According to Luke, "Peter got out of the boat and walked on the water and came to Jesus." But soon he became aware of the storm again, was frightened, and began to sink. "Lord, save me," he cried out. "Jesus immediately reached out his hand and caught him, saying to him, 'O man of little faith, why did you doubt?' And when they got into the boat, the wind ceased" (Luke 8:22–25).

Tintoretto in *Christ at the Sea of Galilee* has captured the spectral atmosphere of the moment when Jesus, his figure attenuated and disappearing at the feet, beckons to Peter. This rapidly painted scene, with its economy of pigment and calligraphic brushstroke, seems almost improvised. Tintoretto's Venetian audiences, accustomed to carnivals and the pleasures of the moment, sought out his brilliant and eerie paintings, for they captured the eternal truths of the Bible yet appeared fresh, as though painted yesterday. This particular story had special significance for the citizens of Venice, who lived in daily dread of the sea and the floods it brought. They needed to recall that even a saint's faith could waver in the face of nature's power but that Jesus is their salvation in the end.

Tintoretto's paintings were not in fact as spontaneous as they appeared. He actually built little stages and placed wax figures on them, so that he could work out the composition and lighting for his works before he began to paint them. It was unusual preparation for a painter, but not surprising for a Venetian artist with exposure to the theater and the opera.

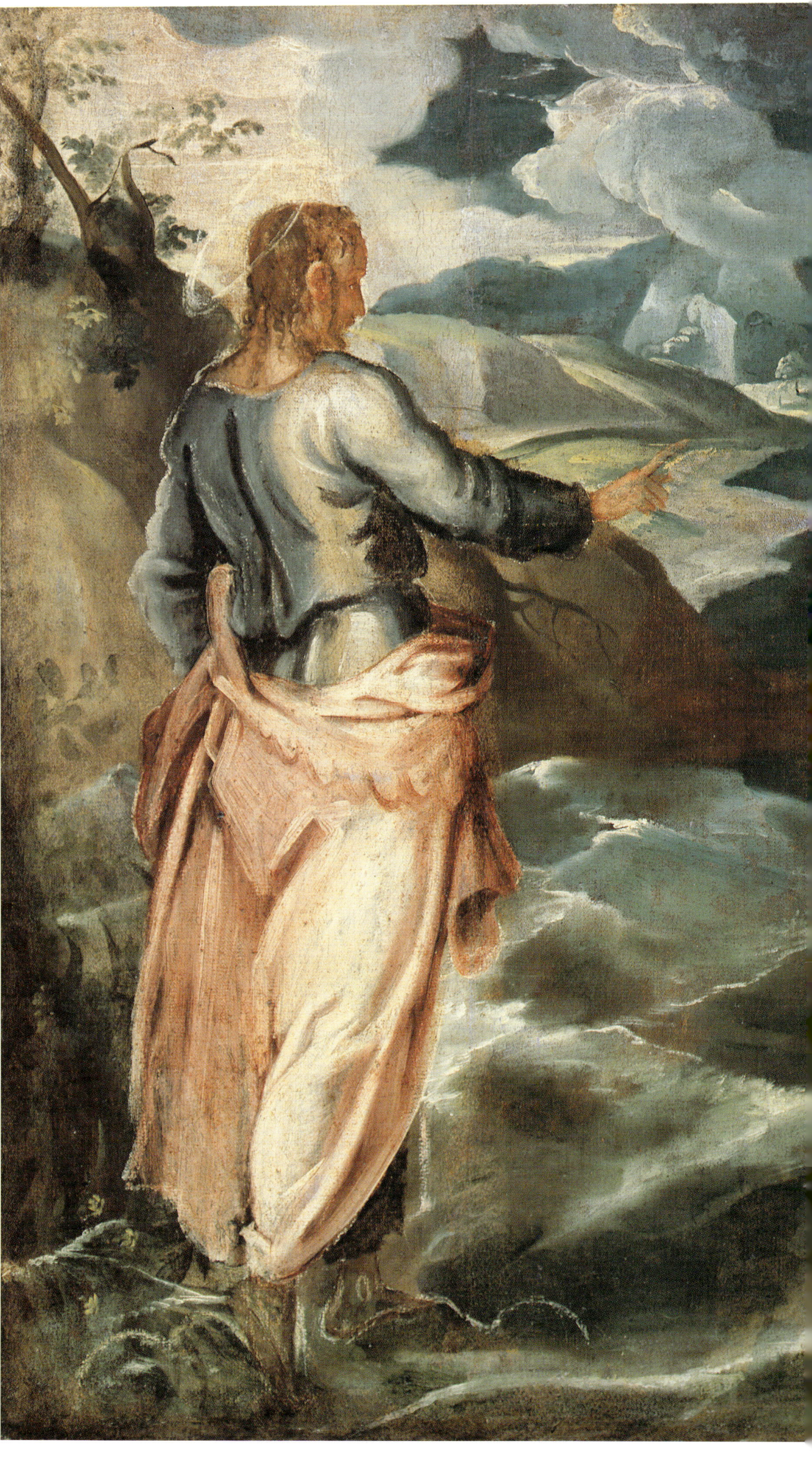

Christ at the Sea of Galilee
TINTORETTO, Italian, 1518–1594
Samuel H. Kress Collection, National Gallery of Art, Washington, DC. Oil on canvas. 46 × 66¼ in.

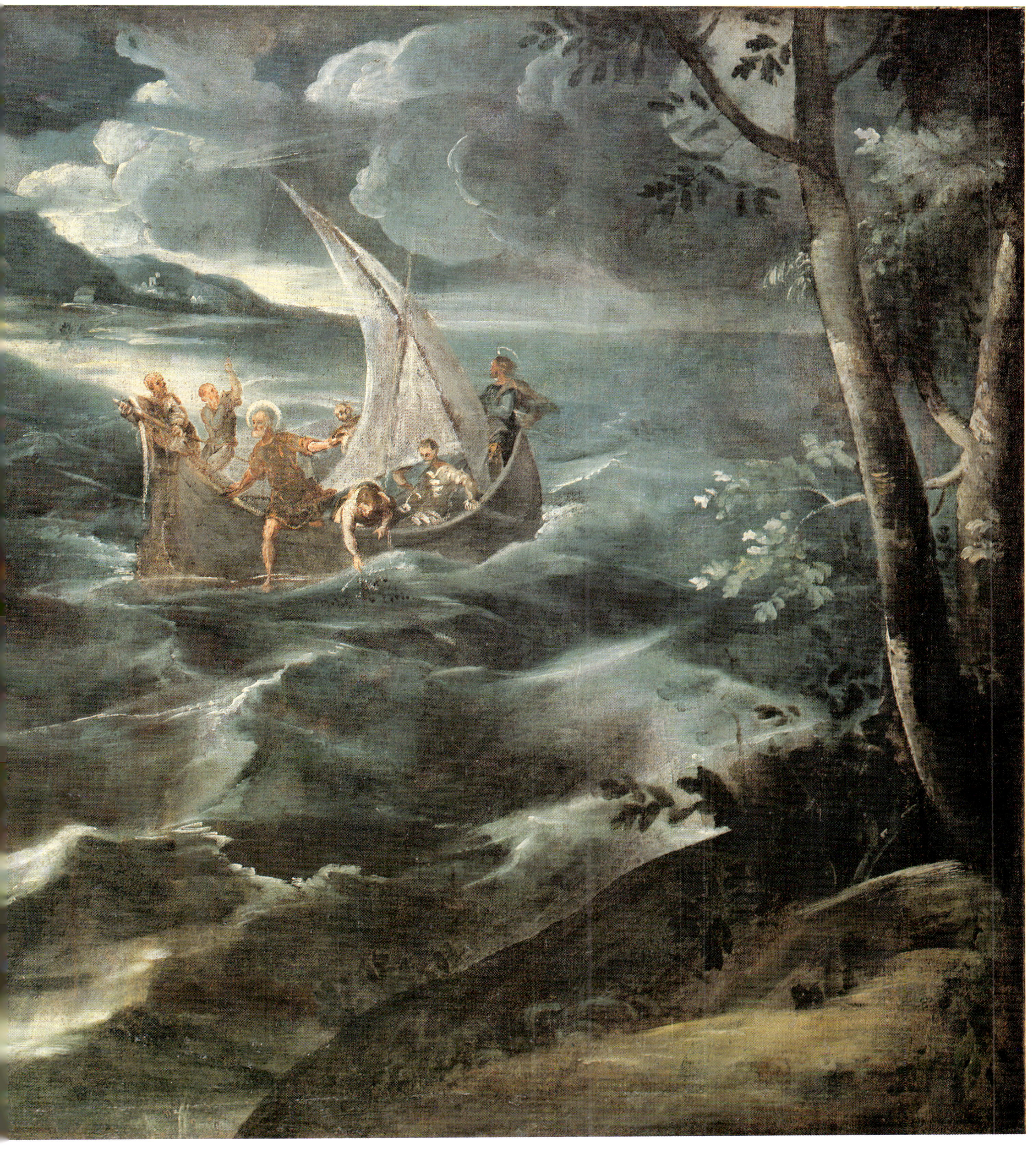

Christ and the Woman Taken in Adultery

Lucas Cranach and Martin Luther were neighbors and friends, and the artist fell deeply under the spell of the great reformer. Luther believed that each nationality should find its own way of expressing the word of God in the vernacular and in art; there was no attempt at a universal language. Cranach sought to do with art what Luther had done with the Bible—to make it accessible in the vernacular. Where Luther had translated the scripture from Greek and Hebrew into German, Cranach introduced German facial types and contemporary costumes into all of his paintings. The result is that the art of Cranach is imbued with 16th-century German form and ethos and illustrates the history and concerns of the German Reformation.

Cranach's *Christ and the Adulteress* draws its inspiration from the story of the woman who was dragged to Jesus in the Temple where her accusers reminded him that Moses had commanded the stoning of adulterers. He replied, "Let him who is without sin among you be the first to throw a stone at her." The men departed, one by one, the eldest leaving first, and Jesus was left alone with the sinner. "Woman, where are they?" he asked. "Has no one condemned you?" "No one, Lord," she answered, and he replied, "Neither do I condemn you; go, and do not sin again" (John 8:1–11).

During Luther's lifetime, many religious sects sprang up in Europe of which he was intolerant. He wanted reform within the church, not new religions. Most disturbing to him were the Anabaptists who were condoning bigamy. His sermons on adultery, which frequently drew upon the story of Christ and the adulteress, were aimed at steering his followers away from such indulgences of the flesh. Cranach probably based this painting more on one of those sermons than on John's Gospel.

By having Jesus grasp the woman by the wrist, Cranach strays from the Gospel account. Jesus' detachment from the woman is what stands out in John's telling of the story, for Jesus was writing with his finger in the dust on the floor while the accusers questioned him. He only looked at the woman after they had left. But Cranach has him grasping her by the wrist, as though yanking her into his presence. His tender expression, however, belies any ill will toward her. He looks as though he is about to cry. Luther often commented on Jesus' profound empathy for sinners, and Cranach succeeds in expressing this.

More than 350 years separate Max Beckmann from his countryman Cranach, yet the former depicts the same story with elements used by the latter. Beckmann, a caustic social critic, has as much disdain for the accusers as did Cranach. Interestingly, he also makes a number of them soldiers, whom he often treated with particular contempt in his paintings. He frequently was hard on religion as well, but here he shows a unique and strong Jesus. Balding, severe, and threatening, he is the exact opposite of Cranach's mild Savior. For Beckmann, painting was an ethical necessity. His personal mission was to uncover the hypocrisy, hatred, and lust of modern society and let it scream out in his art. He hoped this would repel people and drive them to a saner way of life.

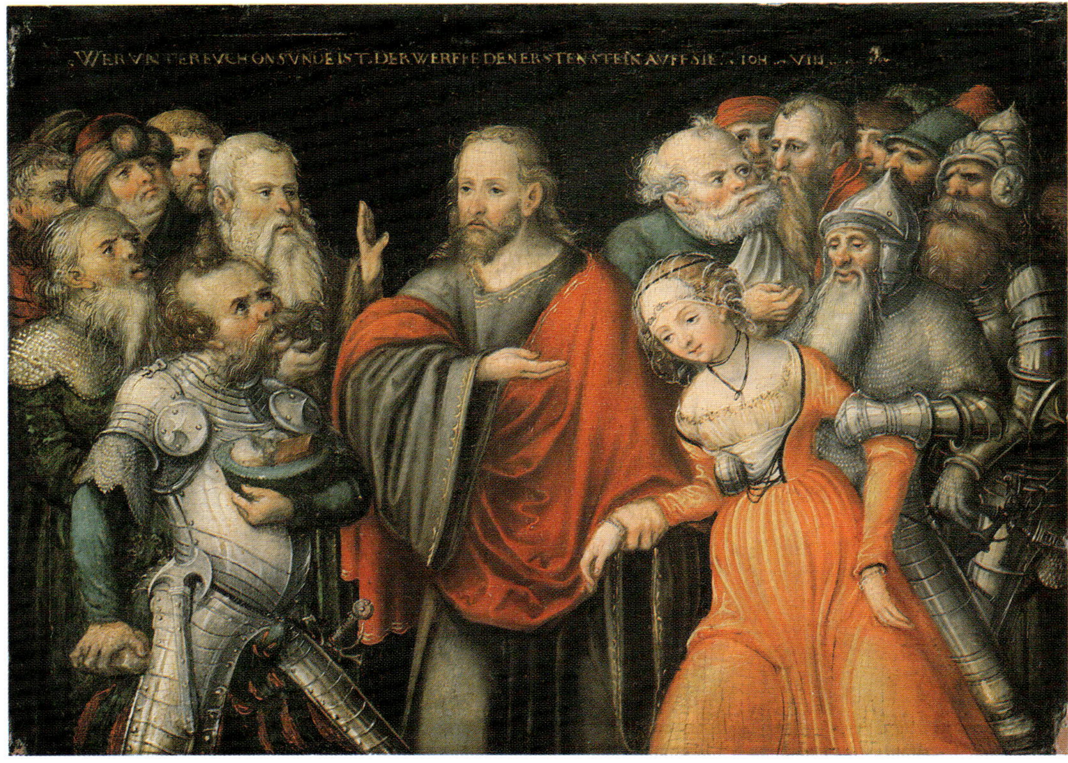

◁

Christ and the Adulteress
LUCAS CRANACH THE ELDER, German, 1472–1553
The Jack and Belle Linsky Collection, Metropolitan Museum of Art, New York. Oil on wood panel. 6¼ × 8½ in.

▷

Christ and the Woman Taken in Adultery
MAX BECKMANN, German, 1884–1950
Bequest of Curt Valentin, St. Louis Art Museum. Oil on canvas. 58¾ × 49⅞ in.

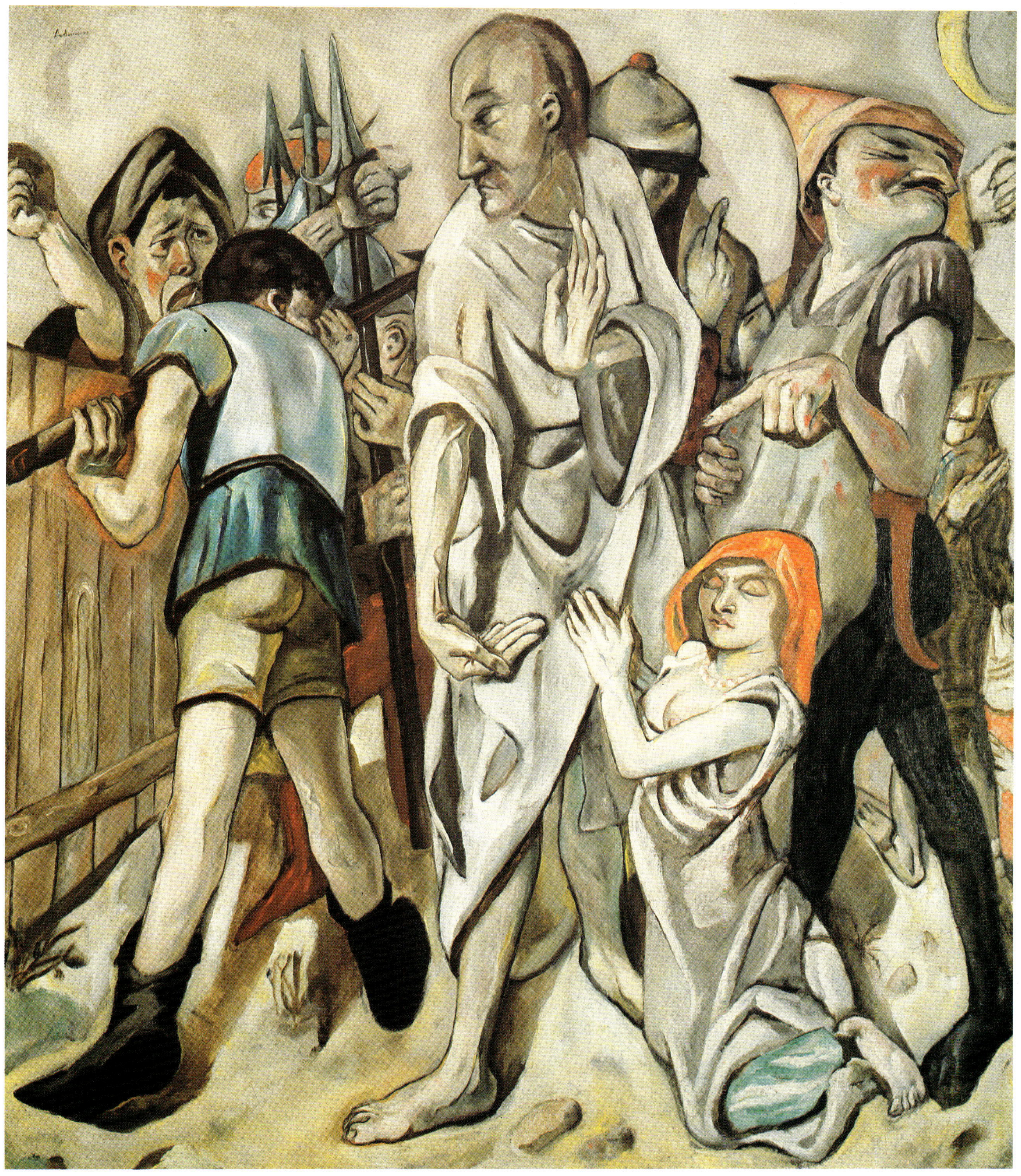

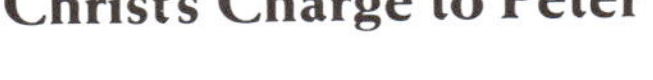

Christ's Charge to Peter

Jesus asked his disciples to describe who they thought he was. Peter's answer, "You are the Christ, the son of the living God," elicited a blessing from Jesus and the charge that is celebrated here: "You are Peter, and on this rock I will build my church, and the powers of death shall not prevail against it. I will give you the keys of the kingdom of heaven, and whatever you bind on earth shall be bound in heaven, and whatever you loose on earth shall be loosed in heaven" (Matthew 16:18–20). In *Christ's Charge to Peter* by Peter Paul Rubens, Jesus presents the key to Peter, who kisses his hand in gratitude, but the great Flemish artist does not try to depict the "binding" and "loosing" of the text, which have been interpreted as meaning church discipline and absolution of sin, respectively.

This episode took place toward the end of Jesus' Galilean ministry, that period of parable-telling and intense miracle-working. But Rubens has combined the story with another one. The wounds on the hands and chest of Jesus place the incident after his death and resurrection, when Jesus met with his disciples and three times asked Peter, "Do you love me?" and three times got the same affirmative answer, "Yes, Lord; you know that I love you." After each answer, Jesus commanded Peter to "Feed my lambs" and "Tend my sheep" (John 21:15–17). Rubens introduces this gentle symbol of the congregation of believers for whom Peter and the others must care as good shepherds, in the lower right corner of the painting near Jesus' left hand. The onlookers are some of the other disciples. It was not unusual to bestow such status on Peter in Catholic art, for he was believed to be the first pope.

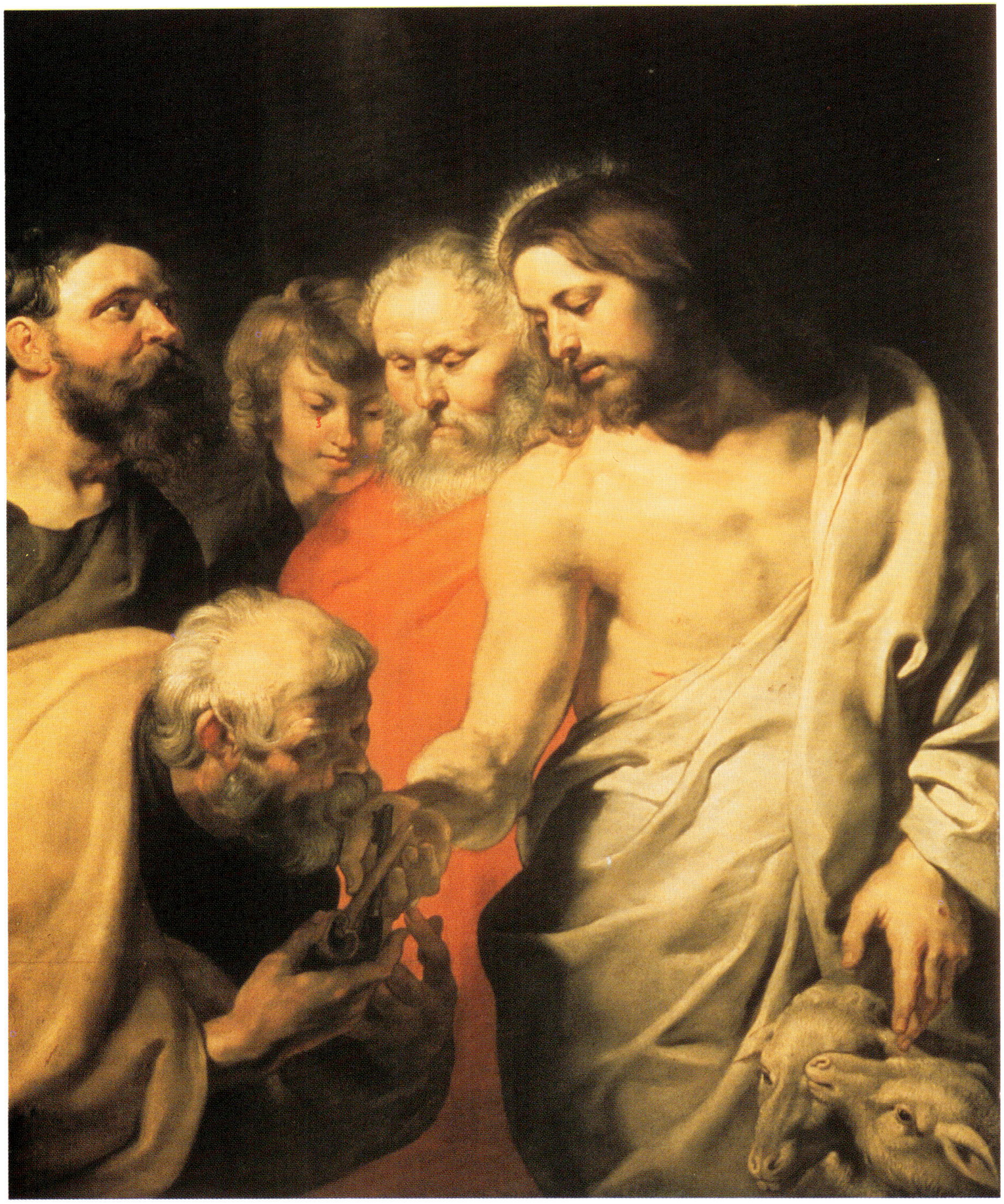

Christ's Charge to Peter
PETER PAUL RUBENS, Flemish, 1577–1640
Wallace Collection, London. Oil on wood panel. 55½ × 45⅛ in.

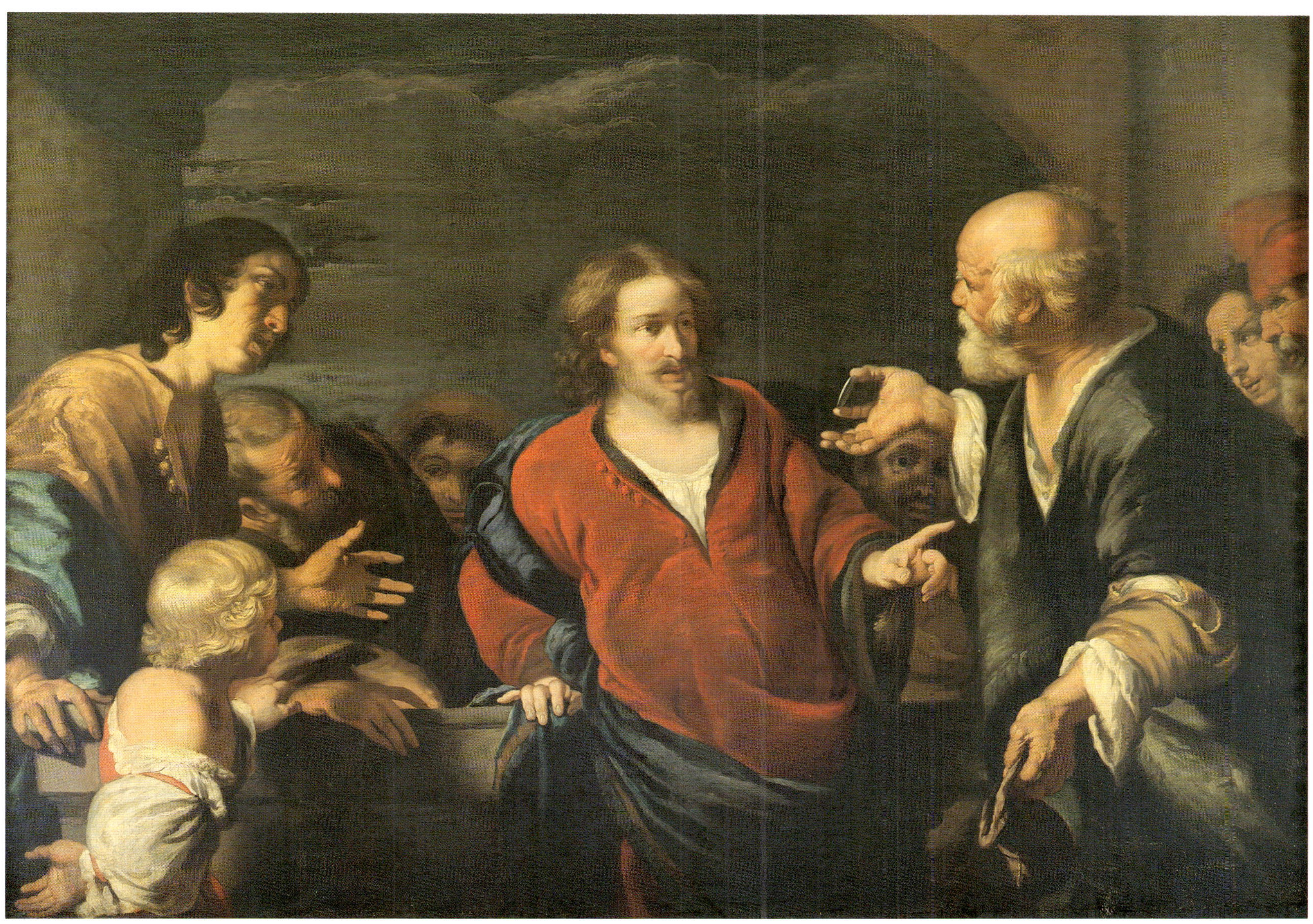

The Tribute Money
BERNARDO STROZZI, Italian, 1581–1644
Nationalmuseum, Stockholm. Oil on canvas.
65½ × 89½ in.

The Tribute Money

Jesus was despised by the Temple authorities, for they believed that many of his parables worked against them. There were times when they could have arrested him, on the grounds that his bold words and actions were without any earthly authority, but they were always afraid of the multitudes that followed him. Nonetheless, they continued to try to entrap him when he spoke. He was aware of their intentions, however, and by being cautious in his remarks he gave his followers words to live by and his detractors food for thought. His most famous dodge was recorded by Matthew, Mark, and Luke, with barely a variation in the accounts.

It came during an encounter between several of the Temple authorities and Jesus. The connivers flattered the rabbi by acknowledging his position as a free agent, beholden to no one. Then they put a question to him that had to do with taxes, a constant reminder to the Jews of their subservience to Rome. "Should we pay them or should we not?" they asked. By way of an answer, Jesus requested a coin so he could look at it. One was shown to him and he asked, "Whose likeness and inscription is this?" They told him it was Caesar's, and he responded, "Render to Caesar the things that are Caesar's, and to God the things that are God's." They were all amazed at what he said.

In his version of that memorable confrontation, Bernardo Strozzi has presented a rendition of Jesus unique in 17th-century art. Seldom is the Savior so apprehensive. At first glance it would seem he is guessing at an answer that will satisfy or confound his enemies, but in fact he is sincerely worried that he will be arrested and his ministry cut short. The embellishment of the purple sash from his arm around his hips is a typical Baroque compositional device. Through its upward diagonal movement, it leads the viewer's eye from the purse of the old man to the face of Jesus. The great teacher leans back, finding support on the ledge of the balustrade behind him, as though wary of the interrogator. Indeed, he should have been, for the Bible states that the Temple officials were allied with partisans of Herod in trying to trick him.

The Parable of Dives and Lazarus

Lazarus was a poor man covered with sores who lay at the gate of Dives, an overstuffed rich man, hoping for crumbs from his table. Both men died, according to Jesus' parable, and Dives went to hell while the poor man "was carried by the angels to Abraham's bosom." Dives was in such agony that he begged Abraham to let Lazarus "dip the end of his finger in water and cool my tongue." Abraham reminded Dives that he had enjoyed good things on earth and that Lazarus had not. Besides, the chasm between them "has been fixed." There was to be no passing from hell to heaven or heaven to hell. Dives then asked that Lazarus be sent to warn his brothers so they would not suffer his fate. Abraham said they had Moses and the prophets to guide them. Dives argued that they needed to see someone from the dead before they would repent. The last words of this parable, spoken by Abraham, not only advised Jesus' followers to model their lives after the lessons of the Bible, it also foreshadowed Jesus' own resurrection: "If they do not hear Moses and the prophets, neither will they be convinced if someone should rise from the dead" (Luke 16:19–31).

Artists were drawn to this story because of the dramatic contrast it presented between Lazarus and Dives, but more so because it afforded them the opportunity to paint a banquet scene. Almost no one but high-ranking church officials, members of royalty, and servants were privy to the great feasts of the courts of Europe, so the public was fascinated by depictions of such events. Domenico Feti would have experienced these rich and elaborate meals firsthand, for at the time he painted *Parable of Dives and Lazarus*, he was artist to the magnificent court of the Gonzagas of Mantua, among the most famous patrons of the arts in all of Europe. He has positioned Dives presiding over the banquet table. His clothes of purple and fine linen and his sumptuous table were described by Jesus in his parable, as was the dog licking the sores on Lazarus' leg in the lower right portion of the painting.

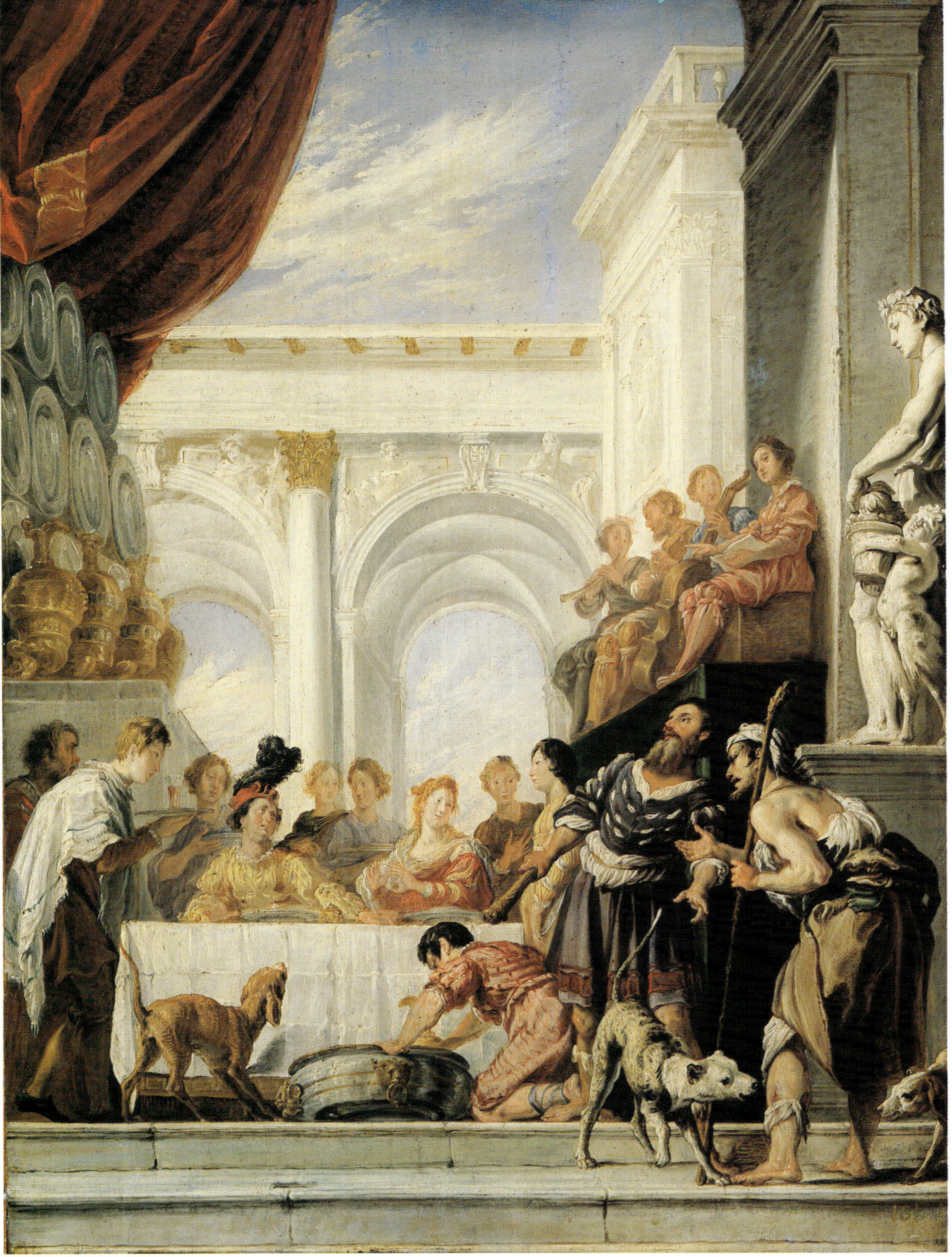

The Parable of Dives and Lazarus
DOMENICO FETI, Italian, ca. 1589–1623/24
Samuel H. Kress Collection, National Gallery of Art, Washington, DC. Wood panel. 23½ × 17⅛ in.

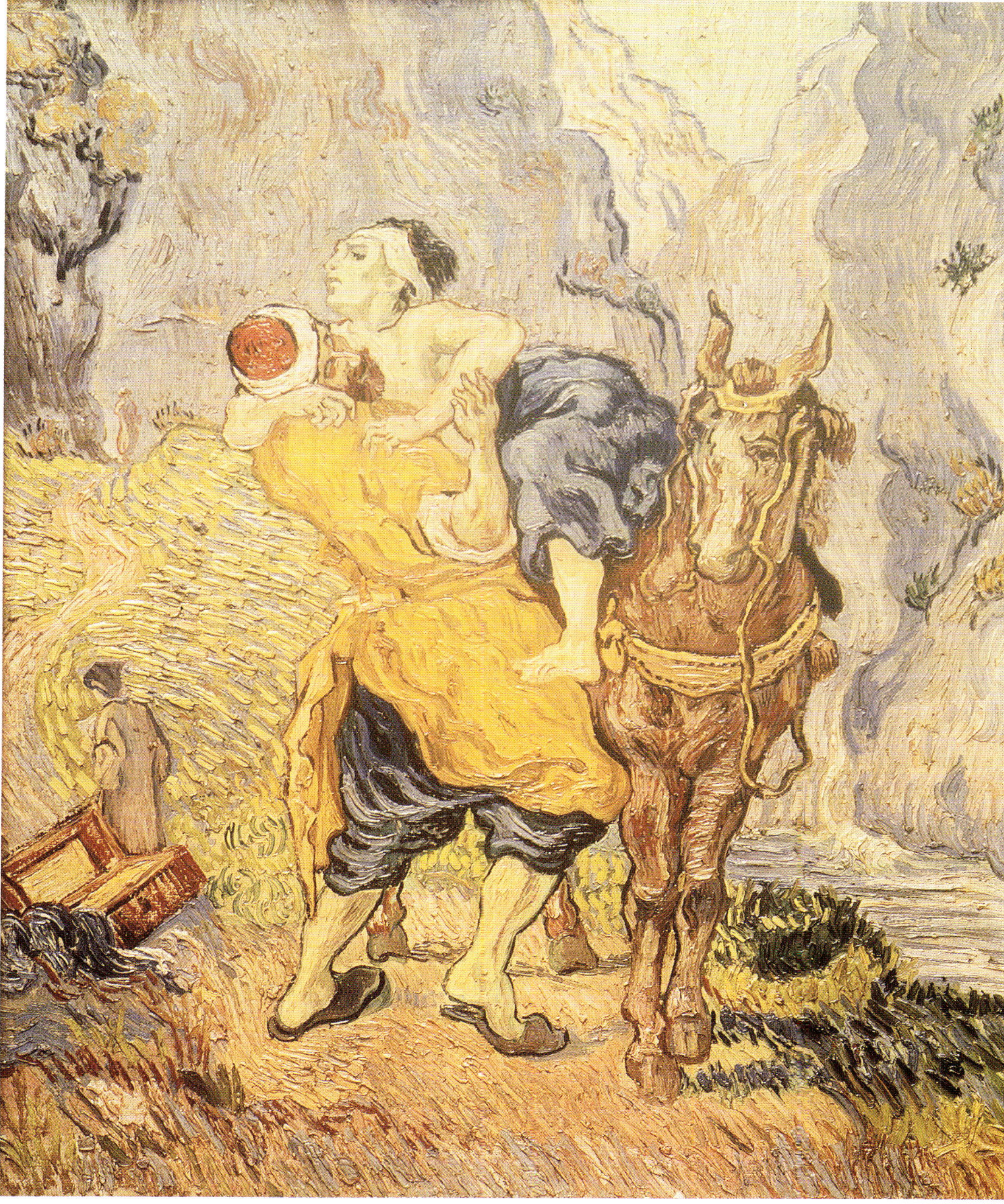

The Good Samaritan
VINCENT VAN GOGH, Dutch, 1853–1890
Rijksmuseum Kröller-Müller, Otterlo, The Netherlands. Oil on canvas. 29 × 24 in.

The Good Samaritan

The son of a Protestant pastor, Vincent van Gogh trained for the ministry but instead became a lay preacher to the impoverished miners of Belgium's grim Borinage district. By the time he was 27, he decided that his vocation was to be a painter, his mission to bring consolation to humanity through art. For the most part, he painted the world around him, but months before his suicide he turned to the Bible for inspiration. Perhaps the stories he learned as a youth briefly helped to assuage his loneliness.

His source for *The Good Samaritan* was the story that Jesus told in answer to a lawyer's question, "Who is my neighbor?" The parable focused on a robbery victim who lay at the side of the road, bleeding. A priest passed him by, and a Levite; van Gogh shows these individuals walking up the road in the distance, beyond the victim's empty suitcase. Finally a Samaritan saw him, nursed his wounds, took him on his own mount to an inn, and provided for his care until he was well. Priests and Levites, who assisted in the Temple, were expected to be charitable, but the Samaritans and Jews were antagonists. Jesus asked which of the three travelers had proved himself neighbor to the unfortunate man. The answer was obvious, and Jesus said, "Go and do likewise" (Luke 10:25–37).

This painting is a copy of a work by Eugène Delacroix, an artist much admired by van Gogh. But Vincent makes the composition his own through his distinctive use of color. The yellow in particular almost vibrates because of its juxtaposition to the lavender and the blue. There is not a single note that is somber or morose. Rather, it is a painting of hope, full of faith that a saviour will come along. Unfortunately, the sense of optimism so evident in this work could not console the artist himself. Two months after painting *The Good Samaritan*, he took his own life.

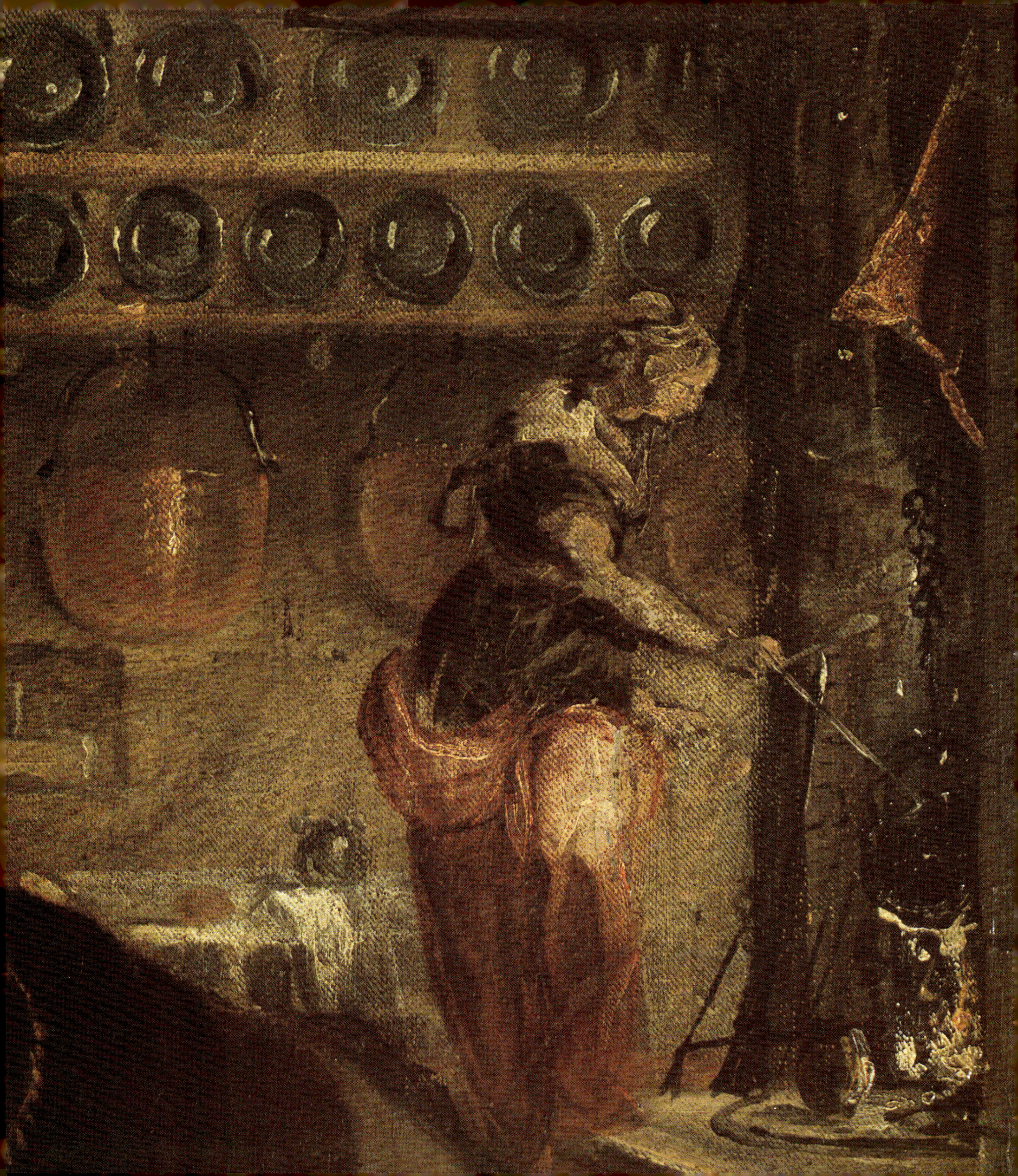

Christ in the House of Mary and Martha

In the Scriptures, the sisters Mary and Martha were such archetypes that it is hard to believe they actually existed as historical figures. There are Marys and Marthas the world over. When company comes, the Marys stay with the guests, listening, commenting, asking questions, and making them feel they are the center of the universe. The Marthas fuss in the kitchen, bustle around tidying things, and endlessly serve wonderful homemade food.

The two sisters were mentioned a number of times in the New Testament, so more is known of them than just their domestic talents. They were the siblings of Lazarus, whom Jesus was later to raise from the dead (see pp. 100–101). They were not poor; Mary was once scolded for anointing the hair of Jesus with very costly ointment. It is likely that Martha was the wife or widow of Simon, who had leprosy, and at whose home Jesus was entertained on occasion.

Of an evening, Jesus was visiting the sisters. Mary was listening to him preach as Martha served refreshments. According to Luke, Martha asked Jesus if he minded that Mary wasn't helping her. Jesus responded that Mary had chosen "the good portion, which shall not be taken away from her" (Luke 10:41), that is to say, Mary's attention was on the kingdom of God.

In *Christ in the House of Mary and Martha*, Tintoretto chooses to depict the moment at which Martha interrupts Jesus' discourse with Mary. The latter, still concentrating on Jesus' words, leans back slightly, affronted by her sister's complaint. Food is being prepared by a servant standing in front of a great open oven in the background; the kitchen walls are lined with dishes. Guests are arriving at the door, and others wait impatiently for their hostesses to serve them.

Tintoretto has arranged his two seated protagonists in postures similar to those used by artists to depict the angel Gabriel and the Virgin Mary in annunciation scenes: the male figure almost genuflecting, leaning forward; the female withdrawing. The expression of intelligent curiosity on Mary's face is also like that of the Virgin in these depictions. This is probably not accidental. Tintoretto was enormously prolific and he visually ravished all of the art available to him for inspiration. Although he seldom left his native Venice, the tradition of art in that city was old and rich. His choice of poses leaves no doubt of his strong religious convictions. Clearly he believed that a moment at the feet of Jesus was a blessed moment, more useful than hours in the kitchen.

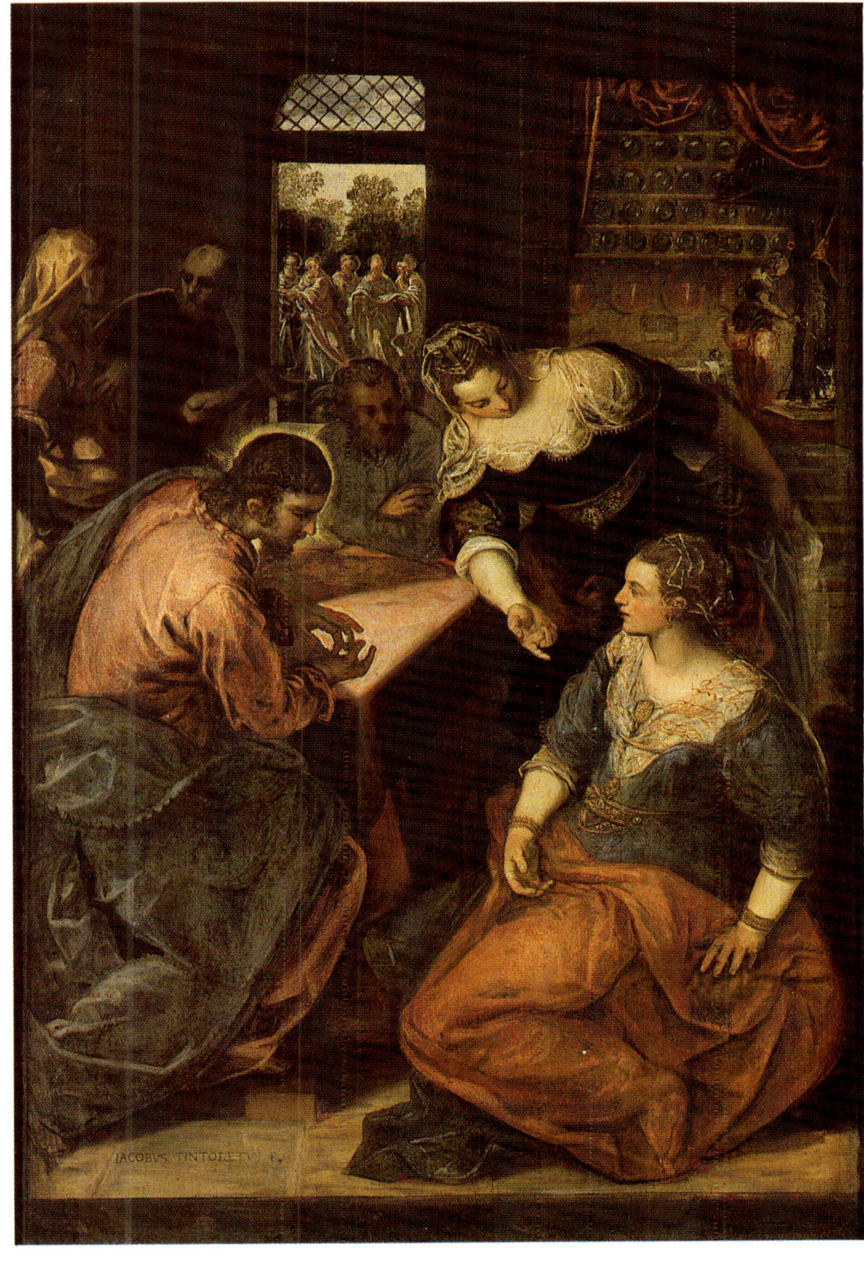

Christ in the House of Martha and Mary
TINTORETTO, Italian, 1518–1594
Alte Pinakothek, Munich. Oil on canvas. 79½ × 52½ in.

◁
DETAIL

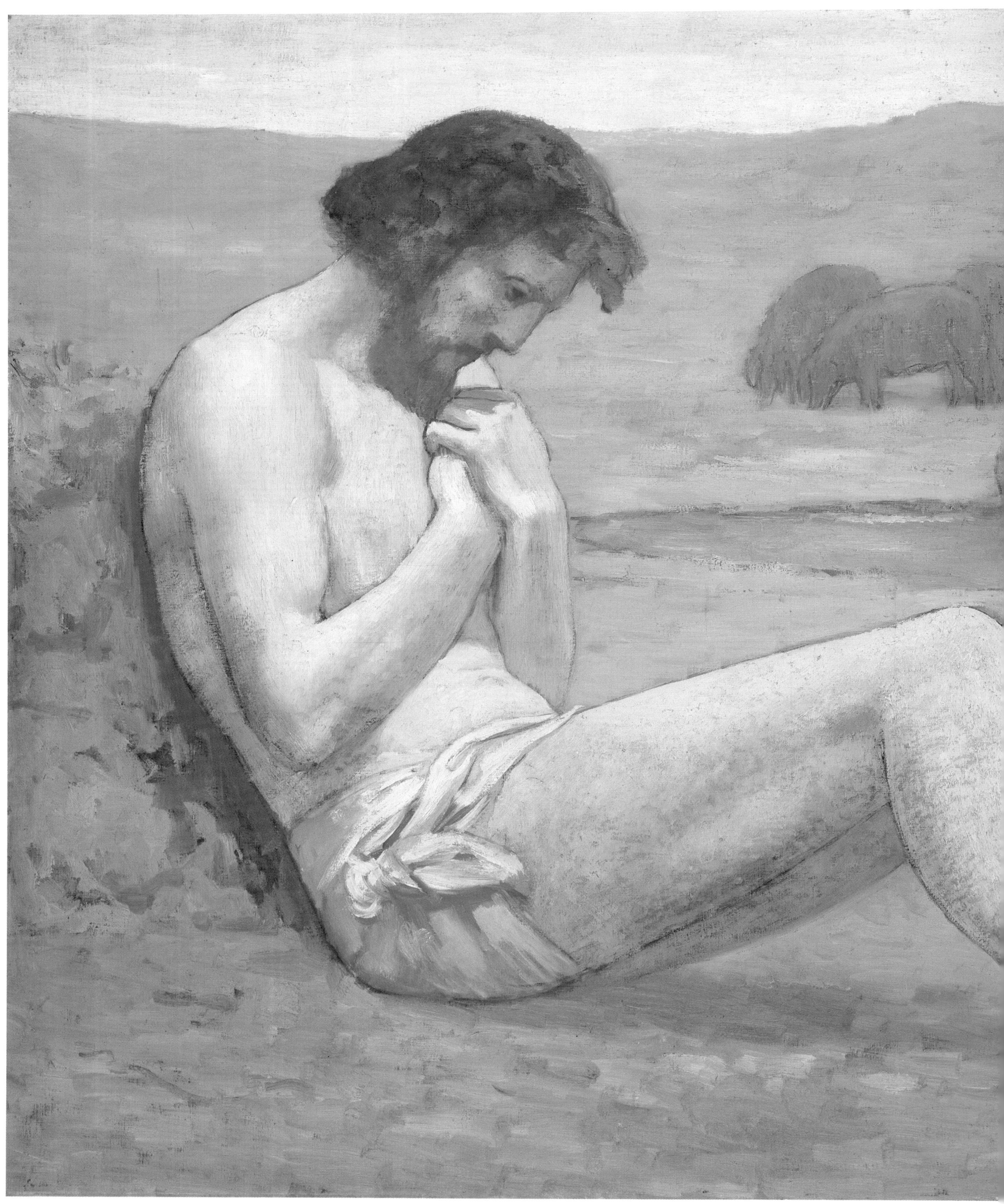

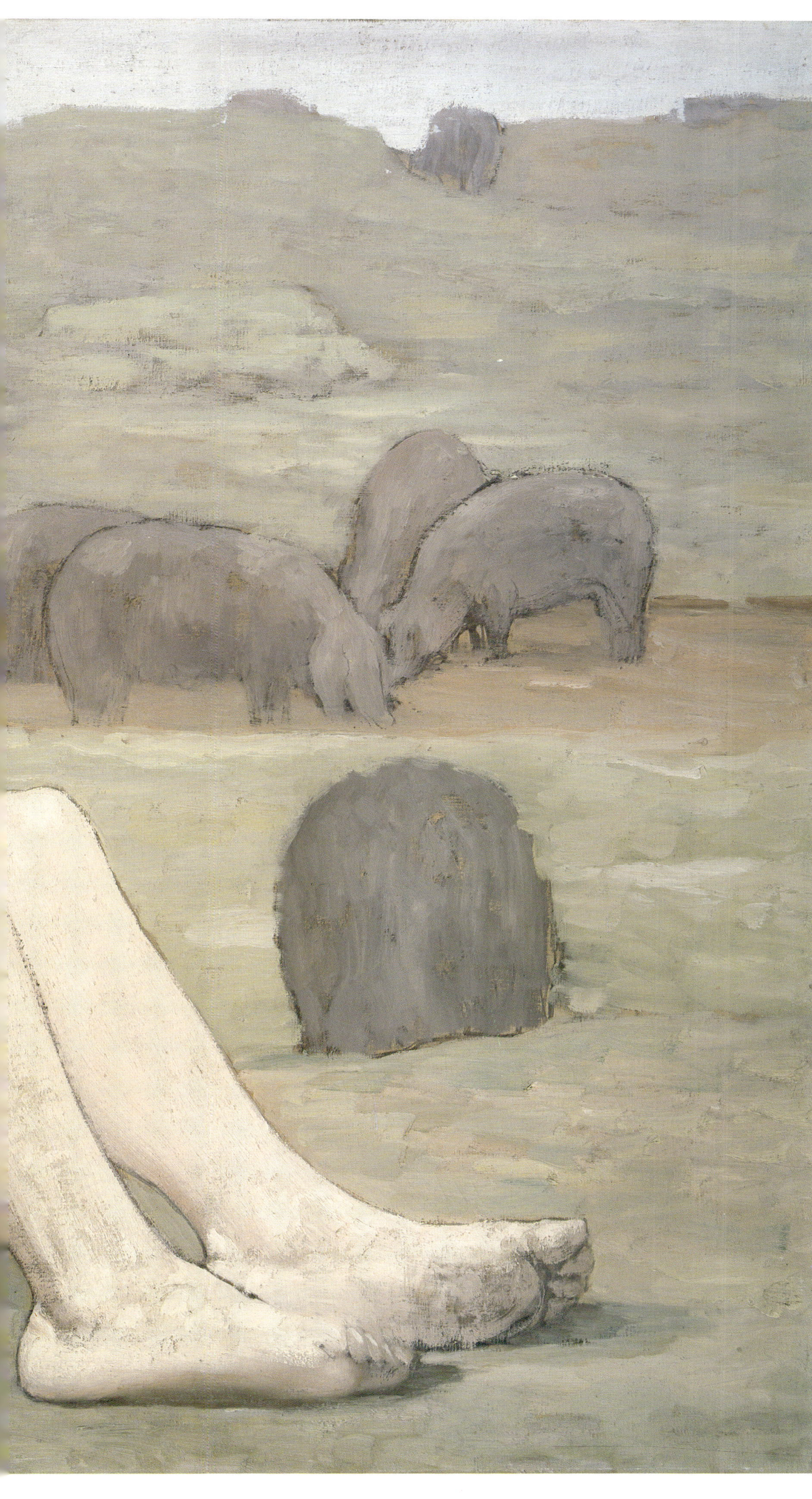

The Prodigal Son

One of Jesus' famous parables tells of a man with two sons. The youngest one asked for his inheritance, went to a far country, and wasted everything. Most artists like to show his dissipations, but not the French painter Pierre Puvis de Chavannes. He seems to understand that the real sin of the young man was not in his loose living but in leaving his father. For, in turning his back on the one who loved him most, the youth was reduced to living with pigs in their sty. In Puvis's *The Prodigal Son*, he is disconsolate, hammering his hands to his chest over his mistake in the traditional mea culpa gesture.

Puvis does not want to stress the squalor of this man's condition, nor does he even suggest the great pangs of hunger the prodigal experienced. He selects a limited palette and simplified forms to capture the mood of spiritual conversion that is taking place. His paint is applied to look flat and without luster, like a plaster wall. The great fresco painters of the past, like Giotto, inspired the artist. Indeed, Puvis became the most important muralist of his age.

In contrast with Puvis's painting, which shows the prodigal in spiritual crisis, *The Return of the Prodigal Son* by Bartolomé Esteban Murillo shows the repentant lad returning home at last. According to the parable, the young son implored his father to treat him as one of his hired servants. "I am no longer worthy to be called your son," he confessed, as his father embraced him. "But the father said to his servants, 'Bring quickly the best robe, and put it on him; and put a ring on his hand, and shoes on his feet; and

The Prodigal Son
PIERRE PUVIS DE CHAVANNES, French, 1824–1896
Chester Dale Collection, National Gallery of Art, Washington, DC. Oil on canvas. 41⅞ × 57¾ in.

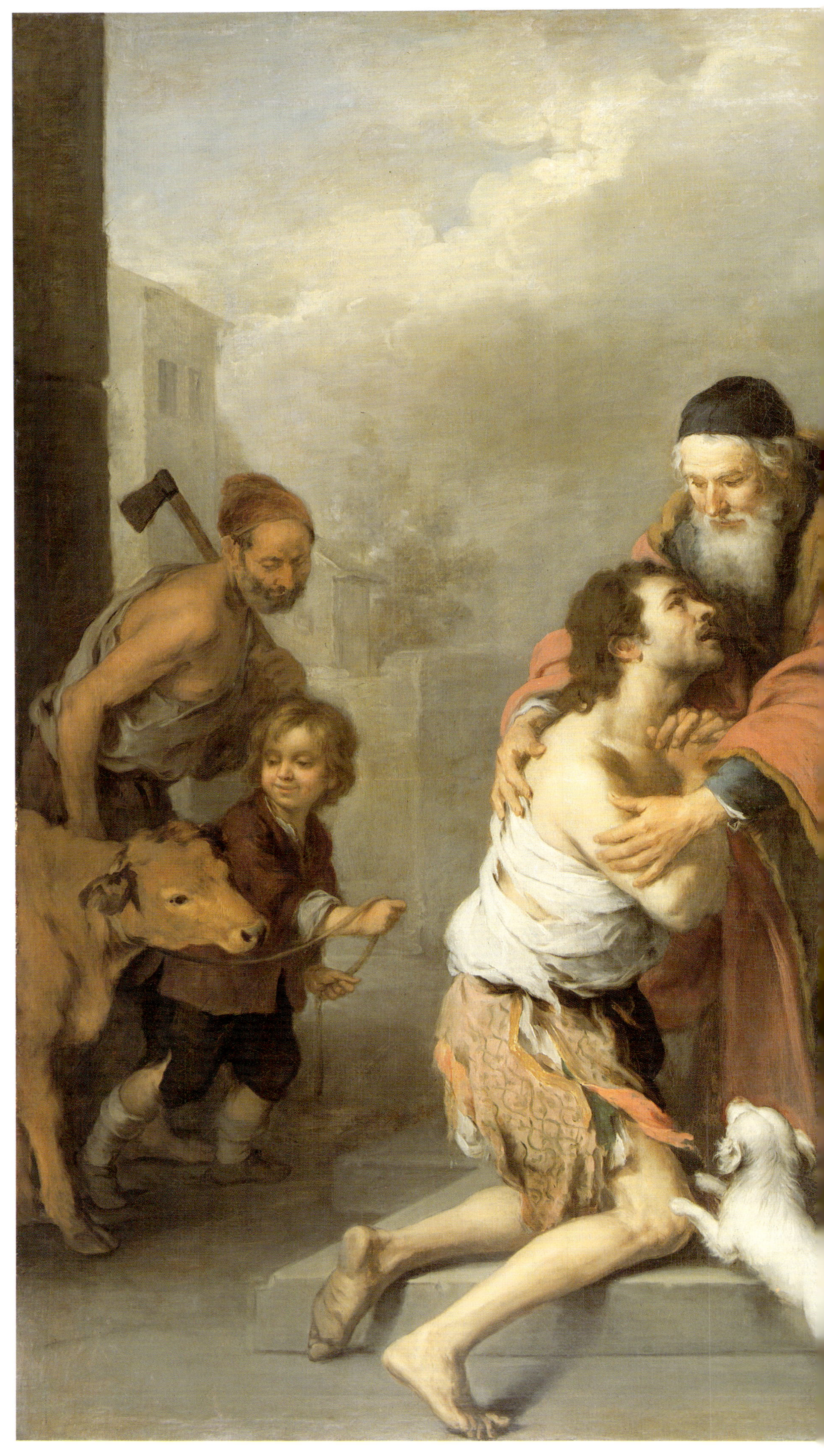

The Return of the Prodigal Son
BARTOLOMÉ ESTEBAN MURILLO, Spanish, 1617–1682
Gift of the Avalon Foundation, National Gallery of Art, Washington, DC. Oil on canvas. 93 × 102¾ in.

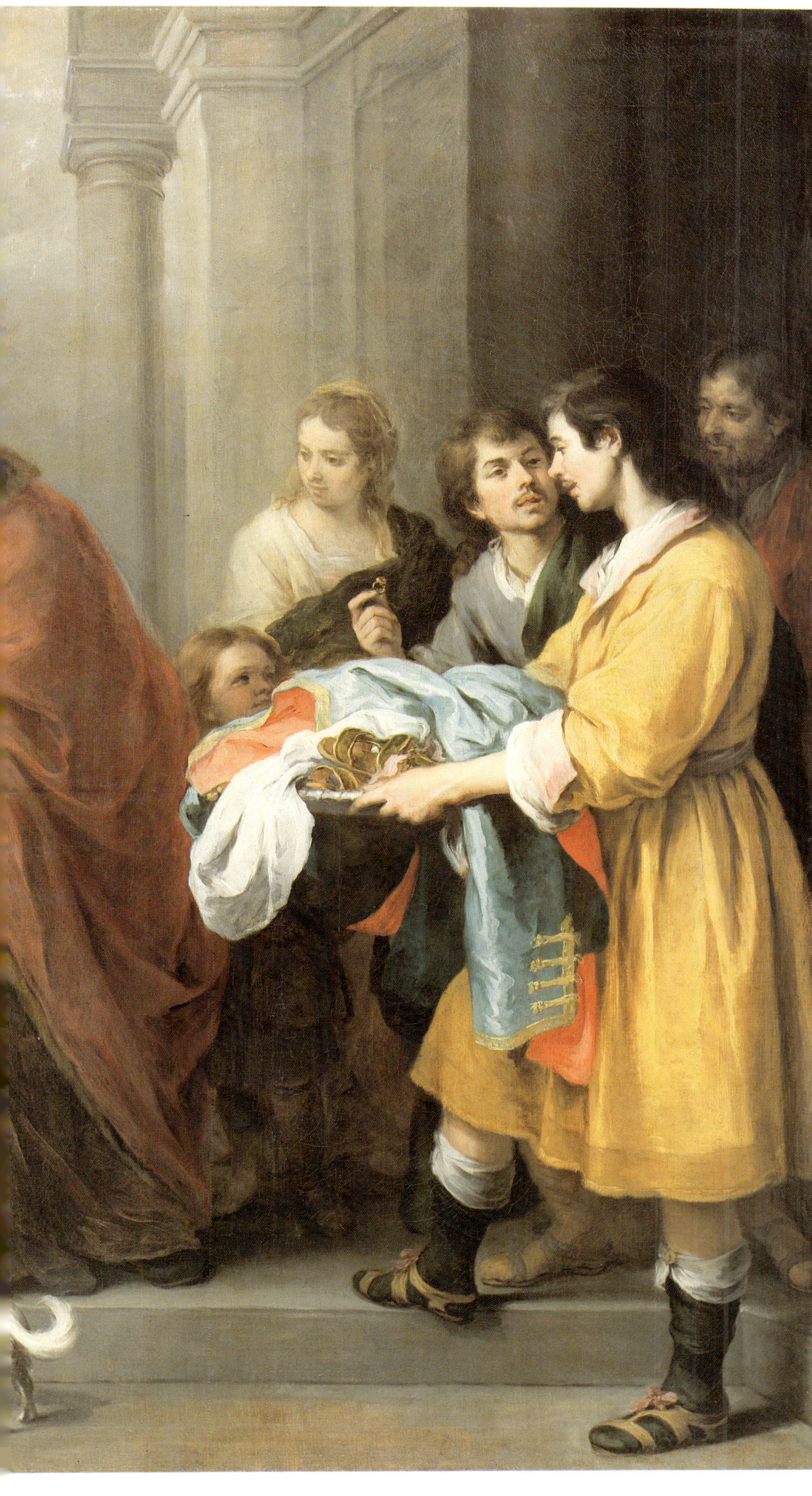

bring the fatted calf and kill it, and let us eat and make merry, for this son was dead and is alive again; he was lost, and is found'" (Luke 15:11–32).

With life-size figures and an appreciation for the sweetness of living, Murillo celebrates this rapturous moment. He even adds to the poignancy of the father's warm greeting by having the family pet join in. The fine ring and garments that will soon adorn the son are admired by the two handsome servants who carry them. Though less brightly lit, the smiling man on the far right and his ebullient companion leading the fatted calf add to the true joy of the moment and emphasize the dignity of the life to which the prodigal has returned.

In light of *The Return of the Prodigal Son*, it is easy to see why pious countrymen found Murillo appealing, and why he earned a favorable reputation abroad before foreigners came to appreciate any of his contemporaries. At one time, Murillo was the most famous of all Spanish artists. Today, however, his works are considered saccharine by many and he is no longer ranked at the very top. Ironically, his declining reputation as a painter may be largely attributed to his greatness as a teacher, for most of his followers and imitators, numbering in the hundreds, lacked his sensitivity and insight and their sentimental works often are mistakenly attributed to him.

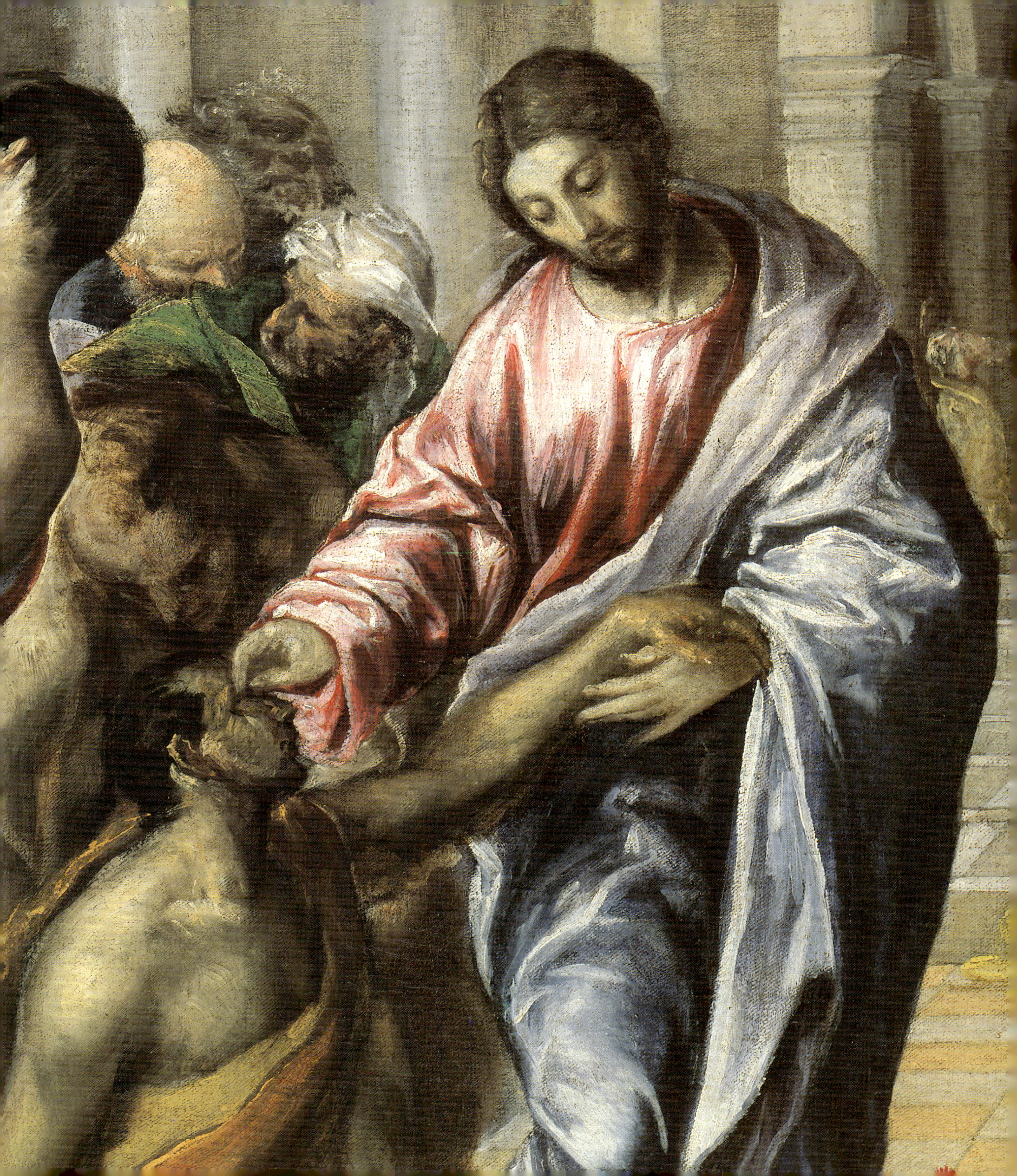

The Miracle of Christ Healing the Blind

Jesus once quoted Isaiah, who said, "you shall indeed see but never perceive" (Matthew 13:14). Thus, for the great teacher, healing the blind was a metaphor for spiritual enlightenment and, at the same time, a reminder that some hearts are hardened to conversion. Jesus restored the sight of several blind people, according to the Scriptures, so it is difficult to pinpoint the episode that El Greco pictures in *The Miracle of Christ Healing the Blind*. Perhaps the object of Jesus' ministrations is the blind man whose story was told in the ninth chapter of The Gospel According to John. He was a beggar who had been blind from birth. Jesus anointed the man's eyes with clay that he made from dirt and his own spittle as he uttered the words, "I am the light of the world" (John 9:5). The couple who stand in awe and wonder at the bottom of the painting would have been the beggar's parents.

This miracle, which took place on the Sabbath, caused a controversy among the religious Jews who learned of it, and they are shown in groups on either side of Jesus and the beggar. The Pharisees, noted in the New Testament for their self-righteousness, huddle to the right, eager to accuse Jesus of dishonoring the Sabbath, for they interpreted the making of clay as work, which is forbidden on the day of rest and prayer. Those on the left accuse him of being a demon. Without the figures of the blind man's parents in the foreground, the painting would have been quite different, with the major emphasis on the conflict between Jesus and his detractors. El Greco instinctively places the parents in the picture in order to keep the focus on the miracle that is taking place. These appreciative human beings also help the viewer comprehend the power of Jesus. The man pointing toward heaven serves a similar function. He is a silent commentator on the source of light as well as Jesus' power to perform an incredible act of mercy.

Born in Crete and trained in Italy, El Greco settled in Spain when he was in his mid-thirties. He remained there as a major artistic force, challenging his contemporaries with a body of highly individualistic and emotionally charged paintings that drew their inspiration—including the elongated figures—from the Greek icons he knew as a child. But the spiritual content of El Greco's works transcends mere stylistic formulas. In *The Miracle of Christ Healing the Blind*, for example, he effectively conveys deep and sincere emotions. As viewers empathize with them, they can accept Jesus' act of healing for what it was—a miracle.

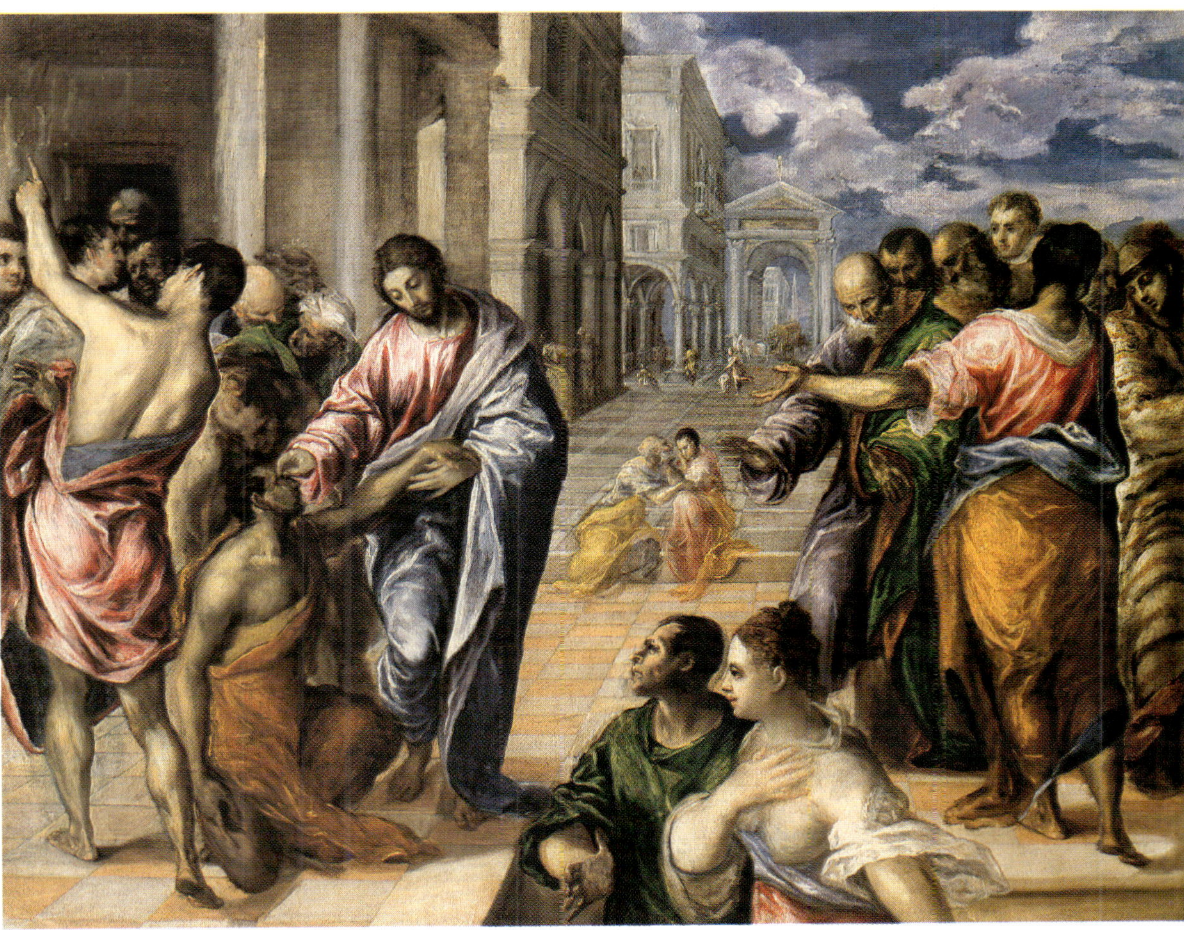

The Miracle of Christ Healing the Blind
EL GRECO, Spanish, 1541–1614
Gift of Mr. and Mrs. Charles Wrightsman, 1978, Metropolitan Museum of Art, New York. Oil on canvas. 47 × 57½ in.

◁ DETAIL

"Suffer the Children to Come to Me"

For some reason, people often assume that bachelors don't like children. Perhaps the disciples thought Jesus, who was of course unmarried, was disinterested in youngsters. At any rate, they rebuked parents who were trying to bring their children to him. The Master was indignant. "Let the children come to me," he said firmly. "Do not hinder them; for to such belongs the kingdom of God. Truly I say to you, whoever does not receive the kingdom of God like a child shall not enter it" (Mark 10:13–16). He then took the children in his arms, laid his hands on them, and blessed them. Seekers after eternal life have ever since looked to this story for the most perfect definition of faith.

Jacob Jordaens was such a seeker, and in his 62nd year became a convert to Calvinism, an unpopular religion in predominantly Catholic Flanders. He apparently kept his conversion secret from all but his family, and continued to serve the Catholic church as the most respected artist in Antwerp, his native city.

In *"Suffer the Children to Come to Me,"* he tells the story of Jesus, the mothers, and their babies through the use of brilliant contrasts. Not only do the somewhat lurid colors sing out in competition with one another, but the differences between areas of light and areas of shadow are exaggerated. The most pronounced contrasts, however, are reserved for Jordaens's treatment of the figures. In order to emphasize the tender age of the babies, he makes some of his disciples considerably older than they probably were. And he portrays the mothers as exceptionally robust. The two closest to Jesus are especially exuberant in the way they approach him. The babies, on the other hand, are docile, dependent, and innocently receptive to what is theirs by nature.

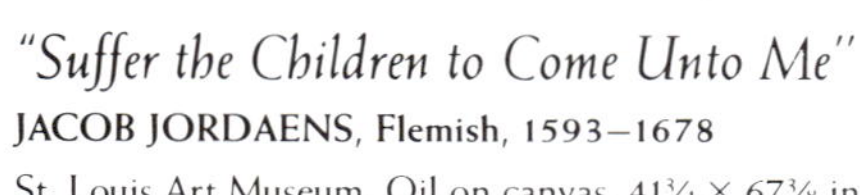

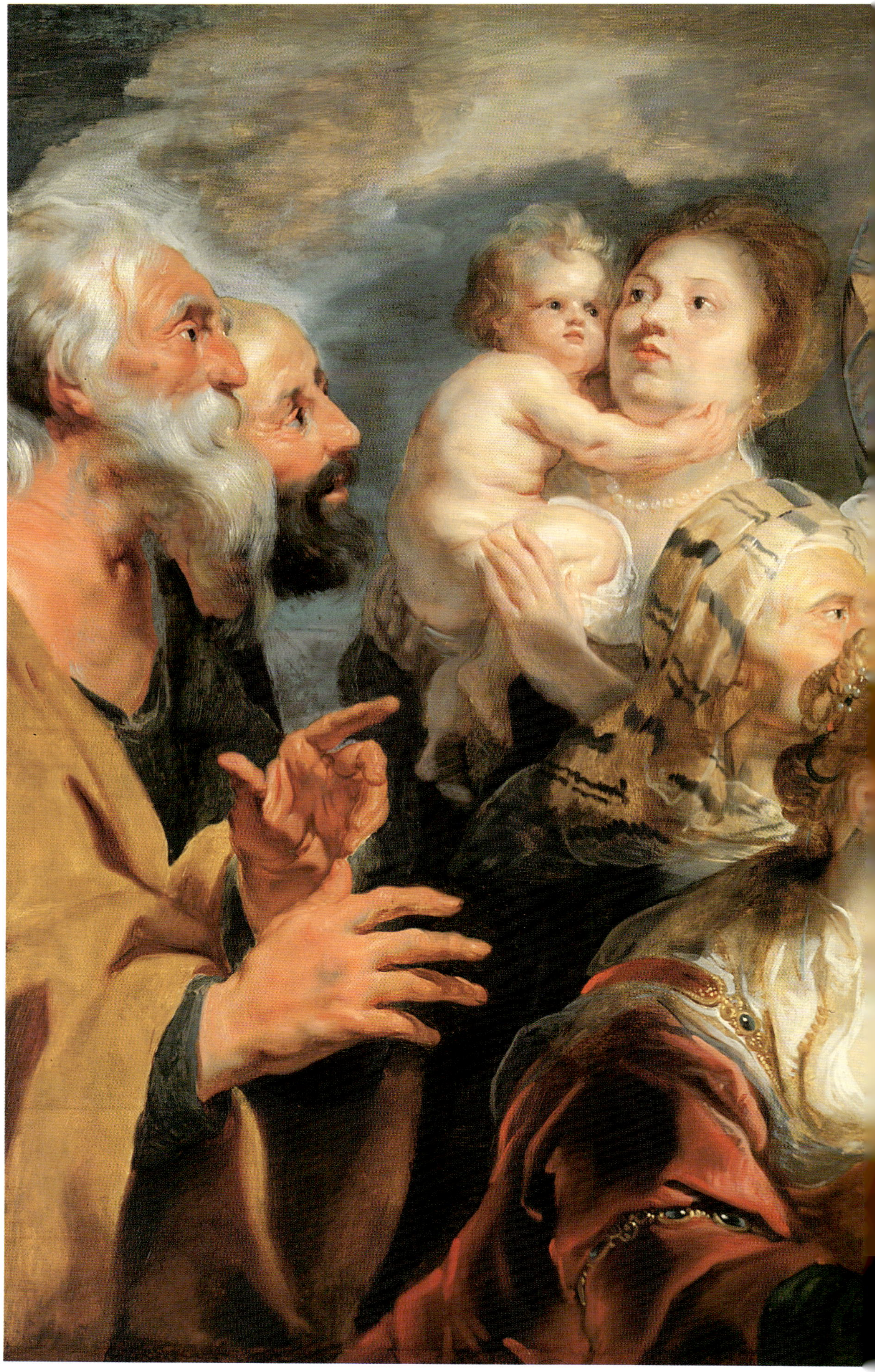

"Suffer the Children to Come Unto Me"
JACOB JORDAENS, Flemish, 1593–1678
St. Louis Art Museum. Oil on canvas. 41¼ × 67⅛ in.

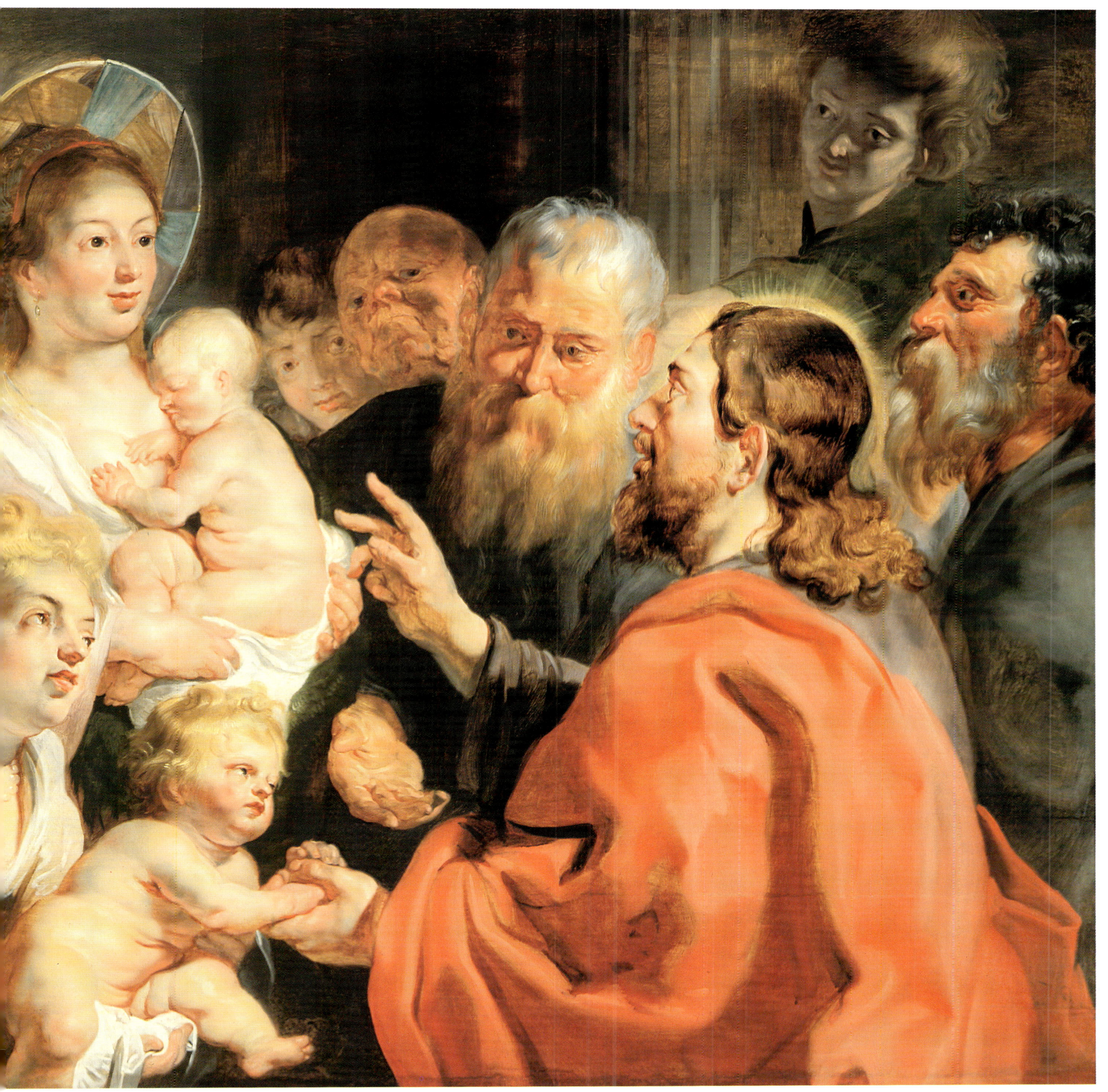

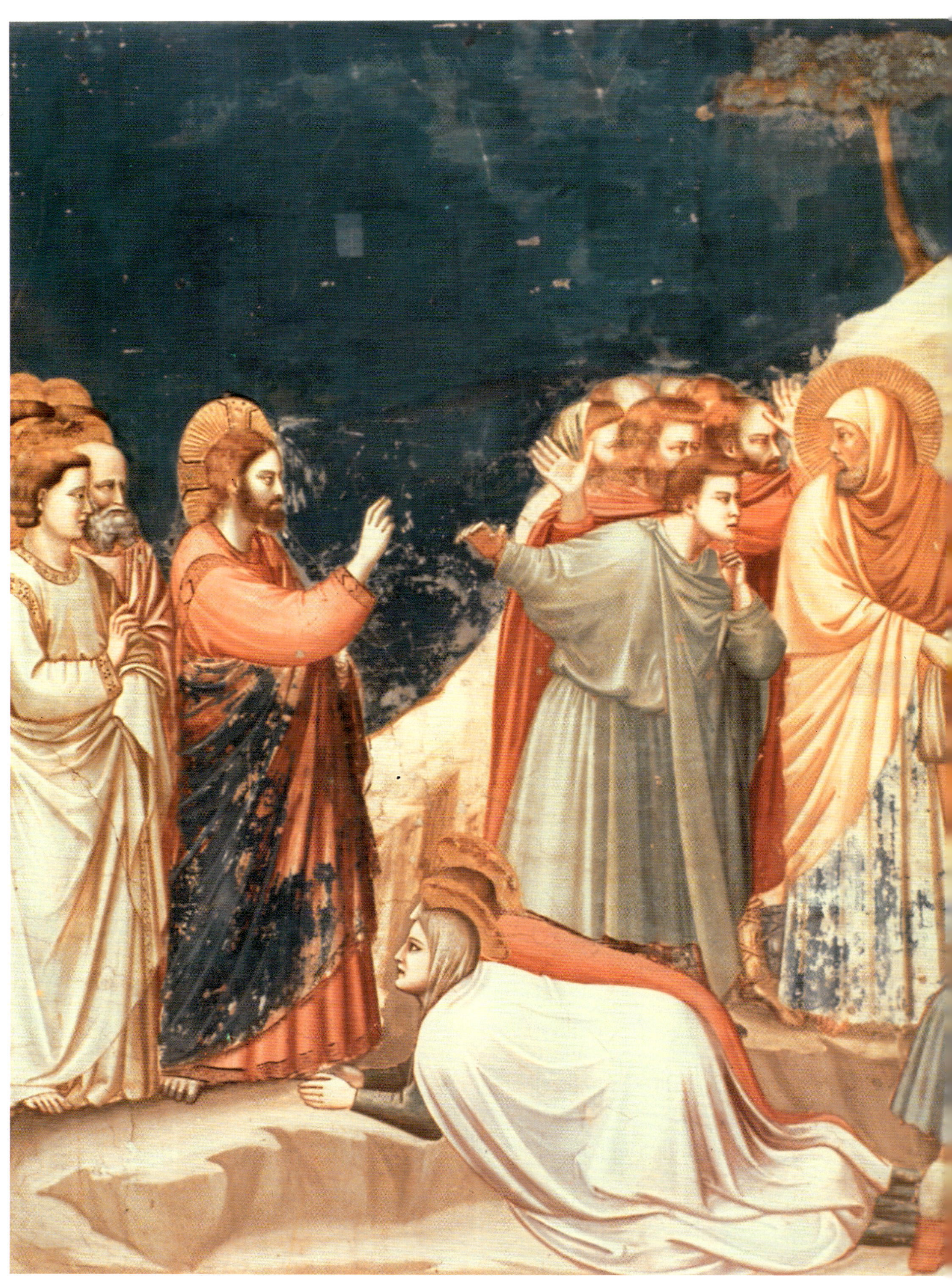

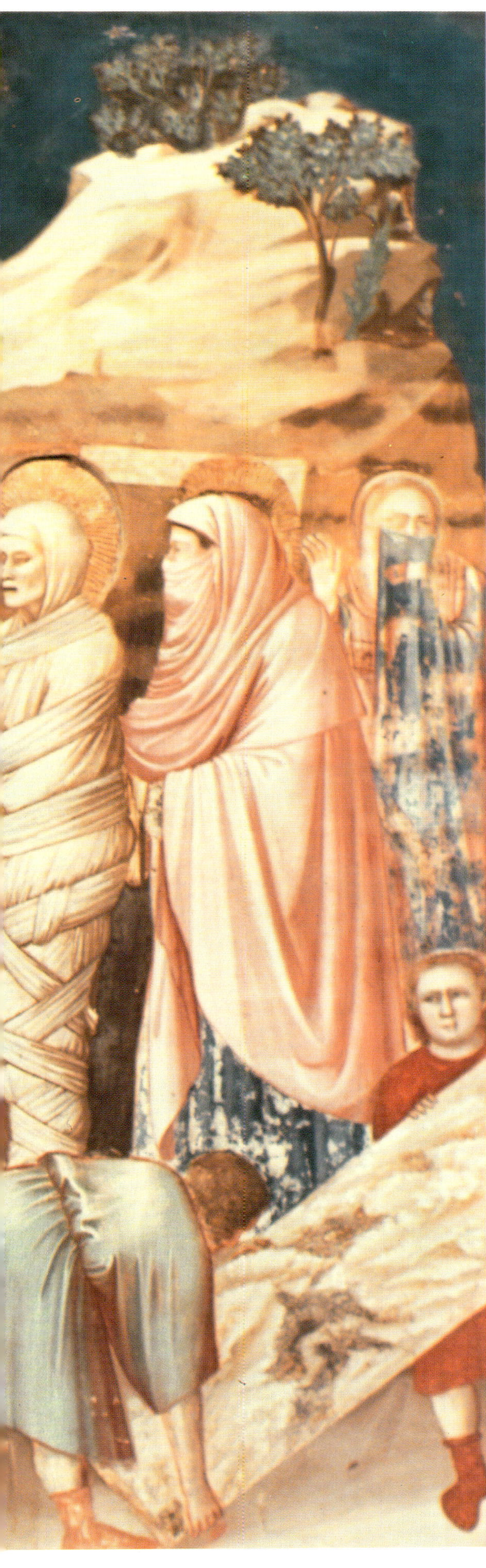

The Raising of Lazarus

The great frescoes by Giotto in the Scrovenig Chapel in Padua are ranked in two rows around the room, the figures in them painted about half life-size, and each scene separated from the next by a border with smaller paintings in quatrefoil decorations. Adjacent to *The Raising of Lazarus*, reproduced at left, is a small picture that shows the Creator bringing Adam to life.

Of the four Gospel writers, John told the most personal stories about Jesus. This one involved three of his best friends, the sisters Mary and Martha and their brother Lazarus. Before anyone told him, Jesus knew Lazarus had died, but he promised the sisters that his close friend would rise again. Mary and Martha thought he meant that all the dead would return to life at the end of time. So when Jesus asked that Lazarus' tomb be opened, they tried to stop him. But Jesus insisted, and in spite of the smell of decaying flesh (Lazarus had been sealed up for four days), he called for his friend to come out. Dressed in his funeral wraps, Lazarus did. Giotto shows the dead man (wrapped like a mummy) looking pale and dazed but alive. Mary and Martha, with their backs to their brother, kneel in monumental gratitude to Jesus. A short time later Mary would assume this posture again, to anoint Jesus' feet with costly oil. The figures behind the workmen cover their noses, and all the others are amazed by the miracle. Many of them were converted to Jesus' ministry.

Giotto was universally regarded in his time as the most talented artist since antiquity. His reputation was based on the realism and truth of his works, which were greater than any that had been created before. Indeed, painting prior to Giotto was flat in appearance, without the illusion of volume in the figures or in the space around them, and the stories were told in standard, conventional ways. To make figures appear to be three-dimensional, even though they were painted on a flat wall, Giotto used a consistent light source that brightened one side of each figure and blended into darker color on the other, to give the impression of shadows. Further, he set these volumetric figures in a convincing environment. Without the knowledge of linear perspective, he invented his own way of treating space, one that made room for each figure on a shallow stage-like setting. In *The Raising of Lazarus*, for example, the setting is deep enough for four or five "layers" of bodies. To accommodate the extras, however, he reverted to the art of the past and just stacked them like playing cards. He also used life experiences, rather than the conventions of the dry art around him, to tell his stories. His success in this regard may be seen in the animated gestures of the monk next to Jesus and the disciple supporting Lazarus.

Curiously, the other Gospel writers ignored the story of Jesus and Lazarus, although it related what was probably Jesus' most significant miracle. By the way, in John's version, it occasioned the shortest verse in the Bible: "Jesus wept" (John 11:35).

The Raising of Lazarus
GIOTTO, Italian, 1266/67–1337
Scrovegni Chapel, S. Maria Annunziata dell'Arena, Padua.
Fresco. 79½ × 73½ in.

Head of Christ

The New Testament does not offer a physical description of Jesus. The earliest verbal portrait dates from the fourth century and is probably no more authentic than any of the painted images of him. Isaiah, writing some 700 years before the birth of Jesus, probably referred more to his lowly and unpretentious life than to his personal appearance when he said, "He has no form or comeliness that we should look at him, and no beauty that we should desire him" (Isaiah 53:2).

Every artist who painted the face of Jesus sought to portray a physical type that would seem authentic to his contemporaries. Rembrandt, for example, searched the streets of Amsterdam's Jewish quarter near his home, to find models for the figures in his biblical paintings. It is not known if a particular young Jew posed for this *Head of Christ*, but the face has an authenticity that would have stemmed from the artist's daily contact with Jews.

Amsterdam was the only city in 17th-century Europe where Jews had complete freedom, so they took up many pursuits that were forbidden to them elsewhere. Book publishing was one field of endeavor at which they excelled. Through this craft, Rembrandt came to know Jews as intellectuals, for he had a passion for learning and the printed word. Thus, in this painting, he chooses to portray Jesus as one whose face reveals intelligence, along with innocent concern. This is the private Jesus. Though he is about to speak, his voice will not be heard by the multitudes. Quiet words will come from his lips, of concern only to the listener.

Rembrandt painted a number of versions of this head and apparently had his students copy these images as an exercise in character study. Hence, of the numerous portraits of Christ attributed to Rembrandt, it is often difficult to distinguish which are actually his.

The subject intrigued him for a number of reasons. He enjoyed painting men and women at various ages in life, and Jesus represented one ideal of man in his prime. Second, he seems to have had a genuine love for the Bible, and therefore he would naturally have been attracted to the figure and personality of Jesus. Finally, he relished the challenge of summarizing character in an unadorned portrait, that is, an image without a narrative based on the subject's life or deeds. Who could have offered the artist a greater challenge in this respect than the magisterial yet simple, profound yet unaffected rabbi?

Head of Christ
REMBRANDT VAN RIJN, Dutch, 1606–1669
Gemäldegalerie, Berlin-Dahlem. Oil on wood panel. 10 × 12 in.

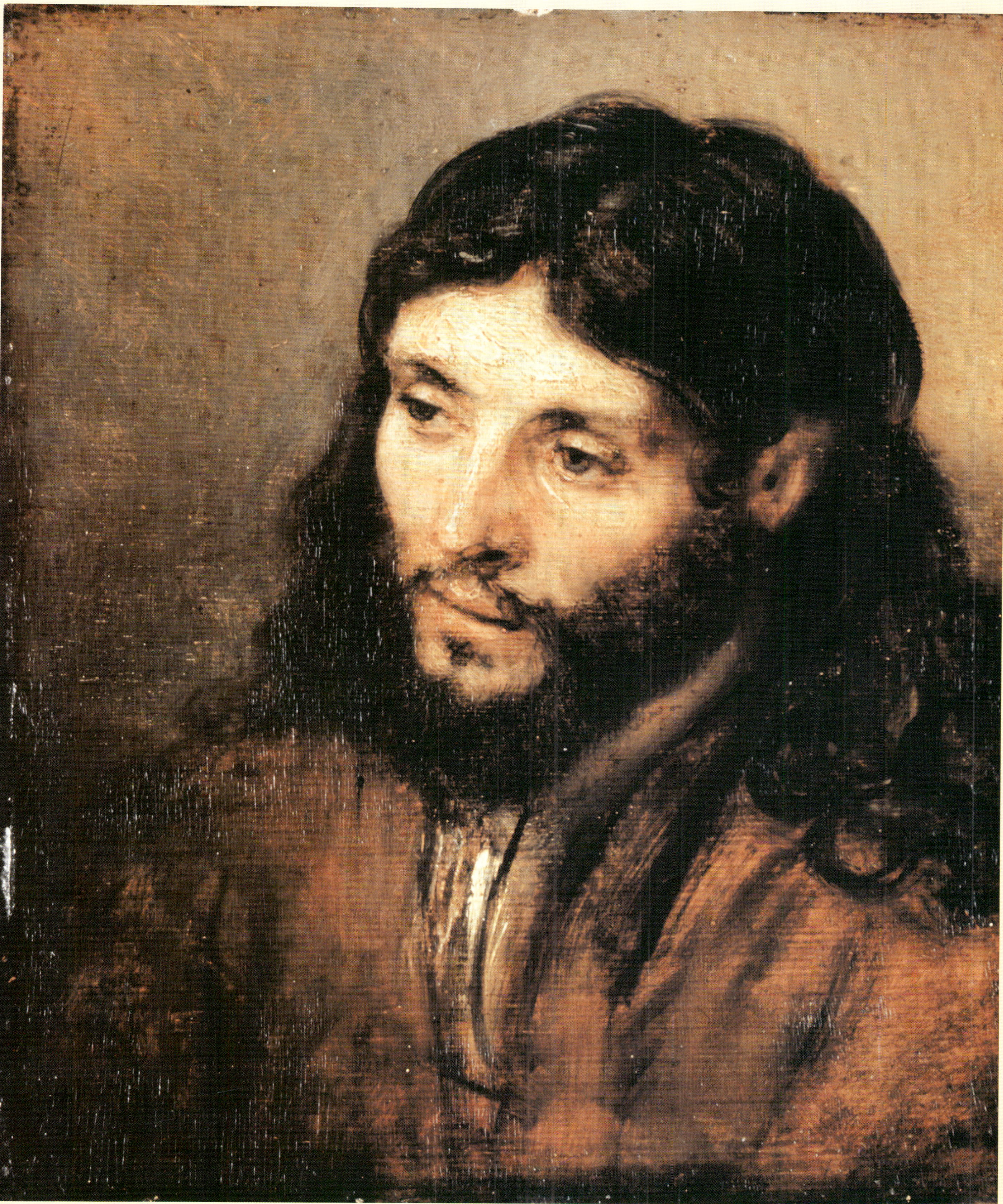

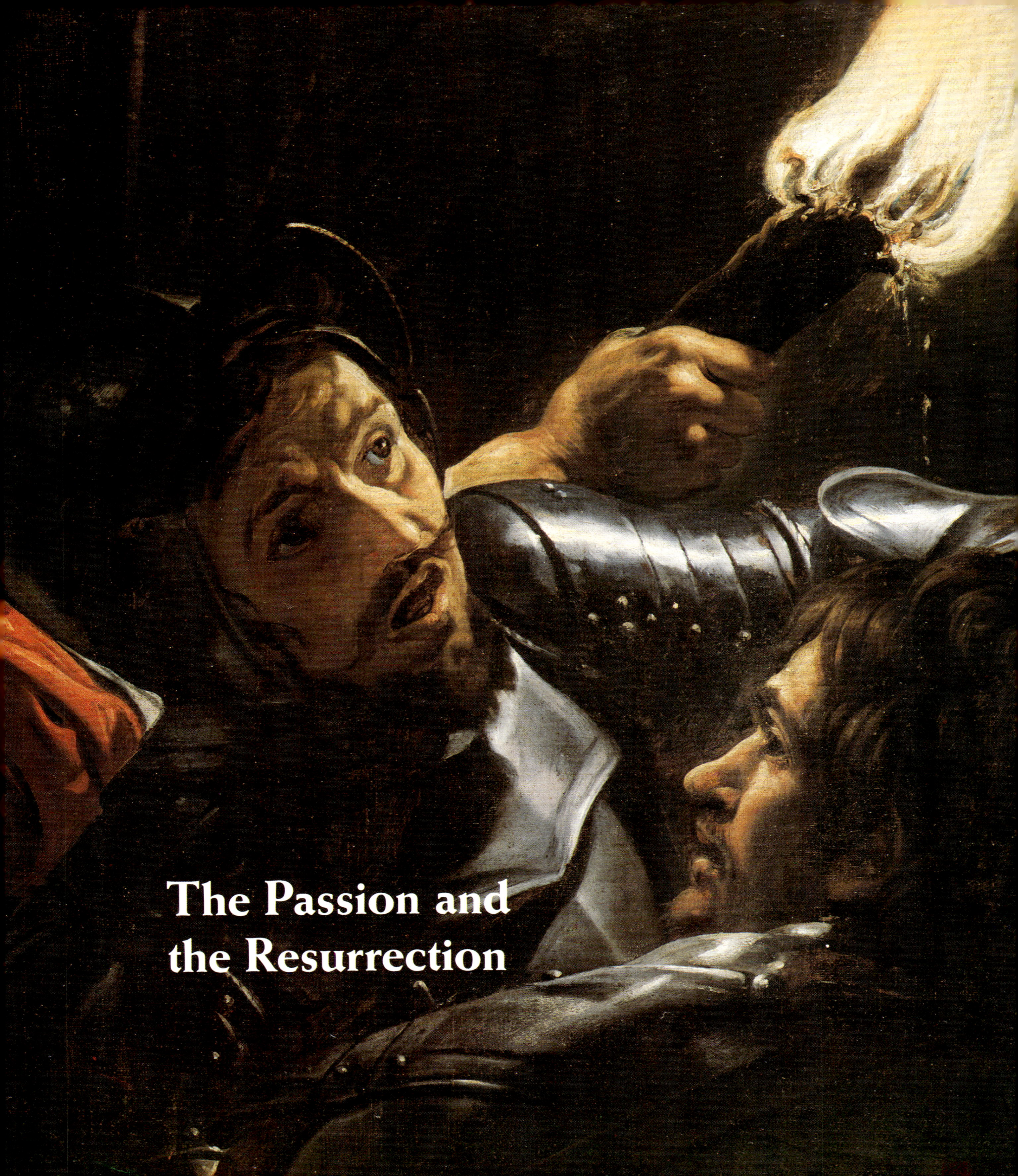

The Passion and the Resurrection

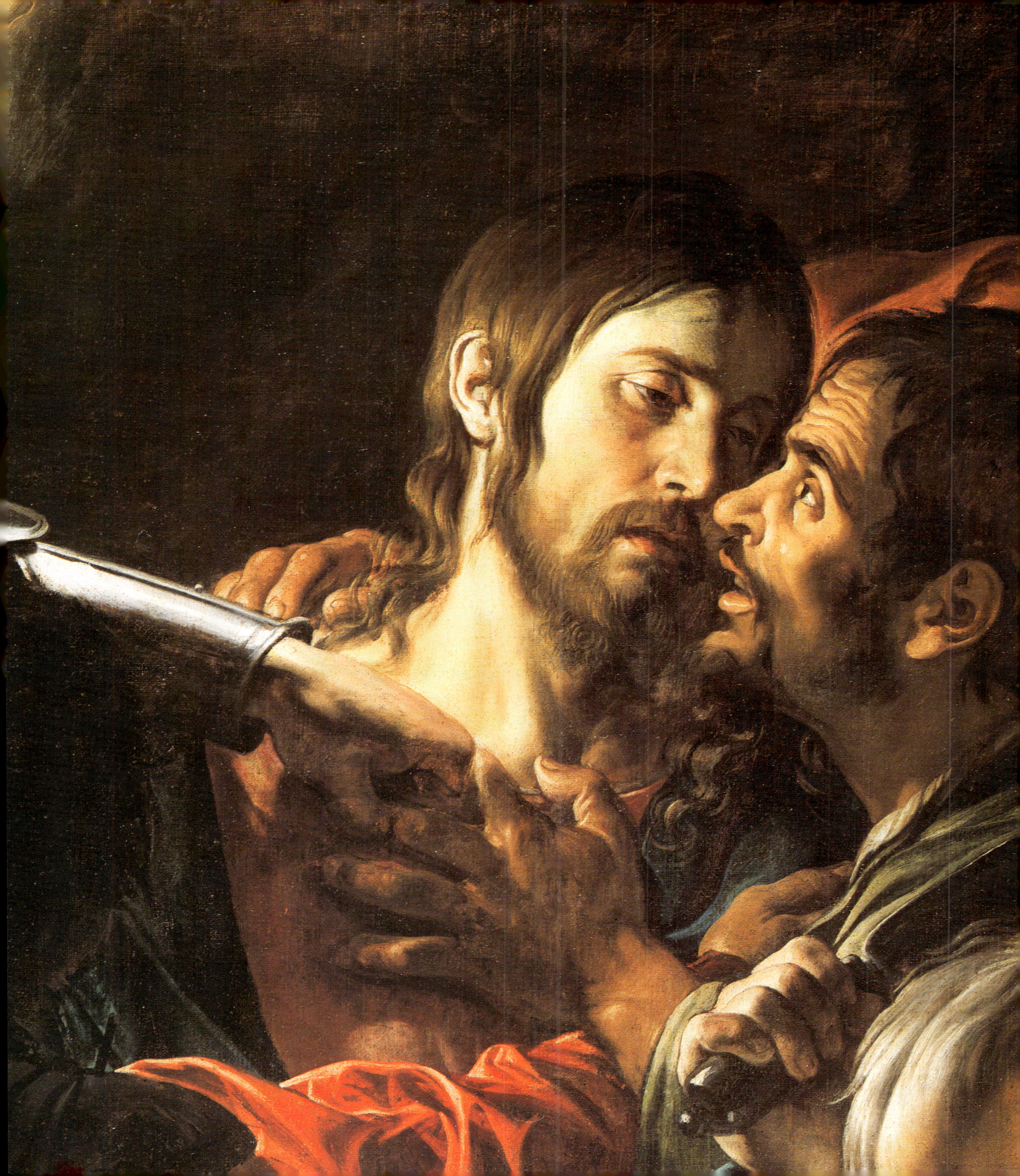

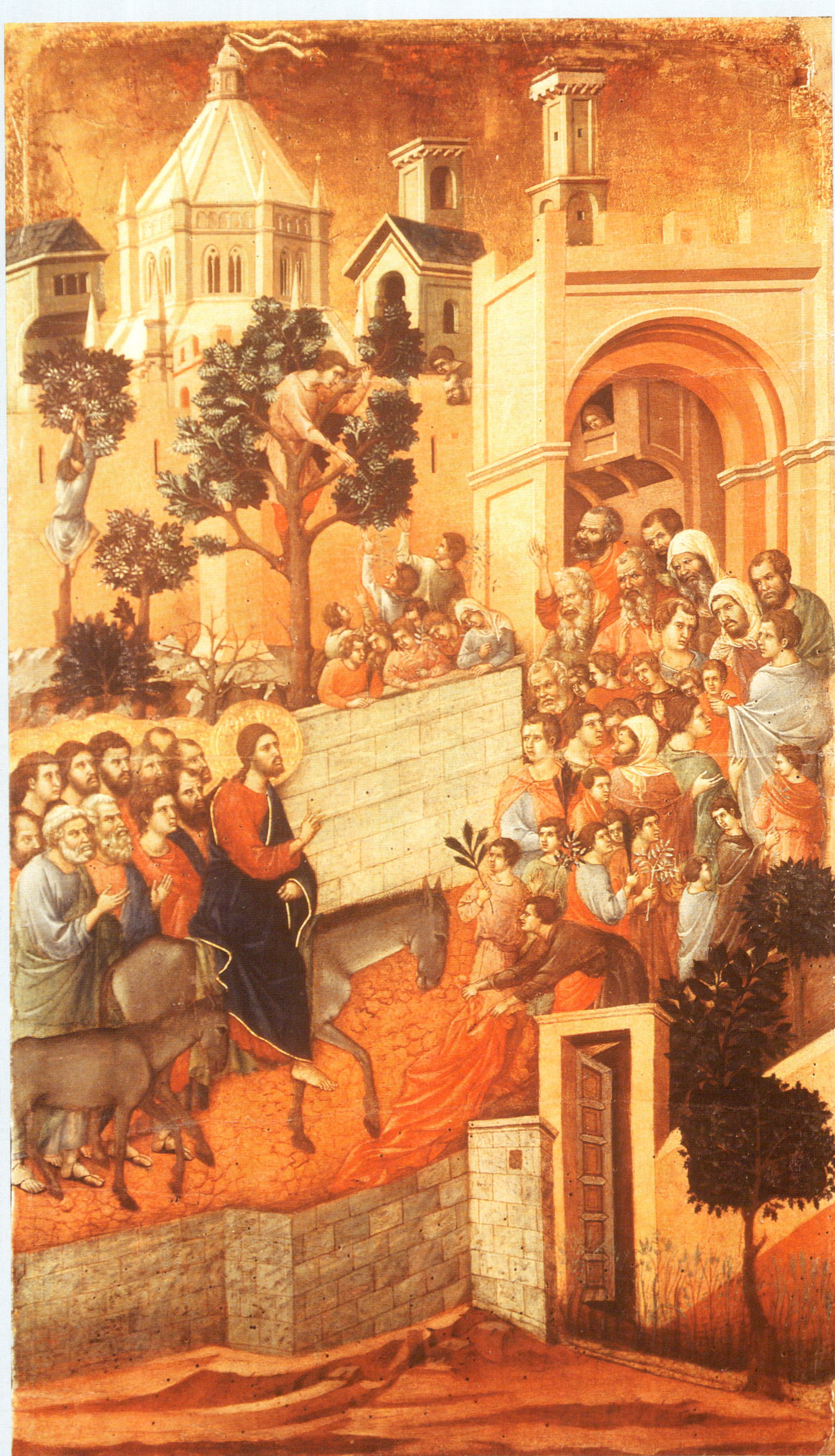

Entry into Jerusalem

Jesus' public ministry—the period in which he preached and engaged in the performance of miracles—lasted about three years. The chronology of the events during this period is not always clear, for the Gospel writers each emphasized different stories and did not necessarily order them in the same sequence. Their narration of the events of the last week of Jesus' life, however, was consistent. It began with his preparations for the observance of Passover with his disciples in Jerusalem.

The entry into Jerusalem was the last earthly triumph in the life of Jesus. This moment has appealed to artists throughout the centuries, in part because it represented a pivotal episode in Jesus' life, and in part because it gave artists a chance to work on a grand scale, with plenty of pomp and circumstance. In the version by Duccio of Siena, Jesus is atop a humble gray ass, a red cloak furled in his way, like a stream of blood. The great teacher looks at it with profound sadness, recognizing the future it portends. He also sees a door ajar in the city wall beyond, his last chance to escape the trial and execution he knows await him.

From trees where they have climbed, followers of the doomed Master yank boughs of leaves to wave as a tribute and sign of victory. But the townsmen are tentative in their greeting, surging not toward Jesus but backward into the protection of the golden gate. A gulf of fear seems to separate these men from the Master and the disciples who follow closely behind him. Triumphal white banners fly from the temple, the only sign of greeting

Entry into Jerusalem, from the back of the *Maesta Altar*
DUCCIO, Italian, ca. 1255–before 1319
Cathedral Museum, Siena. Wood panel. 40½ × 21⅛ in.

that approximates the account of all four Gospel writers of this first Palm Sunday. Clearly this multitude is not singing out "Hosannah" and "Blessed be the King," as the Evangelists reported.

Perhaps at this tense moment Jesus is foretelling the destruction of Jerusalem. "Not one stone will be left upon another" (Luke 19:44), he said, although the artist instead emphasizes the strength of the city walls and the seeming impossibility of this terrible prediction. The wall also serves a more practical compositional function, for its unrelieved passage of gray, placed between Jesus and the Jerusalemites, allows the artist to open up an otherwise busy scene. This stony space is also a quiet reminder of the great gulf that will soon separate Jesus from everyone, even those who stand closest to him now.

This painting is part of the *Maesta*, the famous altarpiece of Siena's cathedral. On one side of it, Duccio shows the Madonna and Child enthroned; on the back, from which this scene comes, the life of Christ is portrayed.

▷
DETAIL

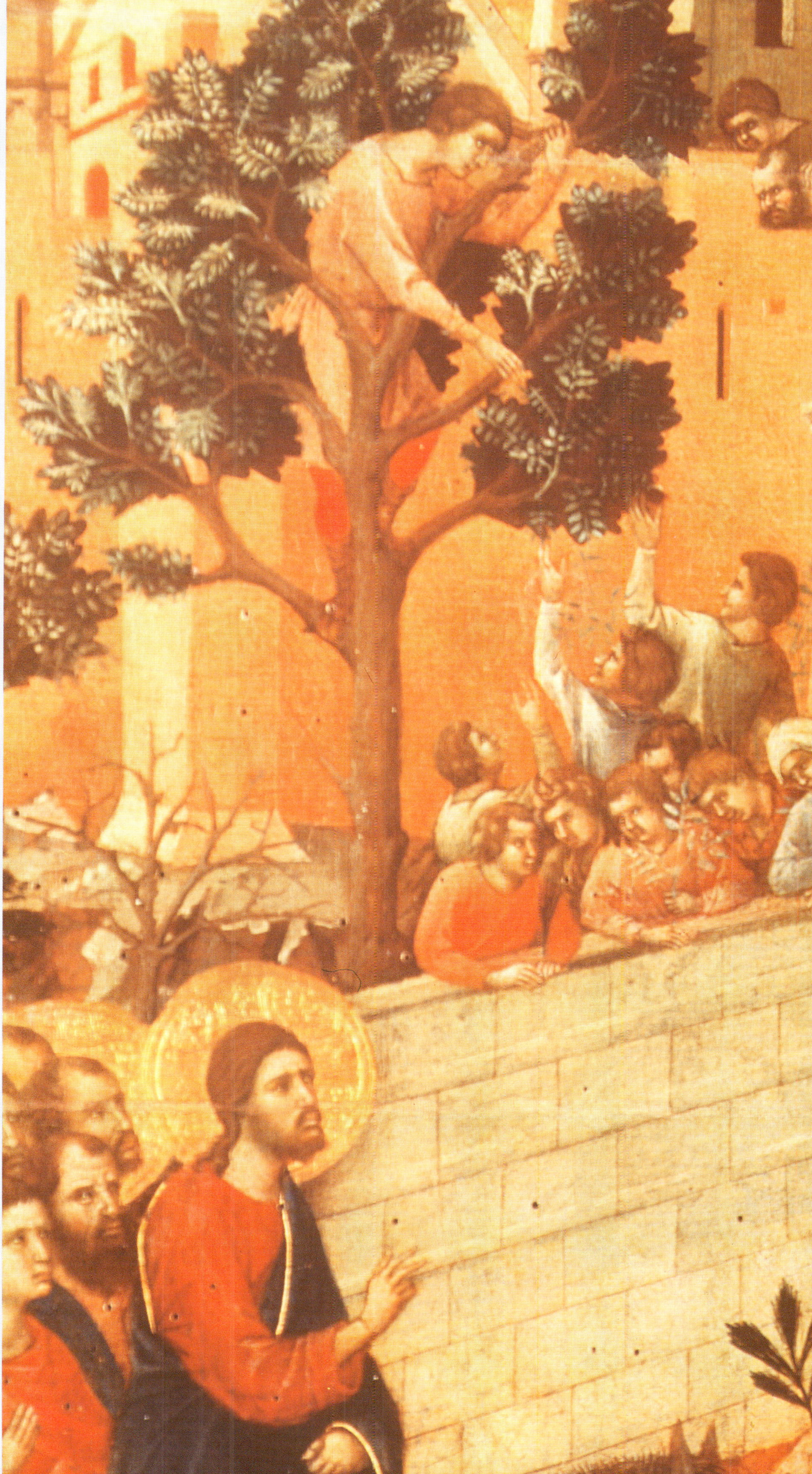

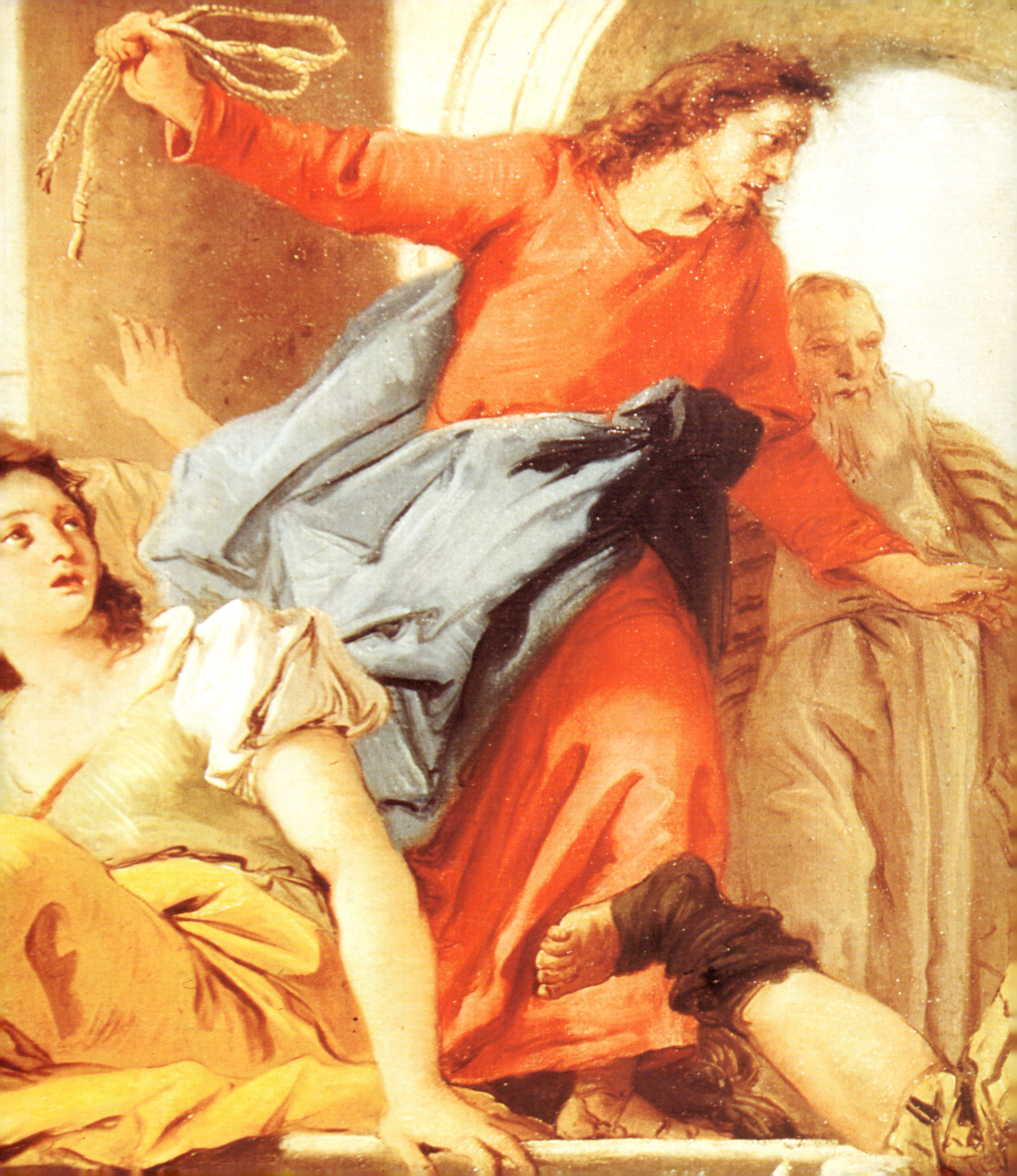

Christ Driving the Money Changers from the Temple

Pilgrims came from far and wide to worship in the temple in Jerusalem. Since only Tyrian coins could be used to make contributions or pay the annual half-sheckel Temple tax, money changers installed booths for currency exchange just outside the Temple. At the High Holy Days, however, they were allowed into the Court of the Gentiles, where this scene by Giovanni Battista Tiepolo takes place. Because their tables took up so much room, Gentiles were precluded from worshipping, one of the reasons that Jesus drove the money changers out. He reminded those who listened that in the Scriptures God's house was called "a house of prayer for all the nations" (Mark 11:17), Jesus also objected to the exploitative surcharges of the money changers and said they made the Temple "a den of robbers." The money changers were not the only subjects of Jesus' wrath. He also lashed out at those who sold pigeons and small animals, which were used as offerings, and at all of their customers.

Tiepolo was one of the greatest palace decorators who ever lived, so he was skilled at painting pictures with odd perspectives for staircase landings and ceilings. In *Christ Driving the Money Changers from the Temple*, he uses perspective to give viewers the rather uncomfortable feeling that the man in the brown vest and his heavy wood table will tumble right into their path. Moreover, by having viewers look up at Jesus from such a low vantage point, he emphasizes Christ's power and authority, but a closer look at Jesus' protruding eyes and firmly set jaw reveal his seething anger. Only in this New Testament story, and that in which Jesus earlier purified the Temple of commerce, was one privy to the violent side of his nature.

According to Mark, the chief priests and scribes heard what Jesus said to the money changers and what he did, and they "sought a way to destroy him; for they feared him, because all the multitudes were astonished at his teachings" (Mark 11:18). In Tiepolo's version of the story the man immediately behind Jesus may be one of these Temple elders. His face is more a drawing than a painting, and it is set in a mask that suggests both disapproval and cunning. For such dark emotions, this is an extraordinarily bright painting. Tiepolo was essentially a sunny artist but he was able, through gesture and expression, to convey even doom.

Christ Driving the Money Changers from the Temple
GIOVANNI BATTISTA TIEPOLO, Italian, 1696–1770
Thyssen Bornemisza Collection, Villa Favorita, Lugano-Castagnola, Switzerland. Oil on canvas. 41¼ × 77½ in.

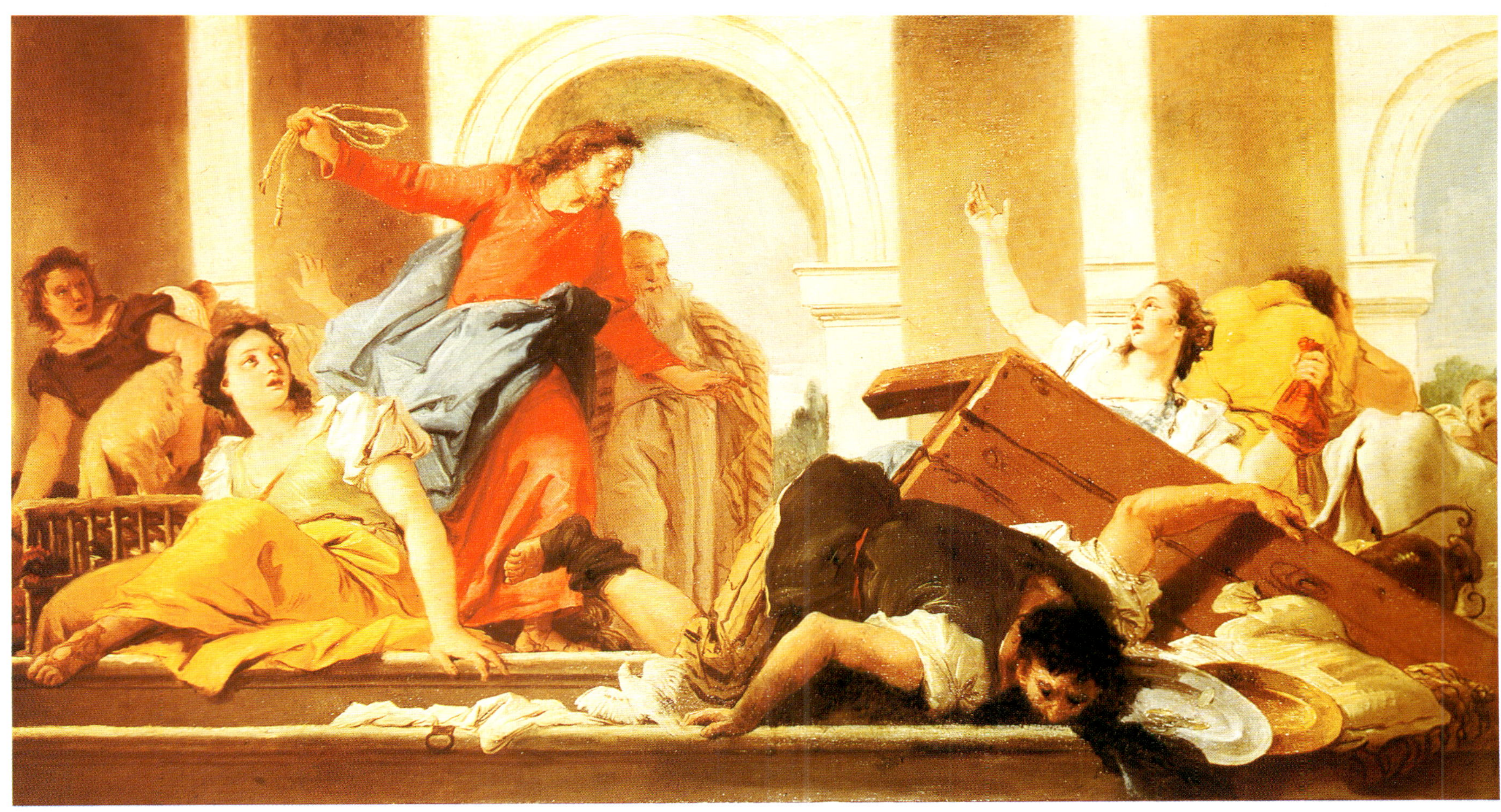

◁ DETAIL

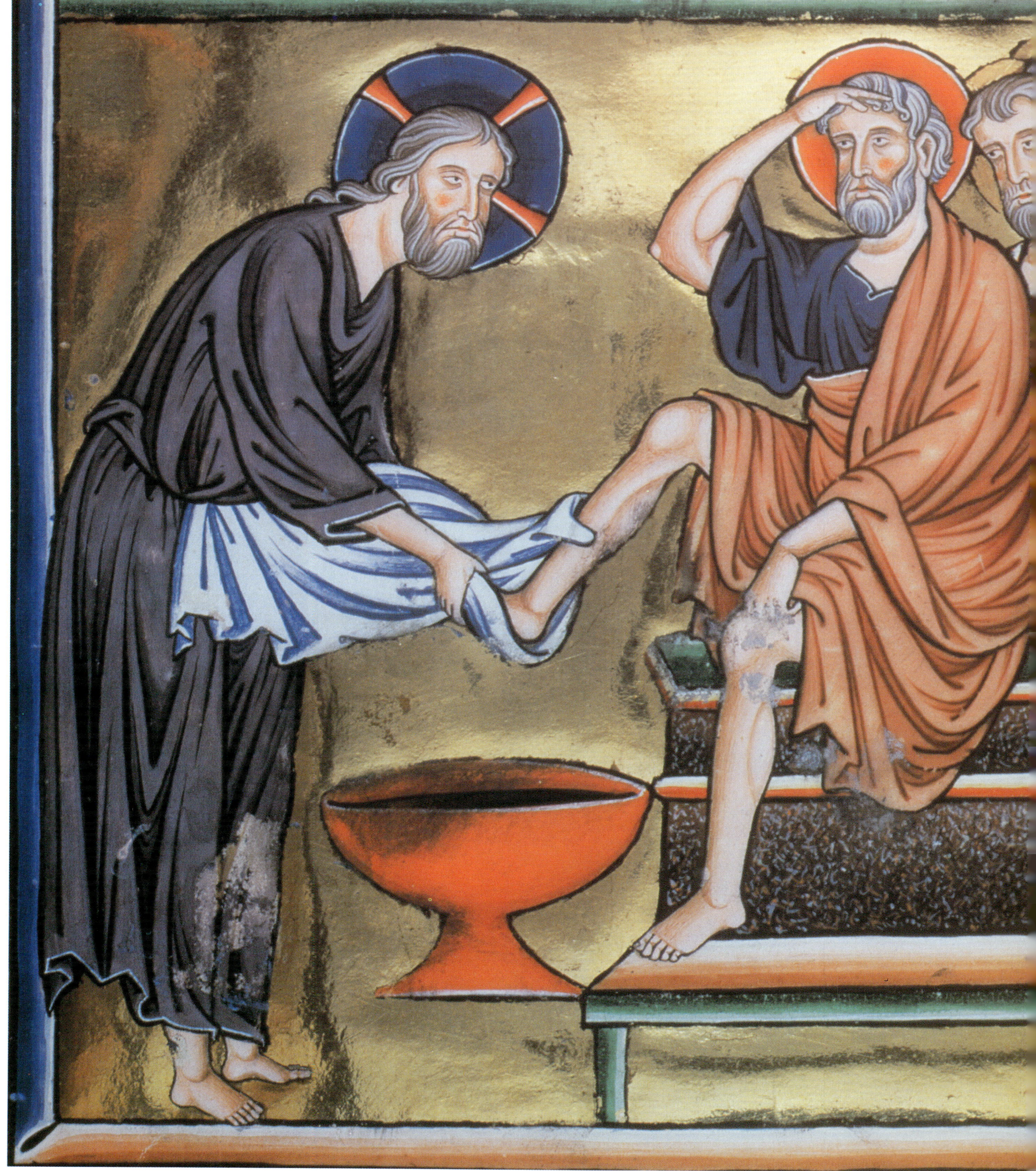

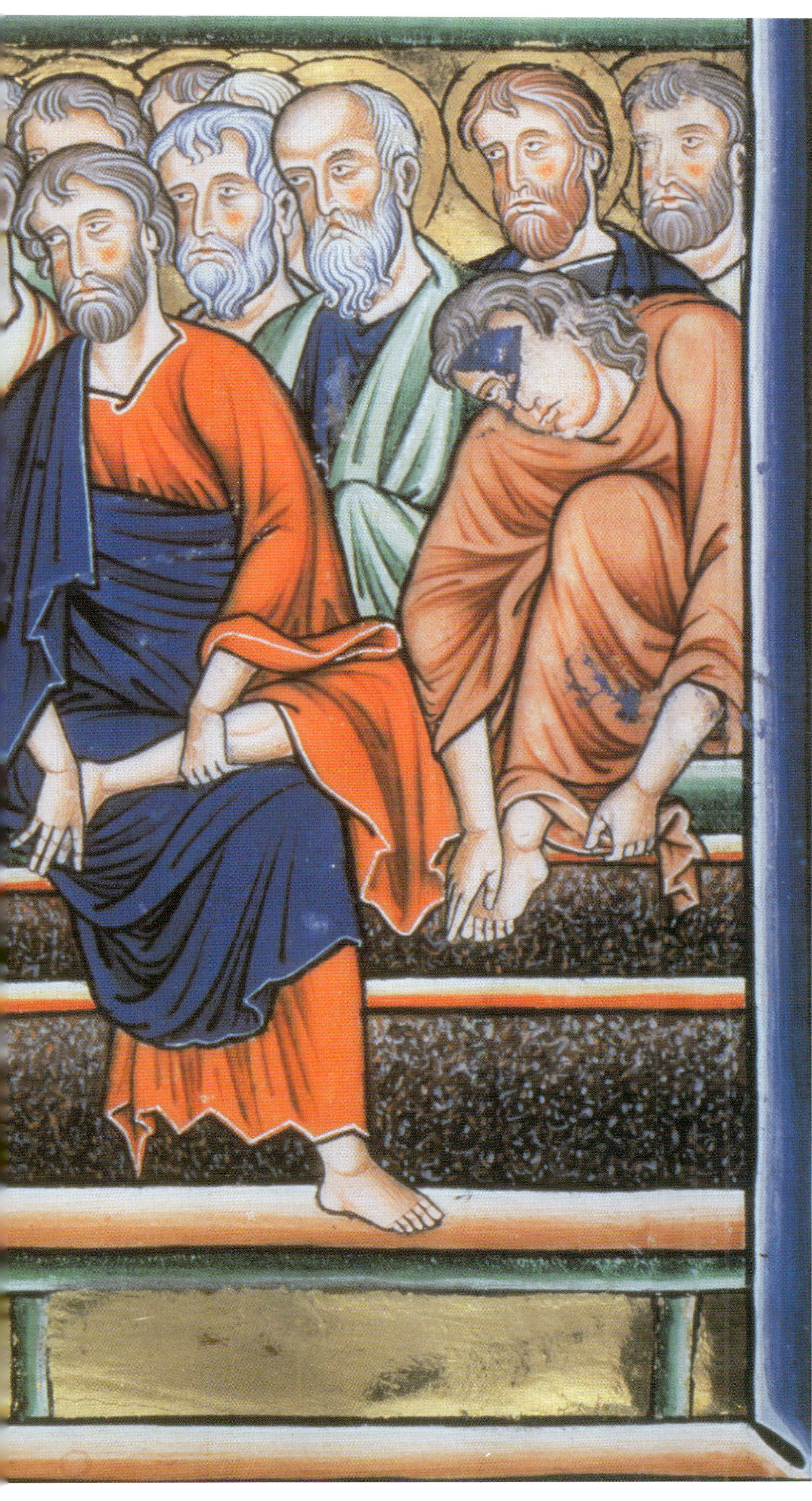

Christ Washing the Feet of His Disciples

John was the closest disciple to Jesus, and only he records the intimate event that took place midway through the Passover meal that is known as the Last Supper. Jesus rose from the table, took off his outer garments, tied a towel around his waist, and began to wash and dry his disciples' feet. John saw this as an outpouring of affection and wrote, "Having loved his own who were in the world, he loved them to the end" (John 13:1).

The tiny manuscript illustration by an unknown 13th-century French artist shows Jesus drying Peter's feet. According to the Scriptures, the fisherman initially objected to his master performing this lowly task, one which was usually done by servants, but he subsequently acquiesced in the face of Jesus' earnestness. The illustration shows the two disciples next to Peter self-consciously wiping their feet with their hands in anticipation of Jesus' ministrations. All of the disciples have the same sad expression on their faces, for Jesus has just spoken the mysterious words, "you are clean, but not all of you" (John 13:10), his first reference to the betrayal by Judas.

At the end of this hospitable but humbling act, Jesus told his disciples, "I have given you an example, that you also should do as I have done to you" (John 14:15). The practice did not catch on, except in monasteries, and in the Vatican. On the Thursday night before Easter, the traditional day that the events of Jesus' last Passover are remembered, Father Superiors throughout the world wash the feet of the monks in their charge, and the Pope publicly washes the feet of the Cardinals of the Church who happen to be in Rome for Holy Week observances.

Christ Washing the Feet of His Disciples
from the *Ingeburg Psalter of Denmark*
UNKNOWN FRENCH ARTIST
Musée Condi, Chantilly, France. Tempera on vellum. 6 × 8 in.

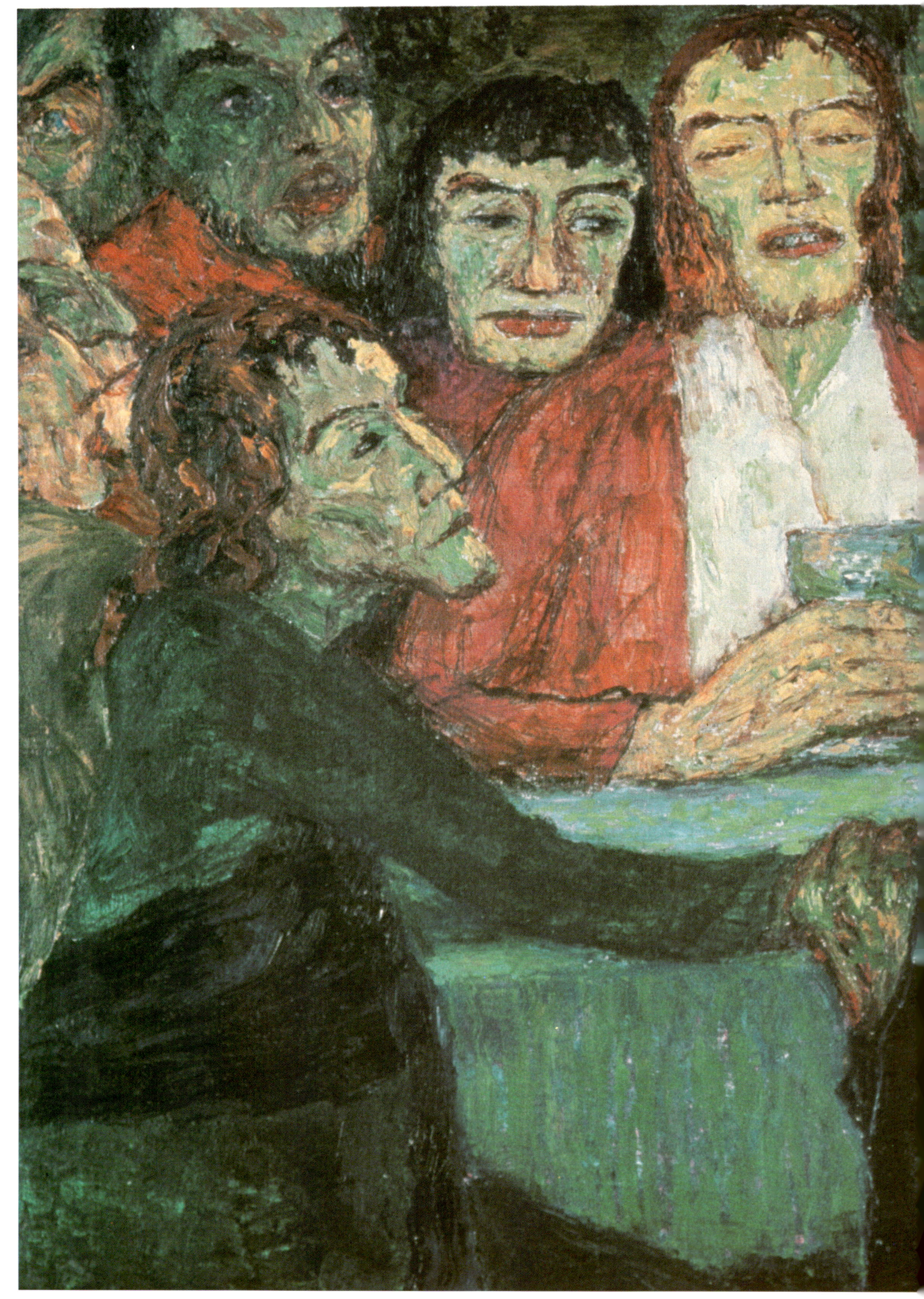

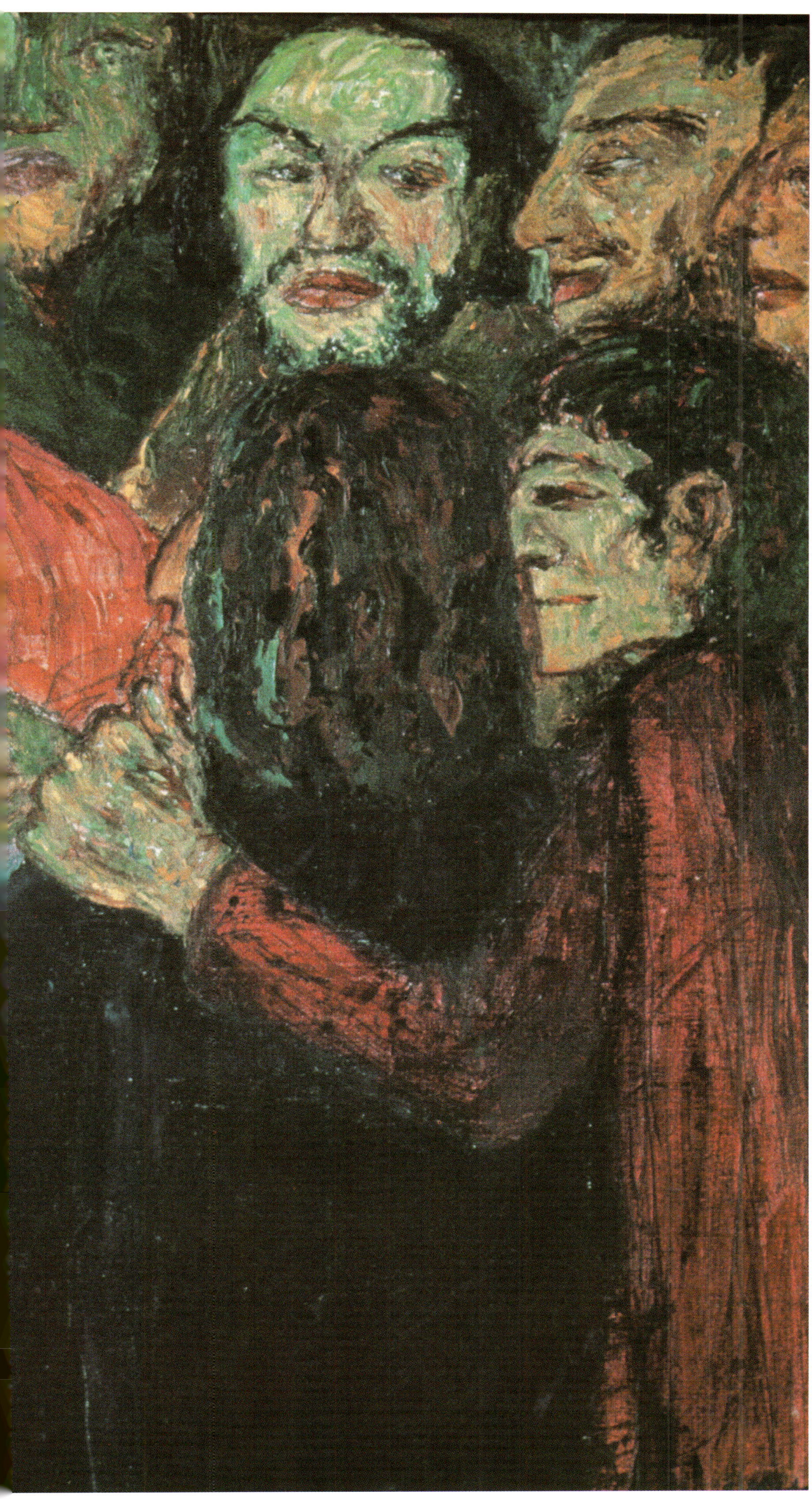

The Last Supper

Jesus' last supper with his disciples was the occasion for the institution of the sacrament called Holy Communion, the Holy Eucharist, or the Lord's Supper. After Jesus announced that one of the 12 disciples would betray him, he blessed the unleavened bread, traditional fare at Passover, and distributed it to his followers, saying, "This is my body." Likewise of the wine, he said, "This is my blood" (Matthew 26:26–27). The ceremonial reenactment of these acts is the central sacrament of Christian worship and has been performed daily for most of the Christian era.

In *The Last Supper* by the 20th-century German Expressionist artist Emil Nolde, the heads of Jesus and his disciples crowd the upper half of the picture, with their hands intersecting in the middle, as if to emphasize the bonds that existed between these men. Nolde has chosen the moment when the Passover Seder is transformed into the first Mass of the Christian era. With great intensity, Jesus holds a vessel of wine and says, "Drink of it, all of you, for this is my blood of the covenant which is poured out for many for the forgiveness of sins. I tell you I shall not drink again of this fruit of the vine until that day when I drink it new with you in my Father's kingdom" (Matthew 26:27–29).

In order to focus the viewer's attention on the figure of Jesus and his sacramental meditation, the artist has drawn upon several devices: he puts Jesus in the middle, he gives the lightest color in the composition to the *tallith* that falls across Jesus' chest, and he enlarges the rabbi's hands well beyond human proportions. Light falls on the table in front of him, as though spilling from his own inner passion. The black forms on either side of Jesus intensify this luminosity. Glancing beyond the Master to the faces of the disciples, one can discover a mixture of emotions—love, wonderment, and acceptance. In the upper-left-hand corner of the painting, one head is turned away from Jesus. It is Judas preparing to leave the room.

The Last Supper
EMIL NOLDE, German, 1867–1956
Stiftung Seebull Ada und Emil Nolde, Neukirchen, Germany. 32½ × 41¾ in.

The Last Supper
MASTER OF THE REREDOS OF THE CHAPEL OF THE CHURCH OF S. FRANCISCO D'EVORA,
Portuguese, 15th century
Museu Nacional de Arte Antiga, Lisbon.

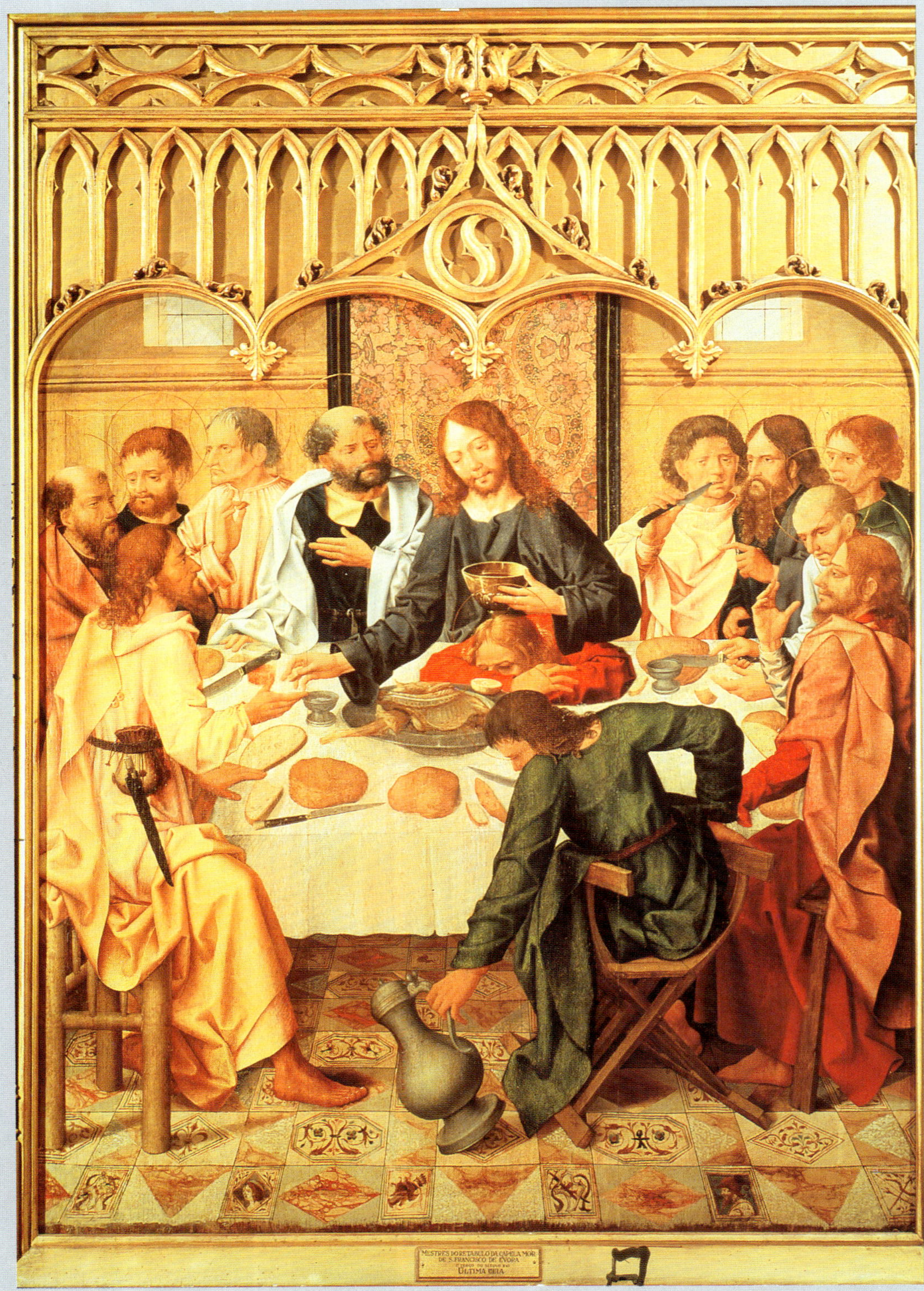

Emil Nolde was born in the far north of Germany and spent much of his long life isolated in the barren wilderness there. A rough and somewhat wild man, he sought to imbue his art with a primitive quality and spirit in the hope that it would speak directly to simple people. This *Last Supper* was painted by him in 1909, a number of years after he had abandoned his career as a drawing teacher and had opted to pursue his work in solitude rather than in association with other avant-garde artists of the day.

Within a Gothic frame of gold, an anonymous artist painted the same scene some 500 years before Nolde, but how differently! He had one moment of the story in mind, described only by John. That moment came at the table when all were seated and Jesus said, "One of you will betray me." John, sitting closest to him—seen here slumped across the table—asked, "Lord, who is it?" Jesus answered that he would identify the man by giving a morsel of bread to him. He proceeded to take a piece of bread, dip it in wine, and give it to Judas (John 13:21–26).

In depicting Jesus' confrontation with Judas, the artist rakes the floor and table so that everything can be seen. He invests considerable imagination in inventing the details of the supper and ascribes a variety of physical types and ages to the disciples. The purse with 30 pieces of silver can be seen strapped to Judas's waist with his dagger dangling beside it. (Judas received the sum for betraying Jesus.) His mouth is clamped shut and his eyes look straight ahead at his former Master. Jesus casts down his eyes reflectively. One disciple picks his teeth with a knife, while his companion points a finger at Judas. Appropriately, everyone has a halo over his head but the betrayer.

▷
DETAIL

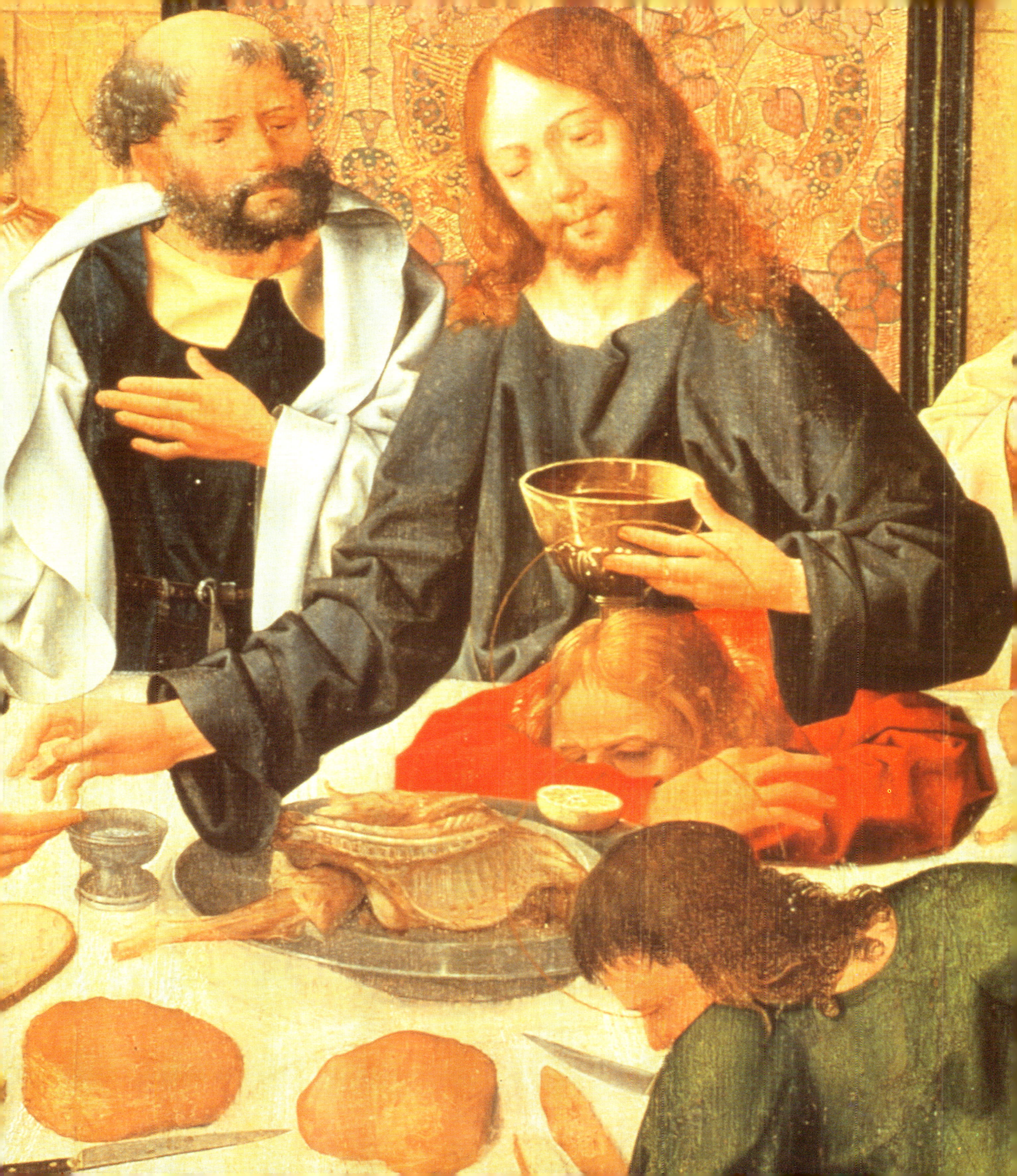

The Garden of Gethsemane

After his last supper with his beloved disciples, Jesus went to the Garden of Gethsemane to pray. It was east of Jerusalem, across the Kidron Valley and the stream called the "black brook" that divided the city from the Mount of Olives. Upon reaching the secluded grove, he took John, Peter, and James aside from the others and asked them to wait and watch. Then, in great distress, he fell to the ground and prayed that his hour of trial would pass. At this point in the story, each Gospel writer added his own details. Luke was the most graphic. He described Jesus as sweating drops of blood, with an angel appearing to strengthen him while the disciples slept on. Luke said they slept out of sorrow, but Jesus was disappointed in them. "The spirit indeed is willing, but the flesh is weak," he told them (Mark 13:48).

In Andrea Mantegna's depiction of this event, Jesus is seen on a ledge, pleading to God that "if it be possible, let this cup pass from me" (Matthew 26:39). Angels hover above him, bearing the instruments that will soon cause him to suffer—a column for scourging and the iron of crucifixion. Meanwhile the disciples sleep quite deeply upon their rocky resting places. Opposite Jesus on the right is Judas leading a group of Roman soldiers to the garden in order to arrest Jesus, as Judas was paid to do.

Mantegna has painted this low moment in Jesus' life with so much visual information, based on his passion for archaeology, that he convinces viewers that he knew exactly where the Garden of Gethsemane was. With steely precision, as though chiseled of pink granite, he provides a mystical setting for Jesus' prayer of agony. But in spite of all his attention to geography, the artist changes the hour, making it early evening instead of night so that all his details can be read.

Mantegna was the most precocious artist of the early years of the Renaissance in Italy. He could apply the newly invented visual illusions of perspective and foreshortening to a painting with greater mastery than any of his contemporaries. This is one of his early works, and it finds its depth and its soul in a literal telling of the Bible story, a tribute to the power of the word. Without a painting like this *Agony in the Garden*, or others that Mantegna executed during his long career, one's visual memory for the settings and details of the critical moments in Jesus' life would be immensely impoverished.

The Agony in the Garden
ANDREA MANTEGNA, Italian ca. 1431–1506
National Gallery, London. Wood panel. 24¼ × 31½ in.

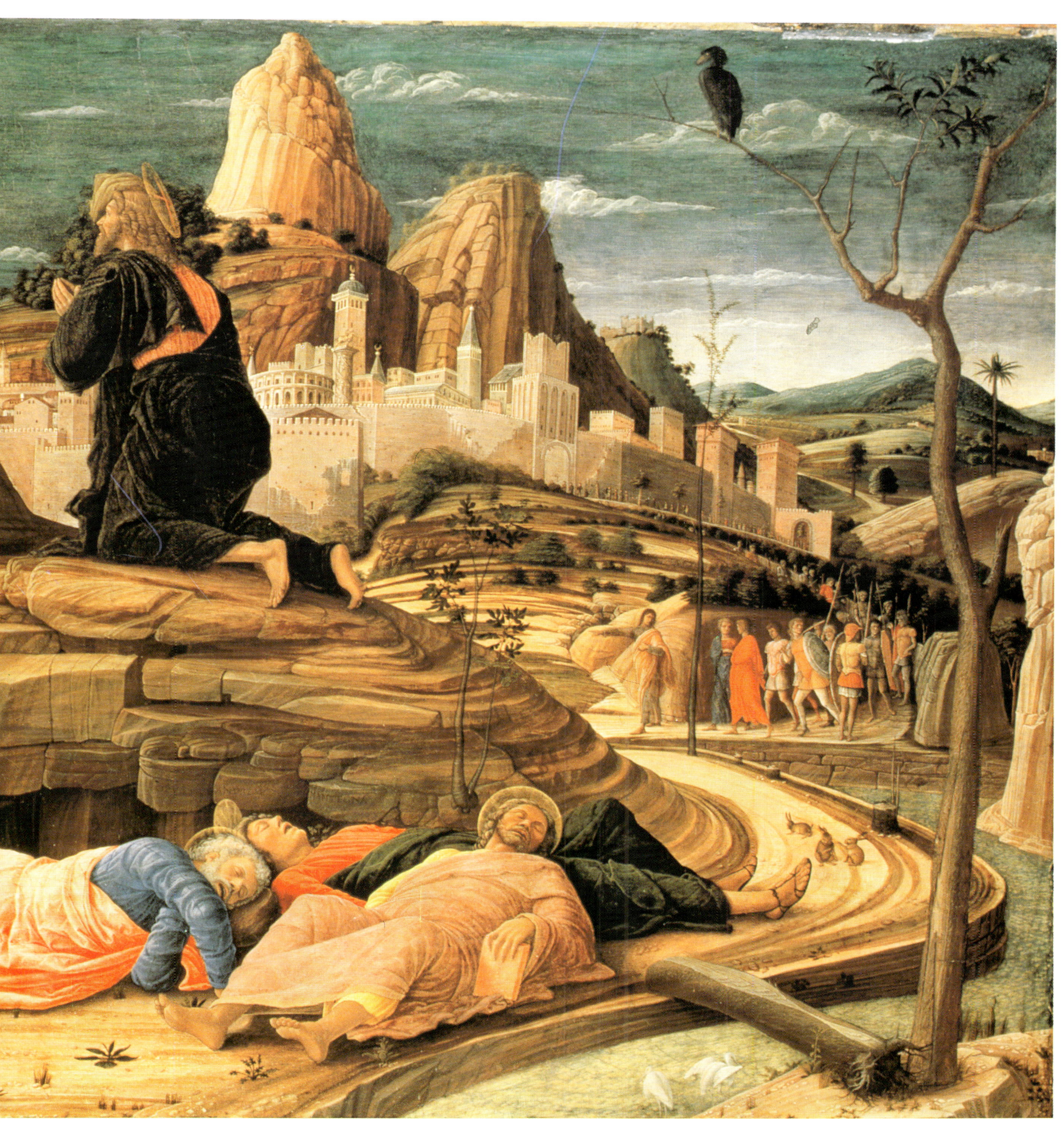

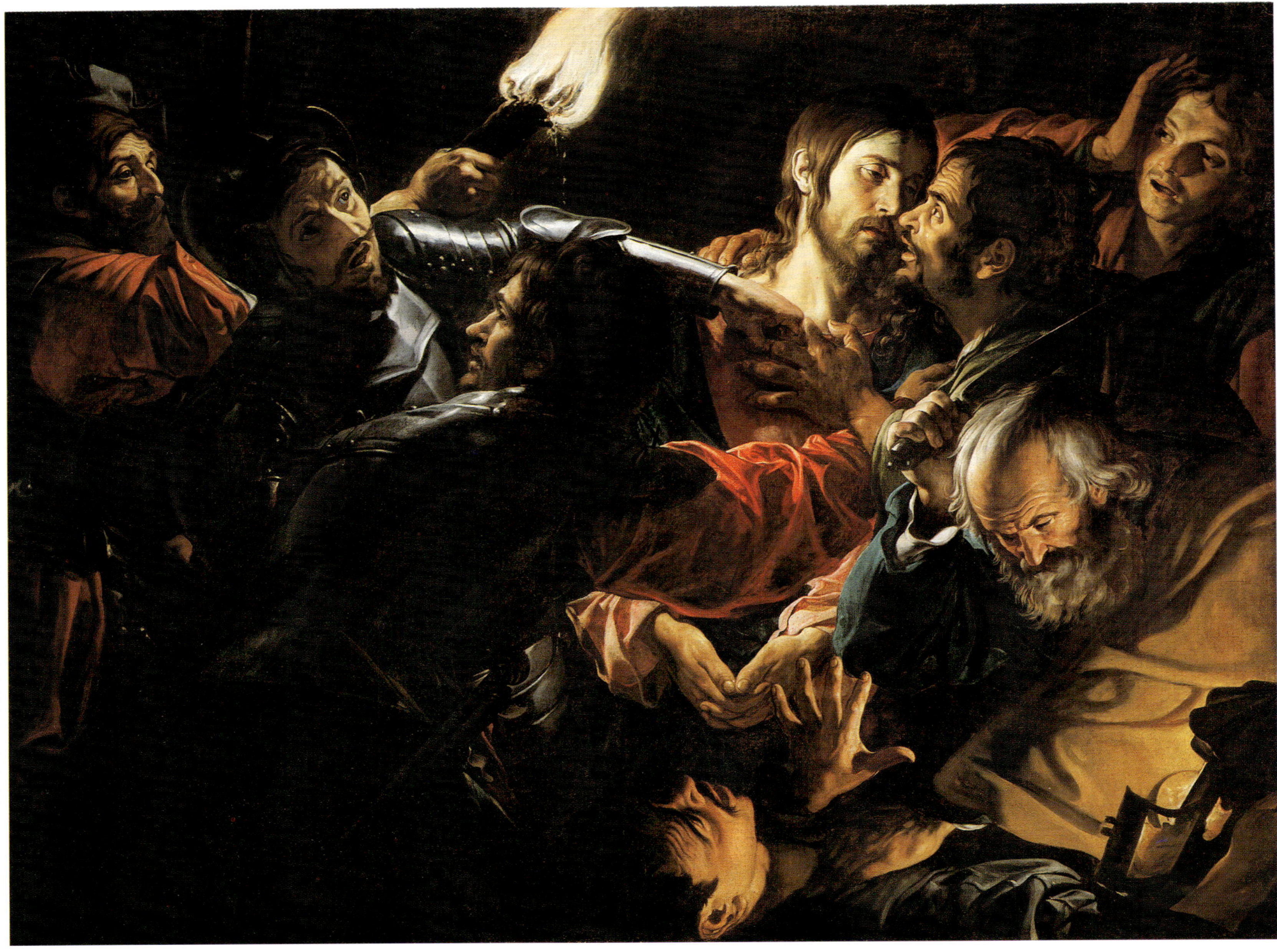

The Taking of Christ
VALENTIN DE BOULOGNE, French, 1591–1632
Juliana Cheney Edwards Collection, Museum of Fine Arts, Boston. Oil on canvas. 58 × 77 in.

The Taking of Christ

Judas had agreed on a sign with the chief priests and their soldiers: "The one I shall kiss is the man; seize him" (Matthew 26:48). Valentin de Boulogne, a French artist who worked in Rome, rushes the viewer into the scene of Christ's betrayal. He does not bother to depict Gethsemane, the site of Jesus' arrest; he is interested in the interior lives of his subjects. With a perspective from above and close in, he allows the viewer to study the faces and emotions of the participants in this pivotal moment in Jesus' life.

The biblical account of the arrest of Christ reported that Peter cut off the ear of Malchus, a slave of the high priest. Valentin shows the angered fisherman attacking the servant in a vain attempt to save his teacher from his captors. Beyond them, Jesus turns his head from the sharp light and acrid smell of a torch that is held close to him to make the identification certain. His face meets that of Judas almost nose to nose, and the betrayer seems frightened by the enormity of what he has wrought.

The surging of the mob is expressed in the back and forth cadence of the figures. Heads, arms, and hands are scattered across the entire surface of the painting in a visual cacophony. This noisy scene, rising up around the quiet and confrontational heads of Jesus and Judas, heightens the drama that ended Jesus' last hours of freedom. According to the Scriptures, Jesus accused his captors of treating him like a common robber. Indeed, Valentin de Boulogne gives the scene the atmosphere of a lynching.

The Denial of St. Peter

At the Last Supper, Jesus told Peter that before the night was over he would deny him three times. And indeed it came to pass. First, during Jesus' trial, he denied knowing his Master to the maid of one of the high priests. Later, he was questioned about being at Gethsemane; again he denied it, and the cock crowed. When the bystanders asked him if he was not one of Jesus' men, he once more swore that he was not. The cock crowed again. Then Peter remembered what Jesus had told him earlier and "wept bitterly" (Matthew 26:75; Mark 14:72).

In *The Denial of St. Peter*, Hendrik Terbrugghen shields Peter from the great shame the Gospel writer imputed to him, by assigning him a place in the background. He is caught there in embarrassment by the earnest wench in the foreground, clearly bringing deep sadness to Jesus, who overhears him from his place across the canvas where he is on trial. These great figures of Christian history are made subsidiary to anonymous soldiers who warm themselves by the fire, the questioning maidservant, and the fire itself. Its crackling warmth was the only comforting note mentioned by the Gospel writers in relation to the trial of Jesus.

This great Dutch master learned dramatic light effects in Italy, drawing inspiration from the work of Caravaggio. Terbrugghen selected stories which allowed him to light an entire scene from the glow of a single flame. Sometimes he had to contrive these settings to achieve this effect, but in *The Denial of St. Peter*, the Bible conveniently furnished him a legitimate subject. It must have taken a Dutchman of great restraint not to show the rooster, so fond were they of barnyard fowl as decorative accessories in their paintings. But, true to the spirit of Caravaggio, Terbrugghen focuses on one salient instant, Peter's first denial, which came before the cock sounded.

Denial of St. Peter
HENDRIK TERBRUGGHEN, Dutch, 1588–1629
Charles H. and Mary F.S. Worcester Collection. Art

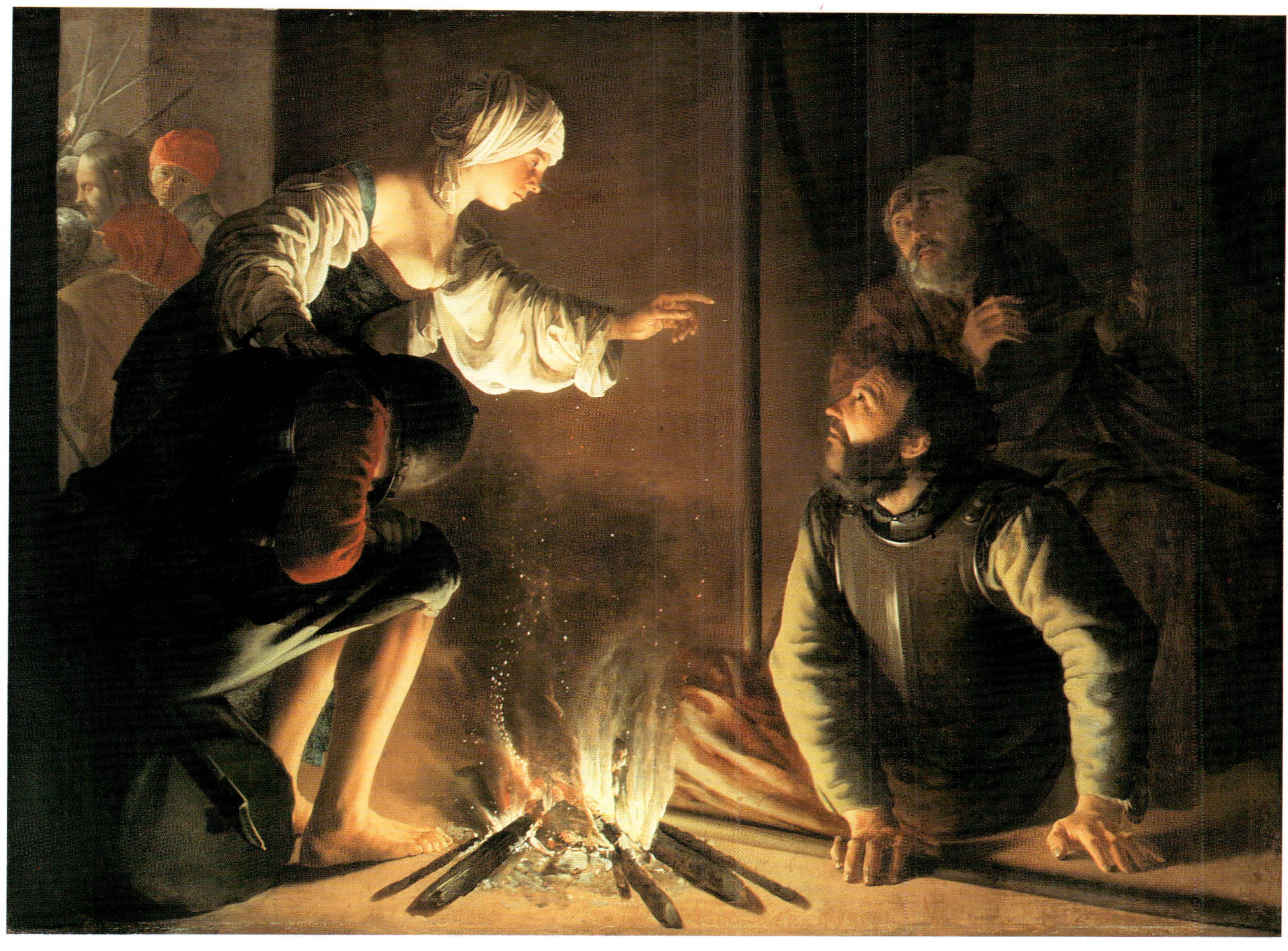

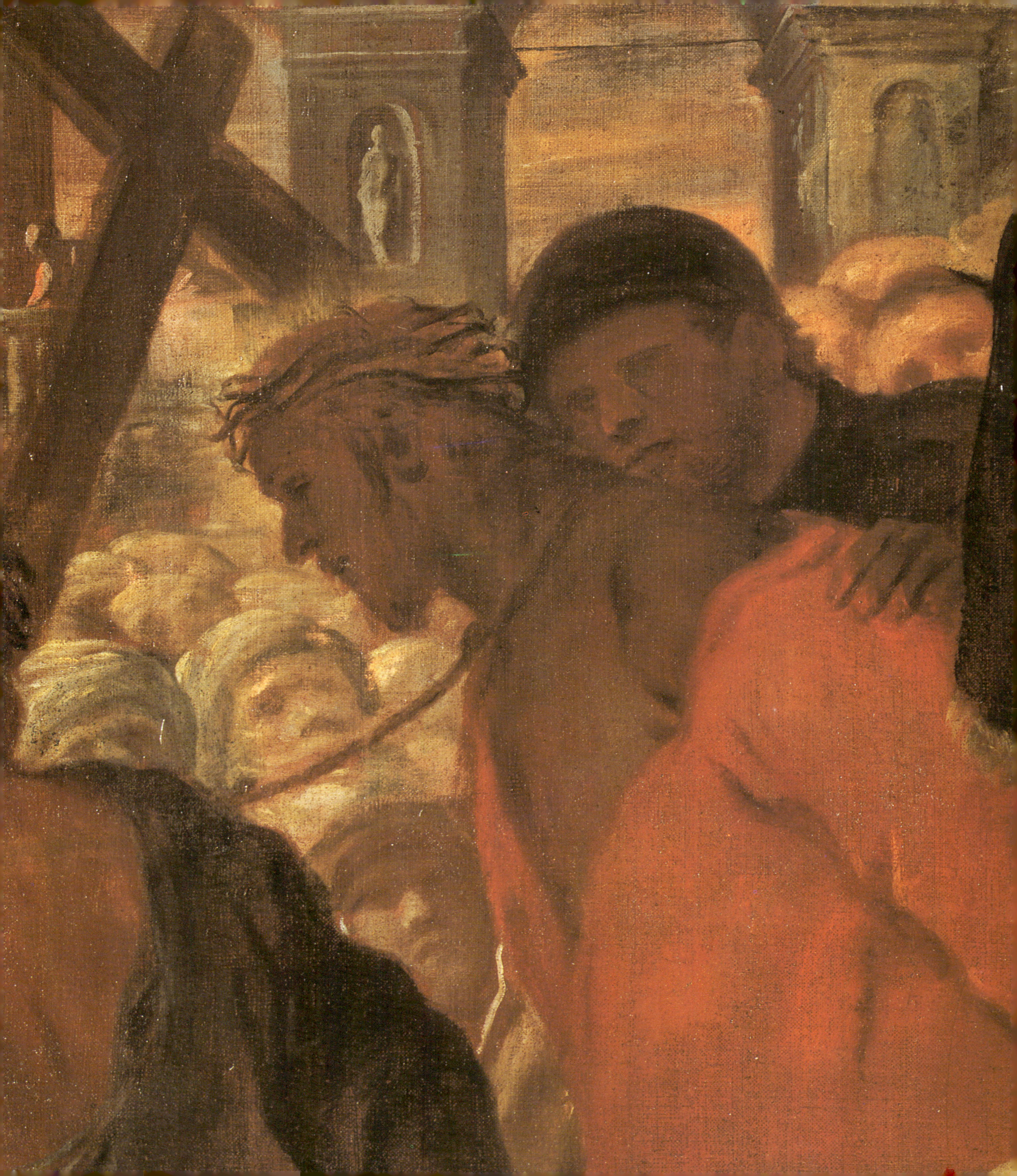

Pilate Washing His Hands

The New Testament viewed Pilate as bloody, vacillating, intimidated by Jesus, and frightened by the rabbi's claim to godhead. But by the second century, Tertullian, the Church Father, described Pilate as "Christian before his own conscience," and in the Coptic church he is venerated as a saint.

Mattia Preti shows him as a powerful politician, boldly outstaring the populace at what was in retrospect the peak moment of his career, his decision in the case of the people vs. Jesus of Nazareth. Clearly the people wanted Jesus to be crucified, but Pilate asked, "Why, what evil has he done?" Soon, however, he tired of this factional dispute among the Jews, called for water and washed his hands of the affair. "I am innocent of this man's blood," he told the crowd, and the populace yelled back, "His blood be on us and on our children" (Matthew 27: 22–25).

If ever there was an instinct in art for capturing the kernel of a story through body language, Mattia Preti has it. The pose of this petty governor of one of Rome's lesser colonies clearly reveals Pilate's pride in his statecraft. He has bowed to the will of the people, yet as governor he has remained above the petty squabbles of his charges. Indeed, he is quite literally above it all, for the artist has had the effrontery to make the viewer part of the mob looking up at Pontius Pilate. Meanwhile, in the lower left portion of the painting, Jesus is being taken away. He is robed in red, wearing a crown of thorns, led by a noose around his neck, his cross awaiting him.

Three figures react as the viewer might. Closest is the old man in armor, impressed by the governor's finesse but recognizing that his sincerity is posed. The young servants, however, seem confused. The black youth wonders why Pilate washes his hands in public, not understanding the man's wiles. The maidservant looks at Jesus with great curiosity. Without her gaze, the condemned man might go unnoticed. So successful was Pilate's performance, that he is remembered in history as much for it as for authorizing the execution of Jesus.

Painting huge frescoes gave Preti a feel for the monumental that was uncommon, even in an age in which bombast and ostentation were the artist's stock-in-trade. He had great success in Naples after the plague had wiped out virtually every other artist there, but he preferred the quiet of Malta, where he lived the last 38 years of his life.

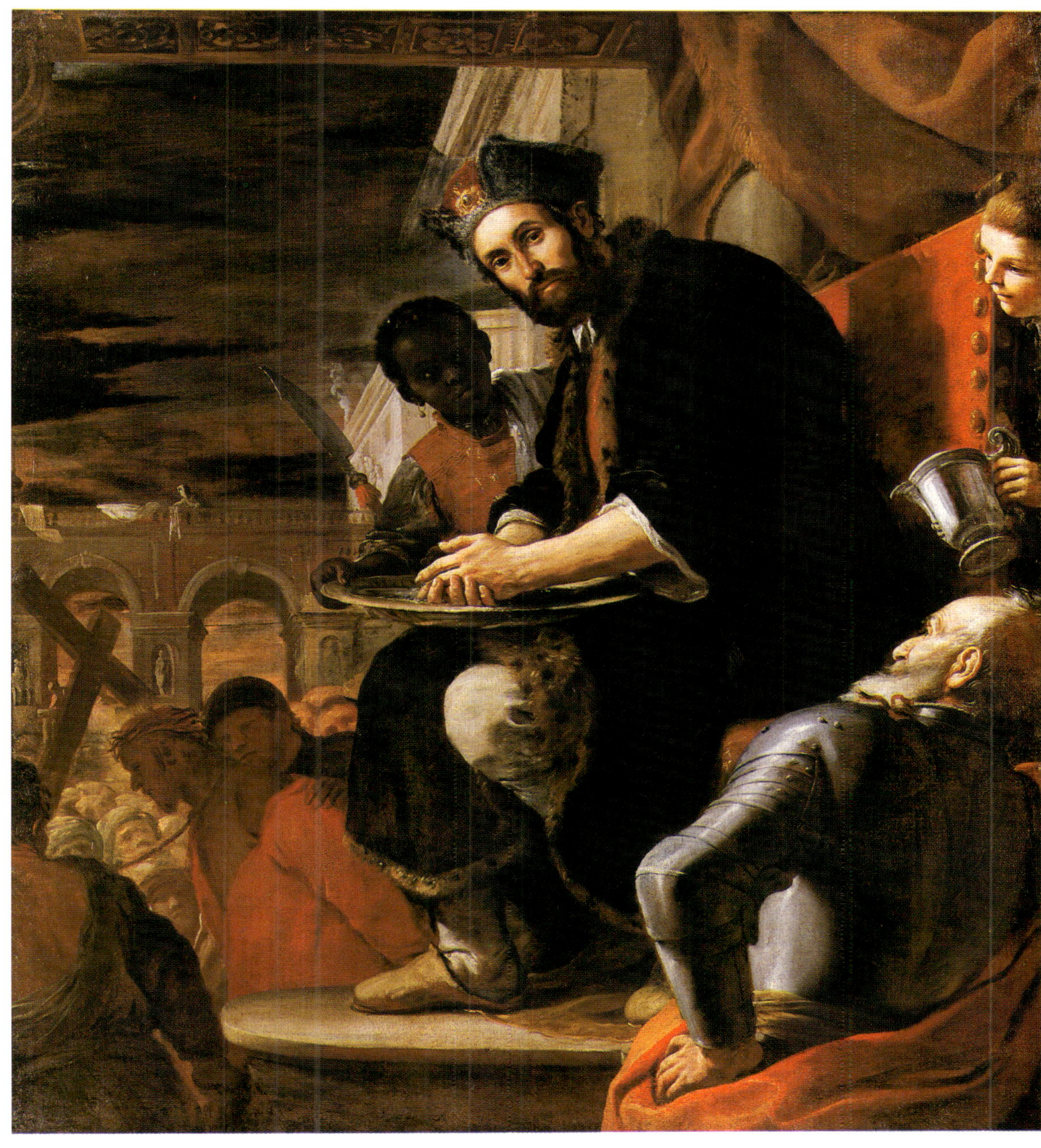

Pilate Washing His Hands

MATTIA PRETI, Italian, 1613–1699

Metropolitan Museum of Art, New York. Purchase, Gift of J. Pierpont Morgan and Bequest of Helena W. Charlton, by exchange, Gwynne Andrews, Marquand, and Rogers Funds, Victor Wilbour Memorial Fund, The Alfred N. Punnett Endowment Fund, and funds from various donors, 1978. (1978.402) Oil on canvas. 81⅛ × 72¾ in.

◁
DETAIL

Christ and the High Priest
GEORGES ROUAULT, French, 1871–1958
The Phillips Collection, Washington, DC.
Oil on canvas. $18\frac{7}{8} \times 12\frac{7}{8}$ in.

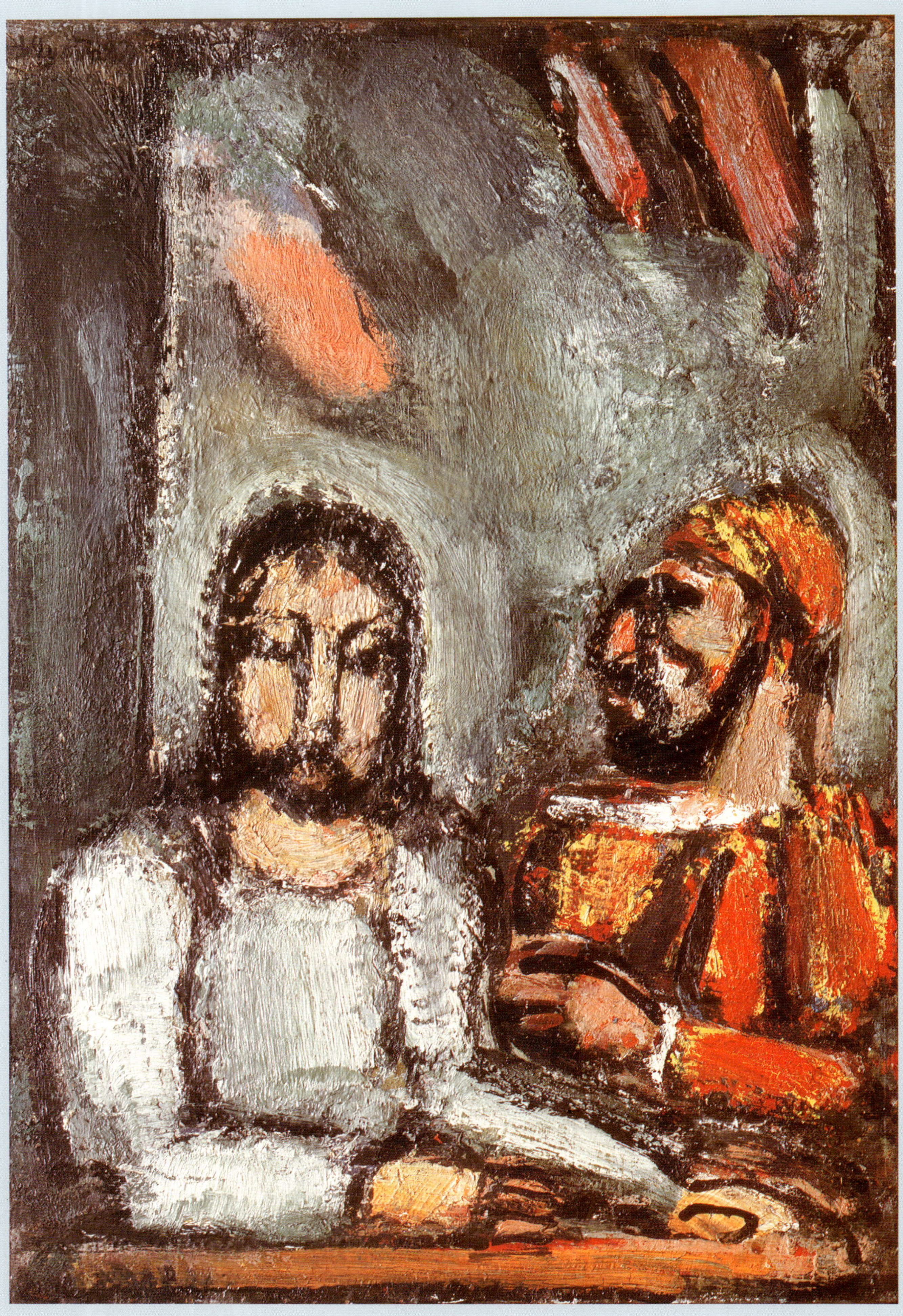

Christ and the High Priest

After one glance at *Christ and the High Priest*, it is clear that Georges Rouault was not interested in the details of Jesus' trial before Caiaphas, the high priest. He shows only two figures, and a sky blotched with blood red. The accuser is in profile, the equivalent in art to second-person singular in grammar; though his eyes are lowered, Jesus faces forward, the equivalent of first-person singular. By this subtle device, Rouault transfers the question of Jesus' guilt or innocence from Caiaphas to the viewers, as though only they are capable of judgment.

Rouault was drawn to outcasts as his subjects. He saw clowns and prostitutes as Christ figures, rejected and scorned by men, but used by them at the same time. Judges were the only subjects he treated with ridicule; depictions of all others were sympathetic and deeply empathetic. Rouault was a devout Roman Catholic, yet the lack of specificity in his paintings and prints causes them to transcend sectarianism and speak to universal emotions.

The artist did not like to give up his works; he never considered them finished. Year after year, he added layer upon layer of paint to a canvas, building up the bold brushwork to an enamel-like finish. At one time, frustrated that he had contracted all of his work to one dealer who demanded paintings to sell, Rouault burned every canvas in his studio in a great bonfire.

The intensity of his working method created a body of icons that are counted by many as the greatest religious paintings of the 20th century. Deeply luminous, they move viewers in much the same way as the stained glass of France's cathedrals. Georges Rouault was the spiritual heir to those magnificent Gothic glassworks. But he was also a modernist. He eschewed the niceties of drawing, correct proportions, and realistic color, for forms that are flat and quickly read, and colors that are strong and direct. Stylistically, he managed to be a figure of his time, but in his religious fervor he was removed from the doubters of the modern age. Hundreds of years from now, historians may find the spiritual core of the 20th century in paintings like this one.

The Mocking of Christ

Between the time of his arrest and his crucifixion, Jesus was mocked three times, first in the house of the high priest, then by Herod, and finally in the praetorium, the fortress that served as Pilate's residence when the governor was in Jerusalem. There, the entire Roman battalion stripped Jesus, dressed him as a king with a crown of thorns, spat on him, struck him, and marched him to Golgotha. The soldiers and their cruel taunts were portrayed by Paul-Gustave Doré and Edouard Manet in the last third of the 19th century.

It is interesting that these two artists painted the same biblical subject within only a few years of one another. Indeed, Doré and Manet shared the same years of birth and death, but their careers were not parallel. Doré made his fame as an illustrator of books, and by 1865 had produced engravings for the entire Bible. This depiction was one of his favorites and he copied the head of Jesus from it numerous times. Manet became one of the most important avant-garde artists of his day and an inspiration to the Impressionists. After painting *Christ Mocked*, he never took up a religious subject again.

At the time Manet painted this work, he was using his art as a vehicle for social criticism. In 1865 he exhibited *Christ Mocked* alongside *Olympia*, a scandalous portrait of a courtesan. In Manet's Paris, courtesans were celebrities and lived and dressed better than the middle classes could. Manet saw both the mocking of Christ and the acceptance of prostitutes as cultural benchmarks, symptoms of the power of ignorance. By exhibiting this work with *Olympia*, he was also following an art-historical precedent, for it was said that Titian's famous *Venus of Urbino*, on which *Olympia* was based, was exhibited in the 16th century next to a painting of Jesus being tormented by his captors.

One of the mockers in Doré's painting is on his knees, saying, "Hail, king of the Jews" (Matthew 27:29). The forbearance and dignity of the condemned man seem to impress the half-naked soldier to the left, for he pauses as though questioning what he is doing. The man in the yellow turban in Manet's scene looks like Georges Clemenceau, whose portrait Manet painted twice in 1865, the same year he painted *Christ Mocked*. The statesman looks directly at the viewer, a sign that, though he is part of the scene, he is there to let the viewer participate in a special way; his look is an invitation to enter the painting. There is no indication that there ever was enmity between the artist and the future prime minister of France, so perhaps Manet is saying that Clemenceau represents everybody. All people are guilty, at one time or another, of not knowing what they are doing.

FOLLOWING PAGES

LEFT
The Mocking of Christ
PAUL-GUSTAVE DORÉ, French, 1832–1883
The Toledo Museum of Art, Ohio. Gift of Rene Gimpel. Oil on canvas. 48¾ × 38⅝ in.

RIGHT
Christ Mocked
EDOUARD MANET, French, 1832–1883
Gift of James Deering, Art Institute of Chicago. Oil on canvas. 74⅞ × 58⅜ in.

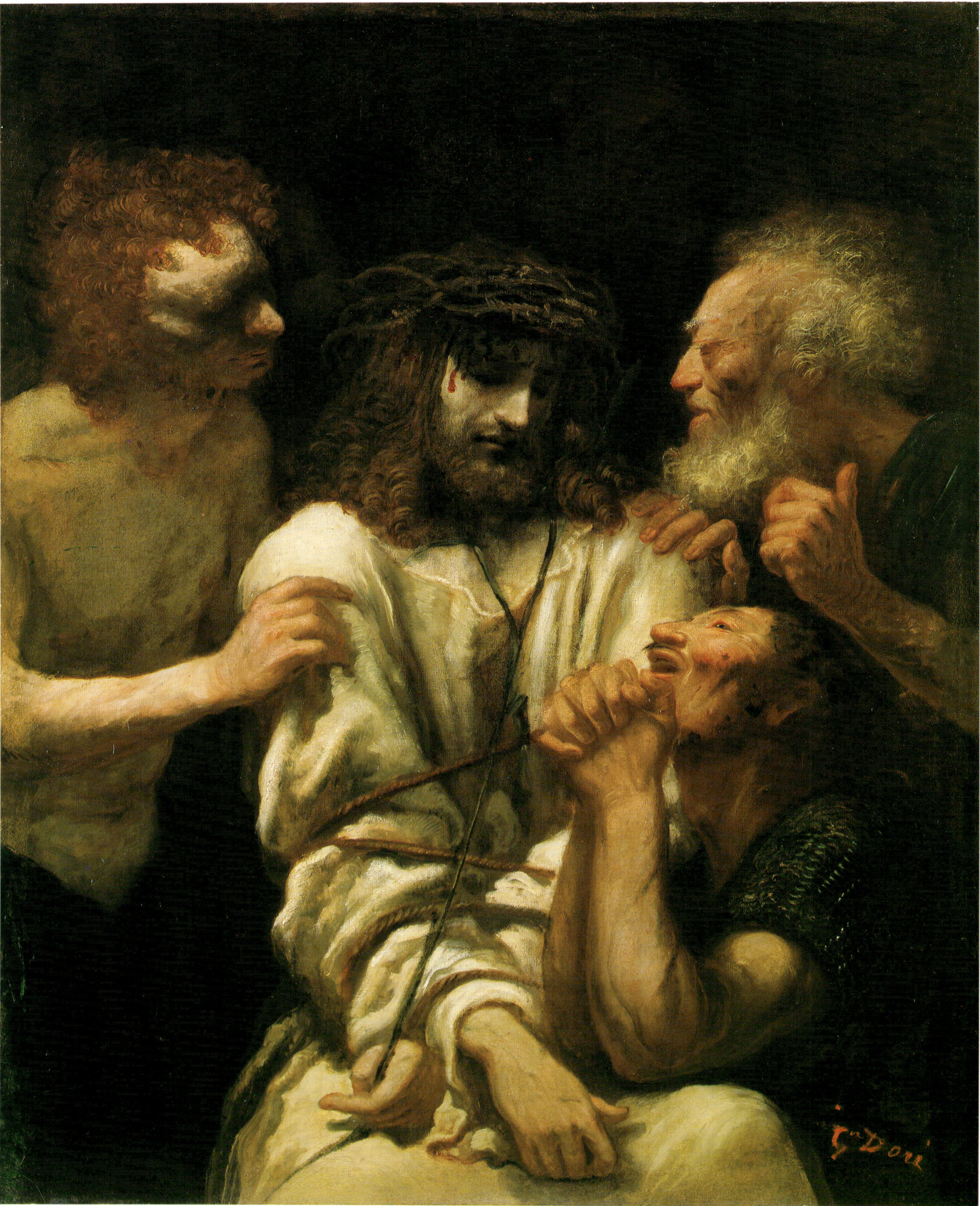

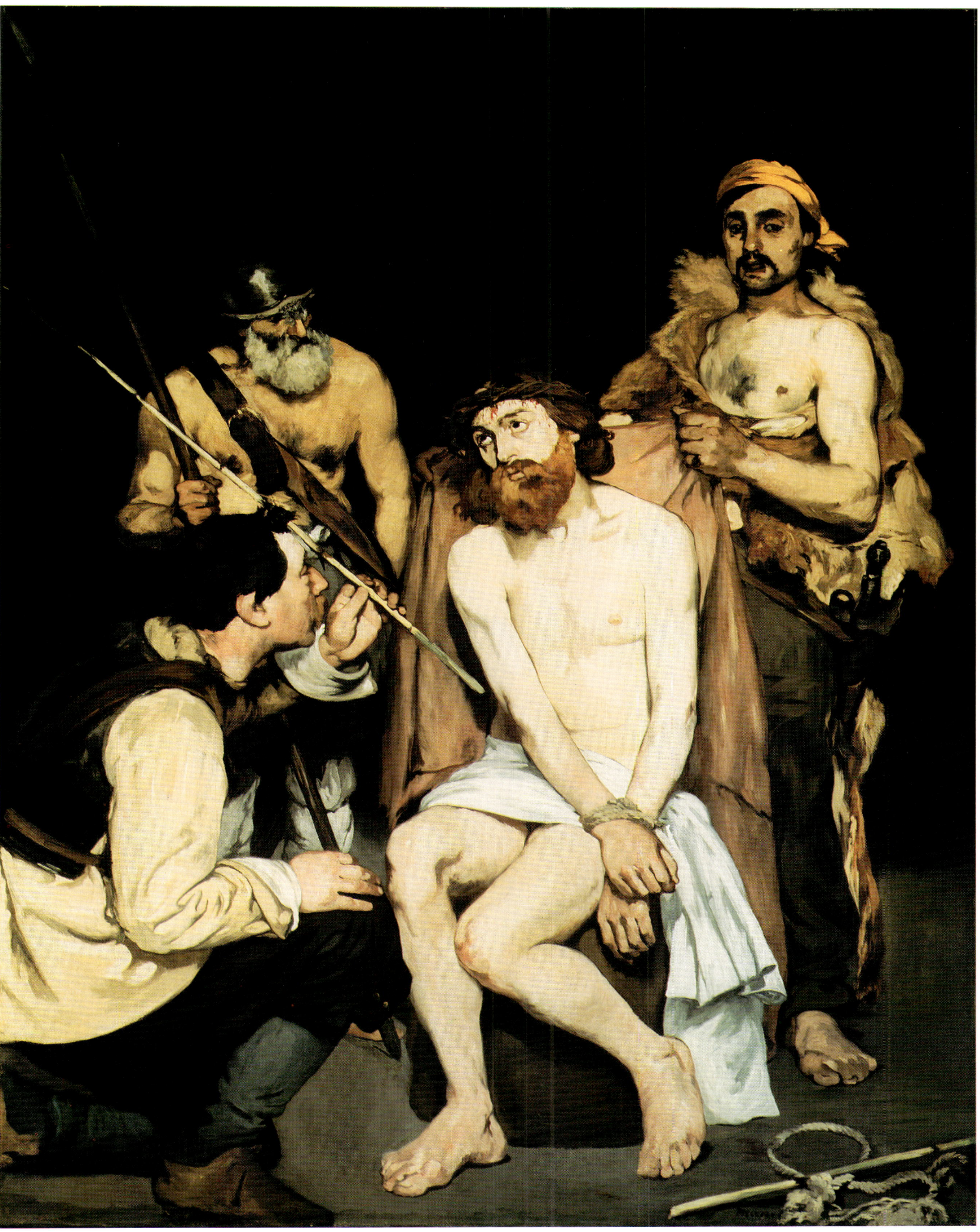

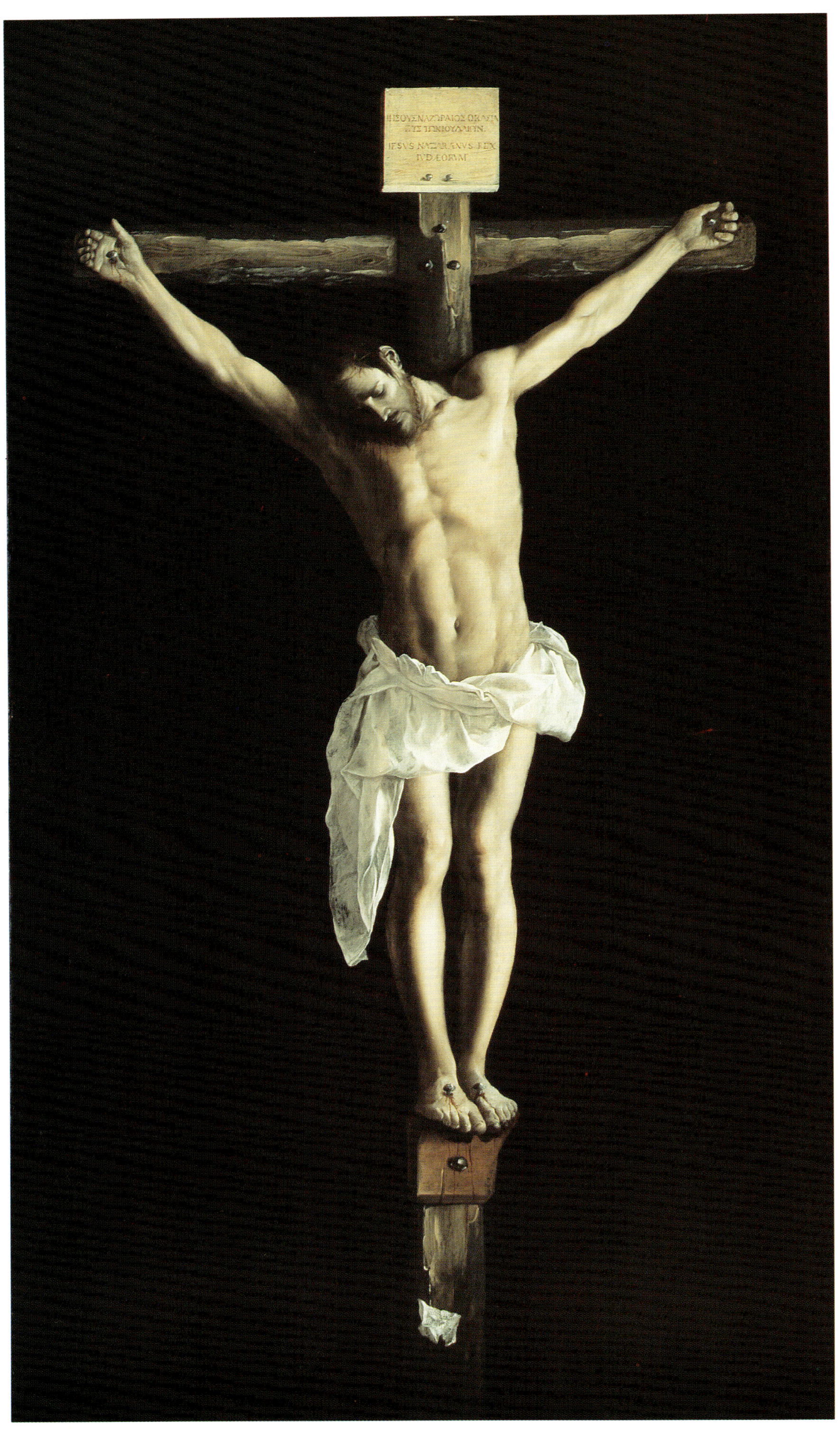

Christ on the Cross

The history of art is so rich with masterpieces covering Jesus' final trials, suffering, and death that it is easy to forget how quickly these events happened. In fact, he was arrested on a Thursday night after supper and executed within 12 hours. If any one incident from that Maundy Thursday and Good Friday has been frozen in time, it is the moment when Jesus hung in death upon the cross.

The painting by Francisco de Zurbarán is one of the quintessential depictions of the crucified Savior and the model for three-dimensional crucifixes that hang in churches, chapels, and homes of the pious throughout the world. So familiar is it that it takes a special effort to see it anew, as though for the first time. In a dimly lit room, the black background disappears and one sees only the wood, flesh, and the white accents of the loincloth, the sign at the top of the cross, and the small piece of paper at the bottom. The stringency of the artist purifies the viewer's mind and focuses it on the peace that Jesus found in death.

As important as the death of Jesus is to Christian theology, the crucifix did not acquire a place in the art and piety of the faithful until the seventh century. Prior to that, the triumphant Christ, clothed in white against the cross, free from the nails and blood of his crucifixion, was the most common image. The form of the dead Christ, so familiar today, first appeared in art around 980 and became standard by the mid-13th century. The devotional literature that centers on the cross, and dates as far back as the beginning of the third century, leads the pious to suffer with Jesus. Savonarola, the

Christ on the Cross
FRANCISCO DE ZURBARÁN, Spanish, 1598–1664
Robert Alexander Waller Memorial Fund, Art Institute of Chicago. Oil on canvas. 74¾ × 58¼ in.

great Italian evangelist and reformer, summed up this attitude in a brief devotion, written in 1498: "I am nailed to the cross with Christ; nevertheless, I live; yet not I, but Christ liveth in me."

The agonizingly realistic painting by the German master Albrecht Altdorfer is more journalistic than meditative in its effect. As a record of an event, however, it present a few unusual details. The mother of Jesus has collapsed to the ground in exhaustion and sits like a peasant woman, monumental and removed from others in the scene. John touches her shoulder, but he is also lost in his own frenzied grief. Kneeling at the foot of the cross, a place often reserved for her in art, is Mary Magdalene. Her yellow dress, covered head, and long, plaited blond hair are highly unusual for she ordinarily is shown with dark hair spilling to the ground, covering her tearful face, and her dress is frequently red, a reminder of her former life as a prostitute. Altdorfer Germanized her and placed her imploring body in such a way as to lead the viewer into the scene and to serve as a model for devotion. Leaning against the cross of one of the thieves who died with Jesus is a tall man holding a lance. With it, he has delivered the final wound to the side of Jesus and now has become reflective.

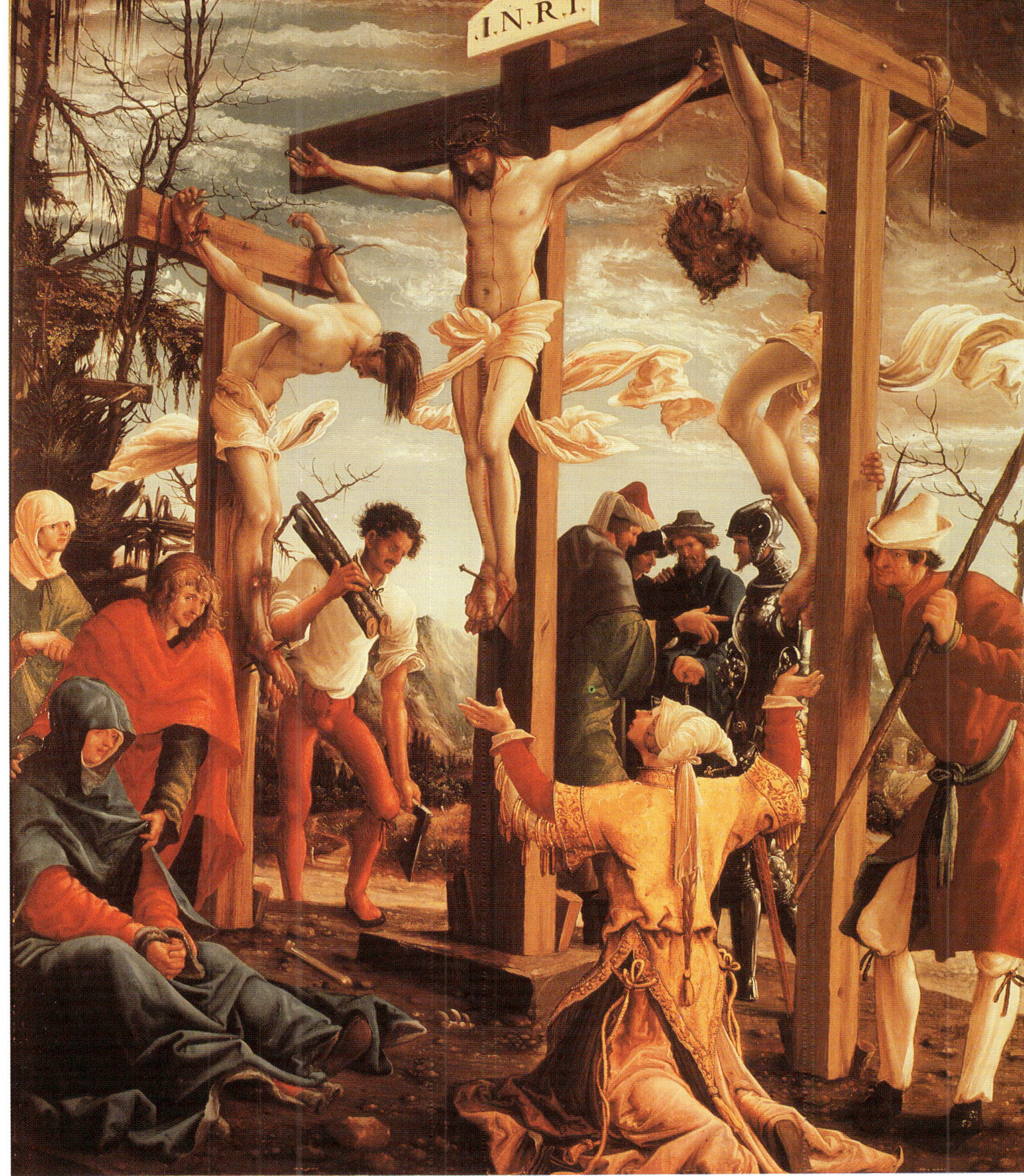

Crucifixion

ALBRECHT ALTDORFER, German, ca. 1489–1538

Monastery Church of St. Florian, Linz, Austria.
Wood panel. 44½ × 37½ in.

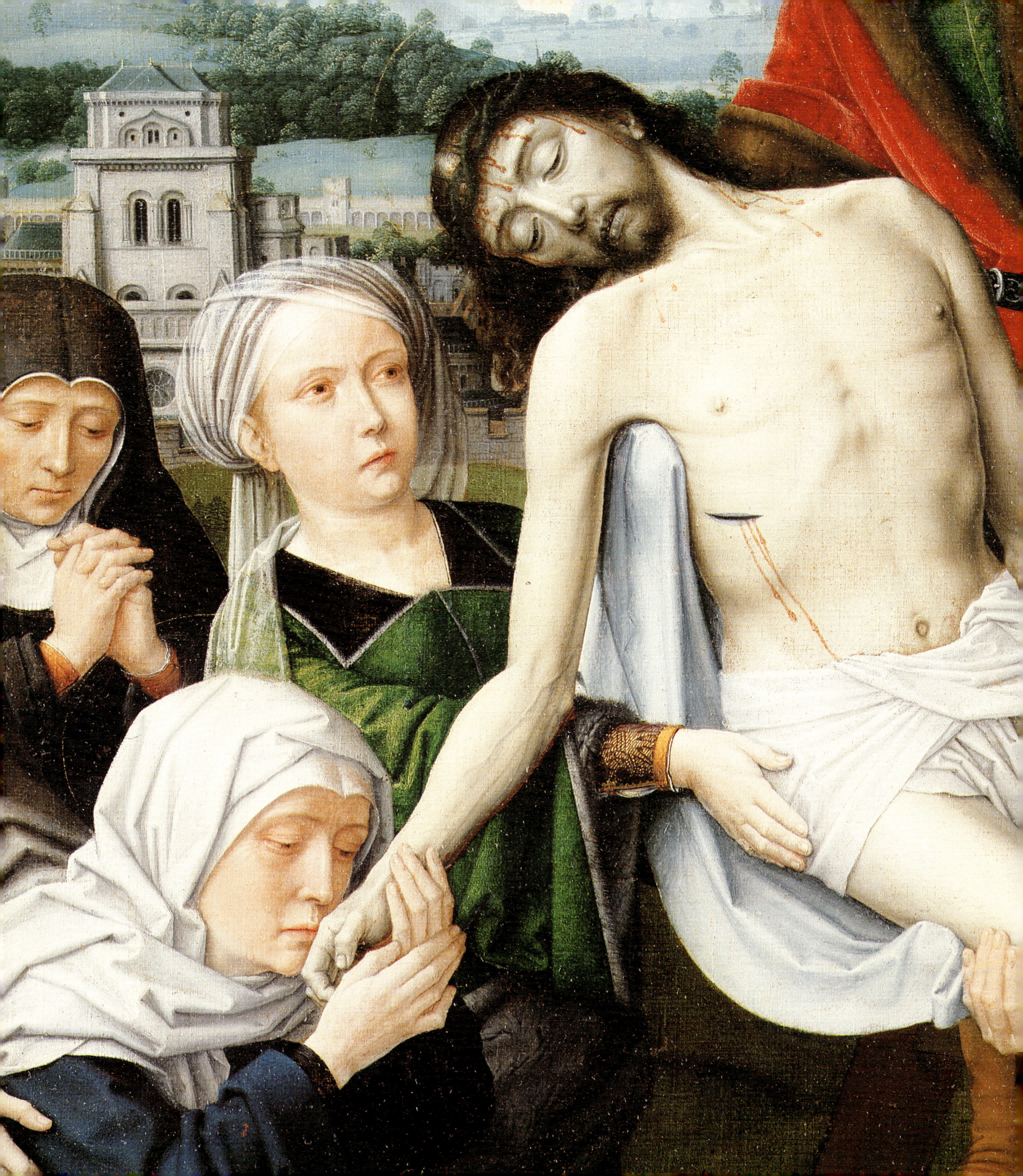

The Deposition

In the history of art, the tragic moments following Jesus' death have been portrayed time and again, giving one an almost freeze-frame sense of these intimate and moving events. The first of these was Jesus' *descent from the cross*, or *deposition*. Next came the *lamentation*, when his body lay at the foot of the cross or near the mouth of the tomb as his family and followers wept over it. The *pieta*, that more intimate scene where the corpse lay across the lap of Mary, is a variation on the *lamentation*. Then came the *entombment*, in which Jesus was buried.

Ordinarily, the executioners would have brought the corpse to the deceased's family, but Jesus died late in the afternoon on a Friday, so there was not time for the Jewish officials to perform their duties before the Sabbath's start at sundown. Joseph of Arimathea, a wealthy, prominent citizen and a secret follower of Jesus, risked everything by going to Pilate for permission to remove his Lord from the cross and to bury him in his own tomb before night. The plan was to return on Sunday morning after the Sabbath, to complete the burial.

This *Deposition* by Gerard David has a strange silence to it. All the figures, save the Virgin Mary, who kisses the hand of Jesus, are somewhat tentative in their actions and expressions. Joseph of Arimathea, the man in purple nearest the foot of the cross, is helped by Nicodemus, a Pharisee who became a disciple of Jesus. Nicodemus wears a green turban, and his red tunic serves to emphasize the bloodlessness of the corpse which is being handed down like a precious porcelain sculpture. The color of the body, so recently alive, has now become as white as the skull and bones that are scattered on the ground. Perhaps that is why the place of the crucifixion was called Golgotha, which means "the place of a skull." Curiously, of the seven mourners here, Joseph seems the most detached, even though it is he who receives the body of Jesus from the cross.

The reflective, almost ceremonial style of Gerard David dominated the art of Bruges for almost 25 years until his death in 1523. He was the last great artist of that city of artists. The dislocations of the Protestant Reformation, the Peasants' War, and the sack of Rome by the mercenaries of the Holy Roman Empire forever ended the taste of the public for an art so sober and reserved.

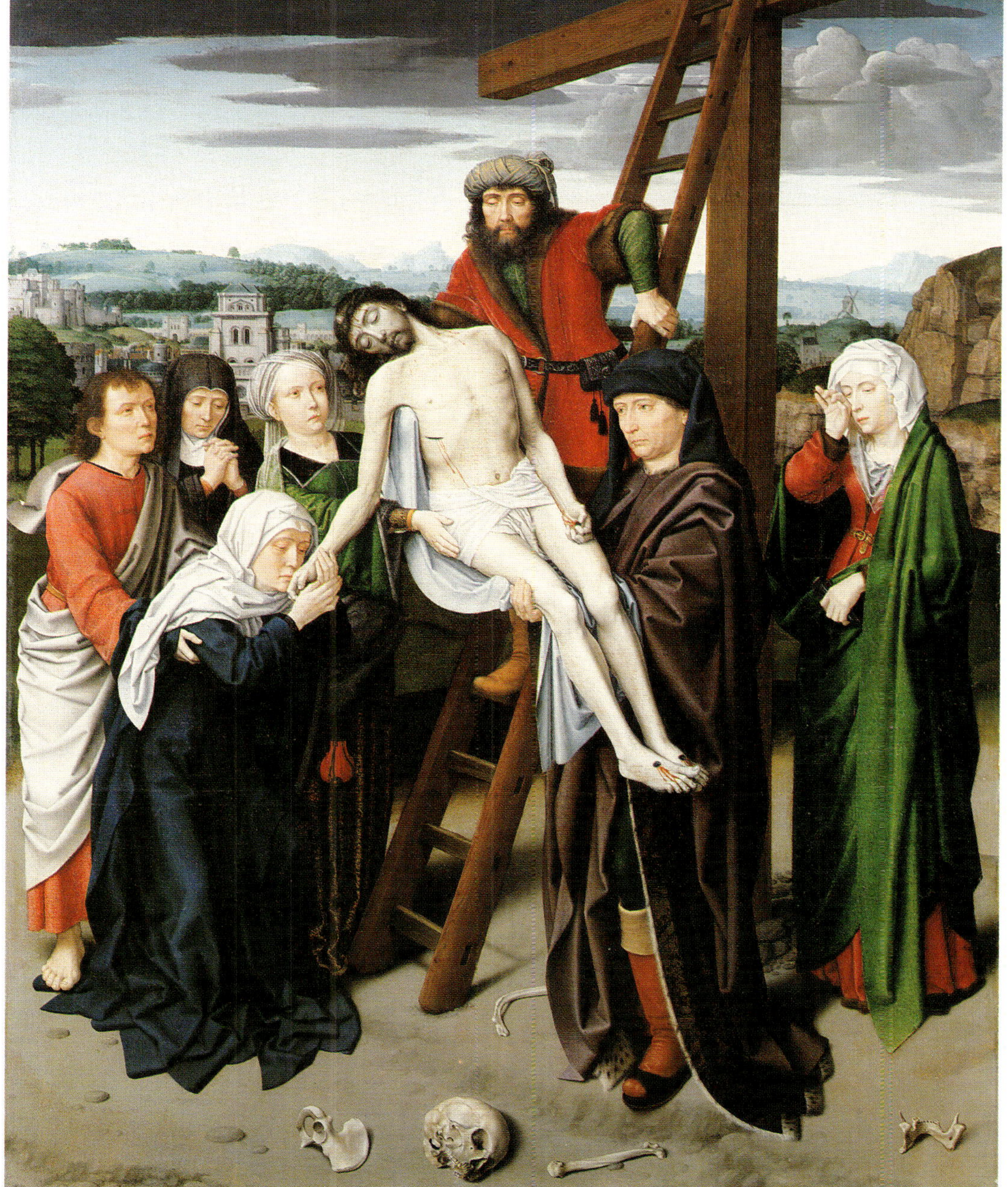

The Deposition

GERARD DAVID, Flemish, active 1484–1523

The Frick Collection, New York. Copyright the Frick Collection, New York. Oil on canvas. 56⅛ × 44¼ in.

◁
DETAIL

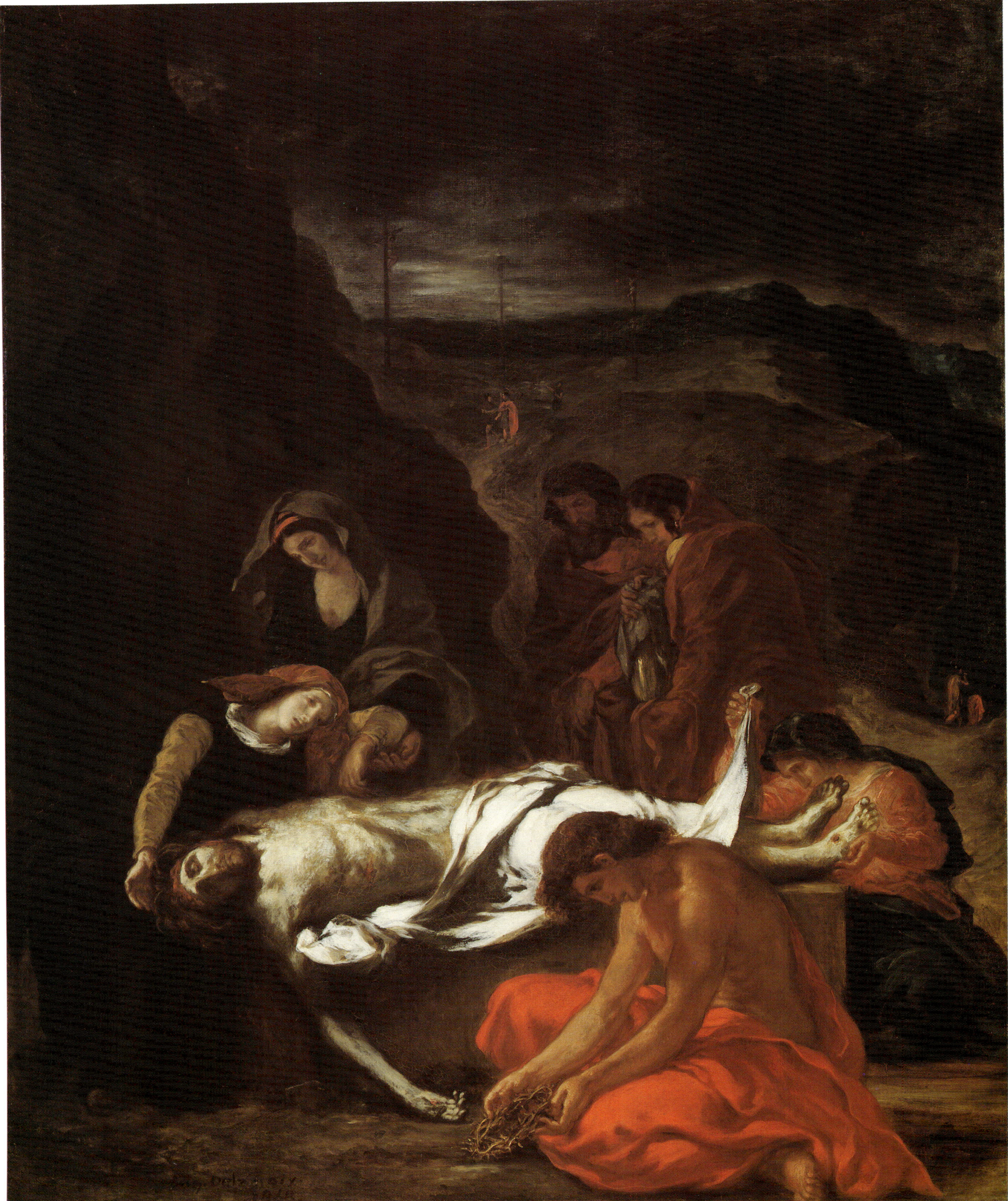

The Entombment

Fra Angelico, a Dominican friar, and his assistants painted the *Deposition of Christ* on pp. 132–133 and about 50 other scenes from the life of Jesus and Mary on the interior walls of a monastery in Florence named after Saint Mark. It is now a museum of Fra Angelico's work. Many of the pictures were in rooms where the monks slept, and others in the common rooms, and they served as a guide to the disciplined devotion of the religious community. This particular fresco has suffered damage across the bottom, resulting in the irregular lower margin.

At the foot of the cross, disposed around the recumbent body of their beloved master to mourn and prepare the remains for burial, are the familiar followers of Jesus, joined by other saints from later Christian history. Joseph of Arimathea and Nicodemus, carrying a jar of spices, confer at the head of Jesus. Mary gives a last embrace to her son. John gently lifts his arms to fold them across his body, while the Magdalene kneels at his feet. There is an almost liturgical aura to the actions and postures of the mourners. They move with familiarity, respect, and restraint, as though to the cadence of monophonic chanting. The walls of Jerusalem are stretched across the background, echoing the posture of Jesus. The landscape is barren, the colors are chaste, and there is a sense of blissful serenity about the scene.

Four hundred years separate Fra Angelico's *Deposition* from Delacroix's painting of the same scene set farther from the cross. Both artists depended on tradition for the placement of their figures and for the actions ascribed to them, but the peace Fra Angelico achieves contrasts with the moodiness of the later work. Where the mourners in the former's depiction are united, Delacroix's are emotionally isolated from one another as they surround the slumping corpse of Jesus.

The even light in the earlier scene gives way to eerie contrasts of light and dark in the 19th-century painting. There is nothing dissonant in the Dominican work, but in Delacroix's scene John's bright red garment seems to leap out of the darkness, and the nakedness of his upper body is as shocking as the color of his robe. Finally, where Fra Angelico focuses only on the cross of Jesus, Delacroix shows three crosses silhouetted against the sky of approaching night. The bodies of the two robbers still hang there.

Van Gogh wrote that "only Rembrandt and Delacroix could paint the face of Christ." Although Delacroix is not remembered for his religious paintings, he concentrated on this monumental work throughout 1847 and finished it the next year. When he saw it in a special exhibition of his paintings at the Universal Exposition in 1855, he wrote that the sight of it filled him with an emotion so strong it surprised him. Indeed, it was one of the most impressive religious paintings to come out of the entire 19th century, a century that was called faithless.

The Entombment
EUGÈNE DELACROIX, French, 1796–1863
Gift by Contribution in memory of Martin Brimmer, Museum of Fine Arts, Boston. Oil on canvas. 64 × 52 in.

DETAIL
The Deposition
FRA ANGELICO

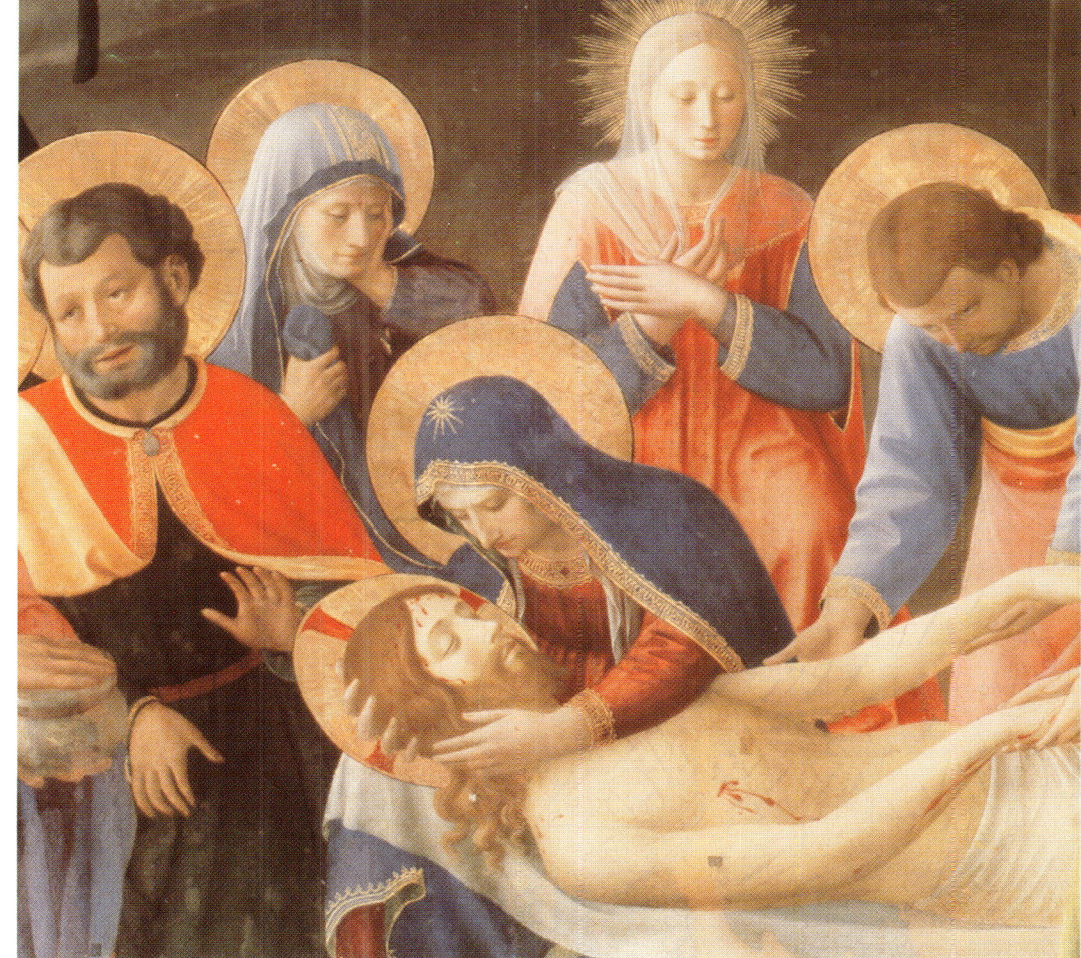

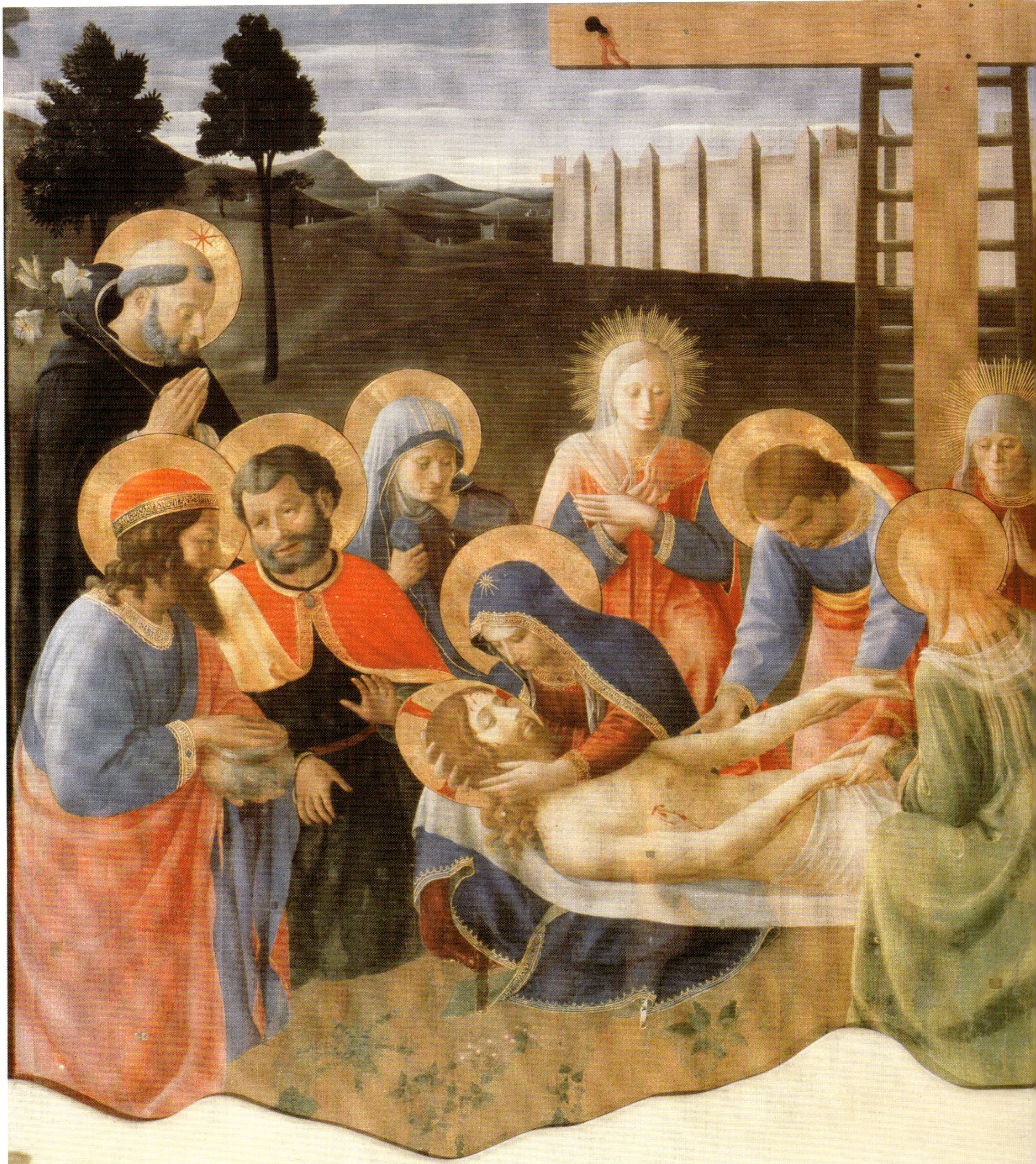

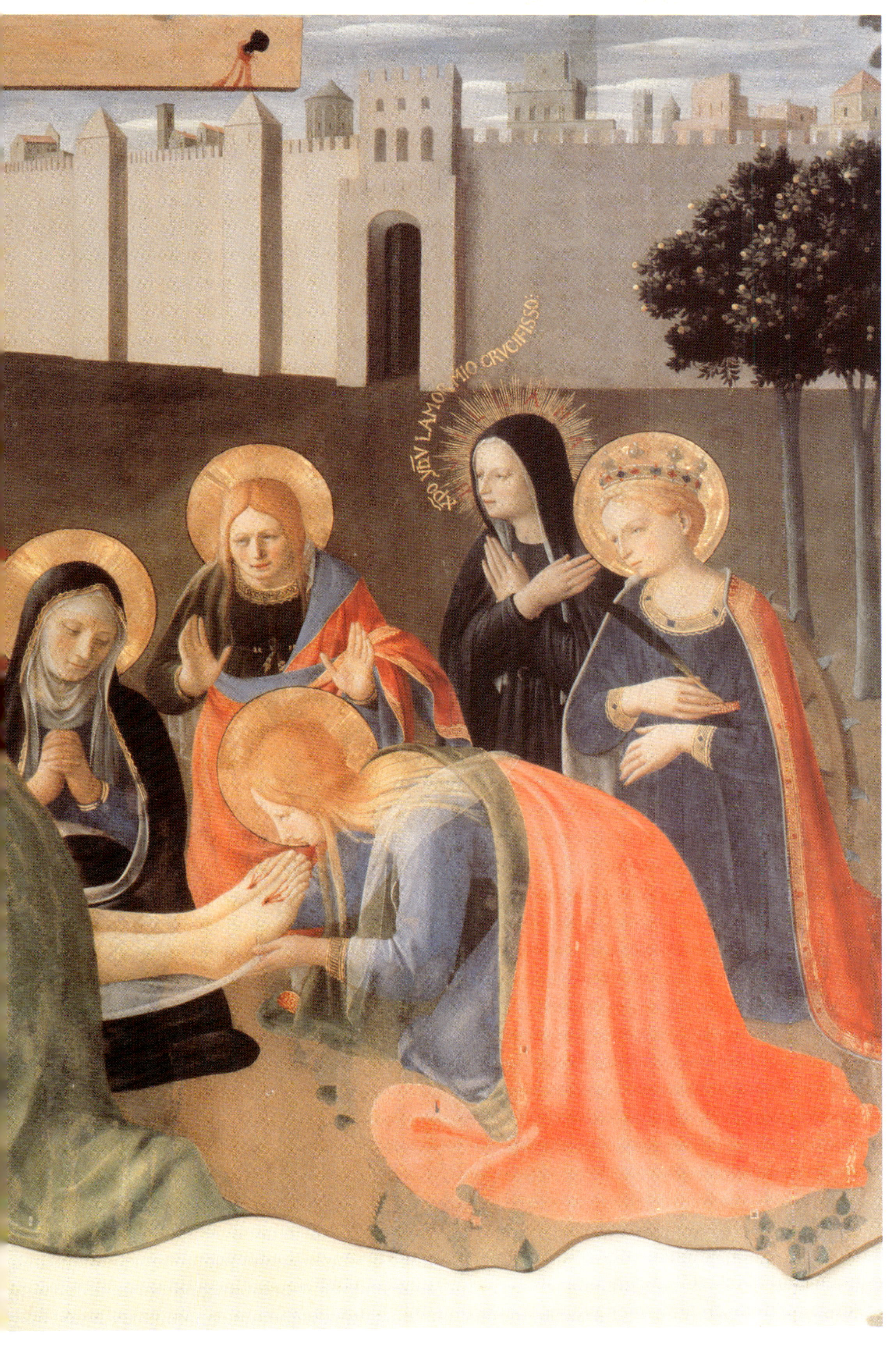

The Deposition
FRA ANGELICO, Italian, ca. 1400–1455
Museo di S. Marco, Florence. 41½ × 65 in.

The Resurrection

Much of the history of 15th-century Europe was dominated by the lives and actions of saints. Two of the most powerful and influential were Bernardino and Catherine of Siena. They so inspired their fellow citizens that the art produced in Siena during their lives has rarely been matched in spiritual intensity. The small *Resurrection* by the Master of the Osservanza is one of the masterpieces of that period.

The subject of this work, Jesus' return to life, is the central doctrine of Christianity, but what actually happened was not recorded by the Gospel writers. The followers of Jesus had not been to the tomb since they laid his body there on the Friday night of his death. On Sunday morning, all the witnesses came to an empty tomb and received reports from angels that Jesus had arisen. The Bible gave no other details except that the tomb was closely guarded, for the temple officials feared that the followers of Jesus would steal his corpse and claim he had risen from the dead, fulfilling Jesus' own prophesy.

The painter here shows Jesus ascending from a sealed tomb. Illuminating the otherwise dark garden is an aureole of golden light on which he floats into the sky. In one hand he holds a fluttering banner of Christian victory and in the other an olive branch, a symbol of life. The wounds from his crucifixion are apparent and his face is set in a passive but almost stern expression of acceptance.

Guards, who have been sleeping, are awakened by the silent radiance, their faces filled with wonder. One kneels in praise. He is linked to the apparition by the color of his tunic, the same gold as the mandorla, and by his proximity to the risen Christ. Since he is dressed differently from the others and has a lance instead of a sword, he is perhaps the centurion in charge. A fourth guard hides his eyes from the light. Dawn breaks over the cold black hills, so evocative of southern Tuscany. Easter has come.

This gifted artist depicts the miraculous event of Jesus' resurrection through an imag-

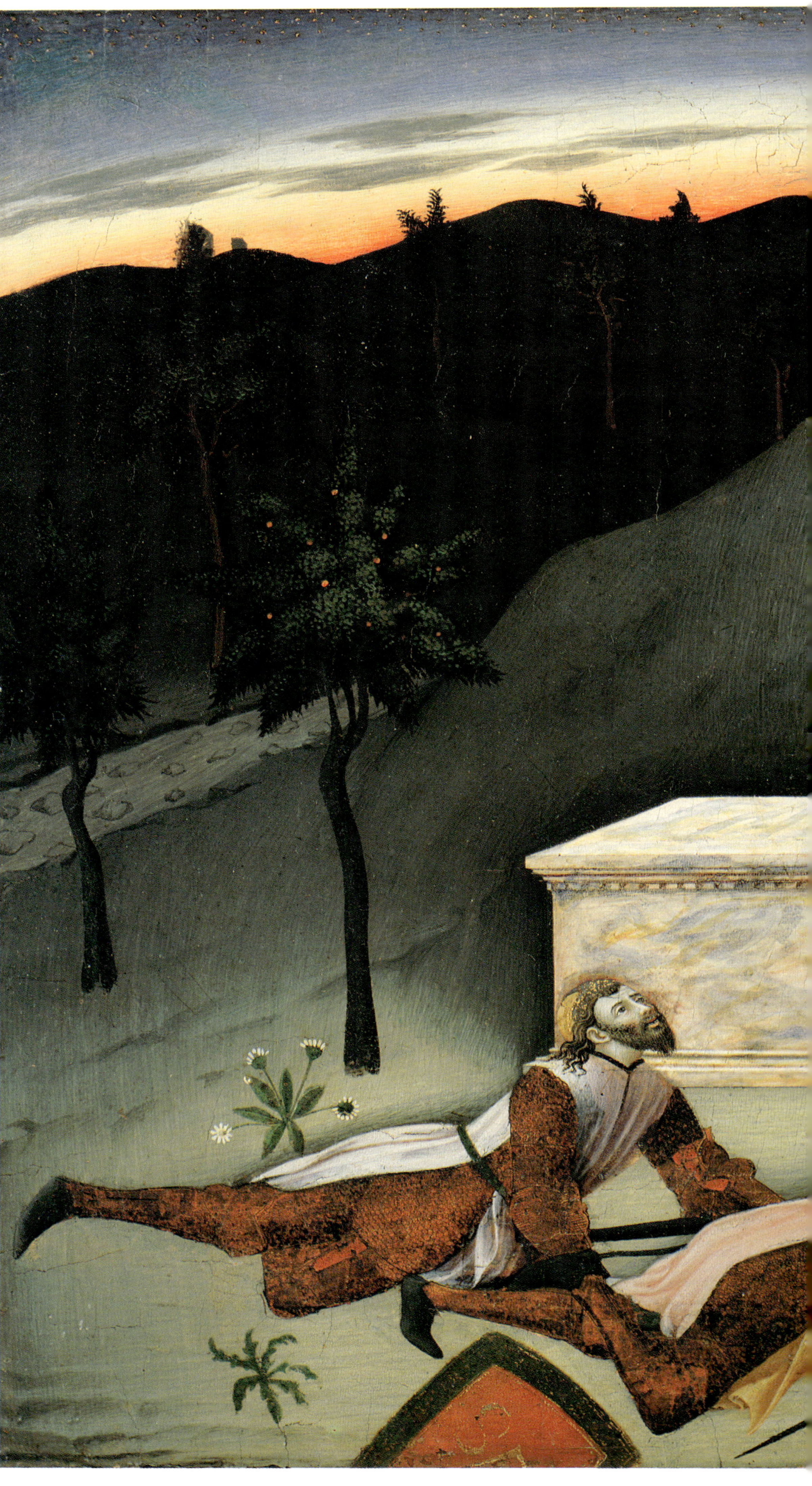

The Resurrection
MASTER OF THE OSSERVANZA, Italian, active ca. 1430–1450
Gift of Mr. and Mrs. Henry Ford II, The Detroit Institute of Arts. Tempera and gold leaf on wood panel. 14¼ × 17⅞ in

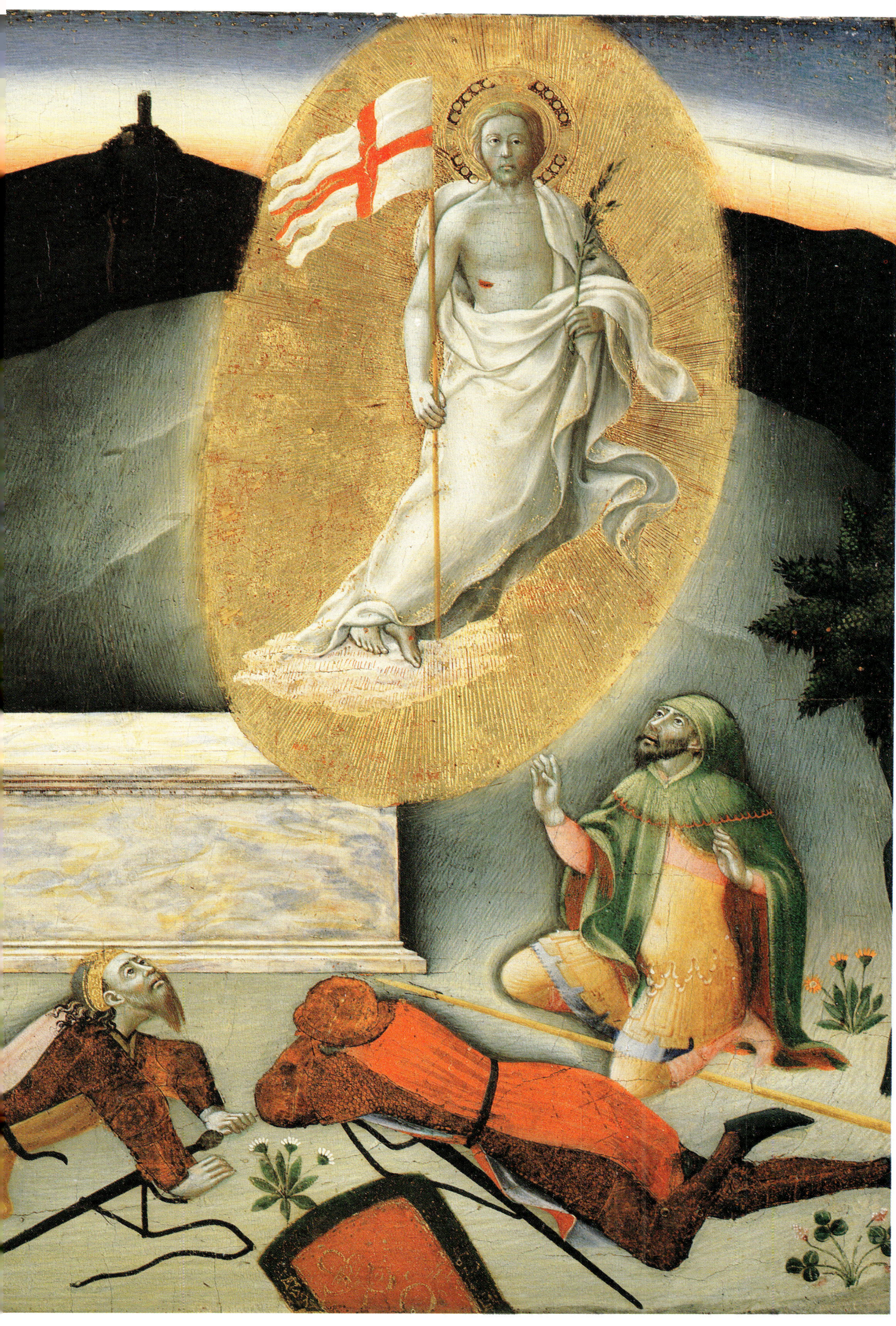

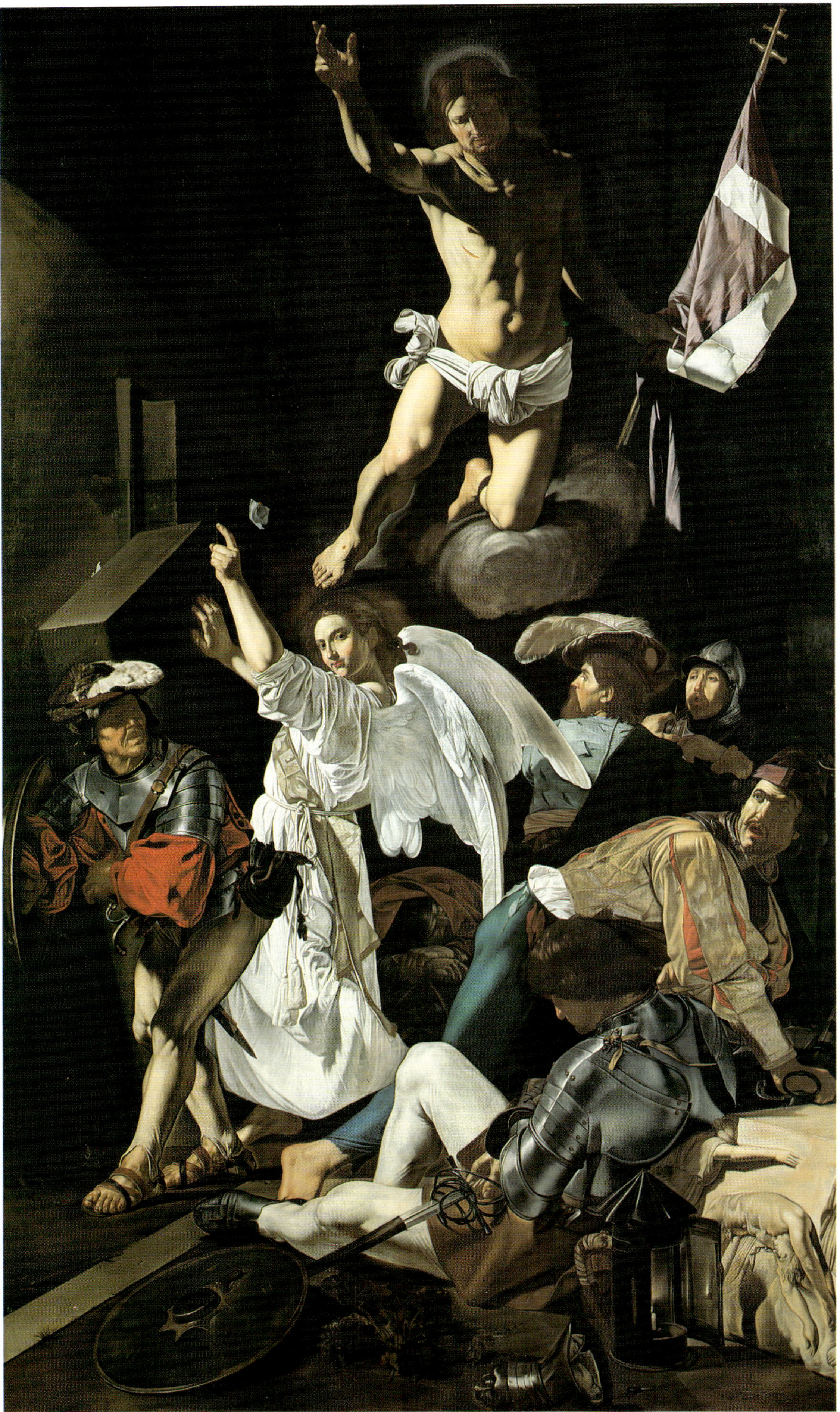

ination filled with faith. Unfortunately, nothing is known of him, not even his name. Since 1957, he has been called the Master of the Osservanza. There is a convent by the name of Osservanza, founded by St. Bernardino, a short walk beyond the north gate of Siena. In it is a large and very beautiful altarpiece dated 1436 which was painted by the same anonymous talent who made *The Resurrection* and a group of about 20 other pictures. Because the altarpiece links all the other works together, the name of the convent has been given to the artist.

The brilliant resurrection scene by Cecco del Caravaggio was contrived to dazzle rather than to mystify. Kneeling on a cloud, Jesus clutches his banner, which juts out toward the viewer. The angel, a brilliant figure of light in the center, points upward, and his radiance reflects from the armor of the soldiers. Their amazed faces contrast with that of the lone guard who is managing to sleep through this unprecedented event. The door of the tomb seems to have been blasted away by the energy with which Jesus rose from the dead.

Scenes of Jesus' resurrection were not common in art until the 15th century. Prior to that, artists had been content to show the empty tomb or the appearances of Jesus to his followers that followed the miracle. The resurrection pictured by the Master of the Osservanza is a mystical one, but by the 17th century athletic resurrections, such as that by Cecco del Caravaggio, became predominant. They are designed more to glorify the church than to celebrate the divinity of Jesus. The Counter-Reformation, that movement in the Catholic world to keep its flock from straying to Protestantism, created a more muscular and glamorous religion than had existed before, and highly theatrical paintings such as this one were a chief vehicle for propagating the reinvigorated faith.

The Resurrection

CECCO DEL CARAVAGGIO, Italian, active first quarter of the 17th century

Charles H. and Mary F. S. Worcester Collection, Art Institute of Chicago. Oil on canvas. 133½ × 78½ in.

The Three Marys at the Tomb

It is not clear from the biblical texts which women were at the tomb on Easter morning. The four Gospel writers were only in agreement about Mary Magdalene. Matthew wrote that she was with "the other Mary"; Mark reported that she was with Mary the mother of James, and a woman named Salome who followed Jesus from Galilee; Luke named Joanna, the wife of Herod's steward, instead of Salome; and John reported that Mary Magdalene was alone, and then fetched him and Peter. John, however, reported that there were three Marys at the foot of the cross, Mary the mother of Jesus, Mary the wife of Clopas, and Mary Magdalene. It is likely that these are the women whom Adolphe William Bouguereau pictures looking into the tomb.

Dressed in modest mourning robes and ready to complete the burial, which was interrupted by the Sabbath, they have come upon the open tomb of Jesus. The great stone that sealed it is ajar and the woman with her back toward the viewer touches it for support. An angel whose "appearance was like lightning, and his raiment white as snow" calls out to them, "Do not be afraid; for I know that you seek Jesus who was crucified. He is not here; for he has risen, as he said. Come, see the place where he lay" (Matthew 28:3–6).

The colors throughout the scene are muted, as though bleached by the dazzling light from inside the sepulcher. The women lead the viewer into the presence of the celestial being whose coming produced this radiance, as well as an earthquake, according to the accounts. Through these three noble figures, the divine mystery of the resurrection becomes accessible.

Bouguereau's reputation is based primarily on his coy paintings of peasant girls, and his rather wanton ones of female nudes, the type that decorated the walls of frontier saloons in 19th-century America. For those familiar with his typical work, a picture with such seriousness and mastery as this comes as a surprise. Although not well known, it is one of the most supreme and highly original religious statements to come out of the 19th century.

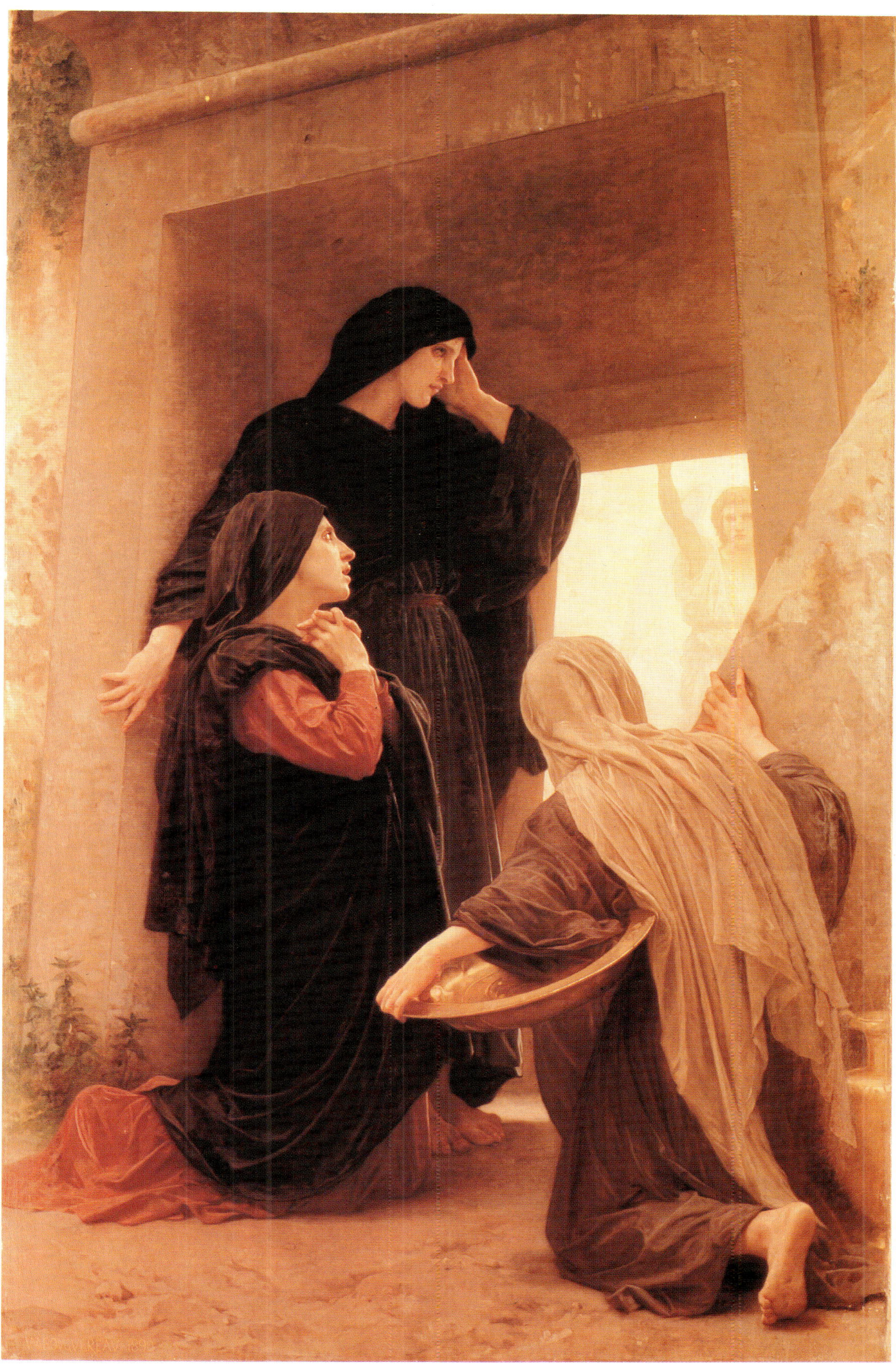

The Three Marys at the Tomb
ADOLPHE WILLIAM BOUGUEREAU, French, 1825–1905
Koninklijke Musea voor Schone Kunsten, Antwerp. Oil on canvas. 103 × 63½ in.

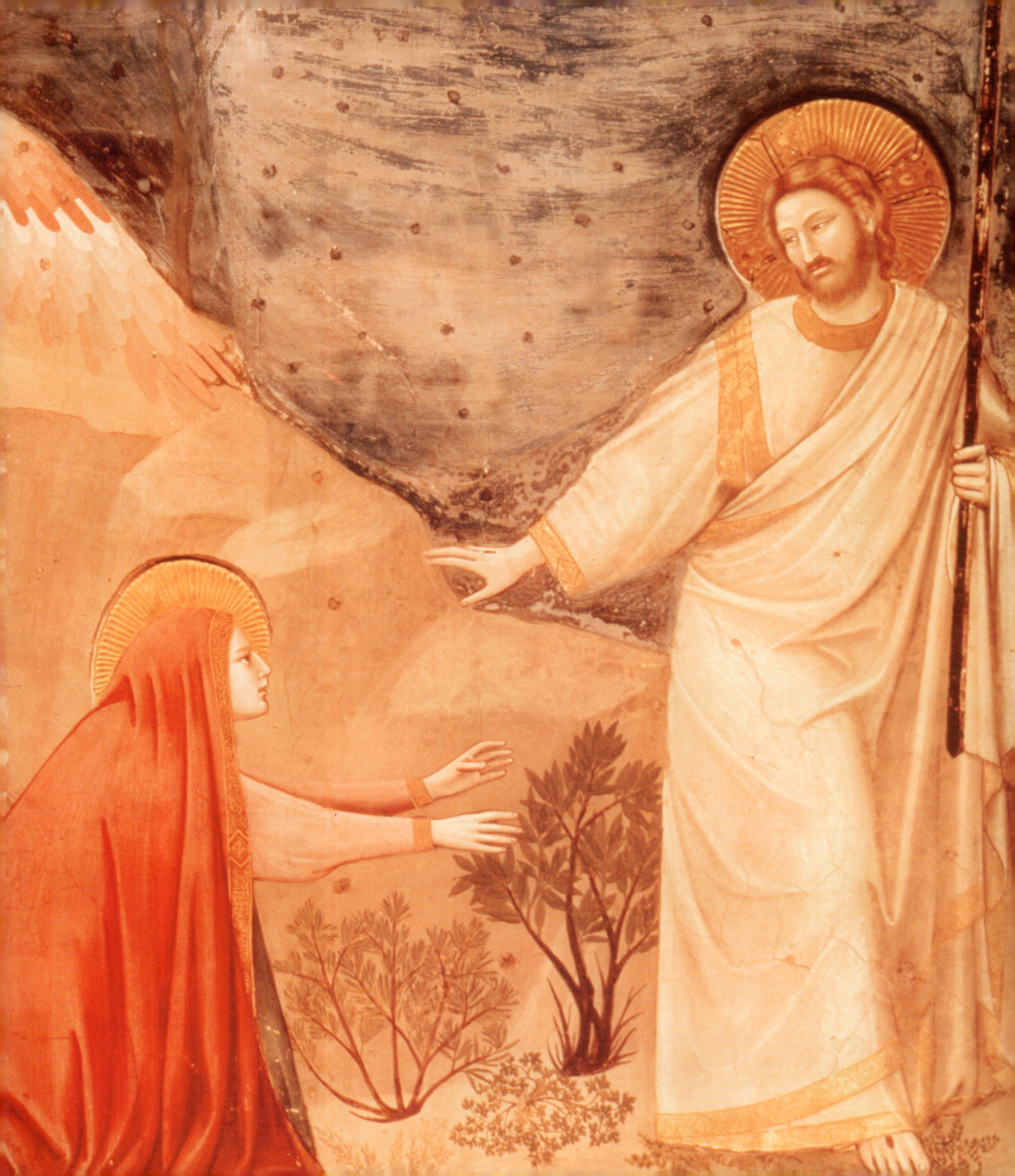

Christ Appearing to Mary Magdalene

Luke reported that two angels were at the empty tomb of Jesus. Matthew added that the appearance of an angel so frightened the guards that they "became like dead men" (Matthew 28:4). But it was John who stated that Mary Magdalene was the first to encounter the resurrected Christ. In *The Resurrection* and *Christ Appearing to Mary Magdalene*, Giotto puts the three accounts together, but the gesture of the angel to the left places the viewer's focus on the latter tender incident. It is a remarkable work both for what it shows and for what it implies in its simple and powerful compositional devices.

When Mary first encountered the risen Jesus, she thought he was a gardener and asked him to take her to her Master, for she had already seen the empty tomb. Jesus called her name. Recognizing him, she said in Hebrew, "Rabboni," which means *teacher*. Jesus quickly warned her, "Do not hold me, for I have not yet ascended to the Father." He then instructed her to tell his brethren that he would soon be returning to God (John 20:15–17).

Giotto hides the Magdalene's famous hair and dresses her in the conventional mourning cloak of 13th- and 14th-century Italy. She reaches out with great spontaneity as Jesus quickly steps away from her, almost out of the picture frame. His posture is ambiguous in contrast to the definite stance of the loving woman. The pose of Jesus as he turns but also withdraws in the opposite direction is one of art's earliest uses of contrapposto. The term comes from the Latin *contra* and *positum*, which in turn are translated from the Greek *antithesis*, a rhetorical usage in which opposites are set against one another, much favored in the literature of Giotto's age.

Jesus' arm, reaching out to forbid Mary's advance, and the angle of Mary's back, form a strong diagonal line. It is countered by another that runs along the edge of the angel's wing and the slope of the hill behind the figures. This invisible X serves the compositional purpose of increasing tension while also enhancing the closeness of the two protagonists.

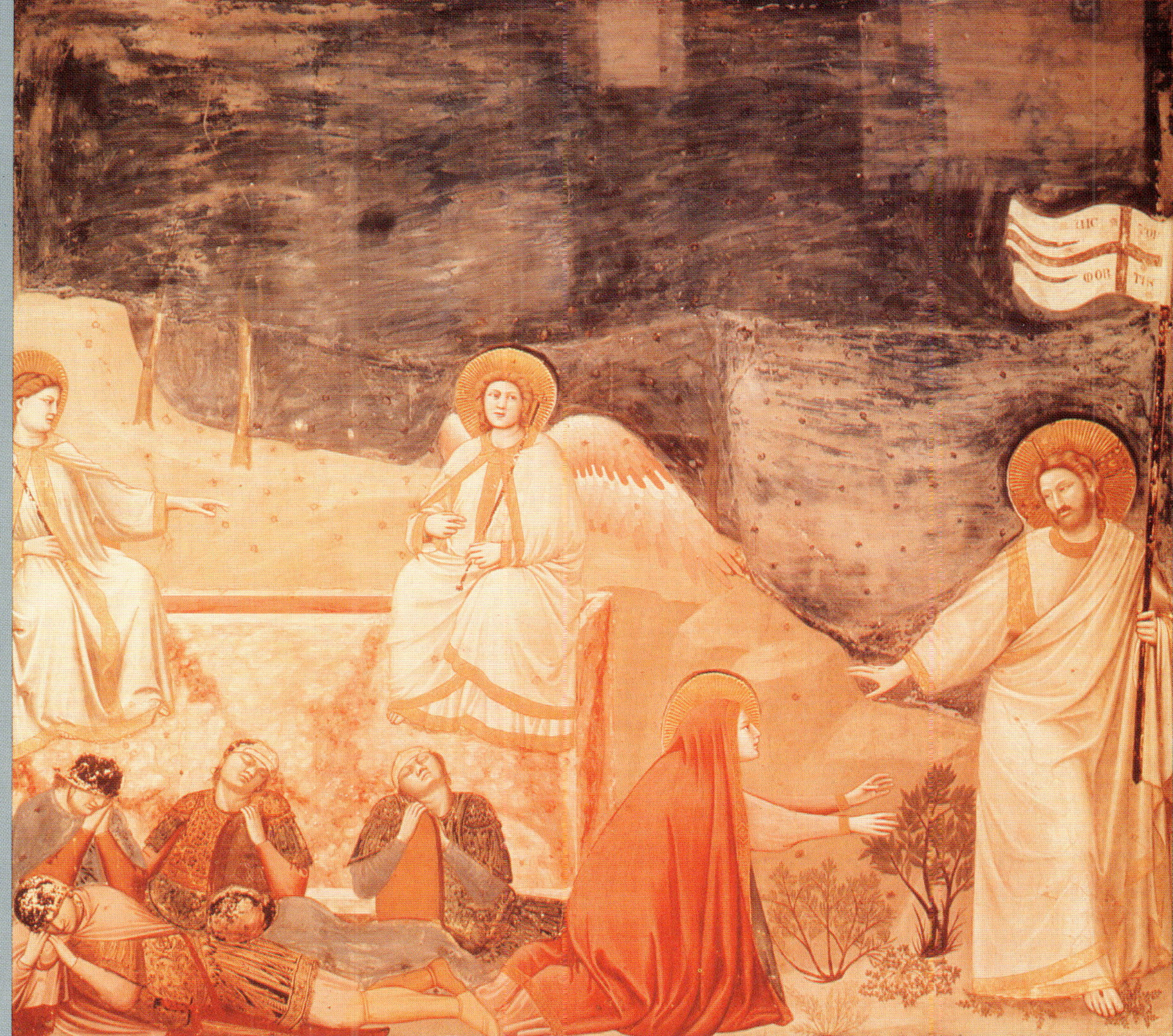

The Resurrection and *Christ Appearing to Mary Magdalene*

GIOTTO, Italian, 1266/67–1337

Scrovegni Chapel, S. Maria Annunziata dell'Arena, Padua. Fresco. 79½ × 73½ in.

◁ DETAIL

Doubting Thomas

Of the 10 or 11 appearances Jesus made to his followers after his death and resurrection, none is as human nor as comforting to the faithful as the tale of Thomas, the disciple who doubted the story of the risen Jesus. "Unless I see in his hands the print of the nails . . . and place my hand in his side, I will not believe," he said (John 20:25). Jesus soon made it possible for Thomas to do that.

The Master's response to his doubting disciple has been repeated again and again in paintings, without an iota of change from the Bible's original telling. Within the week of his resurrection, when the 12 were together in a locked room, he appeared, greeted them, and immediately ordered Thomas to touch his wounds. "Do not be faithless," he said, "but believing." Thomas acknowledged him as his Lord and God, and Jesus responded, "Have you believed because you have seen me? Blessed are those who have not seen and yet believe" (John 20:29).

Bernardo Strozzi's violent illumination of the scene creates jagged patterns of light and dark, which he seems to enjoy contrasting with the soft flesh of Jesus and the tentative, almost nervous touch of Thomas. The three faces in the background, though slashed with shadows, are convincingly real, a reminder that Strozzi was a leading portrait painter of his day.

Thomas, it is said, became a missionary to India. A lengthy book called *The Acts of Thomas*, derived in the third century from Syrian Christian tradition, outlined his apocryphal journeys and repeated highlights of his preaching. Although the book had little historical value, it provided interesting evidence as to how the sacraments were celebrated in the early church. It also portrayed Thomas as unusually abstemious in the pleasures of the flesh, which was odd, it seems, for a man so tactile that he had to touch to believe.

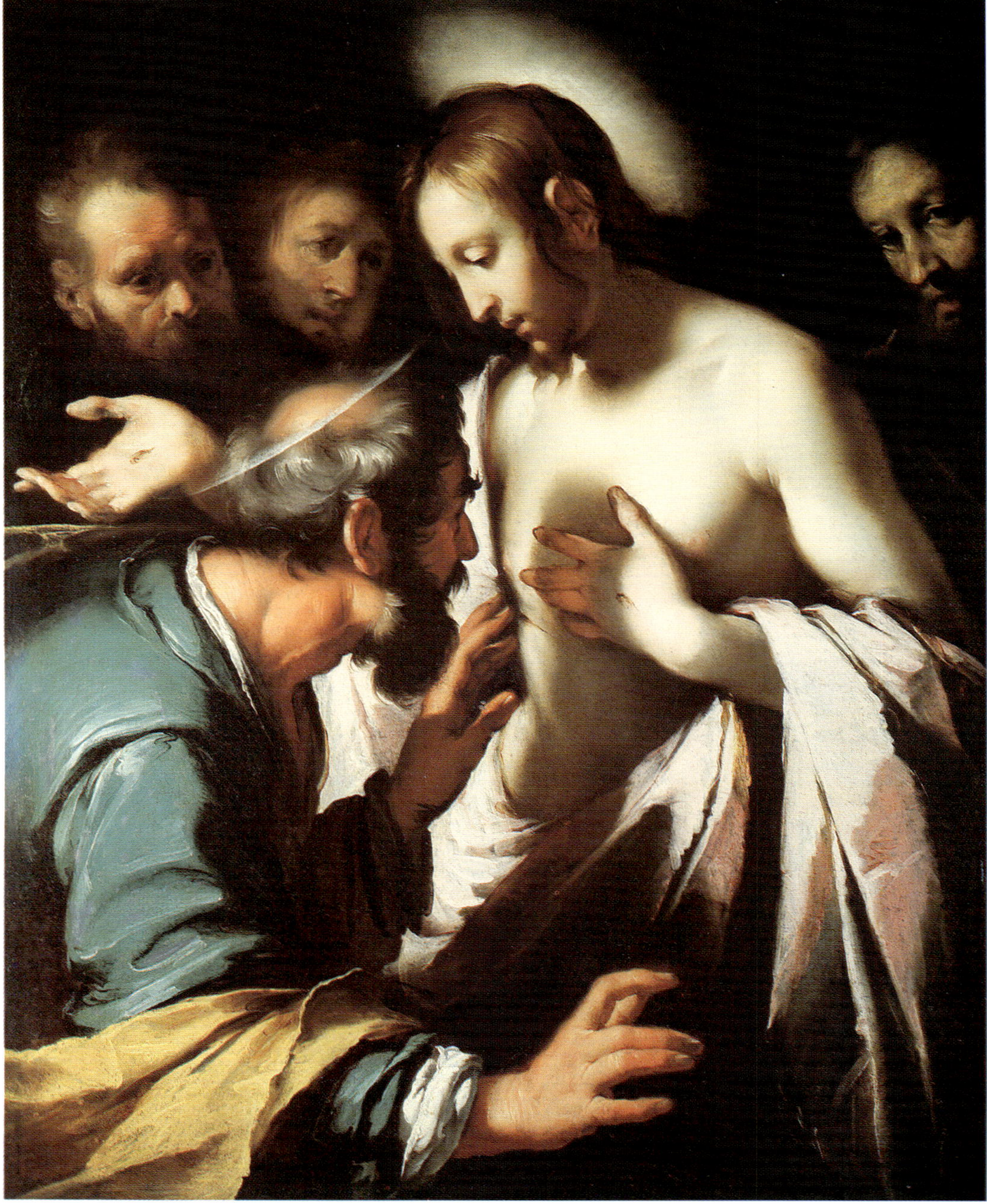

Doubting Thomas
BERNARDO STROZZI, Italian, 1581–1644
Museo de Arte de Ponce, Puerto Rico. Oil on canvas.
43½ × 34¾ in.

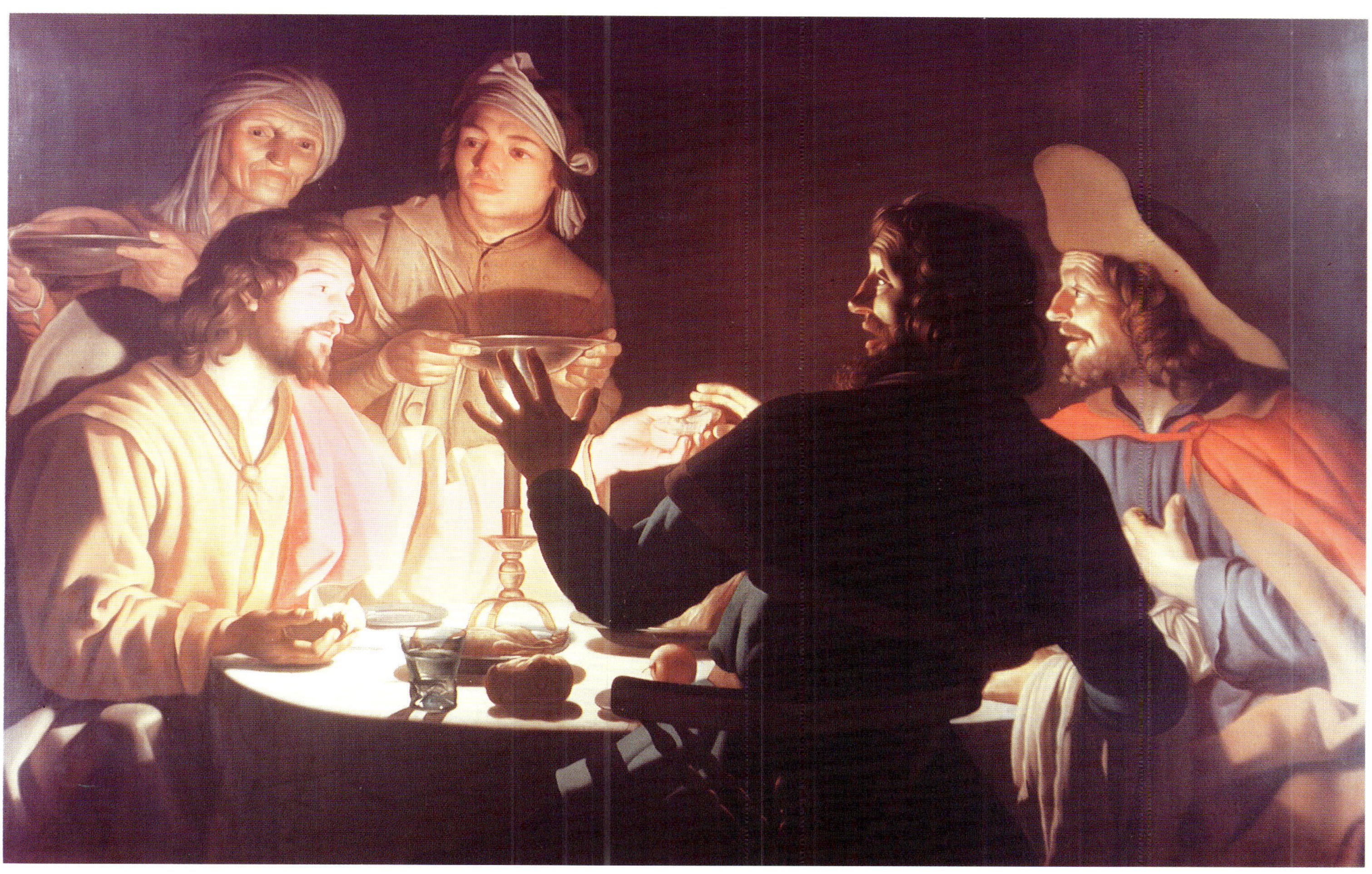

The Supper at Emmaus
STUDIO OR CIRCLE OF GERRIT VAN HONTHORST, Dutch, 1590–1656
Wadsworth Atheneum, Hartford, Connecticut. Oil on panel. 48¾ × 75¼ in.

The Supper at Emmaus

On the very afternoon that he returned to life from the tomb, Jesus encountered two of his followers on the road from Jerusalem to Emmaus. The village does not exist today, but the Bible said it was a 7-mile journey. One of the men that he met was called Cleophas and the other went unnamed, and nothing is known of them but this incident. Neither man recognized Jesus, but upon meeting him on the road they conversed excitedly about the crucifixion and the empty tomb. Accompanying them on their journey, Jesus, according to Luke, "interpreted to them in all the scriptures the things concerning himself" (Luke 24:27). It must have been a long trip. When they reached Emmaus, the men persuaded the stranger to stay with them at an inn. They sat together for dinner. Not until he blessed the bread did the two disciples realize who Jesus was.

While many artists preferred to paint the almost sacramental act of Jesus offering the blessing, Gerrit van Honthorst, full of good Dutch Calvinism, selects the more mundane moment immediately afterward when Jesus' followers recognize their teacher. Honthorst, whose nickname was Gherardo delle Notti (Italian for "Gerard of the night scenes"), for he learned dramatic light effects in Italy, uses the candle to flood Jesus with brilliance and to highlight the silhouetted hand of the man nearest the viewer. The old serving woman and her young assistant realize that they have walked in on a significant meeting, but one wonders if this is a moment of conversion or if they will simply return to the kitchen. This story occurred on Easter Sunday, but Honthorst does not hint at the agony of death that had consumed Jesus only a few days earlier. Here he is shown as a handsome and thoughtful host.

The still life in front of the candlestick shows a frugal repast, and one hopes that there are two more chickens somewhere else on the table, for one is hardly enough for three hungry men. There is also a slight regret that water fills the glass instead of wine. But, as mentioned above, Honthorst was a Calvinist, as were his clients. The orange, no doubt, is a tribute to the House of Orange, for Honthorst was the primary portrait painter to this princely Dutch family. Exotic and foreign to Holland, oranges were usually reserved to clear the palate after rich food.

There is a question as to whether this is an authentic work by Honthorst or one by an assistant working in his studio, or even by a contemporary who admired Honthorst's paintings. Artists taught by having students copy their works, so authorship is often a confusing issue. If Honthorst himself did not execute this work, it is a tribute to him, for it is in his style, full of his ideas.

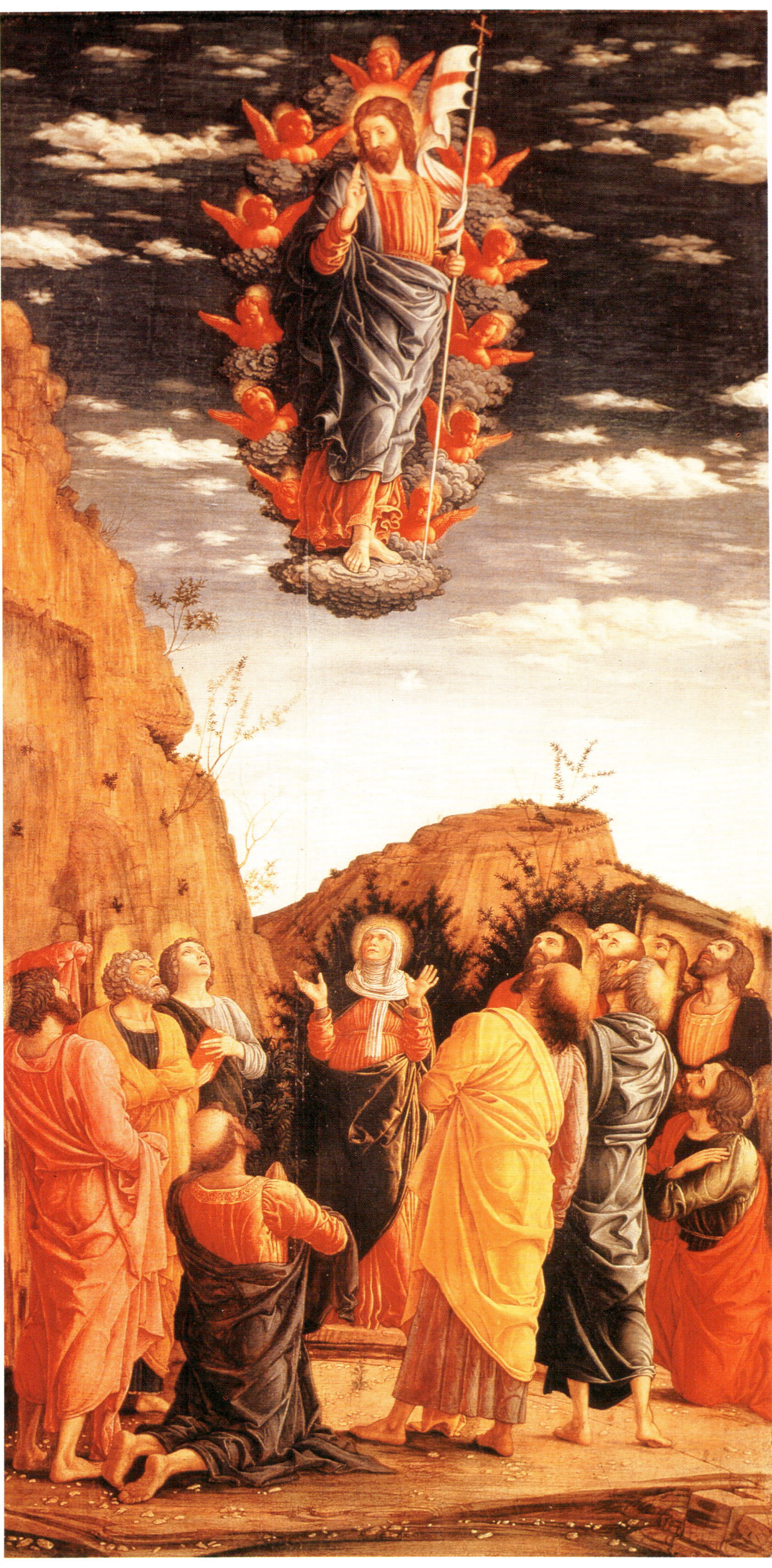

The Ascension

Easter, throughout Christianity, has always held a much higher place of honor as a holiday than the ascension of Jesus. The resurrection was seen as proof of Jesus' divinity, but his return to heaven seemed almost irrelevant, for he said in the very last words of The Gospel According to St. Matthew, "I am with you always, to the close of the age" (Matthew 28:20). Only Luke, of the four apostles, recounted the ascension, and that briefly. "While he blessed them, he parted from them" (Luke 24:51), he wrote, also mentioning that this event took place at Bethany (on the eastern slope of the Mount of Olives). As though he had not given quite enough information in his Gospel, Luke elaborated a bit in the first chapter of his Acts of the Apostles. There he said that a cloud took Jesus out of sight, and after he was gone two men in white robes appeared to tell the disciples that he "will come in the same way as you saw him go into heaven" (Acts 1:11).

Angels helping Jesus with his ascent are not mentioned in the Bible, but artists liked to add them. Andrea Mantegna makes them "angels of day" ("angels of night" are blue), encapsulating Jesus and propelling him upward by the beating of their little wings. The composition would be overly symmetrical had Mantegna not invented the rise of arid mountain to the right. The sharp diagonal of this slope lifts the composition upward and provides a golden glow that seems quite apropos for this final physical parting of Jesus from his mother and disciples.

Jesus' ministry was full of surprises for his followers, and by the expressions on their faces in this painting they seem no better prepared for this one than they were for any of the others. But now they are full of belief in their teacher's divinity. In showing their upturned faces, Mantegna uses foreshortened perspective, removing the viewer from the circle of disciples and placing him high up, opposite the rising Christ. This is an impersonal vantage point but one of privilege.

The Ascension

ANDREA MANTEGNA, Italian, ca. 1431–1506

Galleria degli Uffizi, Florence. Tempera on wood panel. 34 × 17 in.

▷ DETAIL

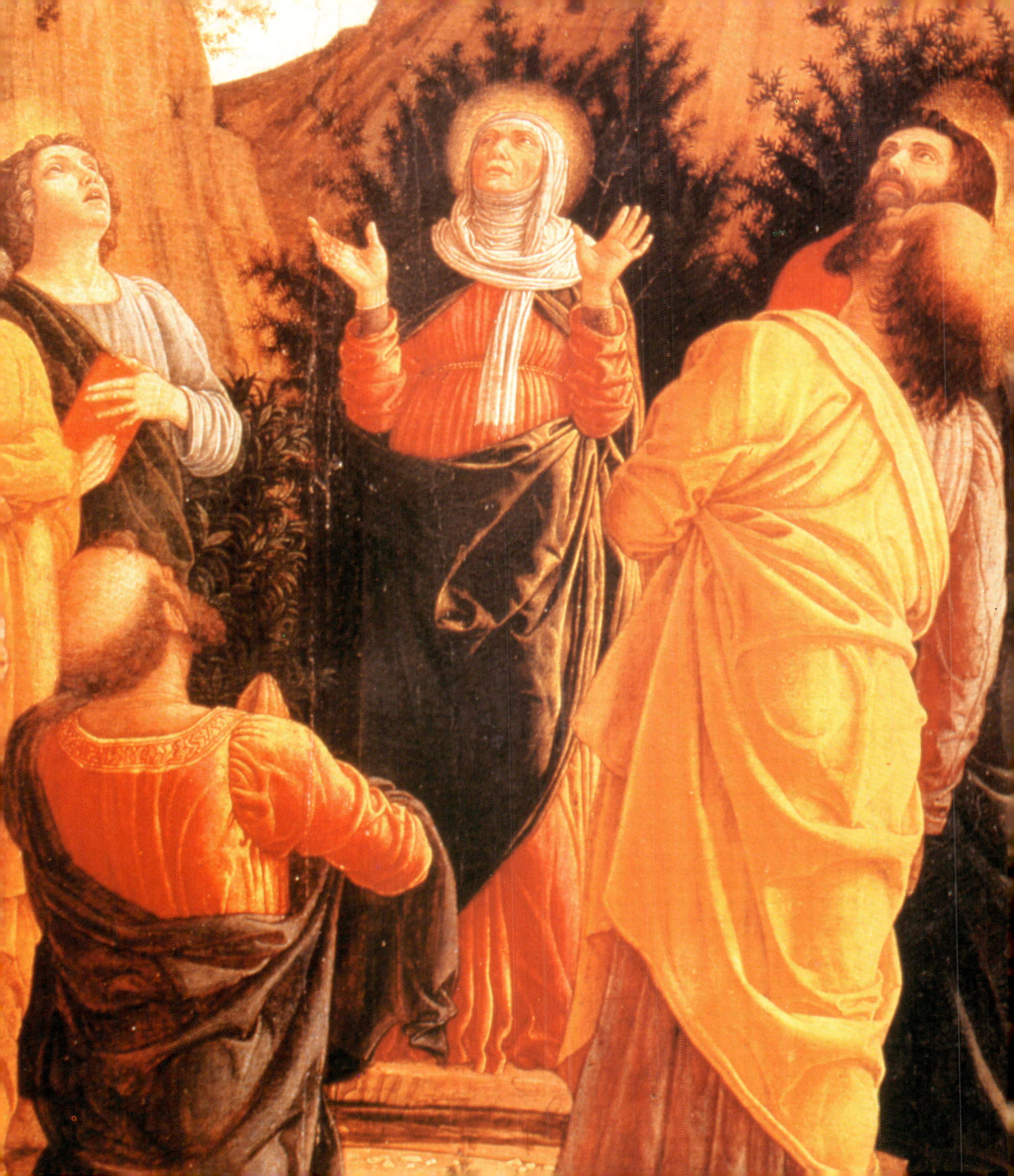

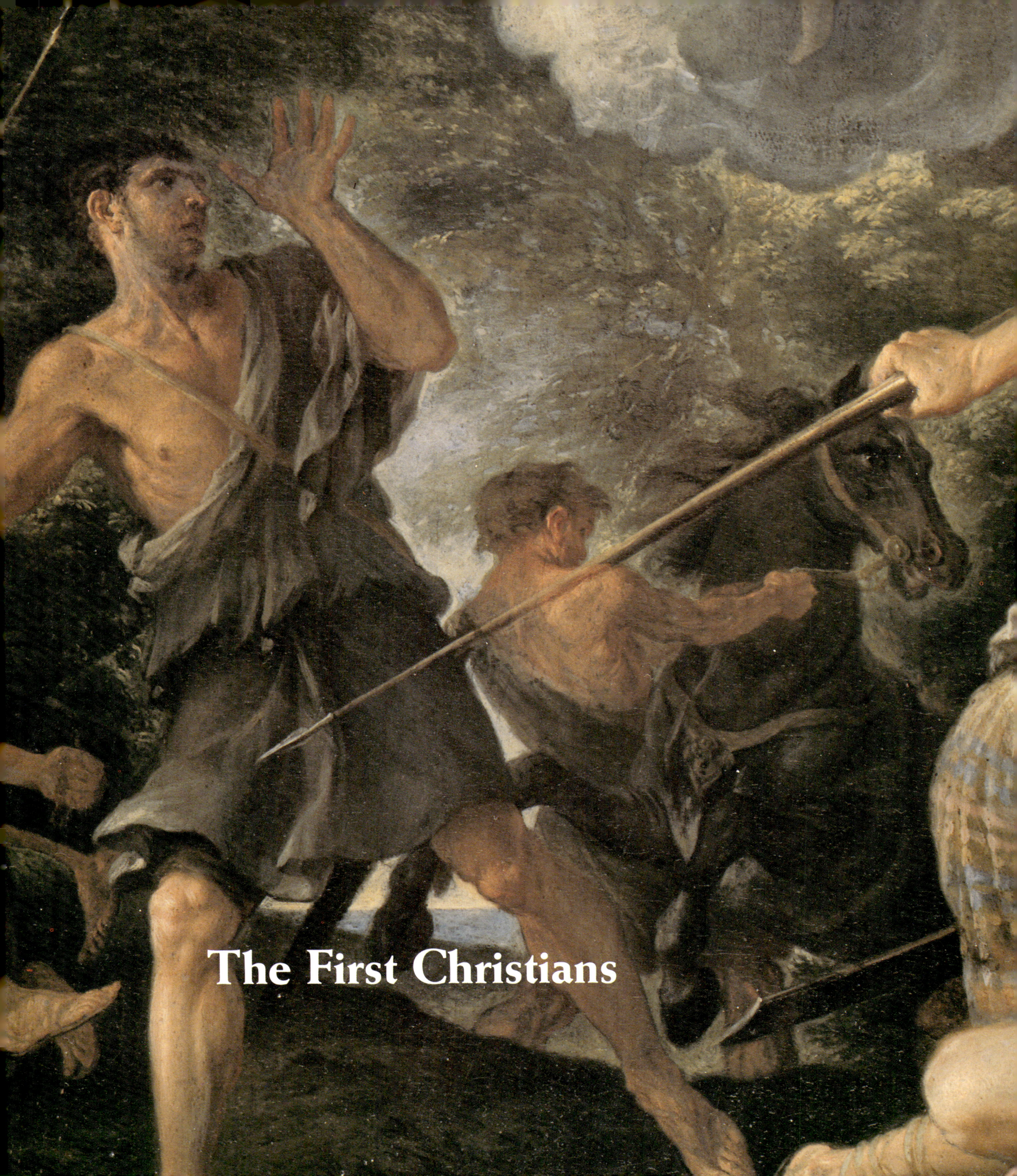
The First Christians

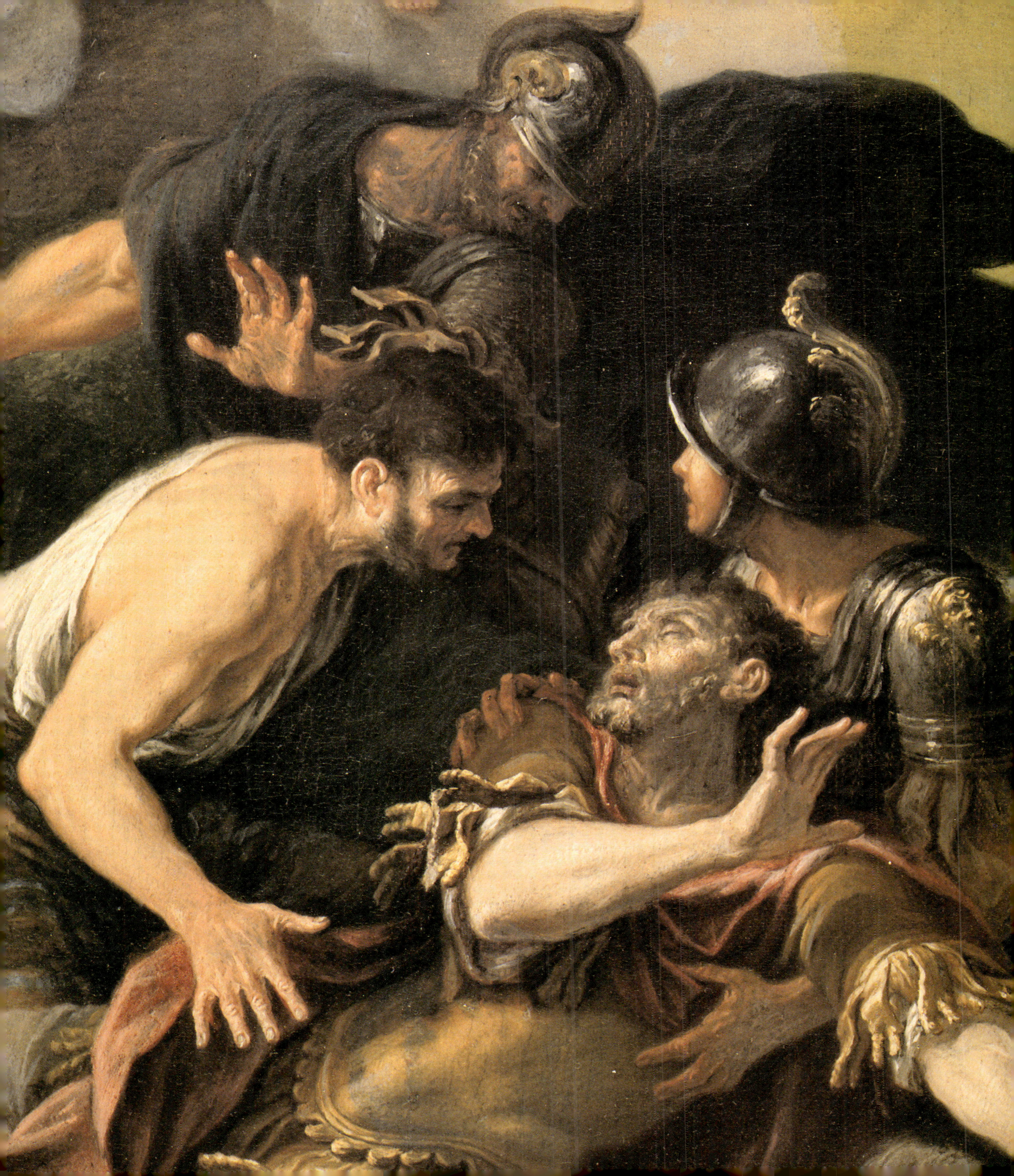

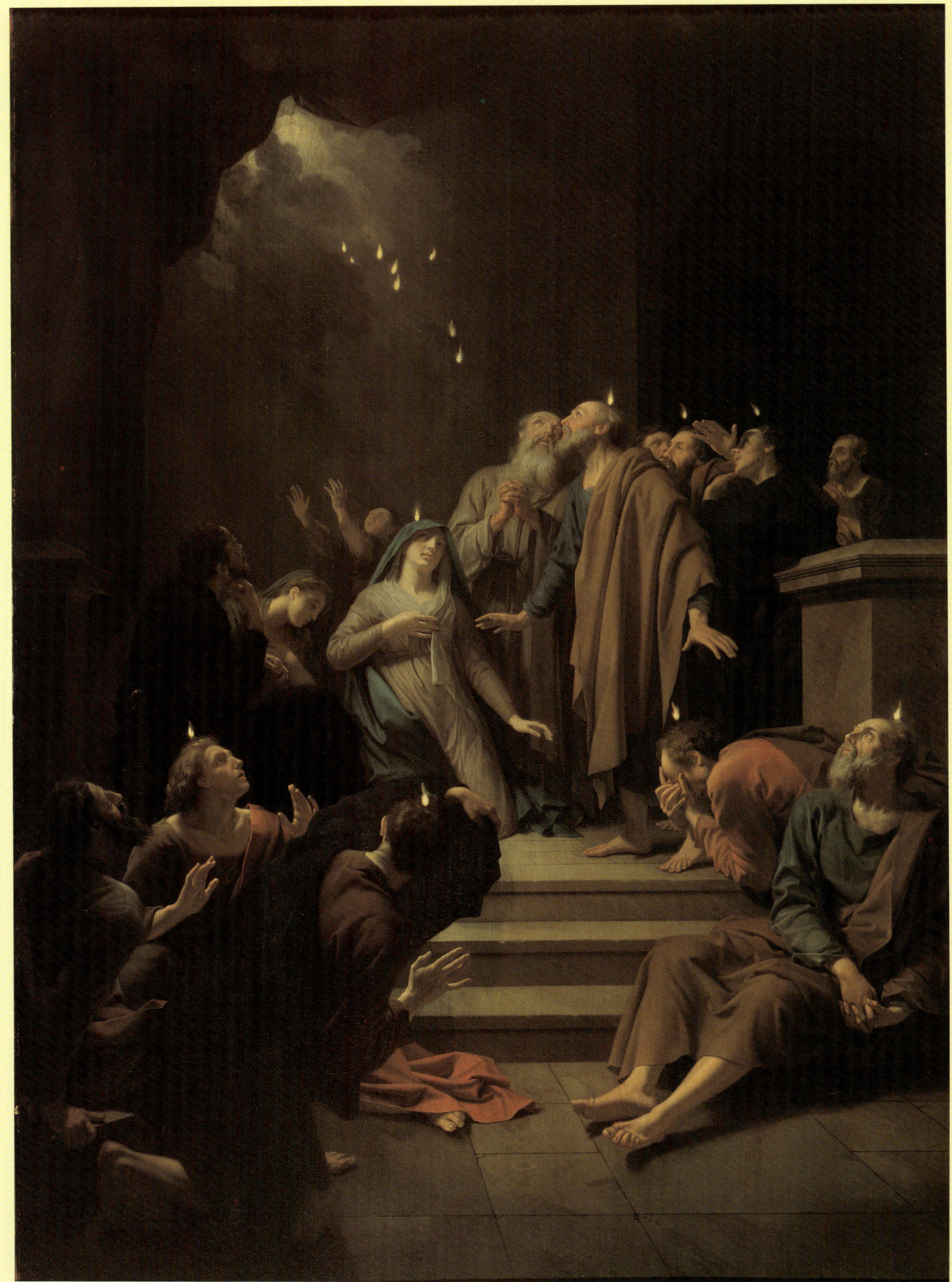

The Pentecost

After his resurrection, Jesus warned his disciples not to leave Jerusalem until "you shall be baptized with the Holy Spirit" (Acts 1:5). Exactly 10 days after his ascension, his followers gathered in a house. Suddenly there was a sound from heaven "like the rush of a mighty wind." Then "tongues of fire" rested on their heads, to use the picturesque language of Luke, who recorded this event in The Acts of the Apostles, written slightly later than his Gospel. He then reports that "They were all filled with the Holy Spirit and began to speak in other tongues, as the spirit gave them utterance" (Acts 2:24).

In *The Pentecost*, Dutch artist Adriaen van der Werff shows eight points of light floating through the dusky haze; the others already rest on the heads of the chosen. The man closest to the viewer hides his eyes and tries to run away; the others are full of praise or meditation. One shields his eyes to look for the source of this peculiar and stirring happening. The disciple at the back of the room, who has not yet received his baptism of fire, reaches out to bring a flame to his head. In spite of all the action this is a strangely silent scene; the gift of tongues has not yet reached the disciples.

Pentecost, after the Greek for "50th day," occurred 50 days after Easter. It was always celebrated as a feast day in the Christian church, but it took on renewed importance to the early Protestants. Since the event could be seen as the start of the worldwide preaching of the gospel, it was a stimulus to the new church's own missionary activities. By the 18th century, when this painting was executed, the commemoration of Pentecost was a major feast day in all Christian countries.

Van der Werff was born at the end of the great "Golden Age" of Dutch painting, but he was more the heir of Raphael than Rembrandt. He introduces a classical grandeur into this scene by combining a magnificent setting, Roman costumes, deep emotions, and dramatic yet decorous gestures. His Dutch clients were cosmopolitan and much preferred the art of France and Italy to the paintings of their own illustrious tradition.

Pentecost

ADRIAEN VAN DER WERFF, Dutch, 1659–1722

Staatsgalerie im Neuen Schloss Schleissheim, Oberschleissheim, Germany. Oil on panel. 30 × 21 in.

PRECEDING PAGES

LAURI: *Conversion of Saul* (detail)

St. Peter and St. John Healing the Lame Man

The New Testament mentions "wonders and signs" attributed to the disciples after Pentecost, but it does not report what the very first miracle was or who performed it. The first one described in detail, however, was a healing by Peter on the steps of the Temple near the entrance called "The Beautiful Gate." Peter and John were on their way to morning prayer and passed the beggars who stationed themselves on the steps from dawn to dusk, hoping the pious would stop and give them money. A man so crippled that he had to be carried and laid at the Temple door asked them for alms. Peter said, "I have no silver and gold, but I give you what I have; in the name of Jesus Christ of Nazareth, walk." He took the man's right hand, helped him up, and the man was healed. Luke, who recorded this event, added, "And all the people saw him walking and praising God, and recognized him . . . and they were filled with wonder and amazement at what had happened . . ." (Acts 3:6–10).

It is typical of French 17th-century painting, with all its restraint and decorum, that it can tell so much. The entire story of the healing and more is to be found in this painting by Nicolas Poussin. The miracle stands in contrast to the usual response of the rich to the poor demonstrated by the man ascending the stairs and proffering a coin to the beggar woman. Meanwhile, at the heart of the painting John points upward as Peter calls on the name of Jesus Christ. The long shadows of early morning, the soft atmosphere, and the measured coming and going of the people bestow upon this act of healing a moral solemnity that is almost sacramental. The surprised reaction of the Temple faithful on the right, by the way, provoked a sermon from Peter, his second in the New Testament. The crowd swelled to more than 5000 to hear him, but the speech earned him a night in jail.

Poussin's paintings had enormous influence on classical-minded artists right through the 19th century when Cézanne said he wanted "to do Poussin again, from nature." When Poussin painted this work, he was living virtually as a hermit, dedicating himself to expressing eternal truths through the almost motionless reserve of his subjects. The prevailing taste of the day was for richer colors, more action, and energetic gestures, yet this artist achieved European fame for the simple and dignified calm of his unique vision.

St. Peter and St. John Healing the Lame Man
NICOLAS POUSSIN, French, 1594–1665
Marquand Fund, 1924, Metropolitan Museum of Art, New York. Oil on canvas. 50 × 65½ in.

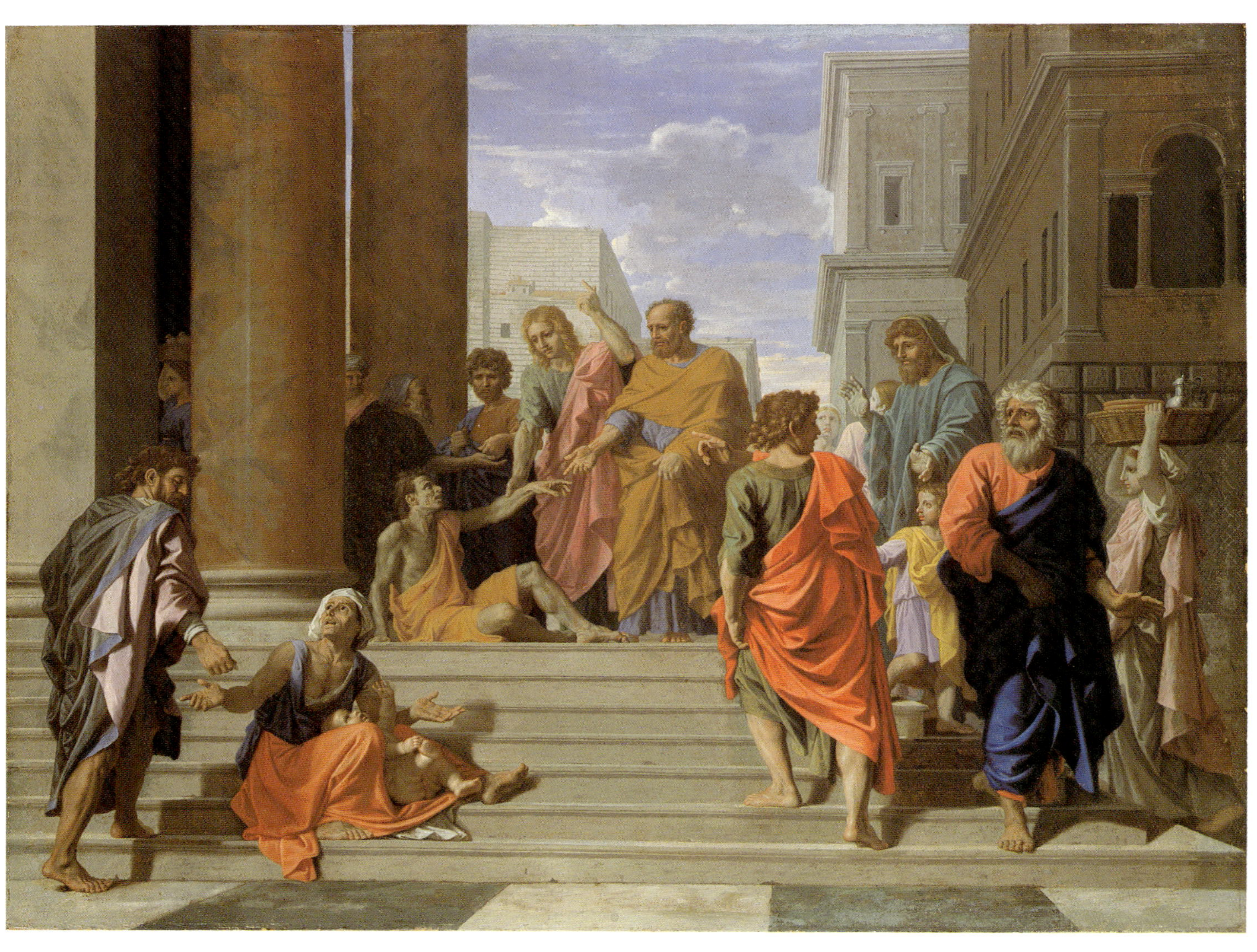

The Stoning of St. Stephen

Stephen had "the face of an angel" and was full of faith and the Holy Spirit. He and six others were elected by the disciples to distribute food to the widows of Greek-speaking Jews, but his work went beyond that. Full of grace and power, he "did great wonders and signs among the people" (Acts 7:8). But he found himself in conflict with members of the synagogue and they plotted against him. His long speech at his trial, recorded in the seventh chapter of The Acts of the Apostles, revealed his prodigious knowledge of the Bible, as well as his youthful recklessness. Calling his listeners "stiffnecked people, uncircumcised in heart and ears," he insisted that "the Most High does not dwell in houses made with hands" (Acts 7:48–51), which insulted their Temple. He was convicted of blasphemy, taken out of the city, and stoned to death, thereby becoming Christianity's first martyr. Luke's graphic description of the event inspired many artists, including the German Adam Elsheimer.

Elsheimer crowds his scene through the use of compressed perspective, so that the figures in the background seem closer to the action. In spite of the distracting details everywhere, the focus is on Stephen. He hurts. His hands are at his side, defenseless. "Lord Jesus, receive my spirit," he prays. And as one of his four executioners stretches his arm to fling the last deadly stone, Stephen cries with a loud voice, "Lord, do not hold this sin against them" (Acts 7:59–60). According to the Scriptures, heaven had opened for him before his stoning and he saw Jesus standing at the right hand of God. Elsheimer repeats this vision to comfort him in his death.

The richly dressed man on horseback is probably Paul (then called Saul), who witnessed this execution and consented to it. Stephen's martyrdom began a wave of persecution against the Christian community, and Saul took an active role in it until his own conversion (see pp. 152–153). He and the others see Stephen, but they cannot see the angels coming to fetch him to heaven. Later Paul would witness a similar vision, one that would turn his heart to Jesus.

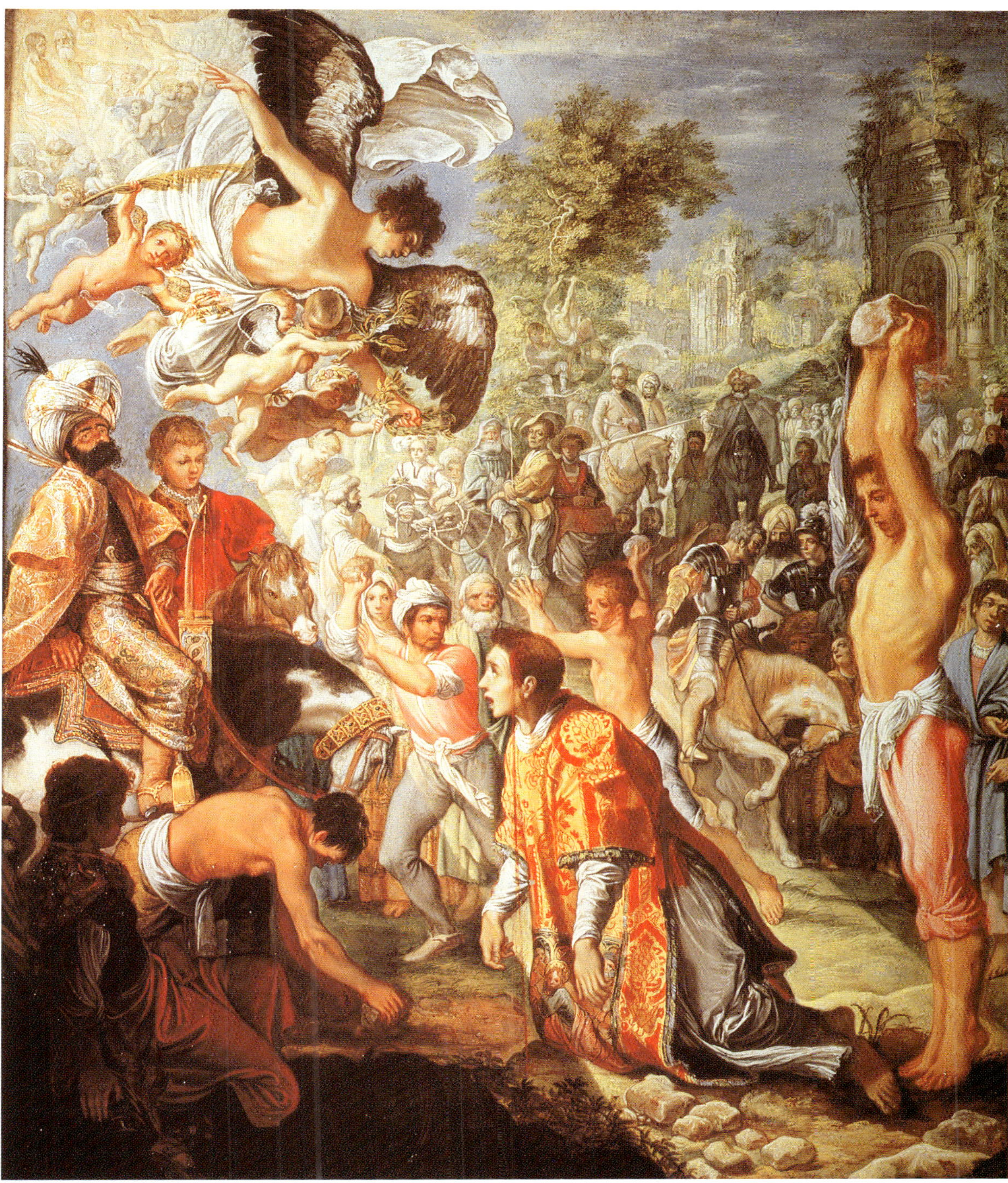

Stoning of St. Stephen
ADAM ELSHEIMER, German, 1578–1610
National Gallery of Scotland, Edinburgh. Oil on silvered copper. 13¾ × 11¼ in.

Elsheimer lived most of his adult life in Rome. The ruins covered with vegetation behind the mob of onlookers are based on buildings he saw there. His works are almost all small and painted on copper, which retains the depth of colors better than wood or canvas. The artist's short life was interrupted by bouts of melancholia, and his output was small. Yet, works he created were copied by Rubens and Rembrandt, the greatest tribute one artist can pay to another.

The Centurion Cornelius

Caesarea, 65 miles northwest of Jerusalem on the Mediterranean coast, was the administrative center of the Roman government in Palestine. A large number of native Romans, called the "Italian Cohort," were stationed there, and one of their officers was the centurion Cornelius. He had a reputation among the Jews for his piety, his liberal giving of alms, and the devotion of his household to God. One day an angel came to him and told him that his prayers and alms had "ascended as a memorial before God" (Acts 10:4) and he was instructed by the heavenly visitor to send men to Joppa to fetch Peter. Even though he did not know why Peter should come to him, he did as he was told. Cornelius called two of his servants and a devout soldier, told them everything that had happened, and sent them to Joppa, a port town about 40 miles south. Rembrandt shows Cornelius instructing his messengers.

Peter had never preached to the Gentiles and believed that only the Jews were to follow Jesus, the Messiah. But while Cornelius's messengers were traveling down the coast, a vision came to him of all kinds of nonkosher animals, birds, and reptiles. Three times a voice told him, "What God has cleansed, you must not call common," so Peter gladly went to Caesarea, preached to Cornelius's large household, and converted them all. They were the first Gentiles to be baptized.

Rembrandt somewhat indiscriminately raided his large collection of exotic costumes to clothe his models for this picture. While a turban is not right for a Roman commander, nor an unmatched and incomplete set of armor for a Roman legionnaire, it is the sincerity in the faces of these men on which the story depends. Cornelius so believed in the message of the angel that when he met Peter he fell down and began to worship him, thinking he was God. Peter quickly set him straight by telling him the story of Jesus. Rembrandt understood a faith so great that it would follow an angel anywhere. By eliminating everything from the painting but the determination of these four men to fulfill a vision, Rembrandt makes a statement about trust and faith.

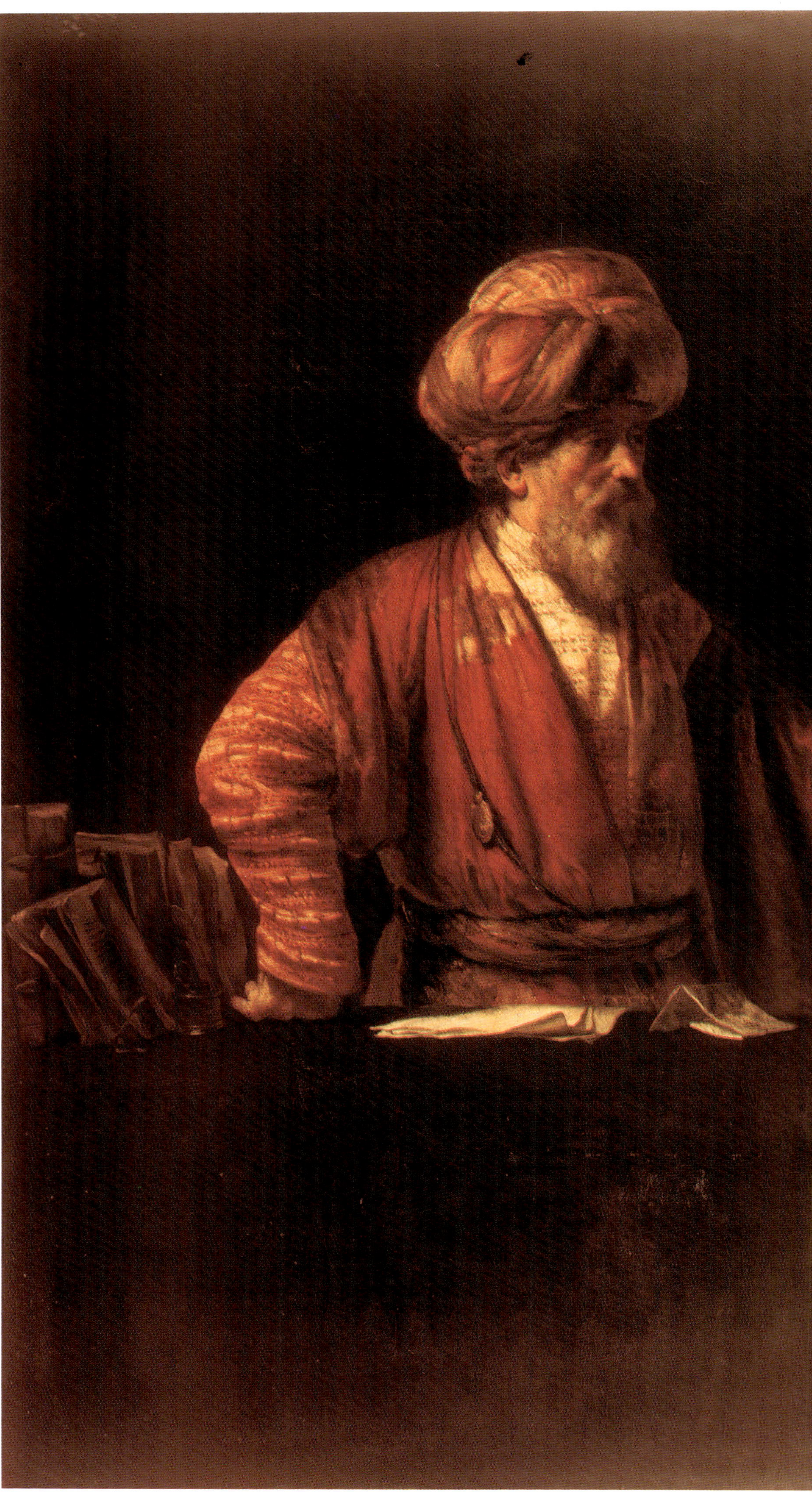

The Centurion Cornelius
REMBRANDT VAN RIJN, Dutch, 1606–1669
Wallace Collection, London. Oil on canvas. 71½ × 87 in.

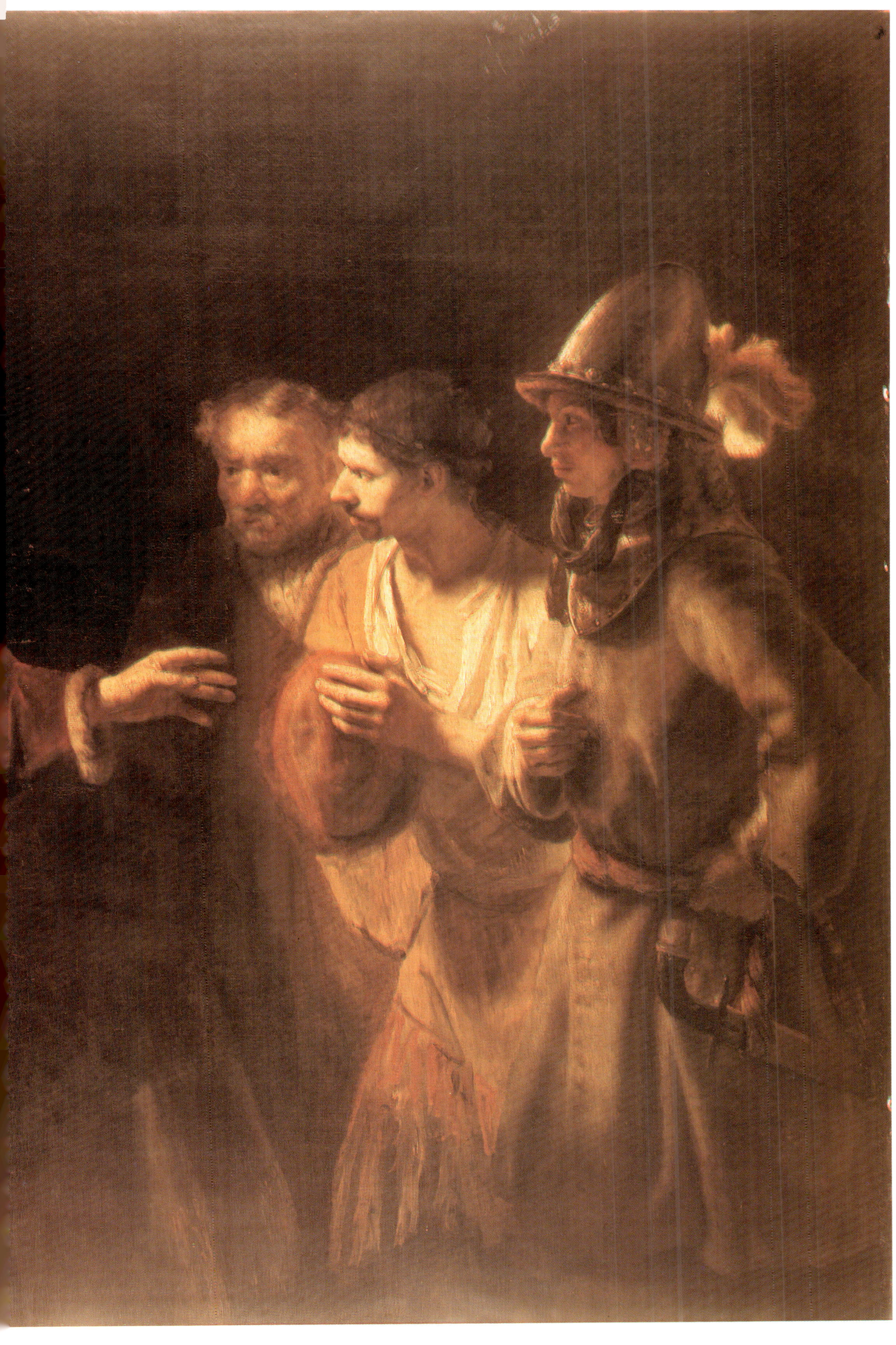

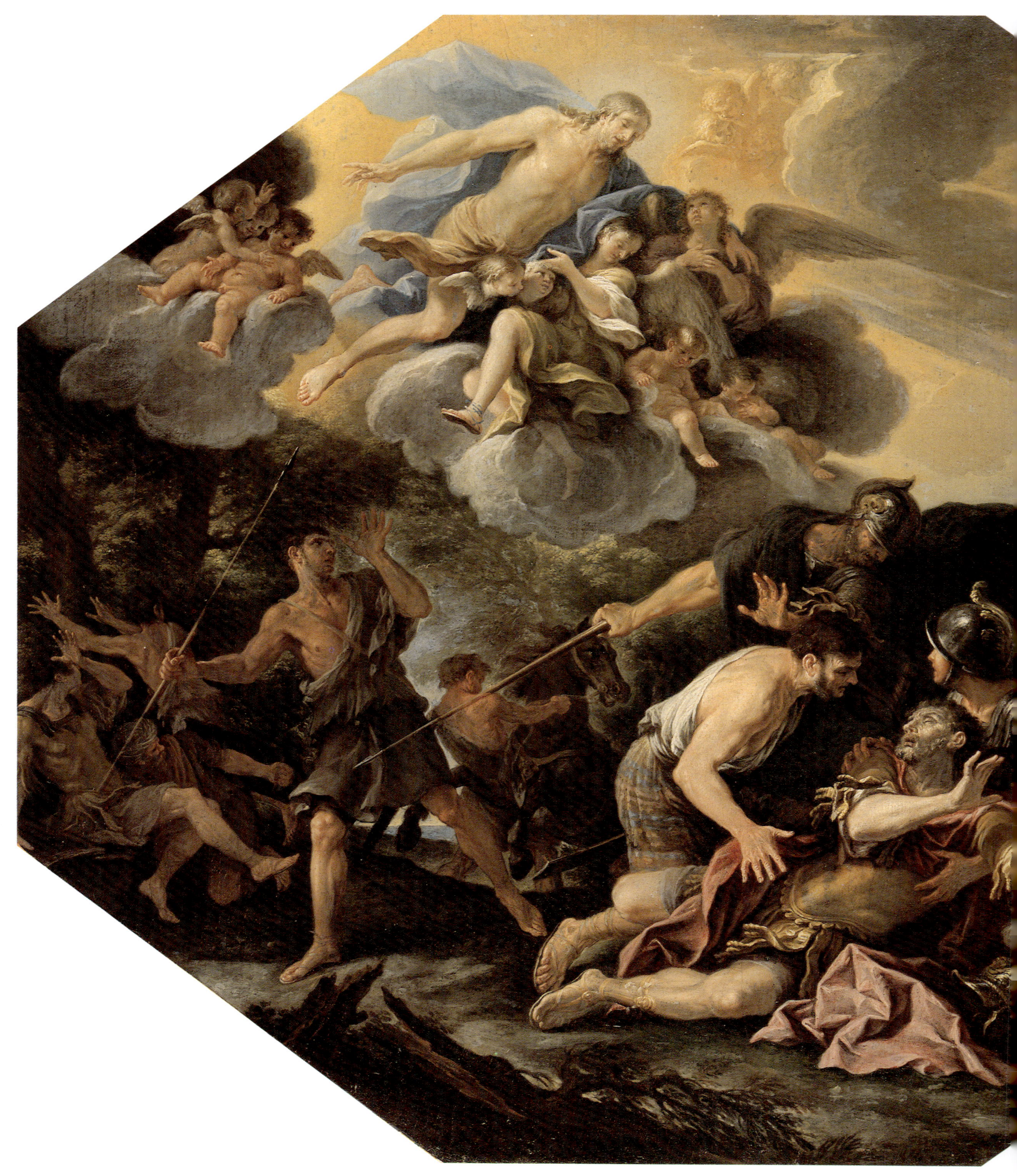

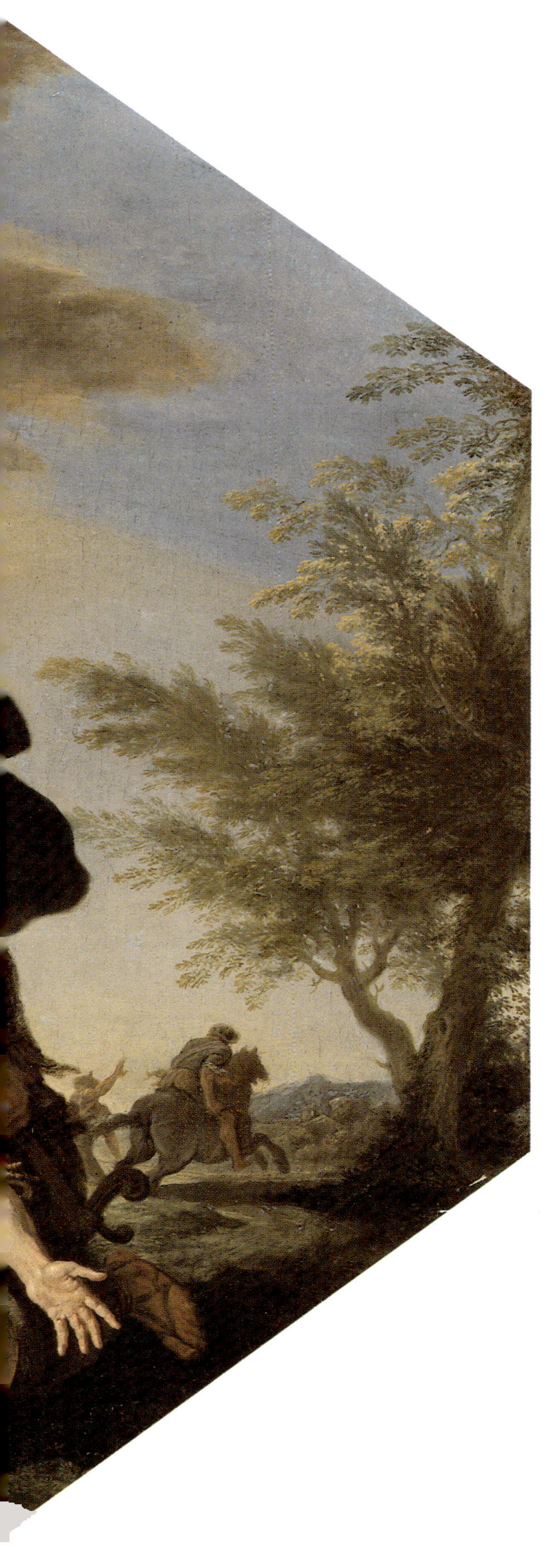

Conversion of Saul

Saul was a Jew of the Diaspora and had received rabbinic training. A strict Pharisee, this anti-Christian zealot had the support of the Jewish officials in his wide-ranging raids against the followers of Jesus. On his way to Damascus to round up Christians for transport to Jerusalem, he was knocked from his horse by a flash of light from heaven. As he lay on the ground, a voice said, "Saul, Saul, why do you persecute me?" When Saul asked who was speaking to him, the voice identified himself as Jesus; he told Saul to go into the city and wait for instructions. Following the incident, Saul was blinded for three days.

Dark broken branches in the left foreground of Filippo Lauri's version of this story suggest the force of the flash, as though it struck like a great bolt of lightning. Saul's horse strains against the efforts of a groom to calm it; two men fall down and a third flees in fear. Clouds descend to the treetops and angels spill from them, as Jesus floats above, supported by these heavenly creatures. He looks directly down at the face of Saul, his yellow loincloth and pale blue cloak providing a visual transition to the golden sky above, with its powerful rays of light.

Filippo Lauri shows Saul as a Roman soldier, with a cohort of men. Indeed, he had Roman citizenship, but he was a bounty hunter for the Temple, not the Emperor. His colleague nearest him realizes that Saul cannot see. The ink-blue cloak billowing out from the soldier with a lance isolates Saul's group from the rest of the composition. It also provides a simile for the darkness Saul would temporarily experience.

Saul went to Damascus as Jesus commanded. There he was cured by Ananias, a disciple of Jesus, who in a vision had been told that Saul was the Lord's chosen instrument "to carry my name before the Gentiles and kings and sons of Israel" (Acts 9:15).

Following the restoration of his eyesight, Saul's conversion was complete. He became the great missionary Paul and is mentioned more in the New Testament than any other figure besides Jesus himself. In this book, he will be seen again in a brilliant painting by Dürer on pp. 160–161. and at the end of his life, in a remarkably sympathetic painting by Rembrandt on pp. 158–159.

Although he had a fondness for secular subjects, Lauri was one of the hundreds of painters who were necessary to supply decorations for the new churches that were emerging thoughout Europe during the 17th century. The building boom was an expression of the Counter-Reformation, making Catholicism more accessible and more attractive to the masses, but it also was in response to a swelling population. This small work was probably shaped octagonally to be used as part of the interior design of a chapel or small church.

Conversion of Saul
FILIPPO LAURI, Italian, 1623–1694
On loan from Mr. Channing Blake to the Museum of Fine Arts, Springfield, Massachusetts. Oil on canvas. 22 × 29 in.

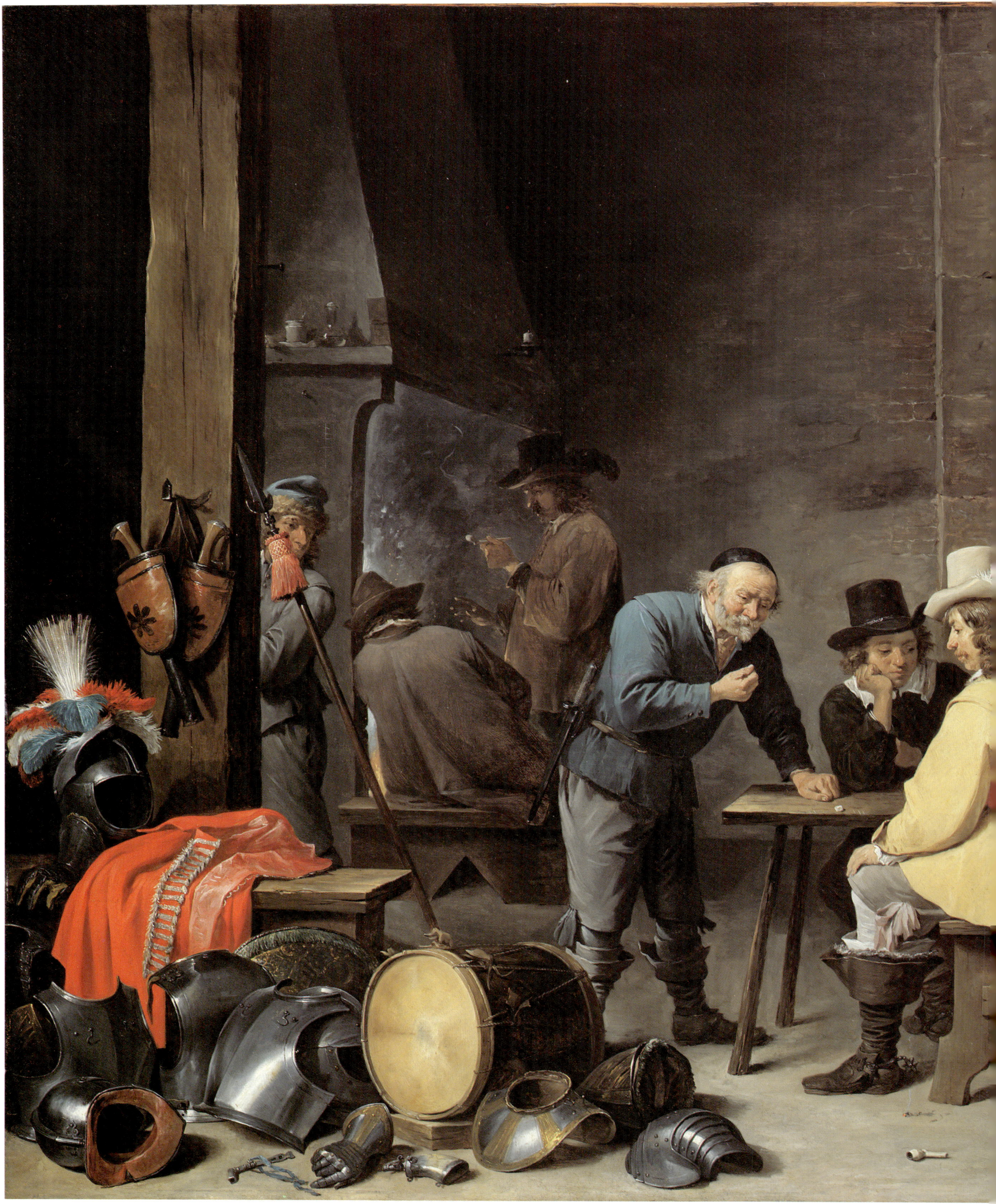

The Angel Releasing St. Peter from Prison

At the height of the first great persecution of the followers of Jesus, Herod ordered Peter's arrest. The disciple had to remain in custody, awaiting trial, under the surveillance of four squads of guards, until after the observance of Passover. Herod was taking no chances. Every door was guarded and Peter was chained in an inner cell between two watchmen. Even Peter never imagined that he could be delivered from this seemingly impregnable jail. So when an angel awakened him and told him to dress he thought at first that it was a dream. But he did as he was bid, and the angel led him past all the guards and into the city. Then the heavenly messenger disappeared and Peter went into hiding. When Herod learned that Peter was gone, he questioned the sentries and had them put to death.

One must search for the story in the *Guardroom with the Deliverance of St. Peter*, but once found the scene becomes tragic. These good soldiers are living their last night, not knowing their fate. Two warm themselves at the fire; four others throw dice. It is a quiet scene, relieved only by the shining pile of armor to the left with a bright red parade uniform, a helmet with red, white, and blue plumes, and a drum. The soldiers' jobs are easy and they are relaxed. The dungeon can be seen in the left background. The room is lighted by the angel's presence as he shows Peter the way out. David Teniers uses soft pinks and blues for this remarkable scene, in contrast to the vivid colors in the foreground.

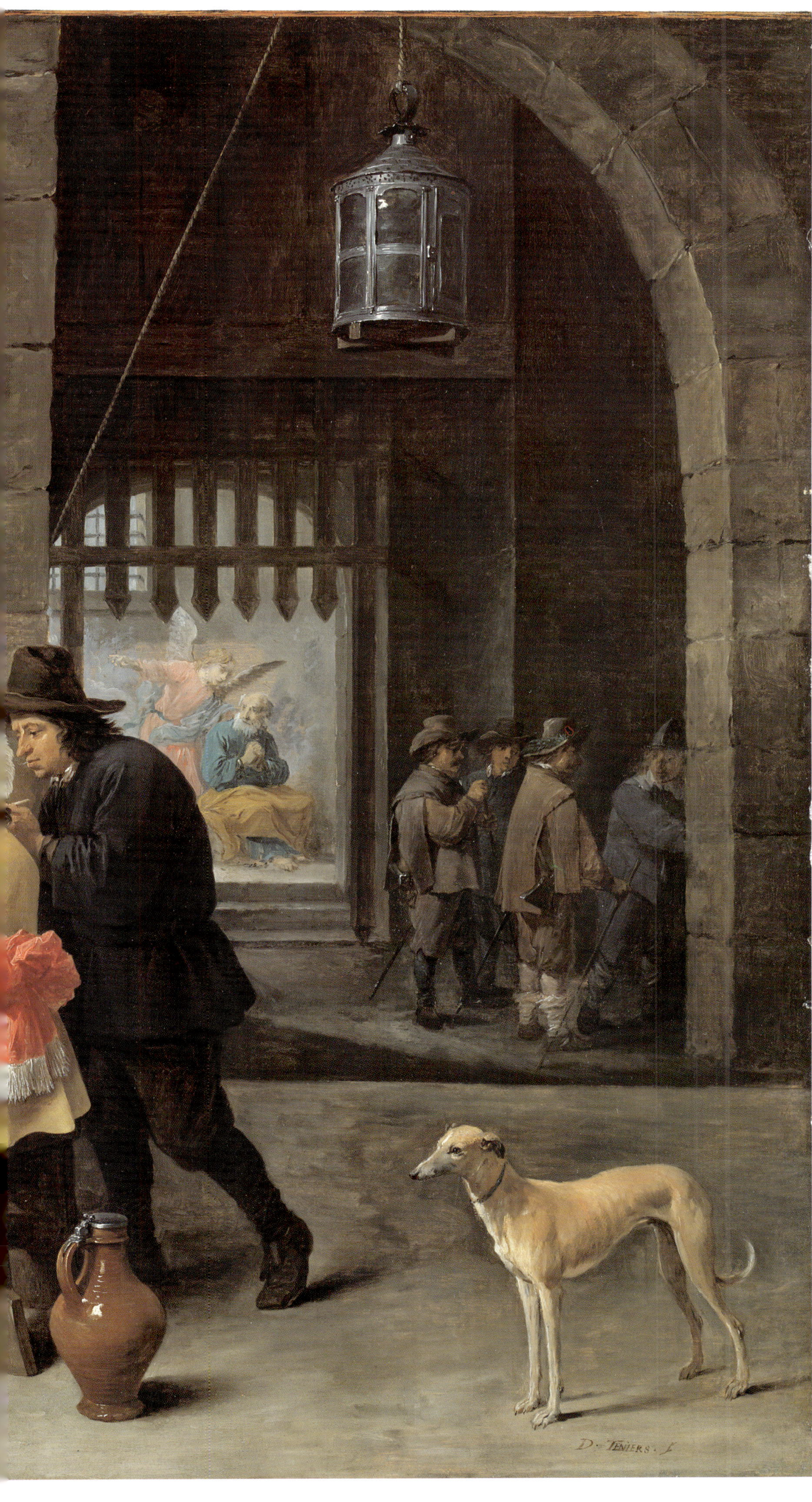

Guardroom with the Deliverance of St. Peter
DAVID TENIERS II, Flemish, 1610–1690
Metropolitan Museum of Art, New York. Oil on wood panel. 21¾ × 29⅞ in.

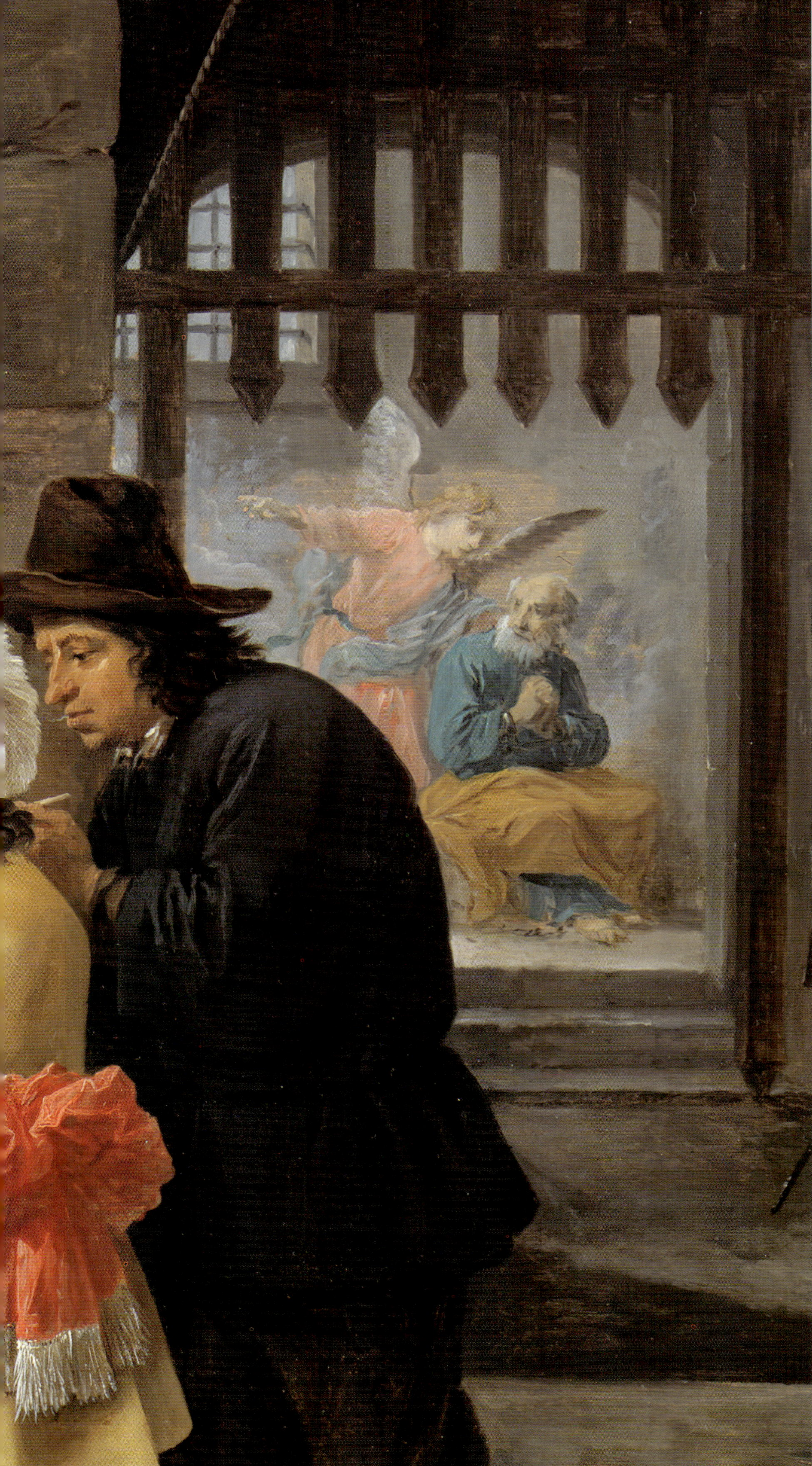

Teniers specialized in painting soldiers, among other subjects, and had the armor and accoutrements of Dutch guardsmen down pat. It is not necessary to read anything unusual into his combining contemporary soldiers with a biblical subject in this painting. He probably thought that the armor of his day was far more interesting to paint than that of the past, and it was certainly easier, requiring no research.

Benjamin West was born in Pennsylvania, but he was living in London when he turned to this story for subject matter. His depiction of *St. Peter Released from Prison* almost appears to be a closeup view of the background vignette in Tenier's painting. West emphasizes the strength of the prison door and walls and the deep sleep of the guards in the dark foreground. The angel, raising the startled Peter from the floor, seems to be the source of the only light in the cell. His hand, held high, is a sign to Peter that he was sent from heaven to perform this act of mercy. This is one of the few New Testament depictions by an American artist during this early period in the history of the new nation.

◁

DETAIL

Guardroom with the Deliverance of St. Peter

▷

St. Peter Released

BENJAMIN WEST, American, 1738–1821

Ellen Kelleran Fund, Courtesy of The Museum of Fine Arts, Boston. Oil on paper mounted on wood panel. 14¼ × 10¾ in.

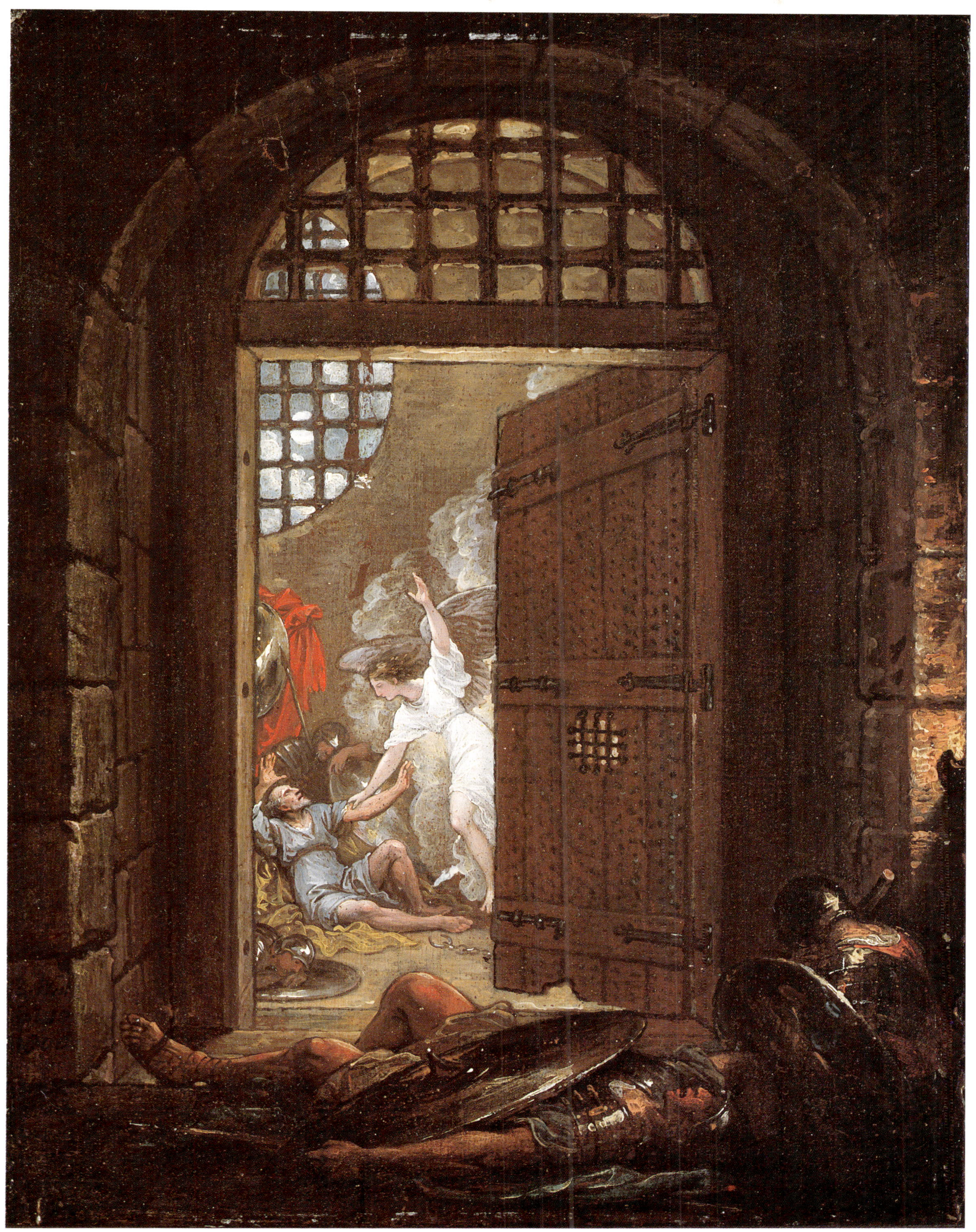

The Apostle Paul in Prison

How can a painting by a 19-year-old provide as much access to the interior life of an old man as does *The Apostle Paul in Prison* by Rembrandt? How could the artist have understood so much so early in his life? Right from the start, it was the genius of this only child of older parents to search for the posture, the gesture, the expression that revealed the personality within, and to capture what he discovered in paint. His subjects were often his own parents and other old people who were neighbors in Leiden, where he was born and raised. After Latin school and a few months at the town's famous university, he set up shop as an independent painter at the age of 17. From *The Apostle Paul in Prison*, executed two years later, it is clear that he was already in full possession of the techniques and insight that would make him famous.

What Rembrandt's painting shows is an apostle who is over 60 years old. He has traveled as a missionary all through Asia Minor and Greece. Though his feet hurt, his strong thighs and back are ready to carry him even further. Right now, however, he is in prison on charges of sedition and profaning the Temple, but he continues his ministry through the written word. With open-eyed concentration and an inner spirit that is as bright as the shaft of light in his cell, he decides how to translate the mysteries of Christian faith into simple words. As usual, he sets forth his own example: "I have learned, in whatever state I am, to be content. I know how to be abased, and I know how to abound; in any and all circumstances I have learned the secret of facing plenty and hunger, abundance and want. I can do all things in him who strengthens me.... And my God will supply every need of yours... The Grace of the Lord Jesus Christ be with your spirit" (Philippians 4:11–23). The 10 letters of Paul in the New Testament are the oldest surviving Christian documents, and four of them, including his last one to the Christians at Philippi, quoted above, were written from prison cells. By tradition, artists have ascribed an attribute or two to many of the saints. These are typically objects with which the individual was associated. Paul's attributes are books and a sword, and they are seen here. The latter refers both to his beheading under the Emperor Nero and his militant Christianity.

The Apostle Paul in Prison
REMBRANDT VAN RIJN, Dutch, 1606–1669
Staatsgalerie, Stuttgart. Oil on wood panel. 28¼ × 23¾ in.

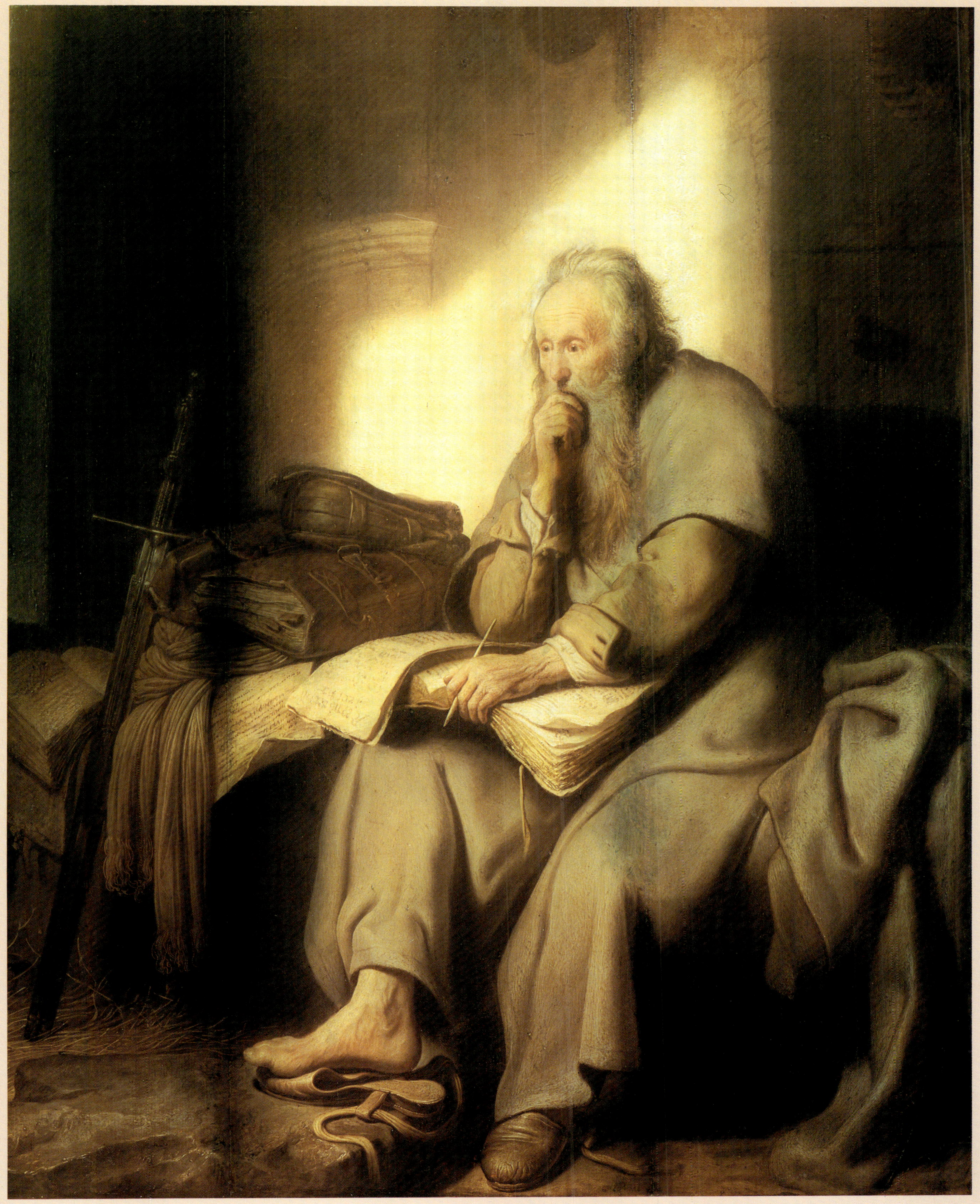

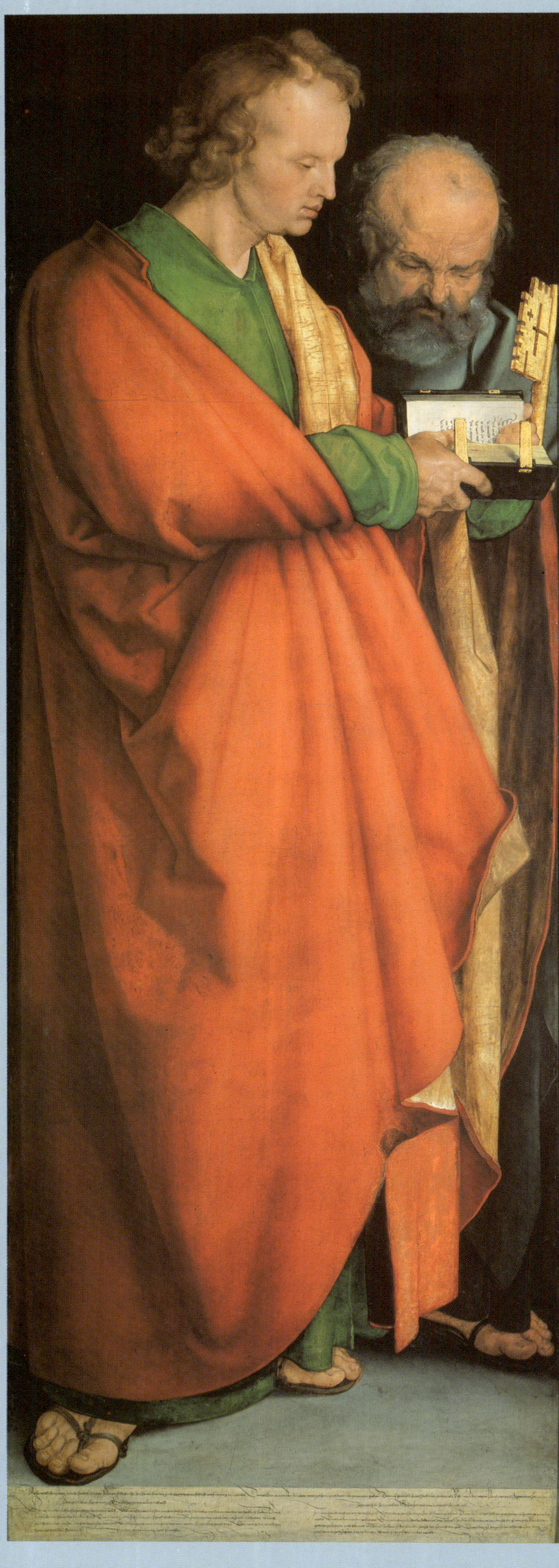

The Four Apostles

Albrecht Dürer was one of the first artists to break out of the medieval mold that placed painters on a social level with bakers, bricklayers, and candlestick makers. He presented himself as a celebrity. Fortunately for him, his talent was equal to his opinion of himself. These two great paintings, *The Four Apostles*, were the culmination of his brilliant career. He worked on them for two years and then, in an unprecedented move, donated them to the town council of Nuremburg, his native city, as a source of inspiration in difficult times. The inscriptions beneath the Apostles come from The Second Letter of Peter and The First Letter of John and are warnings about false prophets. A third inscription from The Revelation to John is a reminder of John's curse that anyone who adds or subtracts from his work will receive the plagues of the Bible. The councilmen did not alter Dürer's work in any way, if that was what he was worrying about when he added such an ominous verse to the painting, but they did sell it about a hundred years after the death of the great artist.

There were, in fact, 12 apostles, not just four, as Dürer pictures them. They were the 11 original disciples of Jesus, and Matthias, who replaced Judas the betrayer. Early Christian apologists saw a corollary between that number and the 12 tribes of Israel. Jesus' charge to the apostles after his resurrection was that they preach the gospel, lead the church, and forgive sins, all under the guidance of the Holy Spirit. After his conversion, Paul spoke of himself as an apostle, and Dürer includes him. He wears a voluminous steel-gray cape and stands next to Mark. Mark, who appears almost disembodied, was not a disciple and apparently did not know Jesus personally, but became prominent after the resurrection as a companion of Paul and

The Four Apostles (Peter, John)
ALBRECHT DURER, German, 1471–1528
Alte Pinakothek, Munich. Wood panel. Each, 85 × 30 in.

Peter. He is the author of The Gospel According to Mark and holds a small scroll in his hand to symbolize that book. Paul's tome is huge in comparison, but he did write much more than Mark. In general, Paul looms larger than the others. He looks at the viewer, and Dürer allots him more space than even John, who is on the left panel in his elegant red wrap next to Peter, holding the great "Key to the Kingdom," his symbol in Christian art. Incidentally, Paul was the favorite apostle of Martin Luther, whose writings brought great religious consolation to Dürer.

Albrecht Dürer devoted much of his career to the design and execution of a series of woodcuts and engravings that were widely distributed by him to famous artists, philosophers, and princes throughout Italy and northern Europe. His great fame could rest solely on their power and importance, but he also painted superbly. Since his youth, he knew of the pursuit of ideal proportion begun in the Italian Renaissance. At the time he labored on these four imposing figures, he was also writing a treatise on measurement and was working on his *Four Books on Human Proportion*, which was published posthumously. But there is nothing didactic about this work. Its power is in its realism, in the convincing volumes of the forms, and in the concentration on the men's faces. Each seems in his own world, like actors in the wings before a performance. In another minute, they will step out, filled with the spirit of God, and begin to preach.

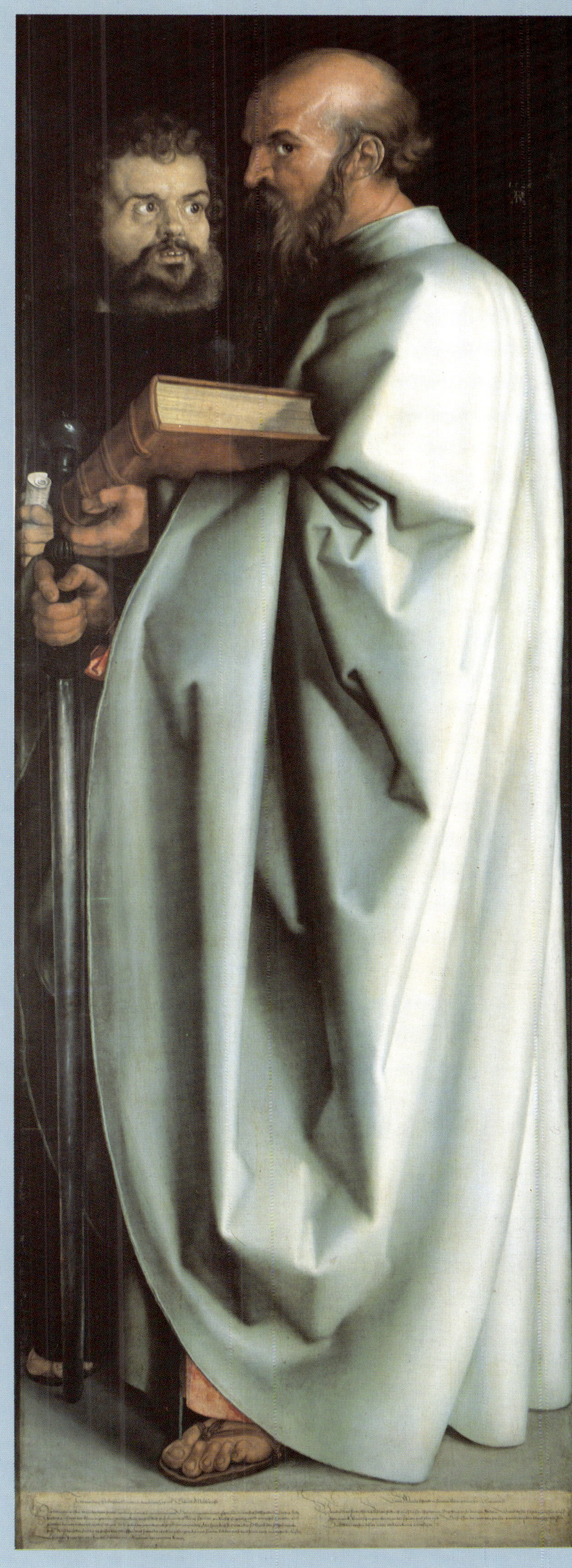

The Four Apostles (Mark, Paul)
ALBRECHT DÜRER, German, 1471–1528
Alte Pinakothek, Munich. Wood panel. Each, 85 × 30 in.

John Called to Write the Revelation

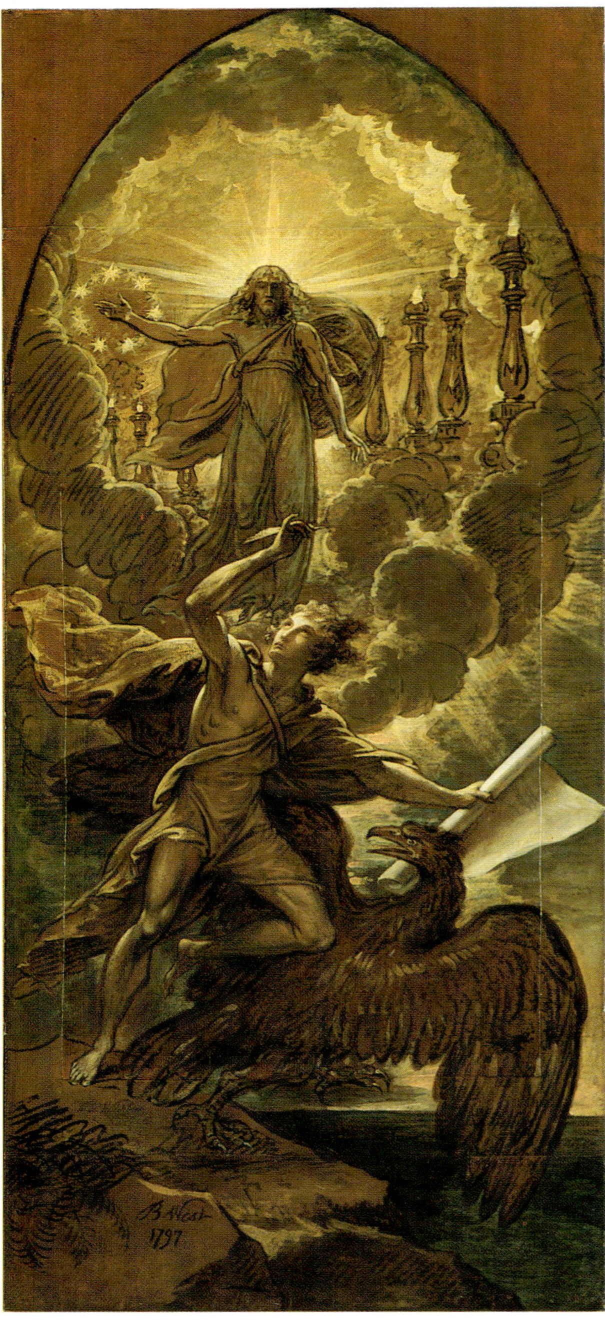

John Called to Write the Revelation
BENJAMIN WEST, American, 1738–1821
Sarah Campbell Blaffer Collection, Houston. Oil on paper
57⅞ × 26½ in.

The imagery of The Book of Revelation, the last book of the New Testament, did not have universal appeal to artists. Many must have found it too specific in its rich detail, not leaving enough room for artistic imagination, and others must have found a drawback in the lack of narrative. The original Greek text and many translations lack polish and are sometimes awkward in describing impending calamities. Certain artists probably shared Martin Luther's view that "Revelation is not revealing." Benjamin West seems an unlikely candidate to be a major illustrator of The Revelation to John, also called The Apocalypse or The Book of Revelation, because he came from a Pennsylvania Quaker background that frowned on anything but the simplest expressions in paint, such as portraiture. But his many years in London as history painter to King George III and as a founder and then president of the Royal Academy gave him fluency in a variety of styles and enormous confidence in taking on new assignments. He was one of the senior artists of the English-speaking world in 1797 when he executed this magnificent oil sketch as one of a series of designs from The Revelation to John, probably intended to be translated into another medium such as stained glass.

The Book of Revelation found John on the Greek Island of Patmos as a prisoner because of his Christian faith, probably during the persecution under the Emperor Domitian (A.D. 95). In the book's first chapter, he described a loud voice that came from behind him. It commanded him to write what he saw and to send it to the seven churches in Asia Minor. What he indeed saw were seven golden candlesticks and a man "clothed with a long robe with a golden girdle round his breast; his head and his hair were white as white wool, white as snow; his eyes were like a flame of fire, his feet were like burnished bronze, refined as in a furnace, and his voice was like the sound of many waters; in his right hand he held seven stars . . . and his face was like the sun shining in full strength" (Revelation 1:12–16). This man identified himself as the Christ and explained that the seven candlesticks represented the churches of Asia Minor and the stars were their angels.

The eagle has long been identified with John as his particular symbol and here in West's painting he supports his left knee upon one. He starts to write with a great flourish of his quill, then pauses to turn around so that he can see who is speaking to him. There stands the awesome figure of Christ engulfed in a mandorla of billowing clouds, his right arm gesturing toward a circle of stars, and his imposing figure flanked by seven enormous candleholders. Glass, with natural light streaming through it, would have begun to capture the radiance of the flames, stars, gleaming metals, and Christ's shining face, but here West depends on contrasts of light and dark to give the impression of brilliance. It is a fresh and heroic vision he captures in his almost monochromatic palette, and one that ignores the atmosphere of persecution and doom that pervaded the biblical text.

The Four Horsemen of the Apocalypse

This volume includes images by a number of artists such as Jean-Baptiste Marie Pierre, Adolphe William Bouguereau, and Adriaen van der Werff, who enjoyed greater fame during their lifetimes than they do now. Jacob von Steinle was another of these, but in the extreme. A very well-known illustrator and popular art figure in his own day, he is virtually forgotten now. While paintings by the others are still exhibited in museums, his have been relegated to the storage vaults. His style is probably too anecdotal and illustrative for modern tastes, but in *The Four Horsemen of the Apocalypse* he demonstrates his poetic mastery of landscape and his ability to summarize stirring descriptions without losing the spirit of the text.

The vision of John that Steinle has painted is one of the most frightening of the apocalyptic prophesies, and one that finds frequent reference in literature but is less relevant in art. John described a white horse with a crowned rider, the Conqueror, who carried a bow. He was joined by a man mounted on a red horse, carrying a sword with which he took peace from the earth. A black horse appeared next. Its rider carried a balance, and he sold wheat at high prices in time of famine. Last came the pale horse whose rider's name was Death. "And they [the four] were given power over a fourth of the earth, to kill with sword and with famine and with pestilence and by wild beasts of the earth" (Revelation 6:8).

Steinle's grim reapers and their powerful, lively steeds face the unknown and each reacts differently. The two in the vanguard are braced for anything, even the abyss at the edge of the cloud, while Pestilence is horrified. Only Death, who is blind, charges on, fearless of what lies ahead, for he has already been there. In the victorious scene at the end of time, described in The Revelation of John, Christ and the armies of heaven will sit on white horses and vanquish even the determined Conqueror of *The Four Horsemen of The Apocalypse*, displacing him for all time and eternity.

The Four Horsemen of the Apocalypse
JACOB VON STEINLE, Austrian, 1810–1886
Städtische Kunsthalle, Mannheim

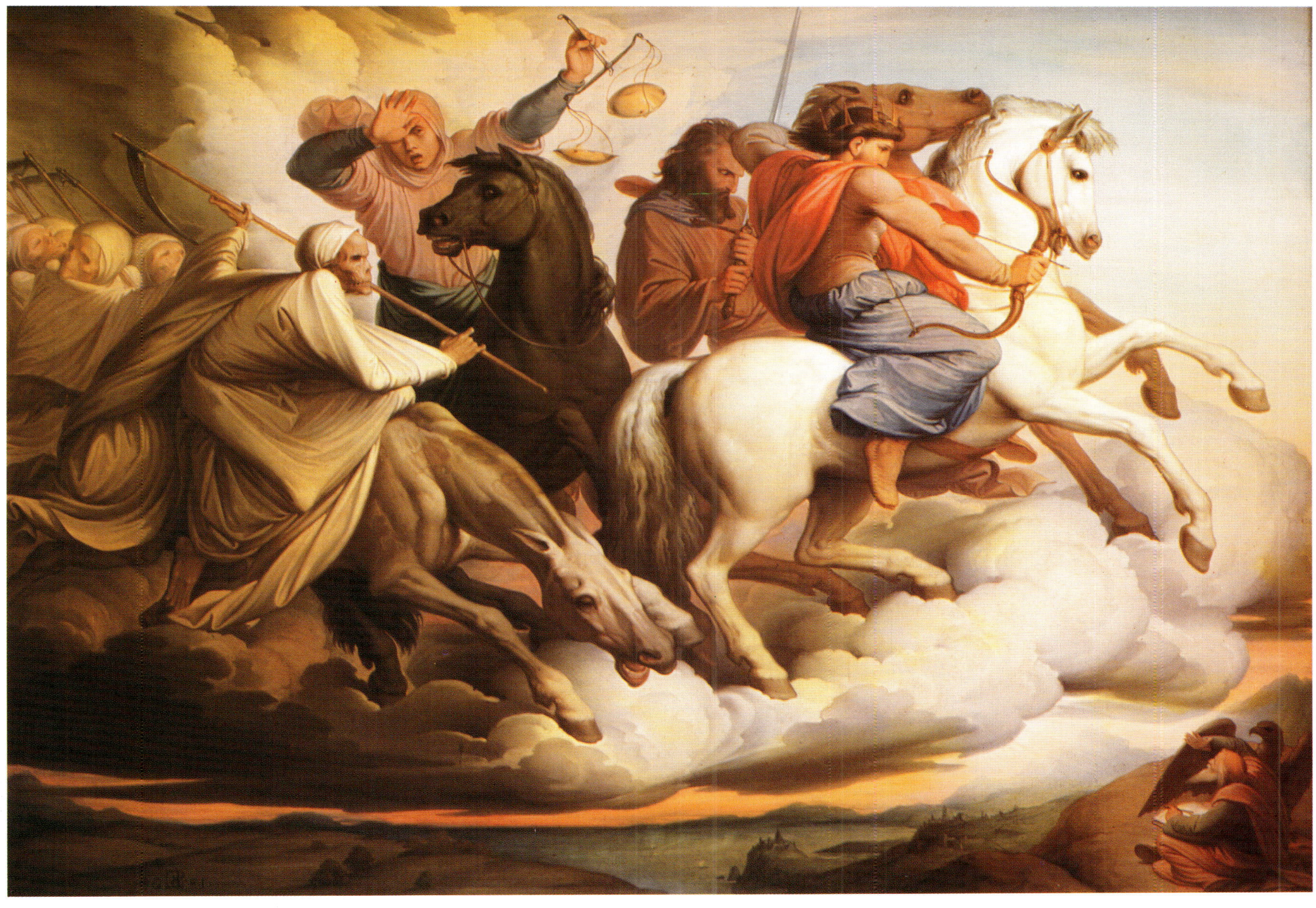

View of Jerusalem

In *View of Jerusalem*, the Austrian Expressionist Oskar Kokoschka takes viewers to the top of the Mount of Olives where one can look across the Valley of the Kidron to the place that is sacred to Jews, Christians, and Muslims alike. This modern Israeli city retains an emotional hold that is far more powerful than the attraction of its historic sites. Though King David made it his capital, Solomon adorned it through a massive building program, and Jesus spent many of his most important days within its walls, there is nothing left of the city they knew. Babylonians, Greeks, and Romans burned, ravaged, and razed Jerusalem, and what Kokoschka shows dates no further back than the early fourth century of the Christian era, and most of it is much newer than that. But in the face of Kokoschka's powerful brushstrokes the architectural history of Jerusalem is irrelevant. He has sculpted a city that seems to have materialized out of the landscape that surrounds it, created in the same way as the stones and boulders in the foreground.

Early in his life, Kokoschka made a name for himself by a group of portraits that laid bare the souls of his sitters. From 1924 to 1931, traveling through three continents, he created a remarkable series of city "portraits," and they, too, reveal more than topography. This painting, which many consider the greatest of his city vistas, has been described as having a spiritualized quality. Indeed, for all of its stoniness, there is something of the mirage about it, like the vision of the "New Jerusalem" in The Revelation to John. But Kokoschka's Jerusalem is not a new creation at the end of time. It is more a symbol of the endurance of the people and the Kingdom of God for all times, past and present. For pilgrims who come here, Jerusalem is still the most authentic terrestrial association they can have with the Bible. The buildings have changed, but it is on this soil that the heroes of the Old and New Testaments walked.

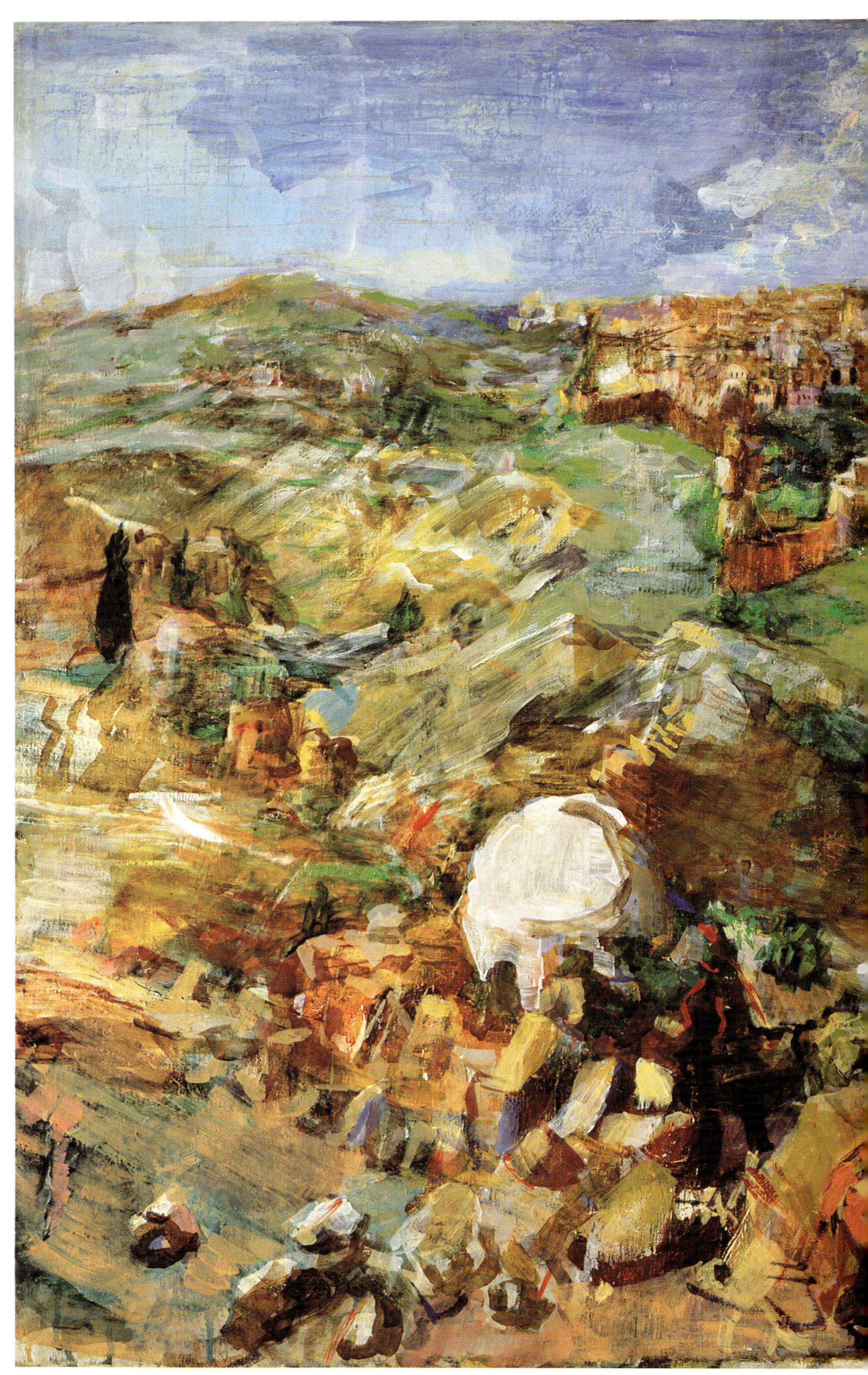

Jerusalem
OSKAR KOKOSCHKA, Austrian, 1886–1980
The Detroit Institute of Arts, Founders Society Purchase, membership and Donations Fund. Oil on canvas. $31\frac{1}{2} \times 50\frac{1}{2}$ in.

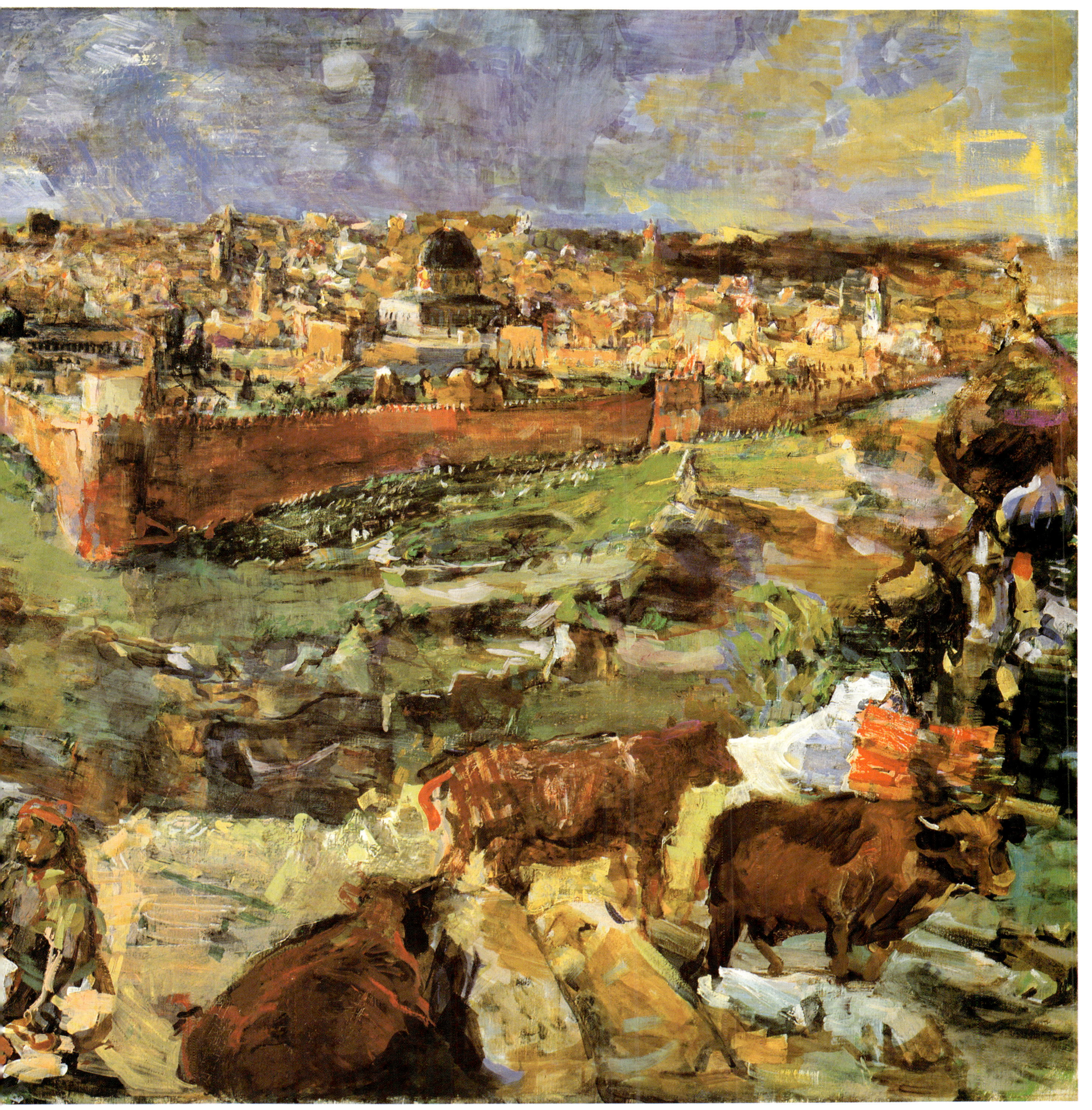

Christ in Majesty

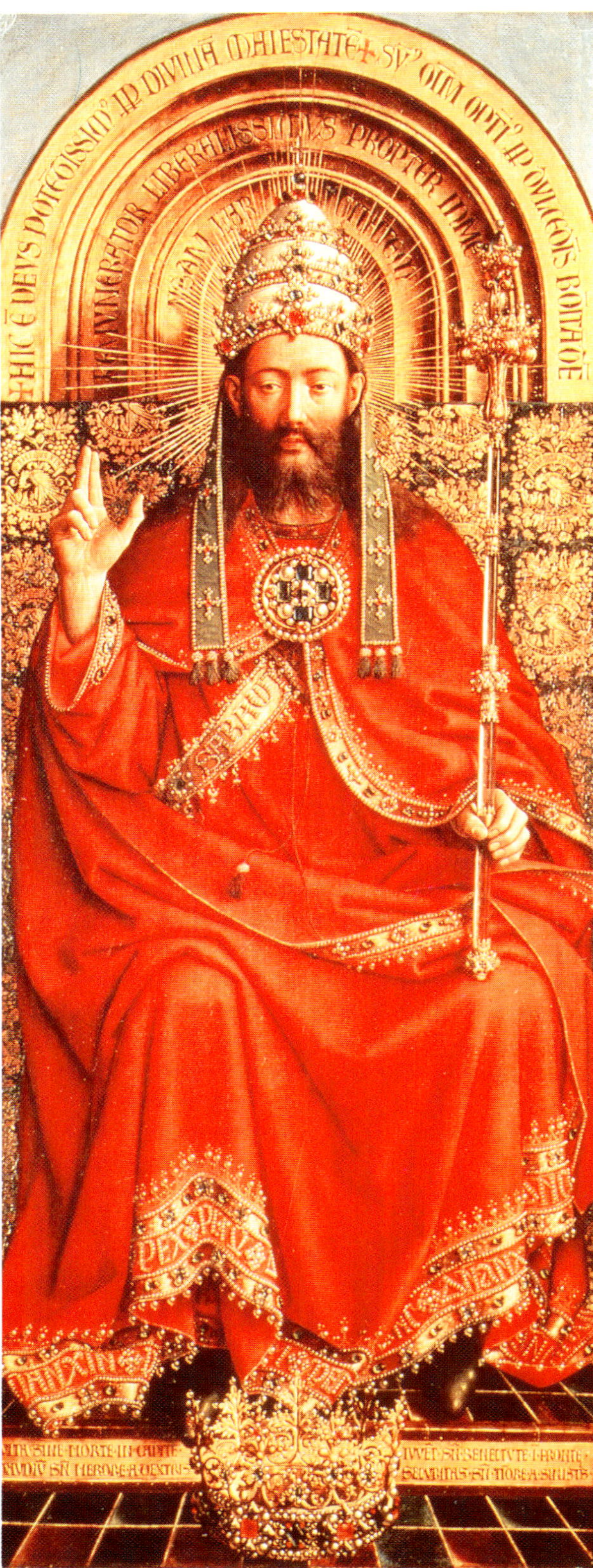

The Lord in Majesty from *The Ghent Altarpiece*

HUBERT and JAN VAN EYCK, Flemish, ca. 1390–1441

Cathedral of St. Bavo, Ghent. Oil on wood panel. 83½ × 31¾ in.

The New Testament begins with the story of the birth of Jesus, king of the Jews, and ends with descriptions of Christ, the judge and king of the universe. But these images of ruler and judge were not common in art until Christianity became a state religion, first through the Byzantine emperors who ruled from Constantinople, and then under Charlemagne, whose legitimacy as emperor came from the Pope. From Ravenna to Rome, and eventually as far away as Spain, figures of Jesus enthroned blessed the faithful from the rounded ceilings of church apses. *Christ in Majesty*, by an anonymous Spanish artist of the 12th century and housed in a Catalonian church, is typical of these stylized, formal, and somewhat fierce images. The richly embroidered garments barely reveal a body under their decorative folds, and correct human proportions were irrelevant at the time this fresco was painted. Thus the hand in this work is enormous, because it blesses, and the feet small, because they are not needed to get the figure anywhere. It is a simple, direct image, but one of theological complexity, rich in biblical references. This great presiding figure is the "Lord sitting upon a throne, high and lifted up" (Isaiah 6:1) of the Old Testament, and at the same time the judge of the end of time, who announced he was the Alpha and the Omega, the beginning and the end. Indeed, these letters from the Greek alphabet are written at the figure's shoulders. The book on his knee is open to a text that reads, in Latin, "EGO SUM LUX MUNDI," so this is also the Jesus who said, "I am the light of the world; he who follows me will not walk in darkness, but will have the light of life" (John 8:12).

Even more complex in its imagery is *The Lord in Majesty* from *The Ghent Altarpiece* by the brothers Hubert and Jan van Eyck, painted some 300 years later than the Spanish fresco. One of 21 paintings that originally constituted this great and famous altarpiece, the figure of Christ enthroned soars above the other scenes when the altarpiece is opened. Wearing the regalia of a pope and of an emperor, his right hand is raised in blessing. In the hem of his garment are words which read in English "King of Kings, and Lord of Lords." This sentiment is also expressed in symbols that appear in the brocade behind the figure, in writing at his feet, over his head, and embroidered on his stole.

While the Christ of the Spanish artist wishes to lead the faithful to light everlasting, the van Eycks have followed the directions of a theologian whose name is no longer known, to paint a Christ who awards glory in his judgment. The most important symbol for the faithful is the gorgeous crown at the feet of the figure. Made of gold which has been worked in the most refined repoussé and inset with jewels, it is the crown that Paul described, the hope of all believers: "There is laid up for me the crown of righteousness, which the Lord, the righteous judge, will award to me on that Day, and not only to me but also to all who have loved his appearing" (2 Timothy 4:8).

Christ in Majesty

ANONYMOUS ARTIST, Spanish, 12th century

From the Church of St. Clement, Tahull, Spain; now at Museo de Arte de Cataluña, Barcelona. Fresco.

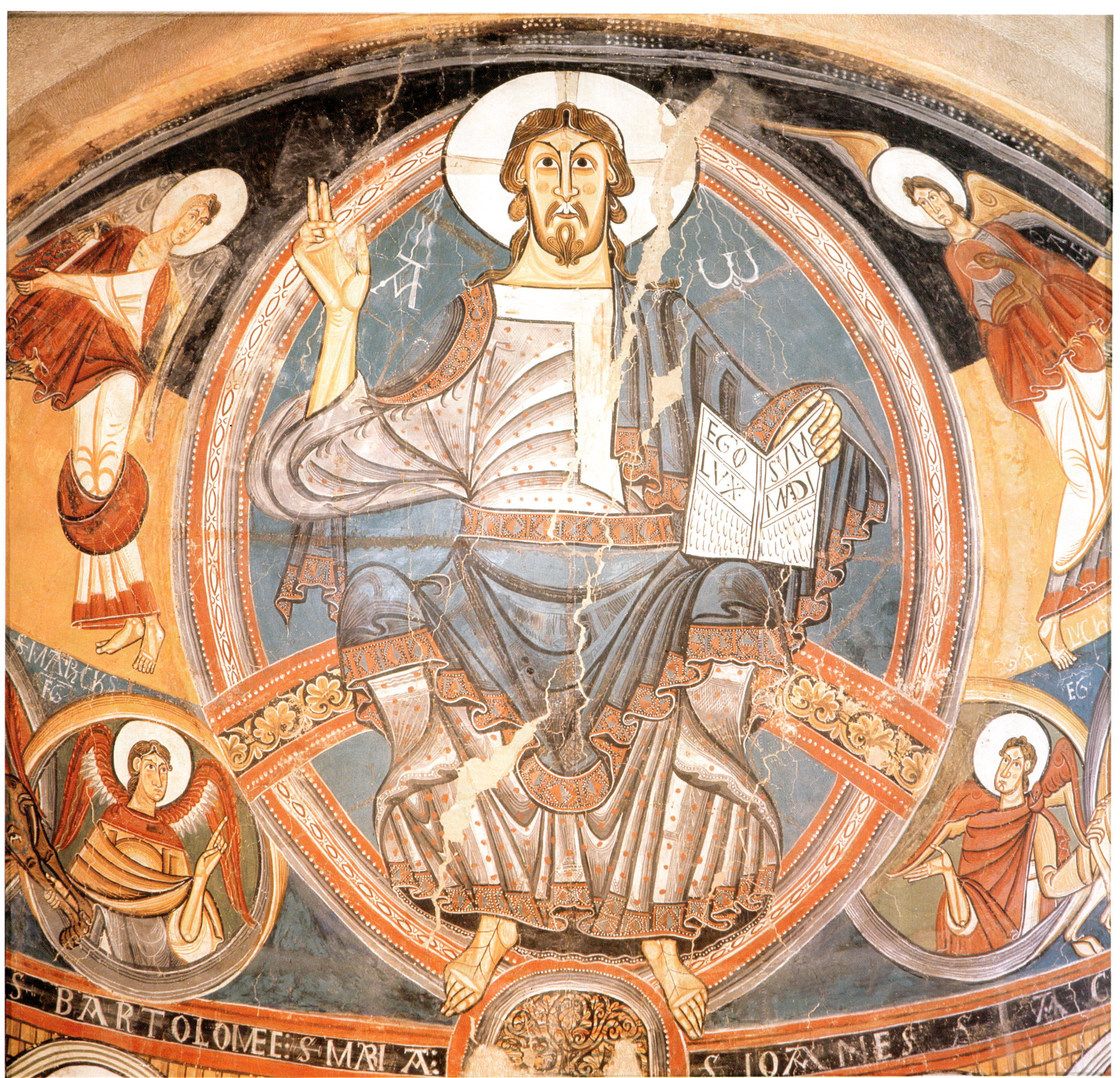
EGO SVM
LVX MVDI
S BARTOLOMEE: S MARIA:
S IOANNES

The Good Shepherd

The earliest known picture of Jesus is on the wall of a catacomb in Rome; it shows him, just as Philippe de Champaigne does in *The Good Shepherd*, carrying a sheep across his shoulders. Dating from the early third century, it is an even older symbol than that of the unrelenting judge on the last day. In the Bible, Matthew combined the two visual ideas of the judge and the shepherd, and described Jesus separating the sheep from the goats at the end of time.

The metaphor of priests and prophets as shepherds tending their flocks is common in the Old Testament, and Near Eastern imagery is full of references to rulers as shepherds. Jesus himself used the bucolic simile in trying to explain his role to a group of disputatious Pharisees: "I am the good shepherd; I know my own and my own know me . . . and I lay down my life for the sheep" (John 10:14–15). Philippe de Champaigne took this potent image and combined it with the parable in which Jesus likened the finding of a lost sheep to repentance: "What man of you, having a hundred sheep, if he has lost one of them, does not leave the ninety-nine in the wilderness, and goes after the one which is lost, until he finds it? And when he has found it, he lays it on his shoulders, rejoicing. . . . I tell you, there will be more joy in heaven over one sinner who repents than over ninety-nine righteous persons who need no repentance" (Luke 15:4–7). The great French artist painted a sublime landscape in which a shepherd runs after the stray. Jesus walks down a path, his blue cloak billowing up behind him, as though he has just arrived from heaven to the joyful sound of an angel playing a violin. The music, however, is not for him, but for the sheep upon his back. The two angels emerging from the dark clouds also rejoice over the one who was lost and is lost no more. A brushfire, common in grazing fields, provides a strangely beautiful but discordant reminder of the alternative to being with the flock.

Though shepherds lived at the edge of every village in 17th-century France, the Parisians for whom this painting was executed were distant from this humble and common occupation. They knew about shepherds, even though they never came into contact with them, just as we know about them today, as working only in rural areas. For many modern people, learning about shepherds comes early. Children become fascinated by these kind and patient men when they hear about them in Sunday school or see them in Christmas pageants. The shepherds on the first Christmas night and the Good Shepherd of the parable are the earliest images of Christianity for many a child, and they stick. This figure of hope is the one most children carry with them through life, so it is a fitting end to this book.

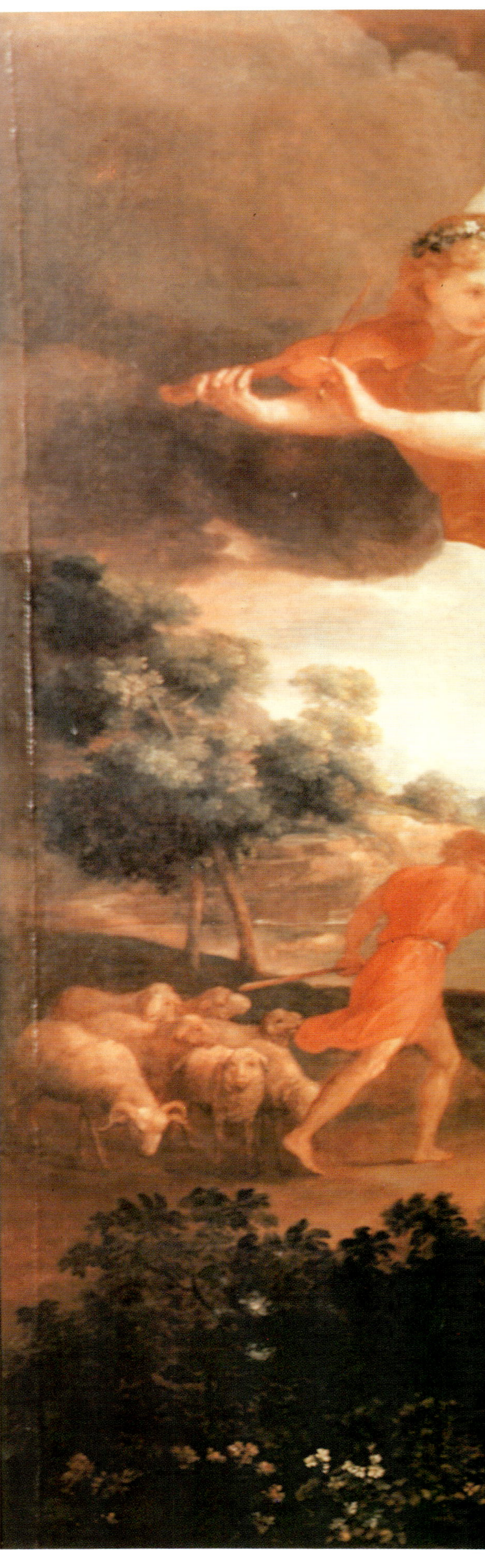

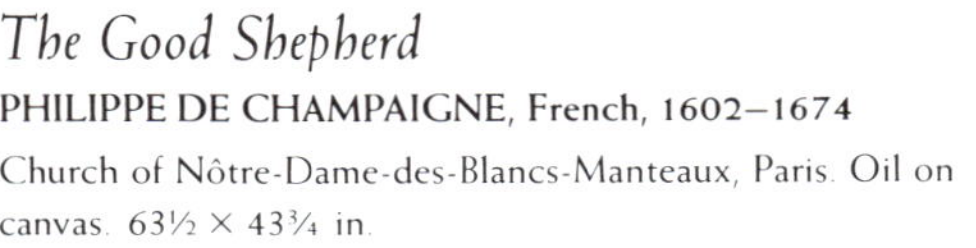

The Good Shepherd
PHILIPPE DE CHAMPAIGNE, French, 1602–1674
Church of Nôtre-Dame-des-Blancs-Manteaux, Paris. Oil on canvas. 63½ × 43¾ in.

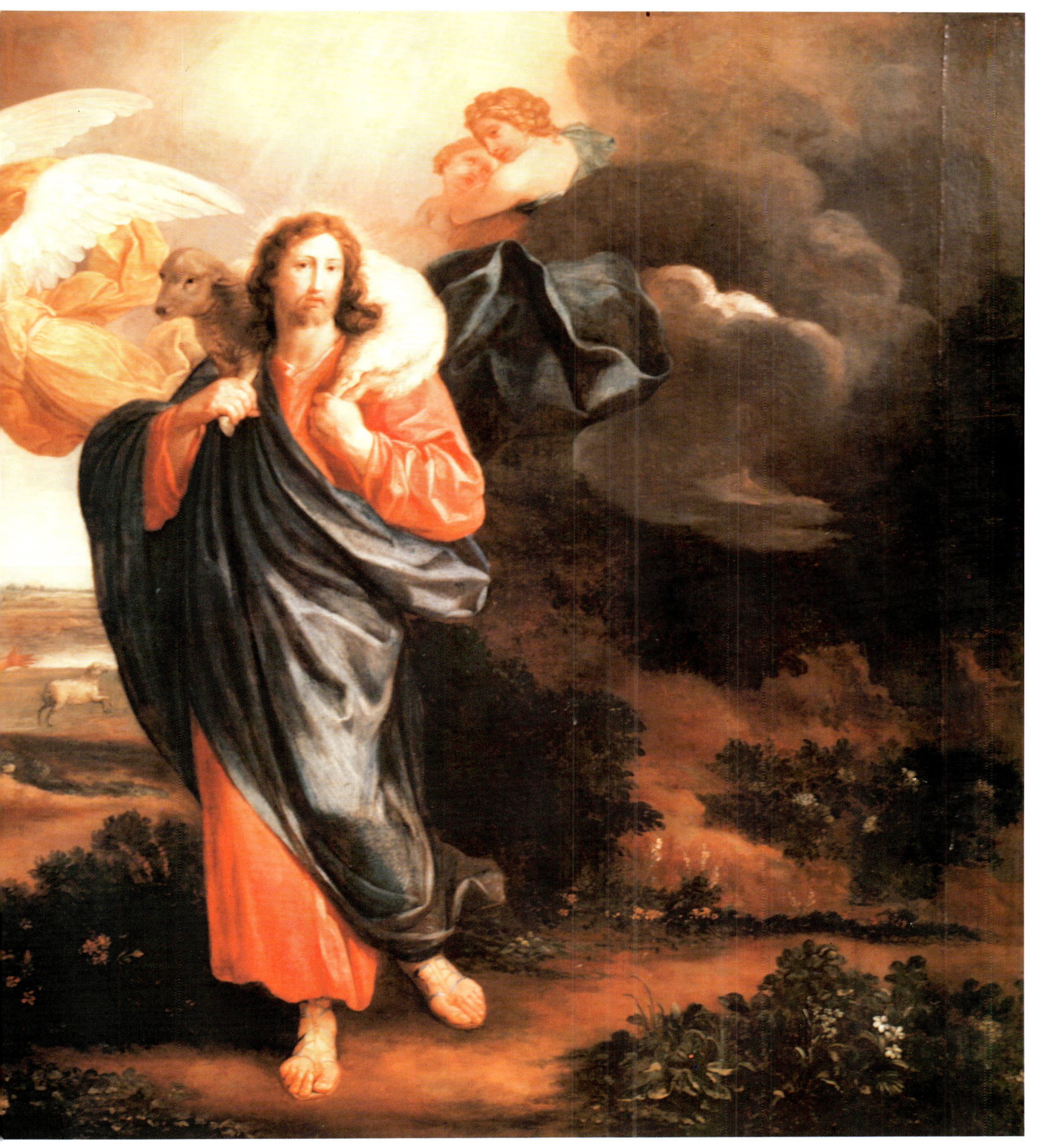

About the Artists

Albrecht Altdorfer, German, ca. 1480–1538 The leading artist of Regensburg, Albrecht Altdorfer was also active in municipal government, serving as mayor and a member of the city council. His style is marked by fully developed landscapes behind emotionally expressive figures. While he is recognized today for his paintings, his works became well known through his engravings and woodcuts.

Fra Angelico (Guido di Pietro, Italian, ca. 1400–1455 A Dominican friar and eventually prior, Fra Angelico headed a large workshop of artists whose pious subjects were painted primarily for monasteries in and around Florence. Known as Fra Giovanni during his lifetime, the appellation "Angelico" was bestowed upon him as a form of praise soon after his death. He was beatified by the Roman Catholic church in 1984.

Max Beckmann, German, 1884–1950 Beckmann's savage, expressive, and highly symbolic paintings stand among the most important statements of social criticism of the 20th century. He escaped Nazi censorship first in Amsterdam, then in New York City, where he taught art at the Brooklyn Museum School. His subjects were often allegorical or biblical, using contemporary figures.

PHILIPPE DE CHAMPAIGNE *The Presentation in the Temple*

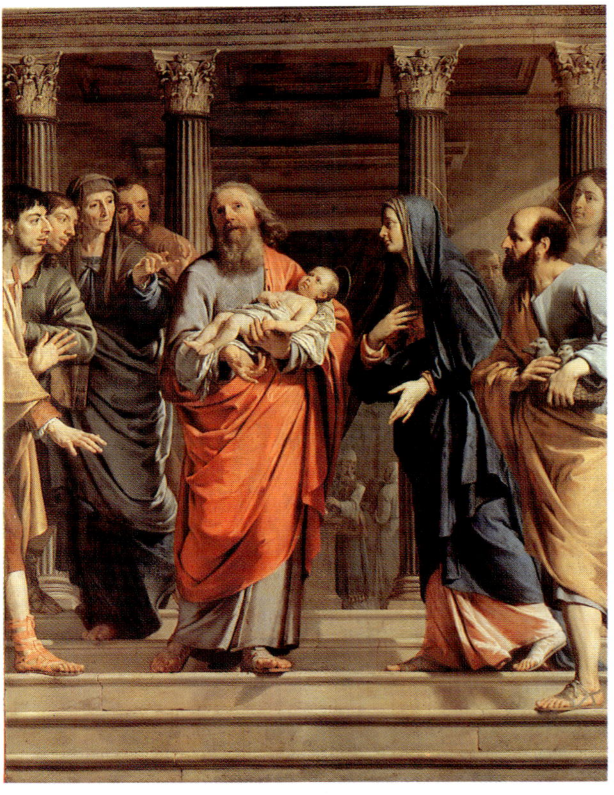

Nicolas Berchem, Dutch, 1620–1683 An influential teacher and versatile artist, Berchem ranged in his work from Italian-style landscapes, winter scenes, and views of dunes to allegorical and biblical subjects. He was famous for his cows, sheep, dogs, and other animals, as well as human figures in landscapes, and often contracted to render such subjects in the landscape paintings of his colleagues.

Adolphe William Bouguereau, French, 1825–1905 Bouguereau was an academic artist who greatly admired Raphael. His early works are drawn mainly from mythology, but he later turned to biblical subjects. His fame, however, derives from his slickly painted female nudes and sentimental figures of peasant girls.

Valentin de Boulogne (or Moïse le Valentin), French, 1591–1632 Valentin de Boulogne went to Rome as a student but preferred the company of Dutch and German artists to that of his countrymen. From the northern painters he learned to depend more on direct observation of nature for subject matter than on tradition, but the greatest influence upon his work was Caravaggio, whose style he continued to imitate long after it had been abandoned by others in Rome. Today he is considered the most faithful of the followers of that influential artist.

Pieter Bruegel the Elder, Flemish, ca. 1525–1569 Universally regarded as one of the great inventive geniuses in Western art, Pieter Bruegel the Elder was befriended by the most important thinkers of his day. Through the use of allegory and proverbs, he faithfully recorded the suffering and misery that befell the Low Countries during the 16th century. His designs were used for engravings, allowing his work wide distribution. He lived mainly in Antwerp and Brussels.

Caravaggio (Michelangelo Merisi da Caravaggio), Italian, 1573-1610 Caravaggio's earliest work was done in Rome and was limited to genre subjects, but he soon specialized in biblical compositions. A revolutionary in his use of unidealized models from the lower walks of life to represent sacred personages, he also pioneered the use of exaggerated light and shadow (*chiaroscuro*) to focus on the most salient aspects of a story. He was the most influential artist of his age, whose students in Rome, especially from France and the Netherlands, brought his style back with them to their homelands where it was imitated, in turn, by others.

Cecco del Caravaggio, Italian, active first quarter of the 17th century Virtually nothing is known of this artist, who took Caravaggio's ideas and highly dramatized them.

Philippe de Champaigne, French, 1602–1674 Born in Brussels, Philippe de Champaigne went to France as a young man and soon became painter to Queen Marie de' Medici, for whom he painted numerous religious works. Many of these commissions, as well as those undertaken on behalf of Cardinal Richelieu, can still be seen in French churches in their original settings. His daughter was a nun whose order was deeply influenced by the Jansenist movement. He, in turn, became absorbed in the austere, sober simplicity of the Jansenists, and this involvement is reflected in his best works.

Lucas Cranach the Elder, German, 1472–1553 The court painter to three successive Electors of Saxony, Lucas Cranach was a friend and neighbor of Martin Luther and is called "the painter of the Reformation." His many portraits of the famous Protestants of his age are among his best works. He was aided by a large studio of students and assistants who executed multiple copies of many of his paintings.

Gerard David, Flemish, active 1484–1523 David became the most important painter in Bruges at a time when that city enjoyed a brisk trade in exporting works of art by native painters. To meet the demand for his conservative and stately compositions, he had many of them copied again and again by his studio employees and followers, who carried his tradition well into the 16th century.

Eugène Delacroix, French, 1798–1863
The leading romantic painter of the 19th century, Delacroix made ravishing use of color, based primarily on that of Rubens, and made a considerable impact on his contemporaries. Though his output was vast, ranging in subject matter from the plays, novels, and lives of major literary figures to religious stories, his best work may be his animals and scenes from Morocco, where he traveled in 1832. The sketches he made there served as the material for paintings for the rest of his career.

Paul-Gustave Doré, French, 1832–1883 Curiously, Doré, the illustrator of some 120 books, including the Bible (1866), was more popular in England than in his native France. Late in his life he became as serious about painting as he had been about engraving, and he gained some critical acclaim in this medium. He was also a sculptor.

Duccio (Duccio di Buoninsegna), Italian, ca. 1255–before 1319 The first great artist of Siena and one of the most inspired narrative painters of all time, Duccio infused new life into the traditional Byzantine style through expressive use of outline and a psychologically sensitive retelling of the stories of Christian history. Works are ascribed to him by their stylistic connection to the *Maesta*, his great altarpiece in the cathedral of Siena, his only documented work.

Albrecht Dürer, German, 1471–1528
Dürer was the most important and famous northern European artist of his day. He brought Italian Renaissance concerns about perspective, ideal beauty, proportion, and harmony to his paintings, engravings, and woodcuts, and his art remained highly influential for generations after his death. Indeed, the quality of his graphic production is still

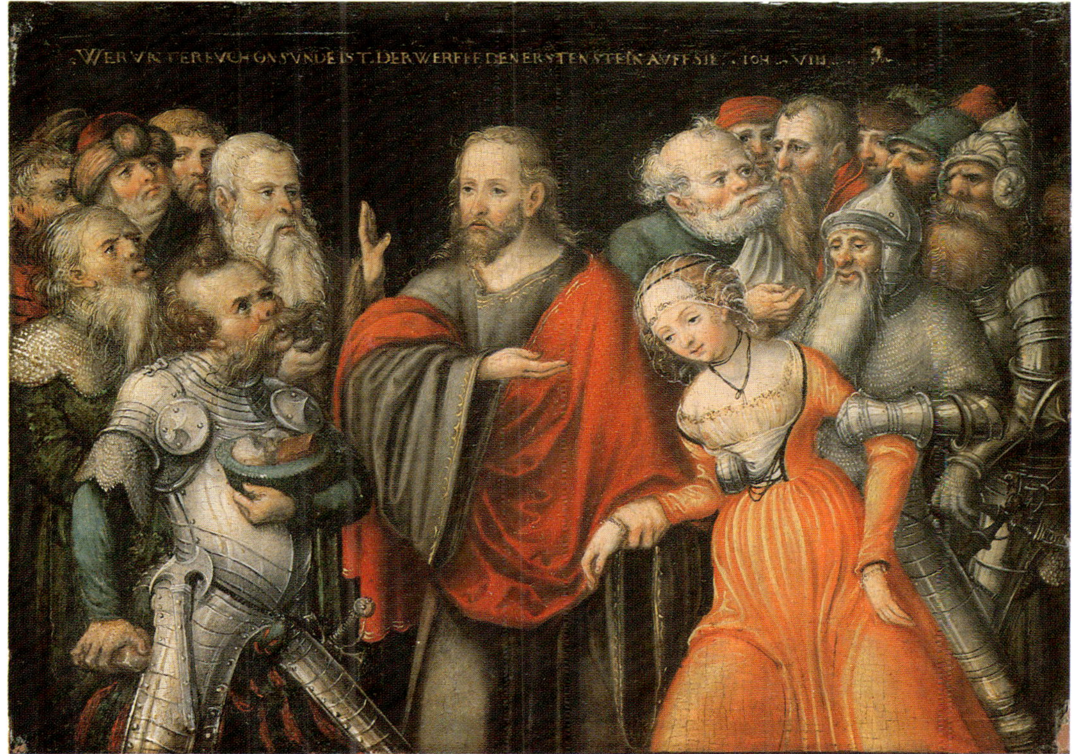

CRANACH *Christ and the Adulteress*

unsurpassed. A native of Nuremberg, where he worked all his life, Dürer traveled throughout northern Europe and Italy on a number of occasions, and his day-to-day diary of one of these trips (in 1520/21) gives the modern reader insight into the goals and problems of this great artist.

Adam Elsheimer, German, 1578–1610
Elsheimer lived most of his short life in Rome, where he came into contact with Rubens and other artists who greatly admired the intense and minutely precise paintings on which he worked very slowly. After Dürer, he is regarded as Germany's most important artist. Most of his paintings are on copper, which preserves the purity of color, unlike canvas and wood, on which colors change with age.

Jan van Eyck, Flemish, ca. 1390–1441
Jan van Eyck paved the way for the development of realism in Flanders by his attention to minute detail, differentiation of textures, and qualities of atmospheric light. He was also one of the earliest artists to experiment with oil paint. Not only was he a painter to the courts of John, Count of Holland, and Philip the Good, Duke of Burgundy, he also served these sovereign lords as a diplomat. His masterwork, the *Ghent Altarpiece*, was done in collaboration with his older brother **Hubert** (?–1426), about whom very little is known.

Domenico Feti, Italian, ca. 1589–1623/24 Although Feti was born in Rome and was painter to the court of Vincenzo Gonzaga at Mantua from 1613 to 1621, he is frequently classed as a Venetian artist because of the great contributions he made to the revival of painting in that city during the last two years of his life. He was responsible for a number of fresco cycles on biblical subjects, but his most characteristic paintings were small in scale and presented sacred stories in the guise of genre scenes, such as *The Parable of Dives and Lazarus* in this book.

Paul Gauguin, French, 1848–1903 At the age of 35, Gauguin gave up a successful career as a stockbroker to take up his weekend avocation, painting, on a full-time basis. Seeking a style not affected by the "disease of civilization," he lived for periods of time in Tahiti, where, in abject poverty, he created much of his best work. His highly personal style is rich in color and linear patterns abstracted from nature.

Luca Giordano, Italian, 1634–1705
One of the most facile palace decorators of his day, Luca Giordano created great interior schemes which can be found primarily in Naples and Spain. He also produced numerous oil paintings, many in the styles of other artists. Charles II and, later, Philip V were his patrons.

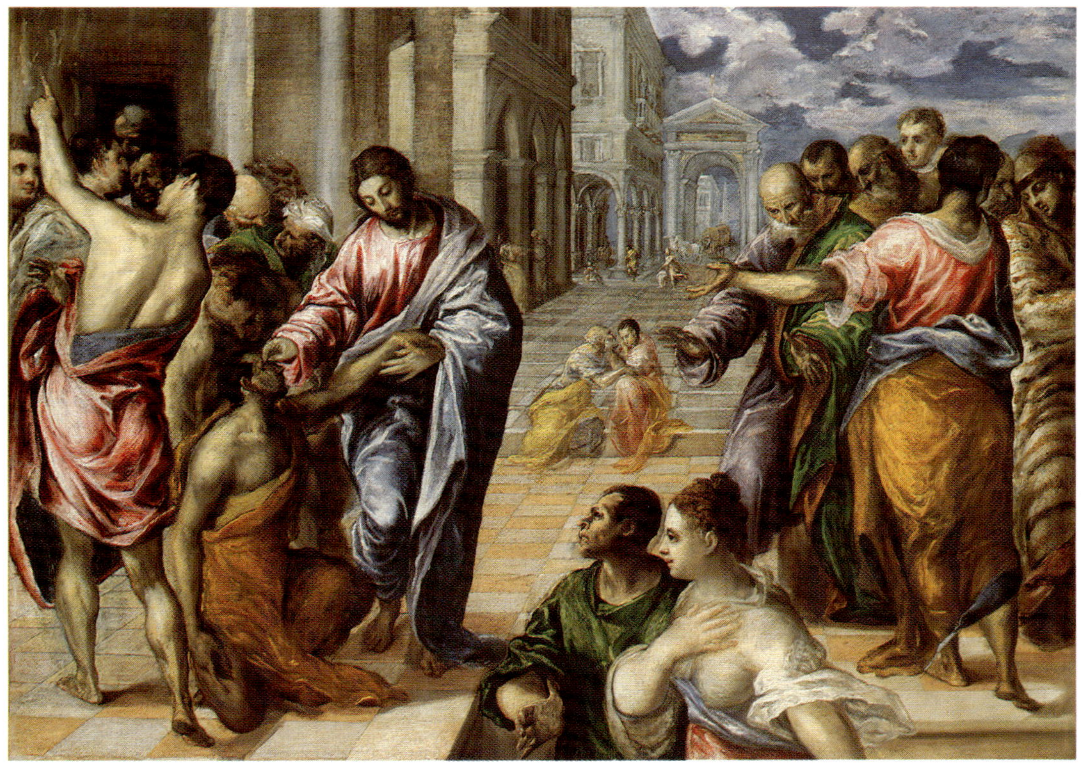

EL GRECO *The Miracle of Christ Healing the Blind*

Giorgione (Giorgio Barbarelli, or Giorgio del Castelfranco), Italian, ca. 1478–1510 Almost nothing is known of this great artist's life, but Giorgione's work influenced Venetian painting for almost 100 years after his death in his early thirties from the plague. He softened outlines and color through the use of pervading atmospheric light, creating works that are luminous and warm. Upon his death, Titian completed at least one of his paintings.

Giotto (Giotto di Bondone), Italian, 1266/67–1337 No artist of any era changed the course of art as dramatically and profoundly as did Giotto, whose figures are more realistically volumetric and more convincingly integrated with the setting than any painted before him. A Florentine, his main works were commissioned in Assisi and Padua and are there still. His last years were dedicated to the design of the cathedral of Florence.

Vincent van Gogh, Dutch, 1853–1890 Although he sold only one painting during his tragic life, van Gogh produced a body of work that is better known today than that of almost any other artist. His paintings are marked by often brilliant, expressionistic color, heavy impasto, and a rhythmic linear pattern. Although inspired by the Impressionists, his style is highly individualistic. His beautiful letters to his brother Théo trace his career and reveal his conflicts and aspirations.

Benozzo Gozzoli, Italian, 1420–1497 First a sculptor assisting the great Ghiberti in Florence, then an assistant to Fra Angelico, Benozzo Gozzoli painted many altarpieces and frescoes as a busy independent artist throughout northern Italy. His highly detailed, often ornamental works are charming and concentrate on the straightforward narration of stories from Christian history.

Francesco Granacci, Italian, 1469–1543 Concurrently with Michelangelo, Francesco Granacci was a pupil of Ghirlandaio and he assisted his teacher in a number of important commissions in Pisa and Florence. Though he was influenced by his more famous colleague-in-training, he kept an earlier, more conservative Florentine style alive through his work.

El Greco (Domenikos Theotocopoulos), Spanish, 1541–1614 Born in Crete, El Greco studied in Venice before settling in Spain in around 1577. His vision uniquely combined old Byzantine and new Italian forms into the most emotionally expressive art of the late 16th century. Because his services were enormously in demand, he required the aid of his son and a large studio of assistants.

Samuel van Hoogstraten, Dutch, 1627–1678 Although Samuel van Hoogstraten was a pupil of Rembrandt, he developed a style which was more precise than his master's, one that appealed to the rich of a generation that was younger than Rembrandt's typical patrons. His treatise on painting and perspective, published during the last year of his life, was widely used. He was also a poet and playwright who worked in England and Vienna as well as in Holland.

Jacob Jordaens, Flemish, 1593–1678 Often a collaborator with Rubens, Jacob Jordaens became the most important painter in Antwerp after the former's death. He received commissions from Charles I of England, the Queen of Sweden, the Prince of Orange, and the burgomasters of Amsterdam, and though he converted to Protestantism late in his life, he was the chief painter to the Roman Catholic church in Antwerp.

Juan des Flandes, Flemish, active by 1496–1519 Though born in Flanders, Juan des Flandes served the court of Isabella of Spain, where all of his known works were painted. He specialized in altarpieces of the lives of Jesus and Mary.

Oskar Kokoschka, Austrian, 1886–1980 One of the most celebrated portrait and cityscape painters of the 20th century, Kokoschka created powerful Expressionist works that played a significant role in the development of modern art. To escape Nazi censorship, he moved to London in 1938, and later lived in Switzerland and New York. After World War II, he established an international summer school in Salzburg, Austria.

Hans Suess von Kulmbach, German, ca. 1480–1521/22 Probably a student of Albrecht Dürer, Hans Suess von Kulmbach lived and worked in Nuremberg and was in Cracow, Poland, for several years as court painter. His characterizations of biblical figures are often highly unusual. He also painted portraits and executed designs for stained glass.

Giovanni Lanfranco, Italian, 1582–1647 Lanfranco is one of the most influential Italian artists of the High Baroque style, whose ceiling and dome decorations, conceived to be visions of heaven, are singularly splendid. These works and Lanfranco's other church decorations are primarily in Rome and Naples but were imitated throughout Europe.

Filippo Lauri, Italian, 1623–1694 Lauri specialized in scenes from ancient history and mythology, and his paintings which illustrated fables were in great demand. He sometimes supplied figures for the paintings of Claude Lorrain.

Claude Lorrain (Claude Gelée), French, 1600–1682 The leading landscape painter of the 17th century and one of the most influential artists of all time, Claude Lorrain lived and worked in Rome, where the patronage of Pope Urban VIII helped him rise in fame. While his poetic treatment of the landscape gave it legitimacy for the first time as a subject of its own, he often added tiny figures from the Bible, ancient history, or mythology, to "elevate" his work to the status of history painting.

Edouard Manet, French, 1832–1883 After studying art in Paris, Manet traveled for five years during which he became absorbed with the works of Frans Hals, Francisco Goya, and Diego Velázquez. Back in Paris, his early work, influenced by these masters, met with public and critical condemnation, but with Emil Zola as his defender, he soon was joined by other young Impressionists, whom he influenced. While his paintings were more subdued than those of Monet, Renoir, and their peers, they had a powerful influence on the development of later modern art.

Andrea Mantegna, Italian, ca. 1431–1506 One of the greatest Italian Renaissance painters and engravers, Andrea Mantegna worked mainly in Mantua and Padua. Known for his bold use of perspective and extreme foreshortening of the human form, his paintings are relatively rare. Of a number of large series that he executed, only *The Triumph of Caesar* still exists (Hampton Court, London).

Quentin Massys, Flemish, 1465/66–1530 An Antwerp painter, Quentin Massys incorporated the influence of Leonardo da Vinci with older Flemish models to produce a calm art of solid figures and soft textures. Portraits and religious subjects make up the body of his work.

Master of the Osservanza, Italian, active ca. 1430–1450 Though this important artist of Siena has not as yet been identified, 20 or so works have been ascribed to his hand on the basis of their stylistic similarity to a three-part altarpiece in the Monastery of the Osservanza just outside the walls of Siena. This great anonymous artist is named after that monastery.

Master of the Reredos of the Chapel of the Church of S. Francisco D'Evora, Portuguese, 15th century This anonymous artist worked in Portugal as a religious painter, but nothing is known of his life. Like the Master of the Osservanza, he is named after one of his works, a *reredos*, or altarpiece, in a church in the city of Evora.

Bartolomé Esteban Murillo, Spanish, 1617–1682 Bartolomé Murillo was the favorite painter of Seville, the city of his birth, where he helped to establish an art academy. While he is best known for his sweet Madonnas, he also painted a broad range of religious subjects, as well as portraits that are considered by some to be his finest works. He is not as highly regarded today as he was in centuries past, but his ability to tell stories in straightforward, simple terms suggests that a reevaluation of his talent may be in order.

MANET: *The Mocking of Christ*

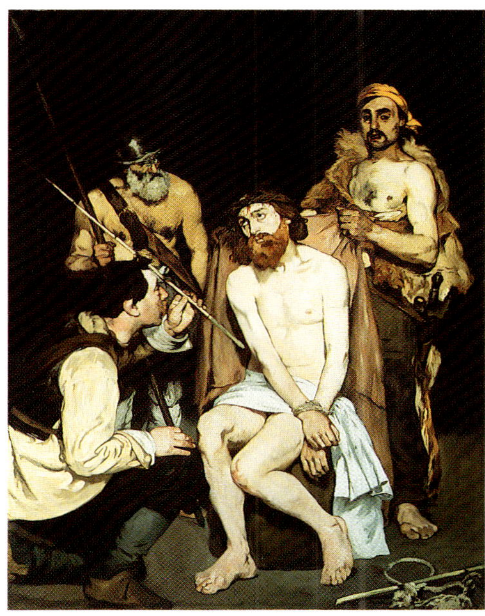

Emil Nolde, German, 1867–1956 One of the greatest Expressionist artists of the 20th century, Emil Nolde was inspired by primitive art and often produced savage, powerful images in prints as well as paintings. Flowers, demonic heads, and religious subjects are among his strongest and best known works. His life alternated between isolation in the wilds of the far north of Germany and the society of avant-garde artists.

Giovanni di Paolo, Italian, active 1420–1482 A highly imaginative Sienese artist with a taste for fantasy, Giovanni di Paolo was guided more by the art of the past than by the Renaissance innovations emerging during his lifetime in nearby Florence. His oeuvre, which was enormous, spanned more than 60 years of activity and consisted almost entirely of religious subjects.

Parmigianino (Girolamo Francesco Mazzoli), Italian, 1503–1540 Parmigianino is known for his graceful, sensuous, elongated figures, whose attenuated features define the style known as *Mannerism*. He was one of the first Italian artists to use the technique of etching, and it was through his prints that his influence reached northern Europe. He fled Rome during the sack of the city in 1527 and thereafter worked mainly in Bologna and Parma (his birthplace and source of his name).

Piero di Cosimo, Italian, 1462–ca. 1521 Early in his life Piero di Cosimo assisted his master, Cosimo Rosselli, in decorating the Sistine Chapel in Rome. Back in Florence, where he lived for the rest of his life, he executed a series of extraordinary and eccentric paintings on the life of primitive man, focusing on the discovery of fire, honey, wine, etc. His reputation as one of the most inventive artists of the Italian Renaissance rests mainly on these works.

Jean-Baptiste Marie Pierre, French, 1713–1789 As the winner of the first-prize scholarship awarded by the French Academy (later called the Prix de Rome), Jean-Baptiste Marie Pierre studied in Italy and upon his return to Paris became an active teacher at and, eventually, director of, the Academy. He served the crown and Madame de Pompadour for much of his career and produced many designs for interior decorations.

Frans Pourbus the Elder, Flemish, 1545–1581 The second of three generations of artists, Frans Pourbus concentrated on religious subjects and portraits. His son, also named Frans, exceeded him in fame and was one of Rubens's chief rivals.

Nicolas Poussin, French, 1594–1665 Inspired by the art of the ancient world, Poussin created scenes drawn from ancient and biblical history which brought him enormous fame during his lifetime. Regarded as the greatest living artist, he worked primarily in Italy, where he formulated the ideas that inspired French classical and academic art for 300 years.

Mattia Preti, Italian, 1613–1699 A powerful Baroque painter, Mattia Preti began his career in Rome, where he studied with Giovanni Lanfranco. Then he moved to Naples. After he became a member of the Knights of Malta in 1641, he moved to that island, where he decorated numerous church interiors.

Pierre Puvis de Chavannes, French, 1824–1896 A student of Delacroix and Couture, Pierre Puvis de Chavannes was primarily inspired by classical art. His sale of a painting to the French government in 1861 brought him widespread attention. Thereafter, he was in considerable demand in Paris and elsewhere. The murals that he created in his chaste and subdued style can be found in the Hotel de Ville, the Sorbonne, and the Panthéon in Paris, and in the Boston Public Library in the United States.

Raphael (Raffaello Sanzio), Italian, 1483–1520 One of the most celebrated artists of all time, Raphael created works that epitomized the harmony and balance of High Renaissance composition. Under Pope Leo X, he was responsible for major projects in the Vatican, including huge paintings in the Stanza della Segnatura. He also designed numerous churches, palaces, and mansions. His fame in the 19th century was based primarily on his numerous renditions of the Madonna and Child.

Rembrandt (Rembrandt Hermensz van Rijn), Dutch, 1606–1669 The leading portrait and biblical painter of the Netherlands, Rembrandt spent most of his career in Amsterdam, where he was a conspicuous figure, initially for his fertile talent and extravagant lifestyle, and later for his public bankruptcy, the breadth of his knowledge, and the depth of his work. As a painter of religious themes, he towers over all others for his ability to empathize with the subjects of the stories.

Georges Rouault, French, 1871–1958 Early in his career, Rouault was an apprentice to a stained-glass maker, and this training greatly influenced his style. The bitter and sorrowful depictions of clowns, judges, and prostitutes that marked his early years gave way to some of the most profound religious expressions of the 20th century. The suffering of Christ was a recurring theme. *Miserere*, his series of about 60 prints on this subject, made his work available to many collectors who could not have afforded his paintings.

RAPHAEL *The Alba Madonna*

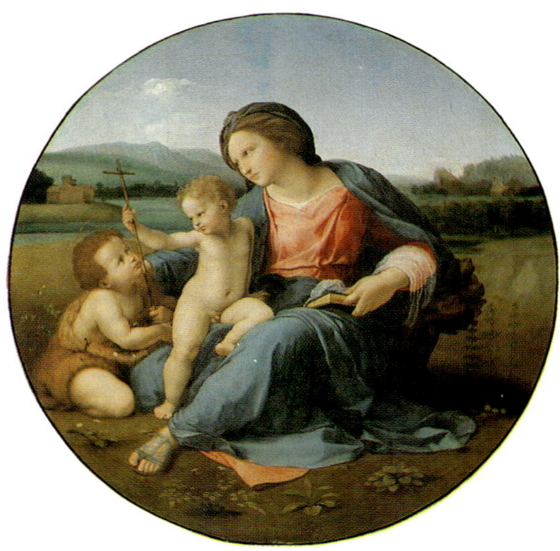

Peter Paul Rubens, Flemish, 1577–1640 The most illustrious artist of his age, Rubens began his career in 1598 in Antwerp, then went to Italy to serve the court of the Gonzaga family in Mantua. On a diplomatic mission for his patrons, he painted in Spain, where he influenced the young Velázquez. From 1608, he resided in Antwerp where he had an enormous studio with many students and assistants. He was showered with honors during his lifetime and lived like a prince under the ongoing patronage of the archdukes who ruled Flanders for the Spanish crown.

Christian Andreas Schleisner, Danish, 1810–1882 A painter of portraits and genre scenes in the neoclassical style, Schleisner also supplied murals to churches.

Jacob von Steinle, Austrian, 1810–1886 A painter and etcher, Jacob von Steinle went to Italy to study the art of Giotto and Fra Angelico. He was the last of the generation of Roman Nazarenes, a group of northern artists who lived monastically, trying to revive religious and moral purpose in art. The painted decorative schemes of many church interiors are to his credit.

Matthias Stomer, Dutch, ca. 1600–after 1650 A student of Honthorst, Matthias Stomer went to Italy in 1615 and worked primarily in Sicily, where he died. His work combines the immediacy of Caravaggio with Dutch solidity.

Bernardo Strozzi, Italian, 1581–1644 Once a Capuchin monk in Genoa, Strozzi later moved to Venice, where he was instrumental in revitalizing painting, which had been in decline since the death of Tintoretto. He was a major portrait painter of his day.

David Teniers II, Flemish, 1610–1690 The leading genre painter of his era, David Teniers II left his native Antwerp for Brussels

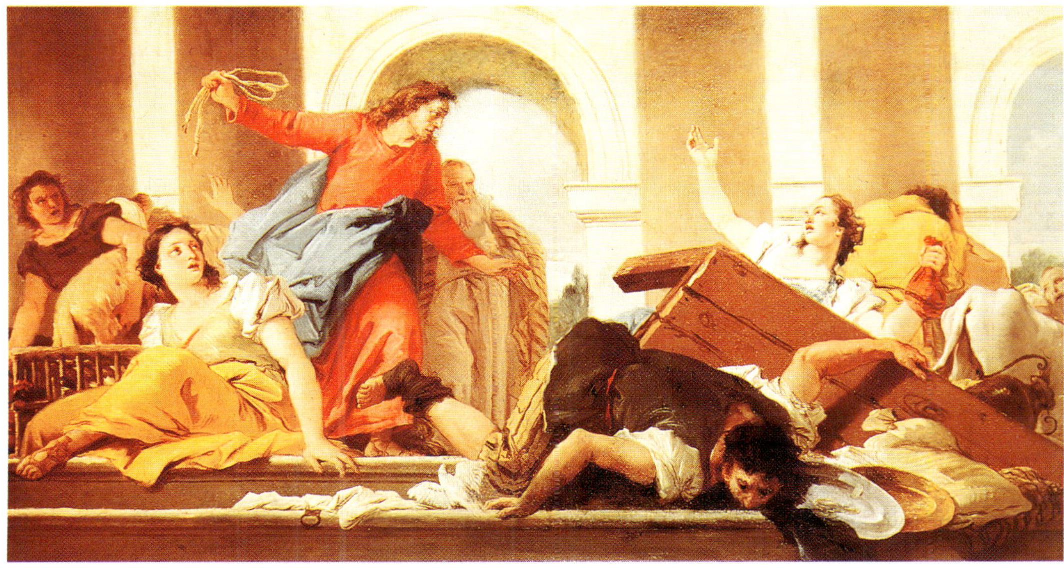

TIEPOLO *Christ Expulses the Moneychangers from the Temple*

to serve as curator and painter to the court of the Archduke Leopold-William, governor of the Low Countries. Teniers founded the Brussels Academy of Fine Arts and died a rich man. He was a prolific artist, with between 700 and 2000 paintings to his credit. Many works ascribed to him are, in fact, copies.

Hendrik Terbrugghen, Dutch, 1588–1629 Terbrugghen was one of the many painters of Utrecht who spent time in Rome, but the only one to reside there during the lifetime of Caravaggio, whose art greatly inspired him. After his return to Utrecht, his simplified but subtle paintings were highly influential in popularizing the new ideas he learned in Italy.

Giovanni Battista Tiepolo, Italian, 1696–1770 Tiepolo was the last and one of the most important of the great Italian fresco painters working in the tradition that began with Giotto. His splendid sense of decoration and his optimistic, light-filled treatments of subjects from biblical and classical history were in great demand throughout Europe. His most famous works are palace decorations in Würzburg, Germany, and in Madrid, Spain, where he spent the last eight years of his life. He was assisted by his two sons, Lorenzo and Giandomenico. The latter gained fame in his own right after his father's death.

Tintoretto (Jacopo Robusti), Italian, ca. 1518–1594 Though he spent his entire life in Venice, Tintoretto painted for many foreign princes. Over 300 of his works survive, most of them large and commissioned by the churches and patricians of his native city. He was known for his swift, linear brushwork, but he carefully planned his paintings, often using small wax models on a stage lighted with candles.

Ugolino da Siena (Ugolino di Nerio), Italian, active 1317–1327 There are no dated paintings by this close follower of Duccio, but Ugolino da Siena is known to have painted for chapels and churches in all parts of Italy. His most famous work is the high altarpiece for the Church of Santa Croce in Florence. His work was very old fashioned in the Florence of Giotto's day.

Diego Velázquez, Spanish, 1599–1660 Recent critics have called him the greatest painter in the history of Western art, a reputation only slightly more exalted than the one he enjoyed in his own lifetime. Highly talented at an early age, Velázquez came to the attention of King Philip IV of Spain, who appointed him his sole portrait painter. The king was younger than the artist and came to depend on him as a warm confidant, raising him to increasingly more responsible positions in his personal service. He was in charge of the royal collections and was able to travel to Italy to seek art. In addition to portraits of the royal family, Velázquez painted mythological and religious scenes.

Stefano da Verona, Italian, ca. 1374–1438 or later Little is known of this delightful religious painter whose career was centered in Verona. Stefano da Verona worked in a decorative and sweet style that was popular in court circles throughout France, Italy, and other parts of Europe.

Paolo Veronese, Italian, ca. 1528–1588 One of the great Venetian artists of his day (Titian and Tintoretto were his contemporaries), Veronese was the most interested in the human figure, striving to give it volume but not great weight. He executed a large number of lengthy series of religious narratives for various churches and is famous for his banquet scenes. He had many assistants, including his brothers Zelotti and Ponchino.

Adriaen van der Werff, Dutch, 1659–1722 A precocious child, Adriaen van der Werff became an independent painter at the age of 17. He was the most famous Dutch artist of his day and served the courts of the king of Poland, the Duke of Brunswick, and the Elector of the Palatinate at Düsseldorf, where he was knighted. He achieved a high level of academic perfection in all of his works.

Benjamin West, American, 1738–1821 West began his career as a portrait painter in Philadelphia and New York. Before he was 22, he had moved to Rome, but eventually he settled in England, where George III became his patron. When he painted scenes of recent history in modern dress for the king, it was a shocking innovation. He helped found the Royal Academy of Art and, in 1792, succeeded Sir Joshua Reynolds as its president.

Roger van der Weyden, Flemish, 1399/1400–1464 One of the great early masters of Flemish art, Roger van der Weyden resided primarily in Brussels, where he enjoyed wealth and prestige. His works are austere and deeply spiritual. They had great influence on the development of painting north of the Alps during the 15th century.

Francisco de Zurbarán, Spanish, 1598–1664 Known for paintings of monks and other austere religious subjects, Francisco de Zurbarán and his large workshop in Seville executed numerous altarpieces. His earliest fame was based on *Christ on the Cross* (1627), illustrated in this book. He is best remembered for his paintings of single figures and for a few exquisite, simple still-life paintings.

Index of Artists and Illustrations